DAUGHTERS OF CALIBAN

DAUGHTERS OF CALIBAN

CARIBBEAN WOMEN IN THE TWENTIETH CENTURY

EDITED BY
CONSUELO LÓPEZ SPRINGFIELD

INDIANA UNIVERSITY PRESS
BLOOMINGTON AND INDIANAPOLIS
LATIN AMERICA BUREAU
LONDON

Published in North America by Indiana University Press, 601 North Morton Street,
Bloomington, Indiana 47404 and in the United Kingdom by the Latin America Bureau
(Research and Action) Ltd, 1 Amwell Street, London EC1R 1UL, UK

The paper used in this publication meets the minimum requirements of American
National Standard for Information Sciences—Permanence of Paper for Printed Library
Materials, ANSI Z39.48–1984.

⊗™

Manufactured in the United States of America

British Library Cataloguing in Publication Data

A CIP catalogue record for this book is available from the British Library.

ISBN 1-899365-15-X

Library of Congress Cataloging-in-Publication Data

Daughters of Caliban : Caribbean women in the twentieth century /
edited by Consuelo López Springfield.
p.   cm.
Includes bibliographical references and index.
ISBN 0-253-33249-4 (cl : alk. paper). — ISBN 0-253-21092-5 (pbk. alk. paper)
1. Women—Caribbean Area—Social conditions.   2. Feminism—
Caribbean Area.   3. Caribbean Area—Social conditions.   I. López
Springfield, Consuelo, date .
HQ1501.D375   1997
305.42′09729—dc20   96-41477

2   3   4   5   02   01   00   99

❖ TO MY DAUGHTERS ❖

VANESSA VILLEGAS LÓPEZ
AND
CRISTINA SPRINGFIELD LÓPEZ

CONTENTS

Acknowledgments   *ix*

Introduction
Revisiting Caliban: Implications for Caribbean Feminisms   *xi*
Consuelo López Springfield

I. Caribbean Women and Women's Studies

1. Decolonizing Feminism:
The Home-Grown Roots of Caribbean Women's Movements   *3*
Lizabeth Paravisini-Gebert

2. Empowering the Mother Tongue:
The Creole Movement in Guadeloupe   *18*
Cynthia J. Mesh

II. Women and Work

3. We Toil All the Livelong Day:
Women in the English-Speaking Caribbean   *41*
Mary Johnson Osirim

4. Reinventing Higglering across Transnational Zones:
Barbadian Women Juggle the Triple Shift   *68*
Carla Freeman

5. Across the Mona Strait:
Dominican Boat Women in Puerto Rico   *96*
Luisa Hernández Angueira

6. Daughter of Caro   *112*
Ruth Behar

III. Women and Health

7. The Power to Heal: Haitian Women in Vodou   *123*
Karen McCarthy Brown

8. Menstrual Taboos, Witchcraft Babies, and Social Relations:
Women's Health Traditions in Rural Jamaica   *143*
Elisa J. Sobo

9. Women, Health, and Development:
The Commonwealth Caribbean   *171*
Caroline Allen

IV. Women, Law, and Political Change

10. The Colonial Legacy: Gendered Laws in Jamaica   *215*
Suzanne LaFont and Deborah Pruitt

11. [Re]Considering Cuban Women in a Time of Troubles   *229*
Carollee Bengelsdorf

V. Women and Popular Culture

12. "Así Son": Salsa Music, Female Narratives,
and Gender (De)Construction in Puerto Rico   *259*
Frances Aparicio

13. Face of the Nation: Race, Nationalisms, and Identities in Jamaican
Beauty Pageants   *285*
Natasha B. Barnes

Contributors   *307*

Index   *311*

❖

ACKNOWLEDGMENTS

I WOULD LIKE to express my deep appreciation to the authors of the essays included in this collection. Special thanks are due to Joan Catapano, Senior Editor and Assistant Director of Indiana University Press, for her trust in the project and her generous editorial assistance. I am grateful to Indiana University's Center for Latin American and Caribbean Studies for its continued support, especially to Judy Summerville, Russell Salmon, Dennis Conway, and Martha Davis, who have aided and encouraged me to pursue Caribbean research and teaching while working toward social and institutional change. I would also like to express my gratitude to Pat Riesenman, Anna Santiago, and Shirley Boardman at Indiana University and to Annette White-Parks, Lizabeth Paravisini-Gebert, Sufen Lai, and Ruth Lewis for their friendship and enthusiasm for my work. To my husband, Rip Springfield, and my aunts, sisters, and daughters who provided undaunted encouragement, I offer my sincere gratitude.

For their permission to reproduce copyrighted material, I thank the Porter Institute, publisher of *Poetics Today*, for Frances Aparicio's "Towards a Feminist Poetics of Listening" (chapter 12 in this volume) and *The Massachusetts Review* for Natasha B. Barnes, "Face of the Nation: Race, Nationalisms, and Identities in Jamaican Beauty Pageants" (chapter 13).

❖

INTRODUCTION

Revisiting Caliban:
Implications for Caribbean Feminisms

CONSUELO LÓPEZ SPRINGFIELD

Somehow, early on, our song makers and tale weavers had decided that
we were all daughters of this land.
EDWIDGE DANTICAT, *BREATH, EYES, MEMORY*[1]

CARIBBEAN WOMEN are "daughters of Caliban," born into a region where all
the "major players" were "newcomers" transported from foreign lands—the African slave, the white merchant, overseer, and colonial administrator, and the
Asiatic "serf"[2] brought in after the abolition of slavery in the British colonies
to work on the huge sugarcane estates). It is an area where natural disasters
wipe out national economies, structural unemployment and underemployment plague the most resourceful workers, and sustained dependency on U.S.
and global conglomerates threatens the survival of local industries and agricultural producers. From the time before conquest up to our contemporary age,
the region has been marked by interregional, hemispheric, and cross-oceanic
migration as people seek or are forced to seek work in other lands. The Caribbean is, thus, a site of permeable boundaries and multiple identities, offering
continuous redefinition of the self and of one's relationship to society.

Based on new ways of thinking about "cultural collisions, interfaces, and
navigable crossings" (Flores, 103), *Daughters of Caliban* bears witness to the
multiplicity of Caribbean women's roles. This interdisciplinary book by feminist scholars in anthropology, sociology, health, law, literature, and culture
studies focuses on issues of direct importance to women: interregional immigrant female labor, the interplay of race and gender in the construction of
national cultures, the impact of developmental policies and colonialist legal
practices on women's lives, and women's creative roles in providing cultural
continuity in exile communities.

Reference to "Caliban" as a cultural signifier is rooted in an earlier time (1960–1970s) when Caribbean intellectuals, struggling with issues of identity throughout the archipelago, turned to Shakespeare's *Tempest* for images embracing *mestizaje*, the process of cultural and racial admixture that shaped Caribbean societies.[3] Caliban, the island's original inhabitant—half-beast, the offspring of a witch who was forced into servitude by Prospero—spoke in utterances; his inability to "master" Prospero's language confirmed his "savage" nature.[4] To twentieth-century Caribbean writers, "Caliban" epitomized the intermingling not only of indigenous, African, and European races but also of African oral and European written traditions, local dialects and standard European languages, a history of colonial oppression and a regional culture of resistance.[5]

Among the "emerging" poets of the Commonwealth Caribbean was Jamaica's Louise "Miss Lou" Bennett, a robust figure in national media politics whose oral performances captured the speech, rhythms, and humor of the island's folk as they debated contemporary issues.[6] Through her use of Creole, "an important element in black identity and cultural unity [and] a major form of defense against dehumanization" (Bush), she reinforced an Afro-Caribbean "rebel consciousness." Although Bennett's poetry was dismissed by Eurocentric critics as dialect poetry in the "minor" tradition, it expressed the subversive creativity of everyday "Calibans" striving to articulate meaning in a hostile world, to establish—in urgent speech—a site free of colonial inhibitions and paternalistic constraints. Since then, Creole as a unifying tool for popular resistance has grown into a movement for social justice in the Francophone Caribbean, inspired, as in the past, by rebellious women.

Athough "Caliban" has been viewed largely as a male construct, we appropriate his legacy of struggle cognizant that identity is never fixed, but fluid. We add to this image a new dimension, one which women writers of the Caribbean remind us of consistently: that we are daughters, reweaving our mothers' stories into our own as we challenge convention. These collective memories help to frame perceptions of feminism and of the ways in which race, ethnicity, economic status, and sexuality affect potential coalitions across class lines. Puerto Rico's Magali Roy-Fequire, one of the few Caribbean scholars to pursue interclass conflict in the development of women's access to voting rights, suggests that class identification has been more powerful than "gender-based" solidarity. "What Creole women desired was a restricted modernization of the gender system," she explains; "what they sought was change and opportunity for the women of their class background" (Roy-Fequire). Elite women negotiated "their enfranchisement at the expense of illiterate, black, mixed-race poor women." As such, they also play the role of Prospero, silencing oppressed women. Merle Hodge recalls having seen "ordinary women go against their political instincts and give in to the point of view of an upper-class woman simply because she has the air of confidence, success, and authority; she can make a room full of ordinary women shut up and listen, like the one man in a roomful of women" (Hodge). Only in a few places has collective action attempted to change class dynamics through government policies; one of them is postrevolutionary Cuba.

Confronting class and racial differences that divide women is the subject of anthropologist Ruth Behar's personal narrative, "Daughter of Caro," which appears in this volume. Born within Havana's small Jewish community in prerevolutionary Cuba, Behar explores, as an adult revisiting her past, both her attachment to her former nanny and to her native land. In the process, she illuminates how upper-class women—employing poor black women to perform housework and childcare duties—reproduce patriarchal patterns of discrimination. Behar describes the intense personal bonds between domestics and the children in their care; at the same time, she reveals an internal struggle to find "home" and wholeness on the borderlands of competing cultures.[7]

The concept of "home" as a site of "contacts and crossings" (Flores) has rarely been addressed by scholars as they struggle to define a "Caribbean identity." Although there are many reasons for ignoring "home" within Caribbean academic discourse, foremost is gender bias within the research agenda itself. It would not be an overstatement to say that most prominent "Caribbeanist" social scientists are men who tend to replicate in their modes of analysis the very patriarchal attitudes that contributed to the ascendancy of colonialism. "Home" is perceived as the private realm or what V. S. Naipaul referred to as the "demi-monde" of women,[8] remote from the dominant discourse of nationalism and its endemic politics. To Caribbean women, "home" is both a site of communal wisdom and a place of sexual oppression. Nowhere is this more evident than in the feminist "immigrant" writing of Puerto Rico's Judith Ortiz Cofer, the Puerto Rican mother-daughter team of Rosario Morales and Aurora Levins Morales, and Haiti's Edwidge Danticat, who capture the strengths and contradictions of Caribbean female culture.[9] While emphasizing women's roles in creatively transmitting culture, they also recognize a legacy of internalized self and sexual denial. As Elisa J. Sobo's "Menstrual Taboos, Witchcraft Babies, and Social Relations: Women's Health Traditions in Rural Jamaica" (chapter 8 in this volume) points out, women promote the sexual control of other women's bodies. At the same time, knowledge of their own bodies allows them power in determining family structures and relationships. Sobo describes life in a Jamaican village where gender-linked role expectations and ideas about the dangers of male-female relationships are perpetuated through bodily discourses and practices. Her research suggests that in order to impede the spread of new health problems (such as AIDS), public health programs must take into account the persuasive power of traditional health beliefs in perpetuating cultural conceptions of morality and social behavior.

Just as every society creates its own cultural systems borne out of unique historical and economic conditions, so does each develop its own concepts of "feminism." Rhoda Reddock's definition of feminism as "an awareness of oppression, exploitation and/or subordination of women within the society and the conscious action to change and transform this situation" (Reddock) is appropriate here as it presupposes that feminism derives its power from the wisdom, resources, and tenacity of the oppressed. I would also add that Caribbean feminism responds to problems that are not always specific to gender oppression. Women are at the forefront of strikes and public protests; in a Caribbean context, these leadership roles constitute feminist action.

Whether through language, labor, or feminist movements, the ways in which women's quest for equality has evolved under local conditions is critical to feminist discourse. Unfortunately, most "case studies" apply Western perspectives to an analysis of island cultures, and writer-activist Merle Hodge's critical remarks still hold true today. "We keep analyzing our society as though it were a Western society. We keep talking about how many women are now 'going out to work,' " she writes. "But women have worked from the beginning. That's what we were brought here for" (Hodge). European American feminist scholars, measuring "feminist" achievements by external standards, ignore the historical salience of grassroots realities.

The first of the five sections in *Daughters of Caliban*, "Caribbean Women and Women's Studies," examines this breach between European American and Caribbean feminisms. Lizabeth Paravisini-Gebert (chapter 1) laments European American feminists' failure to acknowlege the "indivisibility of gender relations from race and class, the intricate connections between sexual mores, skin pigmentation, and class mobility, the poverty and political repression that has left women's bodies exposed to abuse and exploitation." She underscores the Eurocentric bias of much contemporary theorizing; concurrently, she shows how the plantation economy helped to shape local, and often competing, feminist movements. Similarly, Cynthia J. Mesh (chapter 2) argues that the "Eurocentric perspective" of French feminist theory "fails to take into account the geographic and cultural specificities that make women's lives very different in various parts of the world, despite common political and national affiliations." Mesh's essay on the Creole movement in Guadeloupe, led by grass-roots organizer Dany Bébel-Gisler, "epitomizes the possibilities that one person, indeed, one woman, may have to effect real change in the world around her." Bébel-Gisler's extensive activism also raises vital issues about women communicating across class lines—an area in need of urgent study. She relates how Guadeloupe's Creole movement, by promoting the legitimacy of the Creole language, encourages "women, often less educated than men and therefore less adept at speaking French" to "take an active part in their own development and to take advantage of better opportunities for earning money." The language of the oppressed poor majority is, thus, both a powerful means to interpret reality and a tool to redress gender inequities.

The second section, "Women and Work," sheds new light on old debates about the nature of women's work. Several years ago, feminist scholars pointed out that the lines between public (male) and private (female) realms blur as Caribbean women contribute to society in a multitude of ways. Riva Berleant-Schiller and William M. Maurer maintained that the "overlapping of domestic and community spheres renders such a dichotomy useless for understanding sex roles and ideologies" (Berleant-Schiller and Maurer). Nonetheless, household and "public" labor are sometimes treated as separate spheres; and one recent study of female industrial workers in the Hispanic Caribbean goes so far as to contend that housing and daycare fall outside the purview of "women's demands for gender equality" (Safa).[10] In chapter 3, Mary Johnson Osirim abandons the private/public dichotomy, choosing instead to examine the rift between local and international divisions of labor. In her analysis of governmental and grassroots efforts to improve the prospects of women in the labor market, she argues that motherhood must be at the center of scholarly research. She recommends that Caribbean nations adopt a mixed economy, where production and exchange decisions can be made with particular attention to domestic employment and development goals.

Carla Freeman (chapter 4) turns a backward gaze to Maria Mies's house-wifization theory, which described women's work within the international division of labor. The theory held that malleable Third World women's (cheap) labor produced goods which first world women enjoyed as consumer products. Freeman shows how Mies's dualistic model overlooks the effects of transnationalism on Caribbean women's consumption of commodities and styles.

What makes their mass consumption possible, she argues, is their "deeply entrenched involvement in informal marketing and trade." Freeman illustrates how "pink-collar" and "blue-collar" work overlap as women combine wage work in foreign-owned "office factories" with informal dressmaking and marketing. Fashion, often designed and produced in the home and sold in the informal sector, allows data entry workers to cultivate a public "white-collar" appearance; thus, concepts of femininity cross national boundaries, allowing factory workers to adapt local culture to international, corporate styles in the "fashions that they design, produce, and consume."

Daughters of Caliban also examines transglobal societies where women reconstitute networks of relatives and friends in exile communities while maintaining strong ties to their families at home. Although the experiences of Dominican workers in exile have been explored in a number of recent publications,[11] the lives of "boat women" have been much more difficult to examine, largely because of their marginal status in immigrant communities. Sociologist Luisa Hernández Angueira (chapter 5) traces the economic life of "boat women" who brave the deep waters of the Mona Passage between Hispaniola and Puerto Rico in small, overloaded "yolas" (boats) to encounter popular resentment toward the expanding Dominican community in Santurce, Puerto Rico. Her controversial findings establish that single female Dominican heads of households, although less educated than Puerto Ricans, experience more independence than Puerto Rican women. Ruth Behar's contribution, mentioned earlier, is chapter 6.

The third section of *Daughters of Caliban* examines "Women and Health" in the Caribbean. Karen McCarthy Brown (chapter 7) traces women's spiritual and healing roles from slave society to contemporary New York. A cultural theologian, Brown describes how Western medicine breaks apart and parcels out disease "like property distributed to experts with scant attention to the interrelations between the physical, psychological, social, historical, and spiritual illnessess." She contrasts this to Vodou, an Afro-Caribbean healing religion that treats physical and spiritual ailments as one. We are introduced to Alourdes ("Mama Lola"), whose ritualistic healing provides solace to Haitians in exile; concurrently, we see how women's increased autonomy has changed traditional vodou by enlarging women's roles as spiritual leaders. Brown's experimental work in feminist ethnographic writing has helped shape a new body of knowledge about "a female tradition" of spiritual hearings.[12]

Elisa J. Sobo, in her study of Jamaican women's health traditions (chapter 8) also contrasts Western with Afro-Caribbean health traditions. She argues that partly because mothers are generally the first people to whom sick individuals turn for help and also because the healing arts were not wrested from women (as they were in "Western" cultures), Jamaican health traditions are largely female-centered. Based on concepts of menstruation and procreation, they focus on the belly and the blood. Sobo reveals how women use their knowledge about the menses to control each other and so to maintain their social positions. Finally, she interprets spirit impregnation and the role of spiritual healers.

Caroline Allen (chapter 9) takes health and demographic transition models—which exclude gender—to task. Her research is important, since these models (which compare health and demographic indicators across nations) help to determine the allocation of funds to health projects around the world. Allen argues that the health transition models' findings that chronic, noncommunicable diseases such as hypertension and diabetes mellitus prevail in the richest countries are flawed and that if researchers incorporated data on gender, they would find that rates of death from these diseases are significantly higher in the Commonwealth Caribbean than in any other region in the Americas. She insists that development programs consider the changing role of women in the international division of labor, migration from rural to urban areas, lifestyle, and the consumption of imported canned and processed foods at the expense of fresh produce sold in local markets. She exhorts health researchers and practitioners to tackle such social and economic issues as trade policies, the sexual division of labor, and gender stereotyping.

The fourth section of *Daughters of Caliban*, "Women, Law, and Political Change," examines the effects of legal and political institutions on women's lives. Anthropologists Suzanne LaFont and Deborah Pruitt (chapter 10) provide significant insight into the effects of social policy and family laws on the lived reality of Jamaican women. They contend that the nuclear family model—on which these laws are based—is inappropriate, since legal marriage is the exception not the rule in Jamaican families. In a place where out-of-wedlock birthrates are rising consistently and most women have children with more than one sexual partner, fostering the Eurocentric ideology of the nuclear family harms women in their struggle for independence and equality. LaFont and Pruitt break new ground in arguing that Caribbean family laws must address the needs of women and children in culturally appropriate ways.

Political scientist Carollee Bengelsdorf (chapter 11) probes the public/private dichotomy following the steady decline in the Cuban economy. She explains that although the 1959 revolution eroded the boundaries between the public and private spheres, traditional patterns of labor and political representation are increasingly "reasserting themselves." The failures of the "Engelsian paradigm" takes us beyond traditional Marxist economics; feminist cultural studies allow her to glean how racialized narratives of sexuality perpetuate "machista" attitudes, which in turn uphold the "(male) gendered nature of the public sphere."

The fifth section of *Daughters of Caliban* examines "Women and Popular Culture." Frances Aparicio (chapter 12) discusses how popular music reproduces the struggles between men and women in a contemporary urban world where gender identities and sexual roles are being transformed. Her groundbreaking essay is an exercise in what she terms listening woman and listening as a woman. The former posits the task of reading women's representation in Latin popular music, "both the ways in which women are figured . . . and the ways in which such figuring gives representation its force by repressing female desire." She begins by examining salsa music as popular culture and the hermeneutic challenges it proposes for gender studies. She argues that while "Anglo feminism" may dismiss these songs as examples of gender oppression, they must be understood within the social, cultural, and historical contexts of sexual relations in Puerto Rican society. She turns to two contemporary Puerto Rican authors, Ana Lydia Vega and Carmen Lugo Filippi, who employ a feminist politics of listening to salsa: undoing and rewriting patriarchal salsa lyrics from a female-centered perspective.

Natasha B. Barnes (chapter 13) shows how beauty pageants are contested terrains for racial politics. Her essay, reviewing four decades, describes the ideology of beauty in Jamaica. While explaining how an atmosphere of racial pluralism led to pageants celebrating diverse ethnicities, she examines the role of the press and economic communities in shaping and commodifying ideals of feminine beauty.

These studies of Caribbean women's lives contribute to the overall task of shattering the myth of the West Indian matriarch and the passive Hispanic Caribbean woman. As editor, I recognize that much remains to be researched and written about female sexuality, racial and class alliances, criminality, and the expansion of women's labor in bureaucracies and in fast-food industries. This volume is propelled by a guiding assertion that by examining linkages among marginalized groups, we liberate our beliefs and values from ethnocentric epistemologies. These studies are meant to provoke questions and to provide material useful for comparative studies; at the same time, they acknowledge the significance of self-reflexivity in intellectual discourse. Finally, these studies pay tribute to our own daughters and granddaughters, who will retell today's tales, weaving them into their own stories. As daughters of Caliban, they bear the challenge expressed by Julia de Burgos, "to gather dignity and embrace to face the century's cry of liberty."[13]

NOTES

1. New York: Vintage Books, 1994, 230.

2. Gordon K. Lewis used these terms to describe Caribbean populations. He did not include indigenous peoples, since they were largely wiped out by forced labor. See *The Growth of the Modern West Indies* (New York: Monthly Review Press, 1968).

3. Although Gloria Anzaldúa situates *mestizaje* or *mestiza* consciousness within a Chicana framework, it applies to the Caribbean and Latin America as well. See Anzaldúa, *Borderlands/La Frontera* (San Francisco: Spinsters/Aunt Lute, 1987).

4. For an analysis of Caliban in reference to Caribbean feminism, see Sylvia Wynter, "Beyond Miranda's Meanings: Un/silencing the 'Demonic Ground' of Caliban's 'Woman,'" in *Out of the Kumbla: Caribbean Women and Literature*, ed. Carole Boyce Davies and Elaine Savory Fido (Trenton: Africa World Press, 1990).

5. Among the leading literary critics, Roberto Fernández Retamar's essay on Caliban spurred a plethora of critical commentary on the struggle between Prospero (the colonizer) and Caliban (the colonized). See Fernández Retamar, *Caliban and Other Essays*, trans. Edward Baker (University of Minnesota Press, 1989). In addition, Aime Cesaire, one of the "fathers" of Negritude, described Caliban's "viewpoint" as that "of the colonized" in an interview with Charles Rowell, "C'est par le poème que nous affrontons la solitude," *Callaloo* 12, no. 1 (Winter 1989): 63.

6. Bennett, author of *Jamaica Labrish* (Kingston: Sangsters, 1969), began publishing locally in the 1940s. With the substantial increase in women's writing throughout the Caribbean, her contributions to the development of an authentic Afro-Caribbean "voice" have been ignored in recent years, even among feminist scholars. New work on the Creole movement should help to inspire creative approaches to Bennett's poetry.

7. In "Mestizaje in the Mother-Daughter Autobiography of Rosario Morales and Aurora Levins Morales," *Auto/Biography* 8, no. 2 (Fall 1993): 303–315, I situate "home" at the borderlands of two competing cultures.

8. Quoted in Consuelo López (de Villegas), "Matriarchs and Man-Eaters: Naipaul's Fictional Women," *Revista/Review Interamericana* 10, no. 2 (Summer 1980): 220. Naipaul was referring to Jean Rhys.

9. See Judith Ortiz Cofer, *In the Line of the Sun, Silent Dancing*, and *The Latin Deli*; Rosario Morales and Aurora Levins Morales, *Getting Home Alive*; and Edgwidge Danticat, *Breath, Eyes, Memory*.

10. Helen Safa, in *The Myth of the Male Breadwinner* (Boulder: Westview, 1995), 58, argues that throughout the Hispanic Caribbean and "even in Cuba," women's demands are focused "within a domestic framework, emphasizing practical needs such as daycare and housing *over* gender equality."

11. Jorge Duany, ed., *Los dominicanos en Puerto Rico.* (Río Piedras, P.R.: Huracán, 1990); Eugenia Georges, *The Making of a Transnational Community: Migration, Development and Cultural Change in the Dominican Republic* (New York: Columbia University Press, 1990); Sherri Grasmuck and Patricia R. Pessar, *Between Two Islands: Dominican International Migration* (Berkeley: University of California Press, 1991); Juan E. Hernández Cruz, ed., *Los Inmigrantes indocumentados dominicanos en Puerto Rico* (San Germán, P.R.: Interamerican University Press, 1989); Alejandro Portes and Luis E. Guarnizo, *Capitalistas del trópico: La inmigración en los Estados Unidos y el desarrollo de la pequeña empresa en la Republica Dominicana* (Santo Domingo: FLASCO, 1991).

12. The *Ms* reviewer of *Mama Lola: A Vodou Priestess in Brooklyn* (Berkeley: University of California Press, 1991) pointed out that the "largely female tradition of spiritual healing and renewal" was "largely misunderstood and maligned" (July–August 1991, p. 86).

13. Julia de Burgos, untitled poem, translated by Lizabeth Paravisini-Gebert, in Chiqui Vicioso, "Julia de Burgos: Our Julia," *Callaloo* 17 no. 3 (1994): 681.

REFERENCES

Balutansky, Kathleen. "We Are All Activists: An Interview with Merle Hodge," *Callaloo* 12 no. 4 (Fall 1989): 651–662.

Berleant-Schiller, Riva, and William M. Maurer. "Women's Place Is Every Place: Merging Domains and Women's Roles in Barbuda and Dominica," in Janet H. Momsen, ed., *Women and Change in the Caribbean.* Bloomington: Indiana University Press, 1993.

Boyce Davies, Carole. *Black Women, Writing and Identity: Migrations on the Subject.* London: Routledge, 1994.

Bush, Barbara. "Towards Emancipation: Slave Women and Resistance to Coersive Labour Regimes in the British West Indian Colonies 1790–1838," in David Richardson, ed., *Abolition and Its Aftermath: The Historical Context, 1790–1916.* London: Frank Cass, 1985, 27–54.

Cesaire, Aime. "C'est par le poème que nous affrontons la solitude: An Interview with Charles Rowell," *Callaloo* 12, no. 1 (Winter 1989): 63.

Danticat, Edwidge. *Breath, Eyes, Memory.* New York: Vintage, 1994, 230.

Flores, Juan. *Divided Borders: Essays on the Puerto Rican Identity.* Houston: Arte Público Press, 1994.

Hodge, Merle. Review of Karen McCarthy Brown, *Mama Lola: A Voudou Priestess in Brooklyn*, *Ms*, July–August 1991.

Lewis, Gordon K. *The Growth of the Modern West Indies*. New York: Monthly Review Press, 1968.

López Springfield, Consuelo. "Mestizaje in the Mother-Daughter Autobiography of Rosario Morales and Aurora Levins Morales," *Auto/Biography* 8, no. 2 (Fall 1993): 303–315.

López (de Villegas), Consuelo. "Matriarchs and Man-Eaters: Naipaul's Fictional Women," *Revista/Review Interamericana* 10, no. 2 (Summer 1980): 220–229.

Mies, Maria. "Social Origins of the Sexual Divisions of Labour," in Maria Mies et al., *Women: The Last Colony*, London: Zed, 1991.

Payne, Anthony, and Paul Sutton. *Modern Caribbean Politics*. Baltimore: Johns Hopkins University Press, 1993.

Reddock, Rhoda, *Elma Francois: The NWCSA and the Workers' Struggle for Change in the Caribbean in the 1930s*. Trinidad: New Beacon, 1988, 3.

Roy-Fequire, Magali. "Contested Territory: Puerto Rican Women, Creole Identity, and Intellectual Life in the Early Twentieth Century," *Callaloo* 17, no. 3 (Summer 1994): 916.

I

CARIBBEAN WOMEN AND WOMEN'S STUDIES

DECOLONIZING FEMINISM

The Home-Grown Roots of
Caribbean Women's Movements

LIZABETH PARAVISINI-GEBERT

IT IS COMMONPLACE, in these times of increased interest in Caribbean women —ideal canvases, it would appear, on which to theorize on the postfeminist, postcolonial, chaos-driven societies of the twentieth century—to speak of our history, our literature, the quality of our feminism or lack thereof, as if we constituted a homogeneous block, an undivided, unfragmented and unfragmentable entity—knowable, understandable, whole. Caribbean feminism is often discussed in much the same way, as something graspable, perceptible, complete —perhaps different from U.S. and European variables but nonetheless comprehensible, unequivocal. Reference is often made in these discussions to the race and class differences that separate women in Caribbean societies, most often in a perfunctory aside about not assuming that the discussion that has preceded it applies to all women in the region. But these denials can be rather elliptical, managing nonetheless to infer that one could after all continue to seek to understand all Caribbean women through what they share with other women *as women* if we only remind our audiences that the differences allow, like political polls, for plus or minus three percentage points of error.

Lest this sound like accusation or an attempt at polemics, I should avow my own guilt. There is a deceptive ease about generalizations; it is after all part and parcel of the academician's training to learn to draw general conclusions from the particular. Thus I mean it less as an accusation than as a cautionary note, a reminder that the realities we seek to understand as scholars are often much larger than the scholarship we pursue, and that the understanding we offer is at times just approximation, theory based on various fragments of a changing truth. This is not to say that the task of understanding Caribbean women's lives and cultures is futile, fated from the beginning to failure, but that, however fragmentary, scholarship on Caribbean women needs to be rooted in true knowledge of the historical and material conditions responsible for women's choices and strategies in the region, and that the specificities of that process must be well accounted for if our conclusions are going to truly advance knowledge and understanding.

Recently, while preparing an annotated bibliography on Caribbean women novelists that required the reading and summarizing of several thousand items, I was struck foremost by how often explorations of women's movements and women's literatures in the Caribbean seemed rooted in U.S. and European theories developed to analyze different sociopolitical realities (Paravisini-Gebert and Torres-Seda). All too frequently, reliance on these approaches (whether postfeminist, postcolonial, decontructivist) led to de-historicized interpretations that highlighted the "backwardness" of women's movements in the region, the "proto-feminist" quality of women's positions vis-à-vis power structures, while failing to see the specificities of what constitutes feminism for the women concerned. A frequent impression in that extensive review of the critical literature on Caribbean women's writing was that despite the often faultless internal logic of many of the essays I reviewed, the "external" logic—by which I mean the reliability of the assessments if measured against the sociohistorical reality of Caribbean women's lives—was frequently unsatisfactory when not entirely flawed. Unpopular as the thought may be in academic departments that have heavily invested in theory and the concomitant disconnection of the text from the historical materiality of real women's lives, I would posit that as scholars committed to studying Caribbean women we must anchor our work in a profound understanding of the societies we (they) inhabit. The evaluation of a differing reality from the theoretical standpoint of other women's praxes comes dangerously close in many cases to continued colonization. Caribbean feminism must be understood not in the light of other women's feminist histories and goals but in the light of their own experiences and practices. Feminism, if it is to lead to its goal of assuring women as full and multifaceted an existence as possible, must be responsive to the conditions in which that existence must unfold.

Scholarship on Caribbean societies, especially that stemming from current postcolonial and postmodernist approaches, more often than not seeks to relate these societies' attributes and idiosyncracies to past or present links to metropolitan centers. Historical and cultural practices are seen as stemming either from colonial influence or from a desire to shed colonial supremacy once and for all. As Carolyn Cooper has argued, Caribbean literatures and cultures "can become appropriated by totalising literary theories that reduce all 'post-colonial' literatures to the common bond(age) of the great—however deconstructed—European tradition. There are endless interrogations of the text and the prisoner on the stand is always the native. The very idea of 'national' literatures is passé. That old fiction of literature as the product of an age, the ethos of a people, is subsumed in the new reductive fiction of literature as pathology—metastasis beyond remission" (Cooper, 15).

It is not that the conclusions based on these theories lack any validity: colonialism did indeed leave an indelible imprint on Caribbean nations, and anti-colonial struggles have most clearly shaped the islands' political movements, particularly throughout the twentieth century. Caribbean societies, however, have managed to remain profoundly insular despite the colonial onslaught. By this I do not mean that they are unsophisticated, unworldly, or naive societies, but that they are driven as much, if not more, by internal, local concerns than they are by a persistent, continual, and continuous awareness of a colonial past. The peoples of the region have responded to their former colonization with myriad strategies for subverting the very history and identity imposed upon them by their metropolitan masters. It has long been a practice of Caribbean peoples to "carnivalize," at times to "cannibalize," the models imposed by officialdom. In the colonies, "the enthroning and dethroning of [colonial] ideologies was practiced with the greatest haste" (Rodríguez Monegal, 406).

This "enthroning and dethroning" of colonial models extended to patterns of gender relations. Caribbean societies—precisely because of their prolonged colonial status, the far-reaching impact of the institution of slavery on gender roles and family relations, the correlation of race and class imposed by slavery, the gender imbalances created by the overwhelmingly male migration of the first half of the twentieth century, and myriad other factors—developed patterns of gender relations markedly different from those of the colonial metropolis. The standards familiar to the metropolis may have been closely imitated by the small enclaves of Europeanized white or light-skinned middle and upper-middle classes, but were frequently transformed by the masses of the people who wove new configurations out of the fabric of colonial mores. Official culture may have insisted on continuing to represent Eurocentric models as characteristic of Caribbean societies, making them, for example, the prerequisite for social mobility; but the reality was much more complex, more fluid, much more *sui generis*. The image of the closely chaperoned, virginal, white or light-skinned *señorita* that has long since stood as archetypical for Spanish-Caribbean womanhood is as race-, class-, and stereotype-bound as that of the happy-go-lucky unmarried black mother of the Jamaican or Trinidadian yard with her large brood.

Among the Haitian peasantry, to offer a striking example, conventional marriage patterns hold little weight. Legal marriage, Wade Davis concludes in *Passage of Darkness*, has been "beyond the reach or desire" of the overwhelming majority of rural Haitians. *Plaçage*, a "socially if not legally sanctioned relationship that brings with it a recognized set of obligations for both man and woman," is a more common arrangement. But *plaçage* is not necessarily a monogamous relationship. Approximately 75 percent of the Haitian peasantry practices polygyny:

> A woman who shares a man's house is known as *femme caille*. A *maman petite* is a woman who has borne a man a child without living in his house. Depending on the nature of the bond, however, she may live in one of his second houses and cultivate a piece of land. A *femme placée* is a mistress who does not share the same house with her mate, and who has yet to give him any children. Finally, a *bien avec* is a woman with whom a man has frequent but not exclusive sexual contact. . . . Moreover, though on an individual basis there is often bitterness and conflict between rivals, Haitian peasant women fully recognize the rights of their men to have more than one mate, and occasionally two or more placées will share the same courtyard. (Davis, 41, 43).

Rural Haitian women, on the other hand, control the distribution of goods in the countryside and the marketplace, a role that guarantees them a strong voice and considerable power in the economic and social activities of the community, despite their apparent disadvantages in marital relations.

Likewise, in "Slackness Hiding from Culture: Erotic Play in the Dancehall," one of the chapters of *Noises in the Blood*, Carolyn Cooper uses the metaphor of Slackness/Culture to investigate the "high/low," metropolitan/insular divide emblematic of Jamaican society as reproduced "in the hierarchical relations of gender and sexuality that pervade the dancehall." Although the denigration of "slackness" that pervaded Jamaican colonial culture would appear to determine "the concomitant denigration of female sexuality" as manifested in the freedom of the dancehall, Cooper reads images of transgressive-woman-as-Slackness-personified as "an innocently transgressive celebration of freedom from sin and law."

> Liberated from the repressive respectability of a conservative gender ideology of female property and propriety, these women lay proper claim to the control of their own bodies. Further, the seemingly oppressive macho DJ ethic must

itself be problematised as a function of the oppressive class relations which produce what may be defined as a "diminished masculinity." (Cooper, 11)

I underscore these factors, and offer these examples, simply to illustrate the limited applicability of European or U.S. theories of feminism and gender relations to a reality that may have been influenced by European American cultural patterns but which developed in fairly *local* ways in response to a collision between autochthonous and foreign cultures. These *local*—i.e., *insular* or creole— responses to alien influences shaped the varieties of feminisms to be found in the Caribbean, feminisms that often clash with each other as women of different classes and races strive to achieve sometimes contradictory goals. The insular factors affecting the development of feminist movements in the region—the indivisibility of gender relations from race and class, the intricate connections between sexual mores, skin pigmentation, and class mobility, the poverty and political repression that have left women's bodies exposed to abuse and exploitation—seem alien to the concerns of European American feminist thought.

Take, for example, the vital relationship between women and their bodies, the focus of much theorizing and scholarship on women in recent years. Feminist critics have insistently voiced their concerns with inventing "both a new poetics and a new politics, based on women's reclaiming what had always been there but has been usurped from them: control over their bodies and a voice with which to speak about it" (Suleiman, 7). Feminist theories on the body, however, insist on interpreting bodies as symbolic constructs with cultural significance, rather than as a flesh-and-blood entities. The body thus exists as a form of discourse, "fictive or historical or speculative," but "never free of interpretation, never innocent."

The experience of many Caribbean women, historical experience as well as experience translated into literary texts, denies the body's existence as mere symbolic construct. During the media buildup leading to the most recent U.S. intervention in Haiti, U.S. audiences heard, the majority for the first time, of the systematic use of rape by military forces as a means of political control. Haitian readers coming across the persistent and eventually murderous rape of Rose Normil in Marie Chauvet's *Colère* would reject feminist theorizing on the body's symbolism as superfluous, given the immediacy of the connection between women's rape and both historical and day-to-day reality in their country. Haiti's neighbors in the Dominican Republic likewise continue to be haunted by the story of the Mirabal sisters, the three gifted and courageous women murdered by Trujillo's henchmen because of their persistent efforts to oust the dictator. The heartrending account of their lives and deaths offered by Dominican American writer Julia Alvarez in her novel *In the Time of the Butterflies*, draws its strength from its close connection to history. One could argue that the bodies of the Mirabal sisters are accessible to us through the symbolic discourse of texts such as Alvarez's. And this is indeed true, but only to a limited extent—for behind this discourse, however symbolic, stand the flesh-and-blood bodies of three vital young women, whose terror was real, whose bodies were torn apart, only to be used to inflict further torture—and through this torture a political lesson—on those to whom knowledge of their very real pain would bring immeasurable anguish and fear. In Dany Bébel-Gisler's testimonial text, *Léonora, l'histoire enfouie de la Guadeloupe*, Léonora brands her narrative with the many scars left on her body by her husband's abuse, scars that attest to the palpability of her experiences, her very flesh bearing testimony to history (see Romero, 1993).

The flesh-and-blood quality of women like Léonora, Rose Normil, and the Mirabal sisters must be remembered when reading how Caribbean women writers—and indeed most Third World women writers—"read" and "write" the female body. Their depictions of the "body-as-metaphor" must be seen in the context of political systems where women's bodies have been subject to abuse, rape, torture, and dismemberment precisely because this very treatment, through its interpretation as symbolic construct, has been an effective method of political control. Their reading of the body thus emerges from an ever-present threat to their own vulnerable flesh and blood, and the resulting symbolism is too close to the material body to allow for the comfort of seeing this danger merely as metaphor.

A second common element in what I see as problematic assessments of Caribbean women's lives and writings is the insistence on crediting the emergence of feminism in the Caribbean to fairly recent U.S. and European influences, with the concomitant conclusion that the various feminist movements in the islands responded to the same concerns as their assumed models. That these models have been influential, particularly in recent decades, there is no denying. Contemporary middle-class feminist movements in the Caribbean, seeking increased access to education, property, and employment, owe much to U.S. examples, particularly as many young middle-class women from the region have attended universities in the United States or have found employment with U.S.-spawned multinational corporations operating in the Caribbean.[1] These experiences have shaped the nature of their perceptions of their role as women, clashing with and frequently superseding traditional notions of womanhood.

The history of Caribbean feminism, however, is a long and contradictory one with autochthonous roots that reveal the conflicting realities of Caribbean women, conflicts in evidence from the early days of colonial society. C. L. R. James writes in *The Black Jacobins* of the underlying friction between women of different races and classes that characterized the colony of Saint Domingue. "Passion," he writes, "was [the planters' daughters'] chief occupation, stimulated by over-feeding, idleness, and an undying jealousy of the black and Mulatto women who competed so successfully for the favours of their husbands and lovers" (James, 30). The tensions to which James alludes, tensions stemming from profound class and race differences, have played a continuous role in the emergence and evolution of feminism in the region. As a result we can only speak of women's *movements*, since feminist goals have often meant very different things to women of different races and classes. I find "blanket" statements about feminism in the Caribbean most problematic, as they often raise questions about whose feminism is being taken as the norm and how that group's feminism has worked to frustrate someone else's.

Take the early women's movement in Puerto Rico as a case in point. The issue of women's rights began to be debated in the island in the early 1890s, when local newspapers focused on women's right to work, to own property, and to vote and on women's role in the home and society at large. The debate was led by two distinct and frequently opposed groups. One group comprised working-class women who had been incorporated into the labor force, primarily in the tobacco and needlework industries, after the U.S. takeover. They sought union organization to fight economic exploitation. The second group comprised middle-class women just entering the labor force as teachers, secretaries, bookkeepers, and clerks. They sought an end to legal and social restrictions through a quest for the vote. The most glaring example of the split between the two feminist camps—one led by Luisa Capetillo, the other by Ana Roqué—was the support given by the majority of middle-class suffragists to a law that would extend the vote only to women who could read and write. Such a law took effect in 1929. Those who could not read or write—that is, most Puerto Rican women—had to wait until universal suffrage became law in 1935. Poet Clara Lair, writing under the pseudonym Hedda Gabbler in the newspaper *Juan Bobo*, defended the middle-class position from the vantage point of her own self-perceived intellectual superiority:

I am going to declare that if the United States Congress decided to deprive of the vote Puerto Rican men who do not know how to read and write, it is an anomaly to request it for Puerto Rican women who, as a rule, don't know how to read and write either. . . . it is a logical deduction that a woman that doesn't know how to write is a woman that has not wanted to read. And a woman who has not wanted to read is a woman who has not been able to think. This humble and amiable type of woman known as "the Puerto Rican woman," an atavistic servant, servant to a larger or lesser degree, servant to her master or to her father, or to her brother, or to her husband, but always a servant, is not the type of woman who thinks for herself, who acts for herself. (Lair, 15)

It is not the type of statement, addressed as it is against the political claims of another avowedly feminist group, that allows us to speak of *one* feminism in the Caribbean.

By the same token, in yet another example of the complexities of feminist thought in the region and of the profound autochthonous roots of local feminist thought and practice, working-class and peasant women witnessed the co-opting of the middle-class feminist movement in the Dominican Republic, born in 1931 with the founding of the Acción Feminista Dominicana (Dominican Feminist Action), into Trujillo's political agenda, a naive sell-out prompted by the dictator's promise of voting and other civil rights to literate women. Embraced by Trujillo and his movement, the leaders of the AFD spoke solemnly of the "cessation of mocking remarks" and of their pride in hearing people "speak of their ideal and their cause with respect" (Hernández, 114). In 1942 the AFD joined Trujillo's party and issued a proclamation entreating all Dominican women to give their support to the dictator. The movement's energies were channeled toward "feverish activity in favor of Trujillo's re-election: meetings, proclamations, formation of Pro-Reelection Committees, tributes and marches" (Hernández, 115). Trujillo's authoritarian regime would eventually absorb middle-class feminist organizations in the island, steering their activities toward philanthropy, consolidation of the family unit, glorification of motherhood, and exultation of women's capacity for sacrifice, setting these as standards for womanhood that effectively quashed the burgeoning working-class and peasant women's movements in the Dominican Republic for decades.

In Dominica, in sharp contrast, writer Phyllis Shand Allfrey, an avowed feminist and Fabian socialist who founded the Dominica Labour Party in 1955, urged party women to found the Women's Guild, a grassroots political and social organization whose aim was to use its influence to take "the winds out of the sails of [the conservatives'] ship."[2] It quickly became one of the most active arms of the labor movement in the island, an example of the broader definition of feminism in grassroots movements in the Caribbean, concerned primarily with workers' access to power, land, and property. The Women's Guild came together politically and socially, and its activities (most of them still gender-bound) varied from cooking the banquet for the party's annual conference to singing Christmas carols—something which, as their energetic leader Mabel James (later to become a labor government minister) once described it, got the women "in a cheery merry mood" for the holidays. In January 1962 the women led their first public political activity, a "hell-fire counter demonstration" against the just-ousted conservative party, which was protesting taxes passed by the new Legislative Council dominated by Labour Party leaders. The women had prepared twelve placards, none of them centered on women's issues, but addressing the island's central political concerns, which they saw as their own: "Face the facts and pay the tax"; "Caesar Augustus made a decree that all the world should be taxed"; "And Mary and Joseph went to be taxed"; "Little man, let big man fight for hisself"; "Taxes must be paid"; "Roads cannot be built without money"; "We want better homes, better schools, more roads"; "We want a better Dominica"; "Little man is paying, Big man must pay"; "Heaven help those who help themselves"; "Tax them, Brother, tax them"; "When you pay one cent Big Man pay dollar."

The interest in full participation in the region's political and economic activity evidenced by the Dominica Women's Guild's placards brings me to the last point I want to make on the subject of the misrepresentation of women's movements and women's literature that results from a too-determined theorizing of the Caribbean as postmodern, postcolonial, post-something-or-other. And it concerns women's roles in national movements centered on decolonization and autonomy—an area in which non-Caribbean feminist theory can lead to most serious misunderstandings.

A central feature of U.S. feminist theory is that of the emergence of a fully emancipated woman out of the mire of patriarchal culture. It is an image born of the myths of rugged individualism that have shaped the image of the United States at home and abroad. Woman as maverick, as we can see in recent biographies of women like Eleanor Roosevelt, who emerges from the brilliant pages of Blanche Wiesen Cook's recent biography as a symbol of U.S. feminist womanhood in all its mythologizing power: crushed by her husband's affair with her own private secretary following her six pregnancies in the early chapters, Eleanor rises like a modern phoenix to found a furniture factory, build her own house, engage in passionate friendships with lesbian women, run her own school for girls, learn to fly with Amelia Earhart, become First Lady on her own terms. Dizzying stuff. But you can scan your memories in vain for similar images in the Caribbean and conclude that we lag behind the United States when it comes to heroic feminine material. To do so would be to judge heroism by standards that would never apply to the Caribbean region, where heroism, especially female heroism, has been sought in the subsuming of individual aspirations and desires into the struggle for the betterment of the community, and where women have followed a tradition, in history as in literature, of grassroots activism, courageous resistance, and, at times, even martyrdom. More characteristic of the Caribbean historical process are the careers of women like Allfrey, credited with almost singlehandedly bringing democracy to Dominica. In her attempt to wrest control of the Dominican political system from the hands of the landed and merchant elite, Allfrey had repeatedly crisscrossed the island on foot, traveling to near and remote villages and explaining in patois to gatherings of illiterate and semiliterate peasants the manifest advantages of allying themselves with a political party committed to furthering the workers' socioeconomic agenda. The notion, in all its newness, soon took hold among them. A young supporter remembers her campaign to found the Labour Party as the island's "political awakening," a watershed moment in the island's history whose significance may have been lost on the upper and middle classes but not on the peasantry and working class. While the upper class concentrated its fire on questioning Allfrey's political sincerity and accusing her of being a communist, the supported observed, the poor were happy, "drunk" with the feeling she had helped instill in them that "the day of the underprivileged was at hand" (quoted in Paravisini-Gebert, 1996).

Allfrey's career, tied as it was to the Caribbean's embryonic thrust toward political and cultural independence, also illustrates one significant aspect of women's progress toward fuller participation in all aspects of society: the impact of interregional and international migration on developing feminist consciousness and spearheading feminist activity. As a West Indian in London before the growth of a migrant community in the early 1950s, Allfrey had mastered grassroots politics with the leftist branch of the Labour Party, working on campaigns led by birth-control proponents and feminists like Marie Stopes, Edith Summerskill, and Naomi Mitchison. Later she made women's issues the focus of political activity in Dominica, pressing for the dissemination of birth-control information, the availability of safe abortions, and the procuring of adequate medical care for women. As vice-president of the Caribbean Women's Association from the late 1950s to the early 1960s and minister of labour and social affairs during the West Indies Federation, she fostered interregional communication between women in the English- and French-speaking islands of the Lesser Antilles, working tirelessly, for example, to secure a small vessel to facilitate interisland huckster trade. Her activities were representative of a process of transisland cross-pollination that has nourished women's movements in the region. Very often the process of migration, by forcing women into unfamiliar situations, experiences, and struggles, has resulted in a radicalization of political and social perspectives, leading women to assume roles not readily open to them in their home societies. Such is the case, for example, of Dominican women in the Washington Heights section of Manhattan, who have taken leadership roles in the domestic and community spheres which would have been disallowed in the Dominican Republic. The organizational skills and leadership abilities nourished by these experiences have been invaluable, both to their fledgling communities in the United States and to the home communities to which many of these women eventually returned. Feminist leaders like Dominican poet and essayist Chiqui Vicioso, brought up and educated in the United States, have played central roles in grassroots feminist ventures in the Dominican Republic as they have brought back with them often remarkable experiences in feminist activism and the profound knowledge of their home societies to adapt those experiences to Caribbean needs and mores. Vicioso, returning to her home island as a UNESCO officer, organized peasant women into cultural cooperatives that fostered literary and artistic creativity as a means of empowering women to assume a greater level of control over their physical surroundings and economic activities.

Interregional migration has in numerous instances provided similar opportunities for politization and militancy. A number of Cuban prostitutes, prized for their light skins in Haitian brothels in the forties and fifties, returned home to join the anti-Batista movement, leading the effort to combat the exploitation of women, particularly young girls, in the infamous Cuban brothels of that dictator's reign. Dominican women arriving in Puerto Rico to fill the lowest of jobs, often working for middle- and upper-class Puerto Rican women, have been forced to confront the unexpected "otherness" described by Luisa Hernández Angueira in this collection (chapter 5), a process akin to that they have undergone in other islands where Dominicans have migrated in meaningful numbers, such as St. Marteen and Curaçao. More positively, recent interregional efforts to encourage communication and dialogue have resulted in networks of communication that have proven invaluable in disseminating information and pinpointing successful strategies for community action and grassroots initiatives, countering the negative impact of free-zone development, securing information on health care and AIDS, developing ecological protection programs, limiting the alienating aspects of industrial work, and addressing such women-centered issues as abortion rights, child care, restrictions in access to education and jobs, battering, and child abuse.

In this interregional effort we find women writers playing a leading role, as it has been in literature and the arts that interisland communication developed with greater ease and cooperation (perhaps because they were seen as realms less threatening than political or economic collaborations). Like Allfrey, many Caribbean women writers have taken very active roles in feminist and political struggles. Marie Chauvet braved the Duvaliers in denouncing the Tonton Macoutes in *Amour, Colère, et Folie* (1968) and *Les rapaces* (1986). Jacqueline Manicom, known primarily as the author of *Mon examen de blanc* and *La Graine*, was co-founder of the feminist group Choisir and led a movement to make abortion legal in Guadeloupe (it is still rumored, such is the power of myth, that her fatal automobile accident in 1976 was the Silkwood-like result of these activities). Aída Cartagena Portalatín's founding of Brigadas Dominicanas to publish literary works banned under Trujillo placed her in constant danger. In Ada Quayle's *The Mistress*, Rosario Ferré's *Maldito amor*, Paule Marshall's *The Chosen Place, the Timeless People*, Michelle Cliff's *Abeng* and *No Telephone to Heaven*, Elizabeth Nuñez-Harrell's *When Rocks Dance*, and Phyllis Allfrey's *The Orchid House*, among many others, we find the salient elements of an emerging female and feminist historiography that seeks to examine the parameters of Caribbean feminism from a vantage point that is truly Caribbean and appears to owe little to foreign concepts of women's power.

These texts are part of an extraordinarily large body of novels (some fifty texts) written by Caribbean women centering on the plantation, revolving around plantation mistresses or women seeking empowerment in a plantation-bred social system, and focusing on women's roles in the destruction of the patriarchal/colonial power represented by the Caribbean plantation and its legacy. They depict women's struggle to become leading actors in the destruction of the multileveled power of the patriarchal plantation as the metaphor for the struggles of Caribbean peoples to unshackle themselves from the colonial power represented by the plantation and its remnants.

Their depiction of women as the destroyers of the plantation takes two primary forms: the planter-heroines are portrayed as self-immolating/self-destructive heroines that bring the plantation order crashing down (avenging angels like Antoinette Cosway in Jean Rhys's *Wide Sargasso Sea*, Gloria in Ferré's *Maldito amor*, and Clare in Cliff's *No Telephone to Heaven*) or as mediators that make possible the return of the land to the people (as in Allfrey's heavily auto-biographical *The Orchid House*, Chauvet's *Fonds-des-nègres*, and Marshall's *The Chosen Place, the Timeless People*). Both types of portrayals, however, stress women's roles in returning the land, and the power it represents, to the formerly dispossessed, sometimes themselves (as in Nuñez-Harrell's *When Rocks Dance*) but most often to the exploited peasantry (as in *No Telephone to Heaven*).

In "History and the Novel: Plot and Plantation," Silvia Wynter suggested looking at Caribbean history as the unfolding of the tensions between the structures of the plantation (imposed by the colonial powers) and the autoch-thonous structures of the plot system. In these novels, the planter-heroines are portrayed as the vehicles for the return of the land to the plot system of agri-culture, thus redressing the imbalance of power created by the hegemony of the plantation system. This transfer of land and power is often stressed in terms of a shift (not always voluntary but nonetheless unstoppable) from white ownership to black or mulatto control. This change is invariably presented as feminist, a feminism that incorporates as a primary element an assessment of the racial differences and conflicting class interests that separate Caribbean women. A not surprising number of the plots of these novels revolve around woman versus woman conflicts, as these writers bring to the fore of their texts their understanding of plantation societies as the least likely settings for the development of relationships of sisterhood between white, black, and colored women. More often than not, black, white, and mulatto women "were bound to each other in the [plantation] household, not in sisterhood, but by their spe-cific and different relations to its master" (Fox-Genovese, 100). Hence the de-pictions of relationships between women in the plantation underscore the au-thors' understanding that "class and racial struggles assumed priority over the gender struggle, even though class and racial struggles might have been expe-rienced in gender-specific, and indeed sex-specific ways" (Fox-Genovese, 95). The depictions point to a greater complexity in the alliances and misalliances that make up the complex web of historical relations between race and class groups in the Caribbean than we are likely to glean from a cursory attempt at applying traditional feminist and postcolonial theories to the study of Carib-bean women's lives, cultures, and literatures.

Feminist critics outside the Caribbean, after all, lionized Jean Rhys's hero-ines as representative of the Caribbean woman as victim of patriarchal oppres-sion—in sharp contrast to most Caribbean readings of Rhys's texts, which find heroism in her characters' self-destruction—creating a series of tropes that resonate through the critical literature on Caribbean women's writings. Rhys's heroines, however, are *sui generis* heroines, typical of a vision of Caribbean womanhood shared by few other Caribbean writers. Schwarz-Bart's Télumée Miracle, Allfrey's fictional alter ego Joan, and Dany Bébel-Gisler's Léonora, on the other hand, are emblematic of Caribbean women's rejection of victimization and insistence on their power to endure whatever the cost. I see in this oft-repeated trope in Caribbean women's writings the repository of a Caribbean-bound feminism still waiting to be explored. Rhys has given us the rootless and community-deprived Antoinette Cosway's final plunge into the void; Ramabai Espinet, in "Barred: Trinidad 1987," offers a counterpoint. One of the multiple female voices in her beautifully rendered story, beaten and abused by her husband, kills him and flees with her child into the night. Waking up in a bleak savanna at dawn, she sets out in hope of joining the community that will sustain her through what is yet to come. She has, after all, "lived through the long night."

NOTES

1. Some of these industries—the pharmaceutical industry in Puerto Rico and the electronic- and computer-equipment industries in other islands, for example—have favored the hiring of women over men, claiming as their rationale women's dexterity with their hands, their docility, and their reluctance to join labor unions. Women's access to highly paid employment in multinational corporations in the Caribbean has sent many women into the labor force and into the ranks of women's movements in the region, as they seek to defend and preserve their newly acquired rights and opportunities. It has also has had serious repercussions on gender relations, as the power vested in women in the household by their economic power has upset traditional gender roles. As a result, some scholars would argue, the rates of wife and child abuse, male alcoholism, and divorce have risen.

2. Letter to Phyllis Shand Allfrey from Mabel James, May 17, 1961, in Allfrey's Literary Executor's Archive. Quotations are from this document.

BIBLIOGRAPHY

Alvarez, Julia. *In the Time of the Butterflies.* Chapel Hill: Algonquin, 1994.

Chauvet, Marie. *Amour, Colère, et Folie.* Paris: Gallimard, 1968.

Cook, Blanche Wiesen. *Eleanor Roosevelt: Volume One 1884–1933.* New York: Viking, 1992.

Cooper, Carolyn. *Noises in the Blood: Orality, Gender and the "Vulgar" Body of Jamaican Popular Culture.* London: Macmillan, 1993.

Davis, Wade. *Passage of Darkness: The Ethnobiology of the Haitian Zombie.* Chapel Hill: University of North Carolina Press, 1988.

Espinet, Ramabai. "Barred: Trinidad 1987." In *Green Cane and Juicy Flotsam: Short Stories by Caribbean Women,* ed. Carmen C. Esteves and Lizabeth Paravisini-Gebert. New Brunswick: Rutgers University Press, 1991, pp. 80–85.

Fox-Genovese, Elizabeth. *Within the Plantation Household: Black and White Women of the Old South.* Chapel Hill: University of North Carolina Press, 1988, p. 100.

Hernández, Angela. *Emergencia del silencio: La mujer dominicana en la educación formal.* Santo Domingo: Editora Universitaria de la UASD, 1986.

James, C. L. R. *The Black Jacobins: Toussaint L'Ouverture and the San Domingo Revolution.* New York: Vintage, 1963.

Lair, Clara. "Que no voten las puertorriqueñas," *Juan Bobo,* June 17, 1916, p. 15.

Paravisini-Gebert, Lizabeth. "Esquema biográfico de Ana Roqué," in *Luz y sombra,* ed. Lizabeth Paravisini-Gebert. San Juan: Editorial de la Universidad de Puerto Rico, 1991, pp. 151–159.

——. *Phyllis Shand Allfrey: A Caribbean Life.* New Brunswick: Rutgers University Press, 1996.

——, and Olga Torres-Seda. *Caribbean Women Novelists: An Annotated Critical Bibliography.* Westport: Greenwood, 1993.

Rodríguez Monegal, Emir. "Carnaval/Antropofagia/Parodia." *Revista Iberoamericana* 45 (1979): 405–409.

Romero, Ivette. "The Voice Recaptured: Fiction by Dany Bébel-Gisler and Ana Lydia Vega," *Journal of Caribbean Studies* 8, no. 3 (1991–1992): 159–165.

——. "Women's Testimonial Narrative in the French and Spanish Caribbean." Ph.D. diss., Cornell University, 1993.

Suleiman, Susan Rubin. "(Re)Writing the Body: The Politics and Poetics of Female Eroticism." In *The Female Body in Western Culture: Contemporary Perspectives,* ed. Susan Rubin Suleiman. Cambridge: Harvard University Press, 1986.

Valle, Norma. "La organización de las mujeres en Puerto Rico," *En Rojo* (San Juan, P.R.), June 1–7 1977, p. 10.

——. "Viva controversia entre las vertientes del movimiento feminista," *En Rojo,* June 24–30, 1977, pp. 8–9.

Wynter, Silvia. "History and the Novel: Plot and Plantation," *Savacou* 5 (June 1971).

EMPOWERING THE MOTHER TONGUE
The Creole Movement in Guadeloupe

CYNTHIA J. MESH

THE ISLANDS OF the French Antilles are most often evoked by North Americans and Europeans as vacation getaways, with little understanding of the societies of people who currently inhabit these islands. This is often the case for the vast majority of Caribbean islands, whether independent nations or European territories or colonies. Yet in the past few decades, academic researchers have begun to delve deeply into the complex social and cultural phenomena that exist in the Caribbean basin, and have found many points of intersection common among Caribbean islands and even Latin America. An entire field of study has developed, usually referred to as "Latin American and Caribbean Studies." Yet it is notable that this field of study has for the most part excluded discussion of the French-speaking Caribbean, and especially the islands that are still dependencies of France in the form of "départements d'outre-mer," Guadeloupe (with its dependencies: Les Saintes, La Désirade, Marie-Galante, St. Martin, St. Barthélemy) and Martinique (otherwise known as the French Antilles). Haiti is often included in research on the Caribbean, as it is an independent nation, although much of the research focuses more significantly on the English- and Spanish-speaking islands. Research on women and women's issues in the Caribbean in particular has blossomed over the past two decades, especially since the United Nations Decade for Women: Equality, Development and Peace (1975–1985), yet here, too, discussion of the French Antilles most often has been neglected.

In this chapter, I will show how and discuss why the French Antilles (Guadeloupe and Martinique in particular) have suffered a triple exclusion from academic research and theoretical discussion, and more specifically, how issues affecting women and women's studies in the French Antilles have been further relegated to the background. Through discussion of one particular Guadeloupean woman, Dany Bébel-Gisler, and her work in language development and policy, I will argue that the field of Latin American and Caribbean Studies could benefit by the inclusion of studies on women in the French Antilles, especially with respect to issues of language and gender.

Although the French Antilles remain political dependencies of France, they share certain economic, historical, cultural, and linguistic commonalities with other Caribbean island societies that would seem to make them potentially intriguing parallel points of study for pan-Caribbean research. Yet most often, this is not the case. Furthermore, with respect to women's studies, one might expect to find inclusion of French Antillean women somewhere within the field of "French feminist theory," since women of the French Antilles are indeed citizens of France. Yet Antillean women, and other non-European French women, are most often absent from these discussions. The exclusion of the French Antillean islands from academic research, then, occurs on at least three levels. First, because they are still political dependencies of France, the French Antilles are left out of discussions that mainly focus on independent Caribbean nations, especially with respect to political and economic development. Second, and largely because of this general exclusion on political or national grounds, they are also missing from most women's studies research projects written from a pan-Caribbean perspective, although it can be argued that women in the French Antilles share a host of issues with their female counterparts in other Caribbean communities. Third, issues for women of the French Antilles, legitimate citizens of France, are excluded from discussions of "French feminist theory" because these theories are often confined to explorations of women in the abstract or even from a Eurocentric perspective that fails to take into account the geographic and cultural specificities that make women's lives very different in various parts of the world, despite common political and national affiliations.

Contemplating the field of women's studies with respect to the French Antilles brings all of these exclusions to the fore. It is striking that there has been so little research on women's issues in the French Antilles, yet the possible explanations for these exclusions are themselves interesting to explore, as they point to more general issues of cultural bias, patriarchy, and nationalism. This chapter will begin by offering a brief history of Guadeloupe and Guadeloupean Creole, in order to contextualize the analysis of Dany Bébel-Gisler's work and its relevance for women in the Caribbean more generally. Next, I will discuss in some detail the triple exclusion of the French Antilles from various modes of research in order to show where they might be included in the future and how the inclusions might further broaden and add substance both to Caribbean research and to women's studies. Last, I will offer a brief exploration of Bébel-Gisler's work as a sociolinguist, a writer, and a grassroots organizer in Guadeloupe. As one of the few women in Guadeloupe to gain recognition (especially internationally) for her work in traditionally male fields (sociolinguistics, language policy, politics, etc.), Bébel-Gisler epitomizes the possibilities that one person, indeed one woman, may have to effect real change in the world around her. The focus of the chapter will be on Guadeloupe, with some discussion of Martinique as appropriate. Although Guadeloupe and Martinique are often lumped together under the category of the "French Antilles" and indeed share many characteristics, they also have somewhat divergent histories, and the people of the islands generally identify themselves as "Guadeloupean" or "Martinican" rather than as "Antillean." The distinction between the two societies is significant in a number of ways, and rather than overgeneralize, this study will concentrate on Guadeloupe, Bébel-Gisler's birthplace and current home.[1]

A Brief History of Guadeloupe

Guadeloupe has been inhabited since several centuries B.C.E. (see Abenon, 12). At the time of Christopher Columbus's arrival in 1493 on his second Caribbean voyage, the island was inhabited by the Carib people, who had succeeded the Arawaks between 850 and 1000 A.D. Upon their conquest of the Arawak peoples on the various islands of the Antilles, the Caribs are said to have killed the men and reduced the women and children to the status of slaves. The women were kept as mates and supposedly maintained their own language, from which certain Creole words are descended (e.g., *hamac*). Between Columbus's arrival and the first permanent settlement by the French in Guadeloupe, 142 years would pass. The Europeans in the Caribbean were at first occupied with the islands of the Greater Antilles, including Hispaniola (today's Haiti and Dominican Republic) and Cuba in particular. Eventually, the Europeans spread their sphere of influence southward and found a great potential for profit through the cultivation of sugarcane on the islands of the Lesser Antilles. In 1635, France established a colony on the islands of Guadeloupe and Martinique and installed a "governor" to oversee the settlement in Guadeloupe, Liénart de l'Olive. Between this date and 1641, many battles with the Carib people ensued, after which a peace treaty of sorts was concluded and the remaining Caribs retreated to Dominica and other neighboring islands.

Vast numbers of the Carib people were decimated by European disease, forced hard labor, and genocide. Today, only a small number of people descending from the Caribs still live on Dominica. Little by little, France established a stronghold on the islands of Guadeloupe and Martinique, administered by the French West Indies Company, sending colonists from France itself and engaging in the slave trade from Africa for manual labor to work the sugarcane fields for the production of rum and sugar for the European "mainland." The influx of manual slave labor from Africa and, subsequent to abolition in 1848, the importation (often forced) of manual labor from India and China, along with the immigration of significant numbers of Syrians and Lebanese to the islands, have resulted in a heterogeneous society in terms of race, ethnicity, culture, and language. European French culture and language have been predominant by virtue of the political and economic power structure, but this predominance could not halt the development of a new culture and language, Creole, which are characteristic of so many Caribbean island societies populated by peoples of multiple origins.

Between 1759 and 1763, Guadeloupe had become a British colony, along with Martinique, resulting from war between France and England. At the Treaty of Paris in 1763, France gave up most of its North American territories (including Canada) to England in exchange for the return of the Antillean islands. Since this date, Guadeloupe and Martinique have remained French, despite a few short periods of British rule, and were colonies of France until 1946. During the Second World War, until 1943, Guadeloupe was occupied and administered by representatives of the Vichy government, while the people of Guadeloupe developed a vast network of "résistants" who often escaped to Dominica in order to take part in the French Resistance against Germany in Europe itself. After the war, in 1946, Guadeloupe, along with Martinique, French Guiana, and Reunion Island (in the Indian Ocean), was granted the status of "département d'outre-mer" (DOM) and theoretically would become an integral part of European France, politically, economically, even culturally. The main tenet was "assimilation" whereby citizens of the DOM would become indistinguishable from citizens of France except for their geographic residence distant from the "hexagon." While many Guadeloupeans were grateful to become French citizens and expected to reap the benefits, both economic and social, that they hoped this status would bring along, a growing number of Guadeloupeans (mostly Guadeloupeans of color in contrast to the white descendants of the original colonists) found themselves increasingly unwilling and unable to give up their distinct cultural identity for that of their European French counterparts. Departmentalization brought with it a vast improvement in the economy of the island but did not "cure" the problems of unemployment and relative poverty as many had hoped. Although the living and working conditions in Guadeloupe are significantly better than those in other Caribbean islands, there is still a large disparity between these conditions and those enjoyed by residents of European France.[2] To some, the benefits of continuing dependency on France seemed to grow ever smaller. As the population of Guadeloupe continued to grow, many were forced to emigrate to France to find work, mostly in menial positions in domestic and factory work, creating a whole new set of problems for those who would have liked to remain at home on their island but could not for economic reasons. European France benefited from this latest influx of cheap labor and had little interest in giving up the French Antilles even as independence became the order of the day in the late 1950s and 1960s for the many French and British colonies remaining in Africa and the rest of the Caribbean (Abenon, 190–99).

The many problems, political, economic, and cultural, associated with the colonial and ambiguously "postcolonial" situation of Guadeloupe remain today and are passionately debated by members of a number of political and grassroots organizations, in addition to the public at large. It is widely believed that most Guadeloupeans today would not give up the status as a French DOM if a referendum were held. One prime reason cited for this attachment is the fear of falling into an economic and political situation similar to that of Haiti, one of the few other "French-speaking" islands in the Caribbean. Even though many of the characteristics of Haitian society are distinct from those of the French Antilles, both in terms of geography and politics, some Guadeloupeans tend to relate to Haiti more than to other Caribbean island cultures. The reasons for this identification with Haiti are numerous. First of all, as both are former French colonies, there are obvious historical political parallels. Additionally, the official language of Haiti is French (along with Creole since 1986), so there are linguistic ties between Haiti and the French Antilles that do not exist between the French Antilles and other Caribbean nations. In addition to the French language, the French Antilles share with Haiti the Creole language (although in slightly different form), which makes the linguistic and, I would venture, cultural ties even stronger. Furthermore, Haitians have recently emigrated in fairly large numbers to Guadeloupe and Martinique looking for work and have taken agricultural jobs in sugarcane fields that Guadeloupeans, desiring better positions, no longer wish to fill. The Haitians living in Guadeloupe and Martinique are often disdained as immigrants who do not truly belong in

French Antillean society. Since many Haitians cannot speak French or read and write, their full participation and integration into Antillean society is made difficult if not impossible. In contrast, people of the French Antilles generally aspire to a "better" life, often identified with the accumulation of material wealth that seems to be the norm for their counterparts in European France. Not wanting to fall into the same cycle of poverty and political upheaval that they witness in Haiti, many Guadeloupeans (and Martinicans) believe their continued attachment to France will safeguard them from this eventuality.

On the other hand, significant numbers of people believe the continuing dependence on France is precisely what hinders Guadeloupe from realizing its full potential as a nation. They advocate independence from France accordingly. Today there are political parties devoted to the cause of independence from France in Guadeloupe and in Martinique, though they typically earn a small percentage of the vote in local elections. A major contribution of these groups, however, has been to raise the consciousness of the Antillean people about their own Creole culture and language, and major progress has been made, mainly through education and grassroots work, in the reaffirmation of a distinct cultural identity for the people of the French Antilles.

One obvious manifestation of changing attitudes about Antillean culture is the ever-growing, though still far from overwhelming, acceptance of the Creole language. To trace the sociolinguistic history of the Creole language in just a few pages would be an impossible task, yet it is important nonetheless to explain the rudiments of this history to show the extent to which language policy carries with it enormous political and cultural capital in the French Antilles and how the issue of language can be especially significant for women.

Creole Language and Culture

The year that the French established a permanent colony in Guadeloupe, 1635, is the same year that the Académie Française was established. This is certainly not an insignificant coincidence, as the French have long used language as a tool for dominating and trying to assimilate peoples that they have colonized or enslaved. Even in the early days of colonization in the Antilles, the French were intensely aware of the power of language and generally forbade Africans of the same language group from remaining together on a single plantation. Afraid of the possibilities of insurrection if the slaves were able to communicate effectively, the French made it difficult if not impossible for the newly arrived Africans to maintain their first languages. In order for the Africans to communicate with their French masters and with each other, they had to rely on a hybrid language that developed from a mixture of French and West African languages, along with some Arawak.

When people of various linguistic groups come together with no common language, a language of immediate communication generally develops called a "pidgin." This language is fairly rudimentary, allowing for discussion of daily necessities, commerce, and other basic topics. A pidgin is originally no one's first language. Yet as these two or more groups remain together for subsequent generations, the children of the newly mixed group generally learn this pidgin as their first language, which at this point becomes labeled a "creole." Fairly quickly, this language develops into a complex, sophisticated system of communication. "Creole" is both a generic linguistic term and a proper name for a number of creoles which have developed in the last few centuries. Creole languages have sprung up in most colonized areas of the globe, including in the Caribbean, Indian Ocean, and the South Pacific. Creoles that have developed in areas colonized by the French are quite similar, sharing elements of structure, vocabulary, and basic pronunciation. Thus Haitian Creole, Martinican Creole, Guadeloupean Creole, and Reunion Island Creole are all essentially mutually comprehensible, though each also has distinct elements of vocabulary, pronunciation, and grammar that differentiate it from the others.

For many generations, these languages have been regarded as simplified or "deformed" versions of French, often referred to as "petit nègre," "baragouin" (gibberish), or "patois" (see Prudent, 40). Lambert-Félix Prudent, a Martinican sociolinguist and professor, explains that attitudes about the Creole language are corollary to the attitudes about the people who depended on the language, namely African slaves and later Indian and Chinese workers on the islands. He describes the discourse about Creole through the end of the nineteenth century in this way:

> The essential image represented by a majority of authors is founded upon the idea that "Creole is the *corrupted* French of the negroes [nègres]," and the negroes themselves are seen as overgrown children (in the best case) or as dangerous savages, inferior in all ways to the European. (Prudent, 40; my translation)

Although the white planters also spoke Creole and their children often learned Creole from their slave nannies, it was generally considered to be the language of people of color. Since the white planters also spoke French, they did not depend on Creole exclusively for communication, whereas those of African,

Indian, and Chinese origin most often were Creole monolingual. Speaking French, on the other hand, was akin to being French, and one textbook still found in primary schools on the islands, according to Bébel-Gisler, states that to speak French was to be French and to be French was to be human. She discusses the cover of the textbook:

> A typical feature of our societies is that mastering the master's language, French, has been established as the symbol of the attainment of humanity. An illustration of this can be found in a sentence printed on the cover of school books that are still used in primary schools: "School of my country, I'm bringing my soul to you. Make this frail soul, which is weaker than the body it inhabits, a French soul, a human soul." (Bébel-Gisler, 1990, 4)[3]

Those who did not speak French, then, were deemed inferior to the French, and even inhuman. This attitude certainly pervaded the structure of the societies engaging in slavery, and continued to be prevalent well after the abolition of slavery. Creole monolinguals were most often those in the slave and later the working classes of society who did not benefit from private or later public education in French. The widespread, indeed racist, characterization of people of color as intellectually inferior spread to the notion that their language, Creole, was also incapable of expressing complex and abstract thought. Attitudes about people of color and negative assessments of the power of the Creole language originated in one and the same hegemonic scheme.

Attitudes of racial and class superiority have been extremely difficult to overcome, both for the dominant French and for the dominated "Creole" society, yet many of these attitudes have changed over the years, especially as people of color, who make up the overwhelming majority of the population, have taken on positions of power, both politically and economically. Yet negative attitudes about the Creole language, particularly as a symbol of a distinct, non-French culture, have been quite entrenched. However, those advocating independence, in particular, have worked long and hard to eradicate negative attitudes about Creole and to instill pride in the language and the culture and identity which it expresses. There have been many hard-won successes in this area, and a movement to establish a written form and to standardize Creole through grammar texts and dictionaries has been underway for a number of decades. There are currently newspapers published in Creole along with works of literature, and even academic works sporadically appear in Creole. Yet the problem still remains that Creole is most often relegated to "second-class" status and most of the population, although speakers of Creole, does not know how to read the language. Since the only official language is French and the school system in Guadeloupe and Martinique is legislated and administered by the French National Ministry of Education (essentially the same as schools in European France), administrators and teachers in Guadeloupe must follow the national guidelines for each subject matter taught. It was not legal to teach Creole in school until 1982, and many teachers and administrators still hesitate to include a Creole-based curriculum. Indeed, there are currently only two schools on Guadeloupe and Martinique combined where Creole is taught as a formal school subject (both at the middle school level). Additionally, students must have their parents' permission to take these classes, since some parents feel that learning Creole will hinder a student's progress in French and therefore do not approve of the teaching of Creole in school and do not want their children to participate in Creole classes.

Sylviane Telchid, educator and tireless advocate of Creole in Guadeloupe, has written a number of works on Creole, including teaching manuals, a Creole-French dictionary (in collaboration with others), and collections of Creole folktales in a bilingual Creole-French edition. Along with Hector Poullet, she has developed a method for teaching Creole that is distributed by a well-known publisher in France called the Assimil method, *Le Créole sans peine* (Creole without pain). Although she gains fairly little recognition for her work outside Guadeloupe, she, like Bébel-Gisler, has been one of the primary advocates for Creole in Guadeloupe. Together, these teachers and researchers are working toward a greater acceptance of the Creole language, hoping to pave the way for a greater acceptance of and pride in all that the Creole culture expresses.

The French Antilles: Falling through the Cracks

The French Antillean islands hold an ambiguous position in the Caribbean context. As neighbors to other Caribbean island nations and territories, they share many of the cultural, historical, and economic attributes with nearby islands, yet because of their continuing dependency on and political ties to European France, they are often excluded from attempts to forge pan-Caribbean links, both pragmatically and theoretically. The current research on women's issues in the Caribbean is indicative of Caribbean research more generally with respect to French Antillean exclusion and points to the limitations in scope of much of this work. One of a number of works I have reviewed, *The Decade for Women in Latin America and the Caribbean,* published by the United Nations, discusses many issues affecting women in the area. Addressing issues fairly generally rather than by specific country or region, the work attempts to review actions that had been accomplished by 1988, when it was published, and to suggest projects that required further investigation and action. Specific countries are addressed, however, by means of a number of charts and tables in the work which provide a variety of statistics illuminating conditions for women throughout the region. Guadeloupe and Martinique are not cited in these charts and tables, nor are the U.S. Virgin Islands, Puerto Rico, or Anguilla, to name just a few of the other Caribbean islands which are still attached to the United States and European nations (in the case of Anguilla, the United Kingdom). Table 10 is entitled "Latin America and the Caribbean: Proportion of Women in Total Teaching Staff and Students Enrolled by Country, 1970–1980." This table gives the most comprehensive list of countries included in this particular work, and in fact, the word "country" is significant here. By implication, it becomes clear that those areas investigated are only the independent nations of Latin America and the Caribbean, not those areas that remain territories of the United States or European nations. The countries listed are Antigua and Barbuda, Barbados, Bermuda, Cayman Islands, Costa Rica, Cuba, Dominica, El Salvador, Grenada, Guatemala, Haiti, Honduras, Jamaica, Mexico, Nicaragua, Panama, St. Lucia, St. Vincent, Argentina, Bolivia, Brazil, Chile, Colombia, Ecuador, Guyana, Paraguay, Peru, Suriname, Uruguay, Venezuela (Economic Commission, 106–7). Clearly, then, even a work such as this one with a title seemingly encompassing the entire region makes a limitation on its scope by considering only those areas that are now independent nations. Certainly not all works can discuss everything at once, yet the decision to exclude areas of the Caribbean that are not independent nations results in the sense that the territories of the Caribbean are somehow less important or significant and deserving of attention than the independent island nations. The French Antilles clearly fall into this neglected category.

Among the works published in the last two decades on women in the Caribbean, most have offered important contributions in assessing and suggesting ways to improve conditions for women in a number of Caribbean island communities. These titles generally suggest a study of the entire Caribbean region, yet on closer examination it becomes clear that each focuses on a limited number of communities. One of the most recent works, *Researching Women in Latin America and the Caribbean*, explores mainly the English-speaking and Spanish-speaking independent nations (Acosta-Belén, and Bose). *Perceptions of Caribbean Women* (Brodber), *Women of the Caribbean* (Ellis), and *Gender in Caribbean Development* (Mohammed and Shepherd), all concentrate almost exclusively on the "anglophone" or English-speaking Caribbean. The focus in these three works is defined by language, then, rather than by an island's political status as independent nation.

One of the very few works to include discussion of the French Antilles, and other territories in the Caribbean is the 1993 collection *Women and Change in the Caribbean*, edited by Janet Momsen. In the preface and introduction to the collection, Momsen makes clear that this is one of the only collections to include such a broad scope of research with respect to women in the Caribbean. She states: "this is the first [project] to include studies of the English, French, Spanish and Dutch speaking Caribbean and so provides a benchmark in Caribbean gender research" (Momsen, vii). My own review of the research confirms this statement. Momsen includes an article by Huguette Dagenais, "Women in Guadeloupe," that provides an excellent overview of conditions for women in Guadeloupe.[4] In her introduction, Momsen describes effectively and concisely the validity of approaching gender from a pan-Caribbean perspective, despite some of the differences in women's lives in various Caribbean islands:

> Within the Caribbean regional diversity of ethnicity, class, language and religion there is an ideological unity of patriarchy, of female subordination and dependence. Yet there is also a vibrant living tradition of female economic autonomy, of female-headed households and of a family structure in which men are often marginal. So Caribbean gender relations are a double paradox: of patriarchy within a system of matrifocal and matrilocal families; and of a domestic ideology coexisting with the economic independence of women. The roots of this contemporary paradoxical situation lie in colonialism. This book examines these contradictions within a trans-imperial framework. (Momsen, 1)

Momsen and her contributors are attempting to provide a broader perspective for the study of gender in the Caribbean, which is helpful toward understanding how the various historical and political phenomena of these essentially colonial and postcolonial societies have developed and how these developments affect women in particular. The present volume, *Daughters of Caliban*, also provides a broad perspective and will enable even more reflection and ideally action toward the improvement of women's lives in the Caribbean.

Women in the French Antilles have been excluded from practical movements and theoretical discussions not only by their sisters in other Caribbean countries and regions but indeed by their sisters in France as well. French feminist theories (there is not one unified theory of women, but rather a number of prevalent theories) have most often focused on abstract notions of gender and women's conditions in Europe and have failed to take into account the more pragmatic particularities of women's lives, especially for women outside the European context. Claire Duchen, in *French Connections*, translates into English a number of texts by women prominent in the feminist movement in France, texts both theoretical and practical. In doing so she aims to redress for the English-speaking audience some of the negative impressions that French feminist theory has acquired over the years. She explains:

> French feminists have the reputation of paying more attention to theory than to practical questions, and there is some truth in this: when a problem is discussed, more time is spent defining the terms of the debate and the nature of the problem than in looking for any practical solutions. On the positive side, this means that intellectual debate is rigorous; but it also means that feminists in France have been slower than British feminists in "networking," or in setting up rape crisis centres or refuges for battered women. (Duchen, 11)

By elaborating her collection of voices to include discussion of the women's movement in France in addition to the female theorists whose work has often been associated with "French feminism," Duchen offers a more complex view of the work of women on women's issues in France. Yet her focus still remains on European France and does not take into account the female French citizens of political dependencies of France outside Europe.[5] An even broader definition of "French women" needs to be elaborated in order to account for the vastly divergent experiences of French women around the world. Undoubtedly there are points of intersection between issues for women in the French Antilles, for example, and in European France, yet there are also significant differences that need to be considered in order to gain a better understanding of women's status and their particular needs outside of the European context. French feminist theorists have often focused on the issue of language from a very abstract and psychoanalytic perspective but have not generally considered daily problems associated with language, such as bilingualism and education in a bilingual/diglossic society where one language is clearly dominant over the other (in the case of the French Antilles, French dominates over Creole). Bébel-Gisler, one of very few women in her field, has spent much of her life working on the issues related to language and culture for the Antillean people and has begun to gain international recognition for her efforts.

Just as the French Antilles seem to be eclipsed in the vast majority of research on the Caribbean, issues regarding language are not particularly prominent in gender research related to the Caribbean. Yet language and some of the problems associated with bilingualism are of prime importance in Caribbean life and in the field of education specifically. Since education itself is often cited as the crucial locus for the improvement of women's lives, it would follow that a careful consideration of the ways in which language and education intersect is necessary to understanding and eventually improving women's opportunities in education in the Caribbean context. Almost all of the Caribbean communities are bilingual, if not multilingual, by virtue of their "creolized" formation resulting from the mixing of peoples from many geographic origins. The French Antilles, as mentioned, are bilingual societies where almost everyone speaks at least Creole and French. I will consider some of the work that Bébel-Gisler has accomplished in the field of language and discuss the ways in which her work, both academic and grassroots, is especially significant for women's lives in Guadeloupe.

Dany Bébel-Gisler: The Crusade for Creole and Women's Lives

Born in Guadeloupe almost sixty years ago, Dany Bébel-Gisler grew up on a sugarcane plantation and, after years of study in France and work in Paris, returned to Guadeloupe to become a highly prominent figure in the Creole movement in the French Antilles. Having been the first on her mother's side of the family to earn the coveted *baccalauréat* (high school diploma), Bébel-Gisler was encouraged to continue her studies and received scholarships to pursue advanced degrees in continental France, since at the time, there were no institutes of higher education on the islands. Bébel-Gisler earned degrees in sociology and linguistics and was mentored by the anthropologist and scholar Michel Leiris.

In the preface to her first major publication, *La Langue créole, force jugulée*, Bébel-Gisler explains the evolution of her passionate interest in language and her belief in its power as a force for social change. From her experiences as a young student in Toulouse preparing entrance to the Ecole Normale Supérieure in Paris, and through her work with African and Caribbean immigrants in Paris during her advanced studies, Bébel-Gisler became convinced that before other social changes could take place, the issue of language had to be confronted by the immigrant community. Although educational practices in European France with regard to non-French-speaking children are changing very slowly, at the time Bébel-Gisler published her study in 1976, she found that children of immigrants often were relegated to special education classes because of their inability to speak French. As a result, they were put at a distinct scholarly disadvantage relative to children in regular classes. Immigrant adults, by virtue of their inability to speak, read, and write French (or to speak "standard" French), were not able to get decent jobs, and furthermore were made to feel generally inferior because of their linguistic difficulties. But are all of these consequences really only a matter of linguistic ability or deficiency? Bébel-Gisler quickly realized that the difficulties in school faced by immigrant students trying to learn French were not simply a matter of grammar, phonetics, and style. She explains, rather, that the difficulties stem from the social parameters associated with language, and specifically, the social status of the French language. From these early realizations, Bébel-Gisler embarked on what has become a life project to promote a view of language as inextricably bound to sociopolitical forces, and to develop the Creole language, in particular, as a valuable and sophisticated communication system, worthy of writing, standardization, official status, and the utmost respect akin to that conferred upon the French language. Bébel-Gisler is attempting to define and encourage acceptance of Guadeloupean culture and language as distinct from, yet just as valuable as, the European French culture and language forced upon the people of the Antilles from the beginning of colonization through the present.

Specifically, Bébel-Gisler maintains that the separation of Antilleans from their mother tongue, Creole, creates deep sociopsychological troubles that render Antillean development by Antilleans extremely difficult. The interiorization of feelings of inferiority based on the supposed simplistic qualities of Creole and the culture it expresses, endorsed by the idea that French is the only communication system appropriate for official status, puts Antilleans in an adverse relationship to their mother tongue, representative of their distinct culture, that is counter productive to healthy and autonomous personal and societal development. Not until Antilleans reconcile themselves with the value and potential of the Creole language and the Creole culture that it expresses, Bébel-Gisler asserts, will they be able to create the kind of society in Guadeloupe that will allow them to make progress socially, economically, and politically, leading to the end of their dependence on France. In her 1989 work *Le Défi culturel guadeloupéen: Devenir ce que nous sommes* (The Guadeloupean cultural challenge: To become what we already are), Bébel-Gisler discusses in great detail her ideas about language and the importance of recognizing in Creole a tool for communication as complete and sophisticated as the French language. Bébel-Gisler does not advocate the eradication of the French language from Guadeloupe, however, but states clearly that French needs to give up its linguistic monopoly, or rather that Creole needs to take its rightful place along-side French. By equating the monopoly of the French language with the colo-nialism and imperialism of France over the centuries, Bébel-Gisler suggests that the increased usage of Creole, a language formed exclusively in the contact situation between African slaves, Indian immigrants, and French colonists among others, will enable a more coherent sense of Guadeloupean identity, as distinct from French identity, than that which is possible through French lan-guage expression alone. Some may argue that an increasing use of Creole by Antilleans will further isolate them from today's growing global economy. These opponents of Creole development suggest that in order to compete on a global scale, Antilleans must maintain French or another European language. Bébel-Gisler's arguments for the development of Creole are not necessarily contrary to the pragmatic belief that French or English is necessary to Guade-loupe's economic survival in the international market. What is important for Bébel-Gisler is the development of Creole as a means of encouraging Guade-loupeans to take pride in their distinct cultural identity and to begin to realize their own potential to be independent from France. Furthermore, there is a strong sense in Bébel-Gisler's work that the development of Creole as an official communication system will enable much larger numbers of people to take an active role in their own development, since many speak Creole much better than they speak French. If Creole were better accepted as a tool for political, economic, and scientific communication, many more people would be able to participate actively in their own education and government. This phenomenon might especially encourage women, often less educated than men and therefore less adept at speaking French, to take an active part in their own development and to take advantage of better opportunities for earning money and improv-ing their own living conditions as well as those of their families.

Bébel-Gisler's work is scholarly and also activist, as demonstrated through her years of work with immigrant communities in Paris, and currently through her work with the Centre Bwadoubout, which she founded near Lamentin, Guadeloupe. This center is a small school where children and adults who have faced difficulty or even failure in the French school system can learn basic edu-cation and skills in Creole. The only center of its kind in either Guadeloupe or Martinique, this experimental school enables students who may never have finished school to continue their education in a setting that is more accepting of them and that allows them to learn at their own pace and in their own lan-guage. Some of the students return to the French school system after they've mastered basic skills and improved their French (by way of Creole), and others attempt to find jobs in the private or public sectors. In either case, this center gives a small number of students, girls and boys, women and men, a second chance to succeed, while recognizing that their prior failures were not necessarily due to an inherent incapacity to learn, but rather to a school system that alienates its students by denying the validity of the Guadeloupean identity and the language that expresses and defines it.

According to the statistics cited by Huguette Dagenais, there is a distinct gender gap in work for Guadeloupean people. Women typically fill the lowest paid, least prestigious positions, while men enjoy significantly better opportunities for earning money (see Dagenais, 89–95). The connection between language, education, work, and gender must be made. In "traditional" Guadeloupean society, largely modeled on European French agricultural society, girls and boys were not encouraged to attend school to the same degree. Boys were encouraged to continue their studies if the family could afford it, while girls were often cut off from educational possibilities much earlier. Two Antillean novels about growing up in Guadeloupe and Martinique, both based on the lives of real people, convey stories related to this fundamental inequity. *Léonora*, by Bébel-Gisler and *La Rue Cases-Nègres* (Black Shack Alley) by Joseph Zobel both tell of girls who showed promise in their studies in elementary school but were kept from continuing by parents who did not see the benefits in sending girls, destined to become housewives, to school (Bébel-Gisler, 1985; Zobel, 1976). One of the primary effects of ending school early was that girls from the agricultural areas, predominantly Creole monolinguals, did not then have the opportunity to learn French well. As explained earlier, Creole was not, until recently, a written language, so if one did not learn to read and write French, one did not learn to read and write at all. Being illiterate and only slightly proficient in French has severely restricted the kinds of work that women could undertake. Although today, girls and boys attend school in relatively equal proportions (like their counterparts in European France), it will take some time before the attitudes about work change and before women are able to gain more equal access to the prestigious and higher paying positions in the Guadeloupean economic context. In the meantime, the development of Creole and the wider use of this language could enable more women to take better positions in the workforce.

Dany Bébel-Gisler's work, although not predominantly focused on women or on issues of gender, has the potential to greatly affect women's lives, since women have been unduly impacted by the difficulties in negotiating through an unequal (diglossic) bilingual society. Bébel-Gisler's *Léonora* is a testimony-novel about the life of one real woman, now in her seventies, with whom Bébel-Gisler conducted extensive interviews in Creole. These interviews were taped, then transcribed and translated by Bébel-Gisler into French and formed into a literary work published in 1985. This work, which includes many Creole passages in a predominantly French text, is significant for numerous reasons. Most important, perhaps, it exemplifies the life of a peasant woman in Guadeloupe who, under normal circumstances would have little or no access to public discourse of this type. As a black peasant woman, also a Creole speaker (though she does speak some French), Léonora holds a position of relative silence within Guadeloupean society. Yet Bébel-Gisler's work gives her the chance to speak out publicly about her life and her reflections on Guadeloupean history and society more generally.

Bébel-Gisler describes *Léonora* as one element of her own project to define and make acceptable a notion of Guadeloupean culture and language that raises Creole up from the depths of its currently limited and relegated status as "patois." Just as Bébel-Gisler's work with the Centre Bwadoubout shows her commitment to enabling Guadeloupeans to express themselves in Creole, so does her first literary work attempt to provide *Léonora*, a peasant woman, with a public forum for her thoughts and ideas. Furthermore, by using the literary genre of the testimony-novel, Bébel-Gisler hopes to reach a wider audience with her message than was possible through the sociolinguistic, scientific writing of her prior work. By writing it primarily in French, she hopes to make it more generally accessible, since few Creole speakers can, or are willing to, read Creole. Most can, however, read French, and are more likely to read books in French than in Creole.

In addition to Bébel-Gisler's message about Creole conveyed through the novel, the story itself tells the life of a peasant woman who underwent a significant transformation from a girl, forced to quit school at fourteen (though she showed good potential as a student, to a woman who became conscious of her own position in Guadeloupean society as inferior, both by virtue of her sex and by virtue of her position as a colonial (then "postcolonial") subject, and took action to change some of the conditions of her life and the lives of others. Told in the first person, the novel describes Léonora's growing self-awareness. She becomes politically active in the independence movements of the 1970s, believing in the potential for Guadeloupe to become its own nation, and furthermore takes a leadership position in the agricultural union strikes of the same period. Along with other women, she organizes strikes and stands up to the French riot police, in a bold and successful attempt to gain better working conditions for women and men in the sugarcane industry. Léonora's story is quick to point out that the organization of the women, specifically, was crucial to the success of the union efforts. Furthermore, Léonora separates from her abusive husband, and describes their relationship in very perceptive ways that place it within the broader context of gender inequality in Guadeloupe. Léonora herself serves as a powerful symbol of women's resistance, both in the home and in the workplace. This is even more significant since Léonora, a black peasant woman, has had to overcome much oppression in order to take the kinds of actions that she has taken in her life.

This sociological and literary work is only one example of Bébel-Gisler's devoted efforts to improve the conditions of people's lives, and certainly women's lives in particular, in Guadeloupe. As a firm believer in the power of the oppressed to raise themselves up and to take control of their own destinies, Bébel-Gisler is one woman who has already made a significant difference in the lives of many individuals in Guadeloupe. Bébel-Gisler's position as a woman scholar and grassroots activist is instructive and indicative of a larger movement in the islands. Further research on the French Antilles would certainly yield even more stories of women's initiatives to take power and control over their own lives. A comparison of the ways in which these initiatives are similar to and differ from those initiatives taken by women in independent Caribbean island nations might prove quite fruitful for a better understanding of both the specific conditions of women's lives in the Caribbean and the more general problems faced by women in colonial and postcolonial contexts.

NOTES

1. For this chapter, I draw on research conducted through university libraries in the United States and through three months of fieldwork on Guadeloupe and Martinique in spring, 1992. I am grateful for a Yale International and Area Studies Doctoral Thesis Research Grant and a John F. Enders Assistantship that made this fieldwork possible.

2. Huguette Dagenais discusses these disparities in her excellent essay "Women in Guadeloupe: The Paradoxes of Reality." She cites statistics of the 1987 per capita GNP for Guadeloupe in U.S. dollars as $3,190, compared to $4,230 for Martinique and $12,860 for European France (Dagenais 85). This is just one of a number of socioeconomic indicators that describe the relative poverty of Guadeloupe as compared to European

France. The living conditions are clearly better than those in most "third world" nations, and most experts would not describe Guadeloupe as "third world," yet certain communities in Guadeloupe do suffer from severe poverty.

3. Quoted by permission of the author. Thanks to Serge Gavronsky of Barnard College for drawing my attention to this talk and providing me with a copy of the manuscript.

4. Rather than repeat the general information on women in Guadeloupe that can be found in Dagenais's article, I simply refer the reader to it and concentrate my discussion on the work of Bébel-Gisler.

5. I would add here that it is not only the feminist sociological work that has excluded French Antillean women, but indeed the literary work as well, for the most part. None of the compilations of "French women's writing" that I have reviewed for this essay (see Bibliography) includes mention of the many French Antillean women writers (e.g., Maryse Condé, Simone Schwarz-Bart, Myriam Warner-Viéyra, Ina Césaire) who, incidentally, are gaining wider and wider recognition in literary circles worldwide.

BIBLIOGRAPHY

Abenon, Lucien-René. *Petite histoire de la Guadeloupe.* Paris: L'Harmattan, 1992.

Acosta-Belén, Edna, and Christine E. Bose, eds. *Researching Women in Latin America and the Caribbean.* Boulder: Westview, 1993.

Alibar, France, and Pierrette Lembeye-Boy. *Le Couteau seul . . . Sé Kouto sél . . . : La Condition féminine aux Antilles.* Paris: Editions Caribéennes, ACCT, 1981.

Beauvue-Fougeyrolles, Claudie. *Les Femmes antillaises.* 2d ed. Paris: L'Harmattan, 1985 [1979].

Bébel-Gisler, Dany. *Le Défi culturel guadeloupéen: Devenir ce que nous sommes.* Paris: Editions Caribéennes, 1989.

———. *La Langue créole, force jugulée: Étude socio-linguistique des rapports de force entre le créole et le français aux Antilles.* Paris: L'Harmattan, 1976.

———. *Léonora: L'Histoire enfouie de la Guadeloupe.* Paris: Editions Seghers, 1985.

———. *Leonora.* Trans. Andrea Leskes. Charlottesville: University Press of Virginia and CARAF Books, 1994.

———. "Who is the Other? What Does Translating the Other Mean?" Paper for the Seventh International Conference on Translation. Barnard College, New York, 1990.

———, and Laënnec Hurbon. *Cultures et pouvoir dans la Caraïbe: Langue créole, vaudou, sectes religieuses en Guadeloupe et en Haïti.* Paris: L'Harmattan, 1975.

Brodber, Erna. *Perceptions of Caribbean Women: Towards a Documentation of Stereo-*

types. Cave Hill, Barbados: Institute of Social and Economic Research (Eastern Caribbean), University of the West Indies, 1982.

Collins, Marie, and Sylvie Weil Sayre, eds. *Les Femmes en France.* New York: Scribner, 1974.

Dagenais, Huguette. "Women in Guadeloupe: The Paradoxes of Reality." In *Women and Change in the Caribbean: A Pan-Caribbean Perspective.* Ed. Janet Momsen. Kingston, Jamaica: Ian Randle, 1993, 83–108.

Deere, Carmen Diana, et al. *In the Shadows of the Sun: Caribbean Development Alternatives and U.S. Policy.* Boulder: Westview, 1990.

Duchen, Claire, ed. and trans. *French Connections: Voices from the Women's Movement in France.* Amherst: University of Massachusetts Press, 1987.

Economic Commission for Latin America and the Caribbean. *The Decade for Women in Latin America and the Caribbean: Background and Prospects.* Santiago, Chile: United Nations, 1988.

Ellis, Pat, ed. *Women of the Caribbean.* London: Zed Books, 1986.

Evans, Martha Noel. *Masks of Tradition: Women and the Politics of Writing in Twentieth-Century France.* Ithaca: Cornell University Press, 1987.

Jardine, Alice A., and Anne M. Menke, eds. *Shifting Scenes: Interviews on Women, Writing, and Politics in Post-1968 France.* New York: Columbia University Press, 1991.

Kadish, Doris Y., and Françoise Massardier-Kenney, eds. *Translating Slavery: Gender and Race in French Women's Writing, 1783–1823.* Kent, Ohio: Kent State University Press, 1994.

Miller, Francesca. *Latin American Women and the Search for Social Justice.* Hanover: University Press of New England, 1991.

Mohammed, Patricia, and Catherine Shepherd, eds. *Gender in Caribbean Development.* Mona, Jamaica: University of the West Indies Women and Development Studies Project, 1988.

Momsen, Janet, ed. *Women and Change in the Caribbean: A Pan-Caribbean Perspective.* Kingston, Jamaica: Ian Randle, 1993.

Perrot, Michelle, ed. *Writing Women's History.* Trans. Felicia Pheasant. Oxford: Blackwell, 1992.

Poullet, Hector, and Sylviane Telchid. *Le créole sans peine (guadeloupéen).* Chennevières-sur-Marne: Assimil, 1990.

Prudent, Lambert-Félix. *Des baragouins à la langue antillaise: Analyse historique et sociolinguistique du discours sur le créole.* Paris: Editions Caribéennes, 1980.

Randin, Willy. *Développement: L'Avenir par les femmes.* Lausanne: Favre, 1988.

Rao, Aruna, ed. *Women's Studies International: Nairobi and Beyond.* New York: Feminist Press, 1991.

Safa, Helen I. "Development and Changing Gender Roles in Latin America and the Caribbean." In *Women's Work and Women's Lives: The Continuing Struggle Worldwide*, ed. Hilda Kahne and Janet Z. Giele. Boulder: Westview, 1992, 69–86.

Sartori, Eva Martin, and Dorothy Wynne Zimmerman, eds. *French Women Writers: A Bio-Bibliographical Source Book*. New York: Greenwood, 1991.

Status of Women in the Caribbean: Report of Regional Seminar Held at Wyndham Hotel, Kingston, Jamaica, December 10–11, 1987. Bustamante Institute of Public and International Affairs.

Sylvain Bouchereau, Madeleine. *Haïti et ses femmes: Une Étude d'évolution culturelle*. Port-au-Prince, Haiti: Les Presses Libres, 1957.

Telchid, Sylviane. *Ti-Chika . . . et d'autres contes antillais*. Paris: Editions Caribéennes, 1985.

Zobel, Joseph. *La Rue Cases-Nègres*. Paris: Présence Africaine, 1976.

II

WOMEN AND WORK

❖ 3 ❖

WE TOIL ALL THE LIVELONG DAY
Women in the English-Speaking Caribbean

MARY JOHNSON OSIRIM

LIKE THEIR West African sisters, women of African descent in the English-speaking Caribbean have historically been involved in labor outside of the home which enabled them to make important material contributions to their families. Although much of this work remained invisible, arduous, and sex-typed, their labor force participation rates during most of the past two centuries still outpaced that of women in the Spanish-speaking Caribbean and in Latin America (Momsen, 1993; Safa and Antrobus, 1992; Larguia and Dumoulin, 1986). During slavery, Afro-Caribbean women were forced to engage in backbreaking labor on sugarcane plantations alongside men.[1] Even with emancipation and the end of colonialism in the region, women's income-generating activities were largely confined to low-wage, low-status, gender-segregated positions, many of which were concentrated in the informal economy. The declining position of Caribbean primary products on the world export market and U.S. policies, such as the Caribbean Basin Initiative (CBI), have expanded the contributions of women in areas such as tourism and export-oriented industries. Although these women have recently experienced significant improvement in educational attainment and employment, they still face substantial challenges from the domestic and global economies that serve to restrict their socioeconomic mobility and their overall contributions to their families, communities, and national development. Most prominent among these problems are the threats to their economic security posed by austerity and adjustment programs and the passage of the North American Free Trade Agreement (NAFTA).

This chapter seeks to examine Afro-Caribbean women's participation in the labor market from the colonial to the contemporary periods. What contributions have these women made to their societies and to development? What efforts have they made toward empowerment in the public sphere? These questions will be explored within a feminist political economy that draws our attention to both domestic and global issues as explanatory variables accounting for the current plight of Afro-Caribbean women. This analysis will begin by investigating the meaning of work for these women and their historical and modern connections to the labor market. After investigating recent attempts to enhance their status, policy recommendations will be offered to further address the difficulties they experience in the public sphere. Examples of women's work experiences will be drawn most heavily from Jamaica, Trinidad, and Guyana.

The Meaning of Work: Afro-Caribbean Women's Perspectives

The Women in the Caribbean Project (WICP) was the first major effort to characterize women's roles and responsibilities in the workplace and the home (Momsen, 1993; Osirim, 1992; Senior, 1991; Massiah, 1988). Conducted by researchers at the University of the West Indies and the University of Guyana, this study included the collection of statistical information on women's position in the labor market; 1,600 semistructured interviews of women in Antigua, Barbados, and St. Vincent; and thirty-seven life histories and in-depth interviews of women in several areas of the English-speaking Caribbean focusing on their lives in the private sphere. In the latter case, the respondents were asked about their friendships with women, their relationships with men, and the establishment and maintenance of support networks among kin and "fictive" kin (Senior, 1991).

For the purposes of our discussion here, what is most important is the categorization of their labors that Caribbean women revealed. Of the 1,600 participants in the survey, 60 percent cited housework as work (sometimes in combination with other types of work), while 40 percent stated that housework alone was work. Women in the study defined work according to four criteria: income, time involved, necessity, and energy. Like African women and their sisters throughout the Diaspora, Caribbean women critically linked work and the need to labor to their responsibilities as mothers (Bay, 1982; Osirim, 1992; Senior, 1991). In this study, women actually defined work as "any activity which is functionally necessary to maintain themselves and their households" (Osirim, 1992, Senior, 1991; Massiah, 1988). Despite the fact that women's status and responsibilities in the household and family are not the subject of investigation here, this chapter asserts that women's labors in the English-speaking Caribbean must be understood within the broader context of their roles as mothers. While all women in the region are not parents, the centrality of motherhood is and remains a focal aspect of self-identity for Caribbean women. Even those who are not biological mothers often assume the role of "surrogate" mothers for children in the community. Furthermore, this major component of identity exists among women from various class backgrounds.

In the WICP study, women provided an in-depth classification of the types of work. Six categories of work were defined as follows:

1. Not employed—indicates those not involved in an income-generating activity and not involved in home service.

2. Home service—for those engaged solely in homemaking and child-care activities.

3. Home production—for those who supplemented their activities through the sale of handicrafts, agricultural produce, and other activities.

4. Employment in own business/farm—for those operating their own business or farm, with or without paid assistance.

5. Employed by family member—for those engaged in paid labor for a relative.

6. Employed by others—for those working in paid positions for non-relatives.

This definition succeeds in broadening the parameters of what is officially recorded as "work." Not only is housework accorded significance in this definition, but activities in the informal economy that do not receive a regular wage and often go unnoticed, such as handicraft production, are regarded as work in this study. The typology of labor developed in this study is especially noteworthy when one considers that some of these responses were given before and during the Second U.N. International Women's Conference and preceded the third such conference in Nairobi, where much attention was given to the need for national and international recognition of women's unpaid labors. Such ideas had already been espoused by Caribbean women.

Understanding the Nature of Women's Labors in the English-Speaking Caribbean: Historical and Theoretical Perspectives

Feminist theories of development have made a major contribution to our understanding of the types of work in which Caribbean women are engaged. Within development studies, however, such models are relatively recent, when one considers the history of the field.

Major paradigms within the sociology of development can trace their beginnings to the social change literature that appeared with the establishment of the discipline in the work of Auguste Comte (1875). During the past half-century, several perspectives emerged that employed structural and behavioral explanations for the problems of development experienced in the South. Early theories, such as the modernization and psychocultural approaches, measured development in so-called Third World societies according to a Western yardstick—the structures, personality traits, and attitudes noted during industrialization in Western nations were to be emulated in the Southern Hemisphere if development was to occur (Inkeles and Smith, 1974; Eisenstadt, 1973, 1966; McClelland, 1969, 1961; Parsons, 1966).[2] Neo-Marxist approaches in the field employed a different tool in measurement—the development of the South was restricted because of these countries' relationship with the West (Evans, 1979; Cardoso and Faletto, 1979; Gunder-Frank, 1969, 1972). The poverty, deprivation, and overall lack of economic development was a result of historic and postcolonial interactions and the establishment of a world capitalist system that limited production and exports from the Third World to largely primary products. Even with more recent examples of the export of manufactured goods from the South, an international division of labor exists where production decisions, world market prices, and the terms of trade are largely determined by Western powers.

Although neo-Marxist perspectives did begin to examine the realities facing Southern nations, these models, as well as modernization theory and psychoculturalism, completely ignored the role of women in development. Boserup's pioneering work, *Women's Role in Economic Development*, began to set the record straight by investigating the increasing intensity of women's responsibilities in labor markets throughout the Third World. Unfortunately, this exploration accepted modernization as a given and failed to acknowledge the changing nature of capital accumulation in the global economy (Osirim, 1992; Beneria and Sen, 1981; Boserup, 1970).

In the current period, however, feminist political economy has substantially advanced our comprehension of the status of Southern women and their contributions to the development of their communities and their societies. Like their neo-Marxist counterparts, feminist theorists clearly realize the way in which the policies of Western nations, multilateral agencies, and international banks, as external agents, restrict the socioeconomic development of Southern nations. These decisions by the West include but are not limited to the setting of world market prices, especially for primary products; the amount and cost of funding and the conditions for acquiring loans from multilateral and international commercial banks; and the granting of foreign aid. Such actions in the context of an international division of labor operating within the global capitalist system affects class formation and racial, ethnic, and gender relations, as well as other aspects of social structure within Third World nations. Feminist analyses also suggest that we consider how the states' own actions and their adoption of Western-developed policies, such as structural adjustment, and the persistence of patriarchy and local culture within Southern societies often serves to limit the position of women and the poor and the prospects for national development. Perhaps most important, scholars within this tradition have urged us to consider how the global division of labor functions to confine most women to a narrow range of low-paying, gender-typed, largely unrewarding positions in their economies. They have further encouraged us to reject the dichotomy between the personal and the political and the public and the private spheres that has dominated much of the earlier social science literature (Antrobus, 1993). Thus feminist theorists recognize the critical linkage between the workplace and the home and engage in a comprehensive analysis of both external and internal factors to explain development and the status of women in the South (Momsen, 1993; Safa and Antrobus, 1992; Safa and Fernandez-Kelly, 1983; Parpart and Staudt, 1990).

How does such a model inform our study of the historical experience of Caribbean women and the labor market? To understand women's work in the region, one needs to first explore the incorporation of the English-speaking Caribbean into the world economy. This process began in earnest in the sixteenth century with the colonization of the region by Western European powers, the near-total destruction of the indigenous peoples, the Caribs and the Arawaks, and the establishment of plantation agriculture as the dominant economic activity (Momsen, 1993, Senior, 1991; Patterson, 1969). To ensure a steady supply of labor for these plantations and the profitability of these ventures, slaves were imported from Africa and soon became the largest population in the region. By the beginning of the eighteenth century, sugarcane was established as the major product and a monoproduct economy and culture was born in such countries as Jamaica, Trinidad, and Guyana. Reliance on a single primary product then became an early and lasting characteristic of the region, which would shape not only the labor market outcomes for women but also the nature of gender relations in the region for a long time to come.

During slavery, women worked in the fields next to men, doing some of the most backbreaking work imaginable. Despite the fact that "absentee landlordism" characterized many of these enterprises in the British colonies, the general conditions of slavery were much harsher than what was endured in the southern United States (Patterson, 1969). This was especially the case because the tropical climate, with its excessive heat and periods of heavy rainfall, created thicker "bush" that needed to be cleared. In addition, women were involved in domestic labor and petty trading. Plantation work, however, posed the greatest challenges for slave women. Senior describes the extent to which women were involved in plantation agriculture in Jamaica:

> Field slaves were grouped according to strength and endurance, not according to sex. The evidence so far shows that women contributed the largest proportion of field slaves. . . . On one Jamaican plantation in 1789, 70 women out of a total female slave population of 162 worked in the fields, in comparison with 28 men out of a possible 177. Four years later, . . . there were 107 female fieldworkers out of 244, in contrast with 92 men out of 284. Towards the end of slavery, when Jamaican sugar plantations had an excess of female workers, "not only were the majority of Jamaican black women labourers in the field, but the majority of Jamaica's labourers in the field were black women." (Senior, 1991)

In addition to agriculture, petty trading, or higglering as it is called in Jamaica, has a long history in the region that can be traced back to slavery. Slave women frequently farmed subsistence plots in addition to their required plantation work and sold the goods they produced at Sunday markets. The proceeds from their sales were used to "buy freedom" for many slaves and later assisted in the purchase of land (LeFranc, 1988). In fact, such petty trading was perhaps one of the earliest major Africanisms that appeared in the New World. The vast majority of slaves imported from West Africa enjoyed a rich tradition of participation in commercial activities. Many West African women, such as the Yoruba of southwestern Nigeria, had become quite successful in the selling of foodstuffs in the market, while their male counterparts were most often involved in long-distance trade. Such activities in the historic and modern periods have enabled these women to make substantial contributions to the maintenance of their families (Osirim, 1994; Clark, 1988; Afonja, 1981). Afro-Caribbean women continued this rich heritage.

Although emancipation was granted to African slaves in the English-speaking Caribbean in the 1830s, Afro-Caribbean peoples for the most part were still tied to the land. In an attempt to immediately replace the actual and anticipated decline in the "forced" labor market with the end of slavery, British planters in Jamaica, Guyana, and Trinidad in particular imported indentured labor. The first group to be recruited as cheap laborers for the sugarcane plantations were the Chinese. In the case of Jamaica, the earliest population arrived between 1853 and 1854. They were unsuited for the backbreaking plantation labor that was expected of them and, according to some accounts, also appeared unruly (Patterson, 1977). The Chinese were followed by East Indian indentured laborers, who in Guyana, for example, remained largely tied to the land into the postindependence period. East Indians eventually outnumbered peoples of African descent in the country. The descendants of the earliest Chinese and East Indian populations are disproportionately found to dominate the commercial sectors of several of these nations today.

During the middle to late nineteenth century, the majority of Afro-Caribbean women in these societies remained engaged in wage labor on the plantations. In the immediate postemancipation period, for example, 80 percent of the female population was employed in this sector (Senior, 1991). Throughout this period, however, two important factors emerged that would have a significant effect on the working lives of women. First, as these economies entered the modern period, they continued their dependence on sugarcane production. Since the harvesting of sugarcane was largely a seasonal activity, many men, particularly those who lived in areas with one harvest season, began to migrate to other countries in search of work. While some female food sellers were also involved in buying goods in one country to sell in another, the nature of men's migratory labor resulted in their staying in the host nations for a longer period. The lack of stable employment that epitomized the lives of most men in the English-speaking Caribbean had major consequences for the roles and responsibilites undertaken by women. Because of the high rates of male unemployment and underemployment in the region, the percentages of legal marriages and stable unions of long duration remained low among many residents until they approached middle age. Although many men attempted to support their children from common-law unions when they migrated in search of work, they were often likely to establish new relationships and have additional children from these unions. Therefore, women in the original unions most often had to assume the major financial obligations for their children, largely without the assistance of men. So both economic necessity and women's self-concept that focused on the importance of children in their lives led them to participate in income-earning activities outside of the home.

The second major factor that affected the working lives of women was the division of labor that occurred in plantation agriculture. Women did not have the range of occupational choices that existed for men in sugarcane production. The first major division occurred after 1780 with the introduction of machines into farming, when men and not women were forced to use the new technology. With emancipation, women and men continued to work in the fields as participants in slash-and-burn agriculture, but men came increasingly to occupy positions in the sugar factories that were established in several Caribbean nations. In countries such as Guyana where these factories were most often involved in machine repair, as opposed to sugar refining, men still held all the positions in this sphere (Osirim, 1977). Men not only received higher wages for factory work than women did for field labor, but the former positions provided greater job security for men. In addition, factory work trained men in more technical skills and, in general, enabled them to become more familiar with modern machines. Such exposure to modern machines and factory production, as well as the higher wages that these positions afforded, placed men in a more privileged position to occupy a wider range of occupations in the future and to establish their own enterprises. Given their economic advantage, these businesses were more likely to be profitable than women's activities (Osirim, 1990).[3]

In addition to agricultural labor, work in the informal economy became an important area of income earning for women with the end of slavery. Women continued to work in market trade and some higglers became increasingly involved in more long-distance trade throughout the region, purchasing goods in their home country to sell in another. Once the products were sold in the host society, proceeds would often be used to purchase local goods to be sold at home.

Afro-Caribbean women were also involved in dressmaking as a cottage industry. They worked in their own homes, and customers either came there to place orders or the seamstresses would visit the elite clients in their own residences. These entrepreneurs often extended credit to their clients and frequently had to wait a long time before they received payment. This occupation, however, remained a critical area of employment for skilled female workers, especially in Trinidad from the late nineteenth to the early twentieth century. Harewood (1975) estimated that from about 1900 to 1930, dressmaking remained the major occupation for 95 percent of skilled Trinidadian women and for 84 percent of the combined group of skilled and semiskilled working women.

Another important area of largely informal sector activity for women was domestic work. For many women, such labor represented the continuation of the exploitative relationship that emerged during slavery, experienced most directly by those women who were the house slaves. Although employed women would now be paid for such work, the wages were very low, the labor quite strenuous, and for the most part the occupation was unregulated. As a result, rarely did women earn even the minimum wage for work that frequently exceeded a normal eight-hour day. The status of domestic work remained low into the twentieth century and was largely dominated by a female labor force. Society continued not to regard this occupation as "real work," and the concentration of women in the job helped keep the remuneration rates low (Glenn and Feldberg 1989). In addition to live-in domestic work, many Afro-Caribbean women were forced to perform such labor on an even more informal basis, through the taking in of laundry and ironing from middle-class women as a means to sustain their own families.

Agricultural labor, domestic service, and self-employment in such areas as market trade and dressmaking remained the major occupational choices for the majority of women in the English-speaking Caribbean into the mid-twentieth century. While these positions provided women with cash income, they generally kept most women relegated to the bottom of the socioeconomic hierarchy, where they engaged in labor that often remained invisible to official census takers and policymakers. Transitions in the global economy and in the international division of labor would begin to expand women's occupational choices in the late twentieth century. This did not mean, however, that the stigmas of low pay and lack of dignity would be removed from women's work—these labels continue to characterize much of women's endeavors today.

Women and the Contemporary Labor Market

Although women in the English-speaking Caribbean have made great advances over their sisters from a century ago, especially with respect to educational attainment and their rates of participation in the "official" labor market, they still face major inequities when compared with the income attainment and occupational choices of men. As earlier studies have documented, official statistics of women's labor force activity can be rather deceiving. If one were to focus on the percentage of economically active women in some of these societies, especially when compared to their counterparts in other Southern nations (whose rates are often listed in the low 30 percent range), the picture would appear rather optimistic (see table).

Economically Active Women in the English-Speaking Caribbean

Country	% of Population
Antigua and Barbuda	40.1
Barbados	47.2
Guyana*	29.9
Jamaica	45.3
St. Kitts	41.0
St. Lucia	39.1
Trinidad and Tobago*	33.8

*These societies contain larger East Indian populations whose official labor force participation rates for women are lower than those of Afro-Caribbean women. This factor contibutes to lower national percentages of economically active women in these countries.

Sources: Momsen, 1993; *Encyclopedia Britannica Book of the Year*, 1990.

Upon closer inspection, however, one would find that although women have virtually gained parity with men in the educational sphere, this has not translated into more lucrative positions in the employment realm. Women still remain clustered in low-paying service positions, and even when they have been able to enter the professions, they have remained concentrated in teaching and nursing (Senior, 1991; McKenzie, 1986).

What do rates of labor market activity conceal about the actual work that women do in the Caribbean? How have changes in the global economy and the division of labor affected the position of these women in the labor market?

Beginning with the post–World War II period, Southern nations witnessed a shift in the nature of Western nations' involvement with their countries. In English-speaking Caribbean societies such as Jamaica and Trinidad, import-substitution industrialization was attempted in the 1950s as an attempt to diversify these economies and reduce their dependence on the West. Textile and garment-making industries were some of the major local ventures in this era.

At the same time, transnational corporations (TNCs) based in the West ushered in a new wave of imperialism with investment in primary product-related industries and other endeavors in the Third World. In some of the largest nations of the region, namely Jamaica, Guyana, and Trinidad, such corporations became linked to the extraction and refining of major primary products. In the case of Trinidad, TNCs were major partners in the oil industry, while in the former two nations, companies such as Alcan and Alcoa played a major role in bauxite production, especially in the manufacturing of raw bauxite into aluminum. As the price of sugar and its importance on the world market declined, these products emerged as principal export earners for these economies.

These industries, however, were largely male-centered activities and did not provide employment opportunities for women. This was especially problematic because positions in these sectors were stable and generally high-paying compared to the counterpart activities for women without higher education in the service sector and other areas of the informal economy.

What have been the major sources of employment for women from the postwar to the current period? With the decreasing contribution of sugar to national income earning in these nations, women's participation in agriculture also declined. During the past fifteen years, women's official rates in agriculture have ranged from about 30 percent to 40 percent of the female labor force in most English-speaking Caribbean societies. This involvement takes a variety of forms and includes work as farmers as well as farm laborers. Women still produce the majority of food for local consumption, although much of this work remains invisible. They dominate the spheres of food production, processing, and distribution (Ellis, 1986).

Women have clearly made inroads with respect to their participation in the professions and administration. Two factors, however, demonstrate the limited income-earning potential of these fields for women: women remain concentrated in the female activities of teaching and nursing, and the majority of women in these fields are government employees. In periods of economic crisis, such employees are frequently not paid regularly and, under adjustment and stabilization policies, run the greater risk of losing their jobs in efforts to trim state expenditures. Such crises have served as "push" factors leading some women to migrate to the West, where they frequently obtain positions in nursing because of labor shortages in this area in the United States. Others abandon these activities in the hope of earning higher wages through self-employment.

A more recent shift in the international division of labor, the creation of Export Processing Zones (EPZs), began in the 1970s but became most evident in the Caribbean in the 1980s. The establishment of these zones, in conjunction with the Caribbean Basin Initiative (CBI), instituted in 1984, has led to additional areas of employment for women in manufacturing and telecommunications. These more recent developments, however, have not significantly altered the socioeconomic status of Afro-Caribbean women precisely because of the low wages, poor working conditions, and gender-segregated character of this employment.

Export Processing Zones are physically designated areas where goods and services are produced at low to even zero rates of taxation, without any foreign exchange restrictions (Pantin, 1993). These EPZs are examples of world-market production centers that are characterized by foreign investment in areas with a high percentage of young, single women workers creating goods that were formerly manufactured in the West. Particular areas of the South have been most attractive to the establishment of such EPZs, especially those that have a large, low-wage labor force. Unlike the significant positive growth in domestic product that has occurred in areas such as the East Asian Newly Industrializing Countries, manufacturing in EPZs in the Caribbean contributes little value added in production. This is precisely because these activities in the latter case are largely assembly plants—they import semifinished goods from the West and merely complete the production process in the zones. Net export earnings from these activities have also been quite small and, furthermore, only moderate employment growth has been noted in Jamaica, Barbados, and Trinidad where EPZs have been created (Pantin, 1993; Pearson, 1993). By 1986, for example, employment in EPZs of these nations ranged from 2,700 to 8,000 employees (Pantin, 1993).

The CBI has further solidified this development in the global division of labor, since it provides for the duty-free treatment of imports from the Caribbean. Although several categories of goods are exempted from this agreement, for example leather products, clothing, and footwear, textiles that are manufactured in the Caribbean from solely U.S. inputs are allowed to enter the United States (World Bank, 1993). This is especially noteworthy in the EPZs of the Caribbean, such as Trinidad, which had a garment industry since the 1930s, with significant numbers of Afro-Caribbean women involved in sewing in factories and in their homes.[4] The CBI, however, would not allow the use of local inputs from this established industry in production in the EPZs, and thus does not encourage the utilization of locally made goods or indigenous entrepreneurship. What is promoted is increased dependence.

What does this all mean for women who work in the EPZs of the Caribbean?

In addition to the low wages that accompany employment in this sector, the work is labor-intensive, boring, and tedious, providing little or no opppor-tunity for promotion. It is the type of labor that exploits the skills with which women have been stereotypically identified: speed, accuracy, and efficiency in repetitive tasks. The positions that women occupy in these industries have fre-quently exposed them to health risks from dangerous chemicals without pro-viding protective clothing for the women to wear (Ellis, 1986). Meanwhile, women are still clustered in the low-status end of these industries, since the vast majority of managers in these EPZs are male (Senior, 1991; Ellis, 1986; Safa and Fernandez-Kelly, 1983).

Even in the most high tech areas of production in the EPZs, most positions occupied by women offer little remuneration and are associated with many health risks. In the telecommunications industry in Jamaica, for example, data processors at the beginning of this decade earned only about U.S. $.50 per hour (Pearson, 1993). The women worked under constant stress of needing to in-crease the speed with which they worked and suffered from eyestrain, back in-juries, and other problems associated with spending long periods in front of computer screens (Pearson, 1993; Barnes, 1989).

Despite the creation of new industries in the Caribbean, the vast majority of women still participate in the service sector. Over 50 percent of all women working in the region are concentrated in this sector (Senior, 1991; Mohammed, 1987; Ellis, 1986). While more women in the last few decades have obtained for-mal sector employment in this sphere in secretarial and data-processing posi-tions, many women in this sector still depend on the informal economy for their incomes.

Domestic work is still a significant area of employment for women in the region. Although the total number of domestics has been declining over the past few decades, middle-class women who enter formal-sector jobs still hire domestics for housework and childcare. Many have argued that the reality of living in the South without many modern household applicances, where gen-der-role socialization patterns strongly persist, means that women not only bear the brunt of domestic responsibilities, but that these are much more dif-ficult, time-consuming tasks than they are in the West. Consequently, women who hold demanding formal-sector jobs have a difficult time maintaining their households with little or no help from their male partners. Such women, there-fore, are likely to hire domestic workers.

In the Caribbean, such labor takes varied forms. A 1975 study of domestics in Trinidad revealed that they are hired for a day, a half-day, part-time, or on a

live-in basis (Mohammed, 1987; Housewives Association of Trinidad and Tobago, 1975). While the responsibilities that accompany such work are arduous,
live-in workers are generally subject to the most difficult circumstances. This
is because these employees are often expected to work around the clock—employers continue to demand labor from these women beyond the eight-hour
day, and, as a result, it is not unusual to find domestics in these situations working more than twelve hours per day (Mohammed, 1987). As would be expected,
the salaries in this type of occupation remain very low, working conditions are
often poor, and accommodations are inadequate. Domestic workers are seldom
treated with respect from their employers and function without the benefit of
protective legislation (Chaney and Castro, 1989; Walcott, 1988). Live-in workers
further experience significant role strain, since their relationships with their
own children are jeopardized because of the little time and attention they can
give them. In this case, the extended network of support provided by kin and
"fictive" kin has played a significant positive role in the raising of domestic
workers' children.

Many Afro-Caribbean women continue to work as market traders and street
vendors. Although women are still involved in long-distance trading of fruits
and vegetables throughout the region, other avenues for commercial activity
have appeared as a result of economic crisis. In Jamaica, for example, beginning
in the 1970s when scarcity was a feature of the economy, some women became
informal commercial importers of goods from Panama, Haiti, Curaçao, and
the United States (Bolles, 1992; LeFranc, 1988). Unlike their counterparts in
produce vending, the commercial importers were involved in highly profitable
enterprises. Petty trade in foodstuffs still most often yields low incomes for
women.

Higglering remains an important option for Caribbean women with low
levels of educational attainment, and has also constituted an alternative for
women in dead-end white-collar occupations. In fact, many of the informal
commercial importers were previously employed as secretaries and teachers
(LeFranc, 1988).

With the decline in the prices for primary products on the world market,
particularly during the past fifteen years, tourism became an increasingly important source of foreign exchange earnings for the Caribbean. In addition to
the jobs for women in formal services, such as waitresses and housekeepers in
major restaurants and hotels, women also earn income from tourism through
self-employment. Some women in this sector are entrepreneurs who own small
hotels and guesthouses. Women in this sphere commonly generate cash

through the sale of handicrafts, manufactured goods such as T-shirts, and cooked food. They sell these goods in markets and hawk their wares through city streets and along the beaches. The gender-based division of labor is also predominant in this sector—men usually sell the more expensive black coral jewelry and wood-carvings; women sell food and clothing (McKay, 1993). Women's trade based on food and clothing is often less lucrative than men's activities selling more expensive items.

At the close of the twentieth century, then, the majority of women in the English-speaking Caribbean persist in unrewarding, gender-segregated activities that severely restrict their upward mobility.

Trying to Bridge the Gap:
Caribbean Women's Efforts toward Empowerment

Despite the myriad difficulties that Afro-Caribbean women experience in the labor force, they enjoy reputations as strong and resourceful members of their societies (Momsen, 1993; Senior, 1991; LeFranc, 1988; Bolles, 1986; Ellis, 1986). They have formed organizations and waged strikes against employers, as well as organized theater collectives, international development associations, and kinship networks to draw attention to their plight and to support themselves and their children.

The problems of unemployment, outmigration among males, and the resulting prevalence of female-headed households in the region led women to establish networks of support among extended family members and "fictive" kin. These informal groups of women assist each other with childcare and financial support. Perhaps more important, members of these groups provide personal advice and emotional support for each other, building self-esteem and empowering women in their multiple roles. The qualities of responsibility, reciprocity, and dignity that develop in these relationships created a strong foundation from which they could organize to collectively express their problems and pursue their goals as women.

The successful activities of domestic workers to unionize in Trinidad were built on women's experiences with networking in the private sphere. In 1982, they formed the National Union of Domestic Employees (NUDE), which is run solely by women. An earlier study by the Housewives Association of Trinidad and Tobago (HATT) drew attention to problems faced by domestic workers and led to the creation of a Minimum Wages Board. This action resulted in a stipulated minimum wage for domestic employees. Jamaica has also legis-

lated a minimum wage for its workers in this sector, while Barbados has enacted legislation to restrict the working hours of domestics. These laws have
not eliminated the problems these workers face, but the efforts of women have
led the state to take action regarding wages and working hours and have begun
to remove this work from the "shroud of invisibility."

One group that has been influential in focusing attention on the conditions
of domestic work and the other activities in which poor women are engaged
is Sistren, a Jamaican women's theater collective. The collective was formed in
1977 from a group of women participating in the Impact Program, a govern-
ment-sponsored project to create jobs in areas such as street cleaning available
for unemployed women (Sistren Theater Collective, 1988). Sistren has produced plays that depict the lives and working conditions of poor and working-
class Jamaican women. Through their performances, often held in working-
class communities, prisons, and villages, the group "looks at possible solutions
to the problems of women in their day-to-day struggle [and] provides the
members of the collective with the chance to participate in a self-reliant cooperative organization" (Sistren Theater Collective, 1988). In their productions
and in their community work more generally, the members of Sistren acknowledge their African heritage and insist on understanding their past. Moreover,
they recognize the varied and important roles that women fulfill in Caribbean
societies as mothers, workers, partners, daughters, and aunties. Through their
writing and acting, they empower not only themselves but their Caribbean sisters as well by exploring women's lives and engaging in the struggle for social
change.

During the 1980s, many Caribbean governments created women's bureaus
to examine the dilemmas facing women in the region. In Trinidad, for example,
a Women's Bureau was formed within the Ministry of Social Development and
Family Services to provide training, research, and education for nongovern-
mental organizations. Many of these agencies, however, directly benefited middle-class women and did little to address the problems of the poor.

On the contrary, the Women and Development (WAND) Program of the
University of the West Indies Extra-Mural Department in Barbados attempts
to help grassroots women improve their status. Under the leadership of Peggy
Antrobus, WAND has served as a liaison between international development
agencies and the funding of women's income-generating projects. It has placed
an important emphasis on regional activities and has formed broader women
and development projects in the English-speaking Caribbean. In addition, it

has provided encouragement and training for women to begin and sustain microenterprises, thereby generating employment and empowering women.

The creation of an international organization of Southern women, Development Alternatives with Women for a New Era (DAWN) can also be credited in part to the work of Peggy Antrobus and other Caribbean women. The Second U. N.-sponsored Conference on the Status of Women revealed that by 1980, women's conditions worldwide had worsened—they were increasingly displaced from the labor force by new technologies and their rates of poverty and illiteracy had increased. Thus a group of Southern women organized themselves in Dakar, Senegal, in 1982 and established DAWN. Peggy Antrobus and Gita Sen, among other founding members of DAWN, recognized that the efforts of national governments alone would not significantly improve the lives of women. They emphasized the importance of developing a feminist political economy and an organization that critically linked Southern women's oppression to the international division of labor based on gender. DAWN has urged women and development scholars to examine how the global capitalist system has structured and limited the participation of women in the national and international economies. As a result of the policies and actions of nation-states, multilateral agencies, and other key actors in the international economy, the majority of women and children in the South have been thrust into greater poverty, amid efforts to empower themselves.

The Impact of Adjustment and the Possible Consequences of NAFTA: The Quagmire for Afro-Caribbean Women

Although women in the English-speaking Caribbean have made valiant efforts in the quest for empowerment, the improvements made in the lives of poor and working-class women in the modern period have either already largely been eroded or stand in jeopardy of disappearing in the near future. Women occupying low-wage, low-status positions are not likely to witness a positive transformation in their working lives in the short term. Structural Adjustment Programs (SAPs) and stabilization efforts adopted by Southern states, including those in the Caribbean, have eroded many of the small gains made in the recent past, leaving women burdened with additional financial and emotional strains.

What are SAPs and how do they affect the working lives of Caribbean women? Adjustment programs have been instituted by many Southern states upon the strong directives of the International Monetary Fund and the World Bank as a means to improve the states' economic performance. With the massive increases in oil prices in 1973 and again in 1978, mounting international debt from foreign borrowing in the postwar period, and declining prices for primary product exports, many non-oil-producing Third World nations were experiencing major balance-of-payments problems. By the early 1980s, Southern nations were hard hit by the worldwide economic crisis, making a bad situation even worse. To sustain their failing economies, governments were forced to turn to the multilateral agencies for stabilization and adjustment loans. Stabilization loans from the IMF involved drastic short-term correctional measures such as devaluation of the currency and cuts in government spending (Joekes et al., 1988). Structural adjustment loans from the World Bank involve "the mobilization of domestic resources through fiscal, monetary, and credit policies; improvements in the efficiency of resource allocation and use by the public sector; the reform of economic incentives in order to reduce distortions and reform the price systems; and institutional strengthening" (Joeckes et al., 1988). In short, stabilization and adjustment programs in the South have promoted free market policies and massive currency devaluations in an effort to attract foreign investment and to make exports more affordable on the world market. Such actions are supposed to liberalize trade, diversify the economy, and result in less reliance on imports (Iqbal, 1993). Price controls are lifted and state expenditures are reduced through trimming the public sector labor force and cutting subsidies for social programs, such as education, health care, housing, and transportation. It is precisely the "shrinking" of the public sector that has the gravest impact on the lives of women, especially those at the bottom of the socioeconomic hierarchy.

To illustrate how such policies function to further disadvantage women, we will examine one nation's experience with adjustment. One of the first to experience the effects of adjustment was Jamaica, starting with policies enacted in 1977. These programs, which have continued into the current decade, have not controlled inflation and have not reduced foreign debt. As opposed to increasing the demand for Jamaican exports and reducing the nation's dependence on imports, the reverse occurred there in the early and mid-1980s. The EPZs, which have been encouraged as part of the "free market orientation," have not substantially contributed to employment growth in the country.

It is when we consider more carefully what has occurred with respect to employment and social programs that we are best able to measure the impact of these programs on women. First, over 20,000 Jamaicans have lost their jobs in the public sector. Second, in the 1980s, official unemployment grew to 28 percent. Third, devaluation and wage caps resulted in major declines in the standard of living from 1977 to the early 1990s. Iqbal summarizes these problems:

> In view of wage guidelines ranging from 10% to 12.5% and rates of inflation between 30%–60% it must be concluded that the real incomes and living standards of the general population have declined. Real incomes of wage and salary earners fell by 15% between 1983–'85 and by a further 8.4% for private sector workers and 7.5% for government employees between 1989–'90. In June of 1979, the minimum wage just covered the cost of feeding a family of five. By December, 1989 it covered only 58% of the cost, and by December, 1991 only 22% of the cost. (Iqbal, 1993)

How do such employment issues affect Jamaican women, especially those who do not hold positions in the formal sector? Women bear the brunt of employment policies based on SAPs. Since women are clustered in low-wage occupations, they often seek additional support to maintain themselves and their children from partners and extended kin. Although they frequently rely on networks of women for financial and childcare assistance, male relatives, not just partners, are also contributors to the family's well-being. Therefore, men who lose their public-sector jobs and those whose wages do not keep pace with inflation provide additional stress on women, who view themselves and are regarded by others as bearing a primary responsibility for the maintenance of children.

In response to the unemployment problems created by adjustment policies, the state and multilateral agencies encourage the displaced to become entrepreneurs. For many people in Jamaica, this has meant participating in the informal economy as microentrepreneurs. Street vending and other hustling activities have been on the increase on the streets of Kingston, in the markets of Ocho Rios, and on the beaches of Negril. Although some women, such as the informal commercial importers, have financially benefited from the economic downturn, other female petty traders find that they are experiencing increased competition from men, selling the same products, which jeopardizes their already low incomes. This outcome for most women traders has also been noted in many sub-Saharan African countries that are struggling with adjustment (Osirim, 1994; Clark and Manuh, 1991).

The state's reductions in social spending also have a major impact on the lives of women and the poor. In Jamaica, spending on health, education, and social security fell from 622 million Jamaican dollars in 1981–82 to 372 million in 1985–86 (Iqbal, 1993; Boyd, 1988). Expenditures on primary education also took a nosedive, from constituting 16 percent of public expenditures in 1977 to 12 percent in 1989 (Iqbal, 1993; Witter and Anderson, 1991). Under adjustment, the "hidden" costs of going to school escalate, as well as the direct costs in the form of school fees. The increased costs for books, uniforms, transportation, and the frequent imposition of school fees are borne by women. The decline in the construction of low-income housing also meant sustained hardships for low-income residents, who were in dire need of improved living conditions and access to clean water (Iqbal, 1993; Antrobus, 1989). Finally, not only do women experience rising health costs because of the removal of state subsidies, but they are expected to fill the gaps in the provision of health care through their own efforts: "Within current policies of structural adjustment, women's work as traditional health-care providers is used as a justification for cutting primary health care services. It is assumed that women will fill the gaps created by cuts in health services" (Antrobus, 1993).

The passage of the North American Free Trade Agreement also threatens the quality of life for Afro-Caribbean women. Regional economic relationships such as NAFTA tend to focus the attention of the Western powers involved on the specific Southern nations within this sphere, i.e., Mexico. Third World investment opportunities are likely to be sought first in Mexico, as opposed to the English-speaking Caribbean. Many industries are likely to continue to relocate to Mexico, since the possibilities of a cheap labor force and high profits have already become a reality for many U.S. firms. Much of the low-cost labor sought will consist of young female workers who not only earn meager wages but often work in unhealthy conditions. These are certainly not the situations we would advocate for our Afro-Caribbean sisters. Yet this greater attention on Mexico as a production center is likely to result in lost investment opportunities and less employment growth for much of the Caribbean. Furthermore, although part of the impetus for the Caribbean Basin Initiative was the need to limit the potential migration of Afro-Caribbean peoples to the United States, the motivation on the part of the U.S. government in relation to Mexican immigrants is even greater. NAFTA has the potential of not only enhancing the position of the United States in the world capitalist economy but of also satisfying public opinion with respect to stemming the flow of immigrants. For all of these reasons, women in the English-speaking Caribbean are likely to lose in the short run with respect to potential growth in U.S. investment in their region.

Policy Recommendations

As adjustment and stabilization programs (and potentially NAFTA) have taken their toll on Afro-Caribbean women, are there any policies that can be implemented to improve their income-earning prospects and the quality of their daily lives?

Suggestions can be offered to enhance the position of Afro-Caribbean women at both the macro and the micro levels. With respect to the former, the social consequences of adjustment policies on the poor, especially women, require that Caribbean states reevaluate the dictum from multilateral agencies that free market policies are necessary to improve their economies. While the political and economic histories, as well as the racial, cultural, and class composition of the Newly Industrializing Countries (NICs) of East Asia differ from those of the English-speaking Caribbean, the latter can draw an important lesson from the experience of the NICs. That is, these nations did not strictly follow a laissez-faire route to development—in these societies the state played a key role in spearheading development. In many cases, vital industries and utilities need to remain under state control to guarantee a decent standard of living for the majority of the population and to meet national development aims. Leaving the "invisible hand" to control the market often results in much greater hardships for most citizens, who in the South are already living at or below bare subsistence. The best alternative for many Caribbean nations is a mixed economy, where production and exchange decisions can be made with particular attention to domestic employment and development goals.

Given the increased role of regional economic organizations in the world system, it is also important that the Caribbean's own association, CARICOM, be strengthened. This group needs to exert a major role in setting regional development goals—in this interdependent world, small nations, such as those in the Caribbean cannot expect to achieve self-sufficiency. However, they should determine what should be produced, as opposed to this agenda being set from abroad. They can capitalize on their local strengths to produce some of the goods they need and for exports that will yield valued foreign exchange. Regional planning and development goals can be set for areas such as tourism—what activates should CARICOM, national states and/or indigenous entrepreneurs attempt to control? A proactive approach needs to be taken, as opposed to the overarching power of transnational corporations in setting their priorites in the region. This is not to argue that there is no role that TNCs can play, but that role needs to be clearly defined by Caribbean states themselves given their regional (and not just national) priorities. In such activities, CARICOM also needs to create more occupational alternatives in the region, especially for women (as attempted previously by WAND) that would increase their salaries and their employment status. Regional training centers can also be established to provide particularly low-income women with the technical and management skills they need to succeed in these new positions.

Even if these new and greater opportunities are created in the private and public sectors for women, they are not likely to seek or be able to accept such positions unless broader change occurs at the societal level. Gender-role socialization practices need to be eliminated in all their forms in all spheres where they exist—at the level of the family and household, the church, the school, the workplace, and the state. Although enrollments are about equal for young women and men in Caribbean primary and secondary schools, the numbers of students do not guarantee quality education nor assure equal access to nontraditional education for women. Instruction in fields such as construction trades, engineering and computer and telecommunications technologies needs to be made available for women, and they need to be encouraged to pursue these fields. Secondary and tertiary-level institutions should also be more sensitive to the needs of pregnant women and young mothers and provide them with opportunities to continue their educations in a suppportive environment. Further, all vestiges of the colonial education system, especially the O-level examinations that serve to restrict students from not only higher education but from many positions in the labor market, need to be completely phased out in favor of examination and placement systems that reflect the realities of developing economies.

In addition to ending gender-role socialization patterns, the pejorative connotations, such as "unskilled labor" associated with women's work must be eliminated. This extends to all categories of labor—both blue- and white-collar work. While this chapter delineates the necessity to create more and varied job opportunities for women, there is little doubt that some categories of labor associated with women will remain. Rather than calling for an end to such occupations as domestic work, what is suggested in the short run is the full implementation of laws guaranteeing minimum wages and maximum working hours to such positions. The state should acknowledge the importance of housework and childcare in maintaining society and the need for all individuals to realize that regardless of gender, they do have responsibilities in this area that they need to fulfill for their families. Afro-Caribbean women's conceptions of their own labor that appeared in the WICP could serve as an important guide to redefinitions of women's work. These actions would not only improve the status of household labor, but would go a long way in making such work visible.

Although these recommendations do appear to entail additional expenditures for already strained Caribbean states, rethinking and reorganizing their priorities in terms of national and regional aims should enable them to achieve many if not all of these goals. Such changes will not only transform the lives of Afro-Caribbean women but will clearly enhance their contributions to regional development.

Using a feminist perspective, this study examined the historical and modern roles of Afro-Caribbean women in the labor market. The contemporary evidence demonstrates that their activities are clustered in gender-segregated areas that provide low wages and low status and that frequently subject these women to unhealthy working conditions. Despite the attempts of these women to empower themselves in their positions and to draw attention to their plight, the adoption of stabilization and adjustment policies, as well as the ratification of the NAFTA by the United States, poses additional challenges to their well-being now and in the future. Efforts by CARICOM in conjunction with Caribbean states to pursue indigenous development goals and to strive toward the elimination of patriarchy can significantly advance the position of women in the labor market and enhance their contributions to their communities.

NOTES

1. Although women of African descent reside in all areas of the Caribbean, the term "Afro-Caribbean women" is used in this chapter interchangeably with the term "English-speaking Caribbean women" to refer to women of African descent in the former British colonies.

2. With respect to psychocultural theory, scholars such as David McClelland believed that if individuals in the South were not "achievement-oriented," they could be taught such traits in achievement motivation workshops. The need to achieve was viewed by theorists in this perspective as a requisite characteristic for entrepreneurial success, a critical element in the development equation.

3. Research on this topic in Nigeria has demonstrated that men's formal sector connections, gained through greater access to education and employment, provided

them with additional advantages that women lacked. For men, this translated into larger, more profitable small-scale enterprises, compared to women's business activities.

4. The garment factories that were established in Trinidad after 1930 were owned, with few exceptions, by the Jewish and Syrian-Lebanese populations who came to dominate local commercial enterprises in this period.

BIBLIOGRAPHY

Afonja, Simi. 1981. "Changing Modes of Production and the Sexual Division of Labor among the Yoruba." *Signs*, vol. 7, no. 2.

Antrobus, Peggy. 1989. "Gender Implications of the Development Crisis," in George Beckford and Norman Girvan, eds., *Development in Suspense*. Kingston: Friedrich Ebert Stiftung/Association of Caribbean Economists.

Antrobus, Peggy. 1993. "Gender Issues in Caribbean Development." In Stanley Lalta and Marie Freckleton, eds., *Caribbean Economic Development: The First Generation*. Kingston: Ian Randle.

Barnes, C. 1989. "Data Entry Demands." *Sistren Magazine*, vol. 2, no. 3.

Bay, Edna, ed. 1982. *Women and Work in Africa*. Boulder: Westview.

Beneria, Lourdes, and Gita Sen. 1981. "Accumulation, Reproduction and Women's Role in Economic Development: Boserup Revisited." *Signs*, vol. 7, no. 2.

Bolles, A. Lynn. 1992. "Common Ground of Creativity." *Cultural Survival Quarterly*, vol. 16, no. 4.

Bolles, A. Lynn. 1986. "Economic Crisis and Female-Headed Households in Urban Jamaica," in June Nash and Helen Safa, eds., *Women and Change in Latin America*. South Hadley, MA: Bergin and Garvey.

Boserup, Ester. 1970. *Women's Role in Economic Development*. New York: St. Martin's.

Boyd, D. 1988. *Economic Management, Income Distribution and Poverty in Jamaica*. New York: Praeger.

Cardoso, Fernando, and Enzo Faletto. 1979. *Dependency and Development in Latin America*. Berkeley: University of California Press.

Chaney, Elsa, and Mary Castro, eds. 1989. *Muchachas No More: Household Workers in Latin America and the Caribbean*. Philadelphia: Temple University Press.

Clark, Gracia, ed. 1988. *Traders versus the State*. Boulder: Westview.

Clark, Gracia, and Takyiwaa Manuh. 1991. "Women Traders in Ghana and the Structural Adjustment Program." In Christina Gladwin, ed., *Structural Adjustment and African Women Farmers*. Gainesville: University of Florida Press.

Comte, Auguste. 1875. *The System of Positive Polity*. London: Longman, Green.

Eisenstadt, S. 1966. *Modernization: Protest and Change.* Englewood Cliffs: Prentice Hall.

Eisenstadt, S. 1973. *Tradition, Change and Modernity.* New York: Wiley.

Ellis, Pat, ed. 1986. *Women of the Caribbean.* Atlantic Highlands: Zed Books.

Evans, Peter. 1979. *Dependent Development.* Princeton: Princeton University Press.

Girvan, Norman. 1992. "Liberalization Increases Jamaica's Hardships." *Caribbean Contact.*

Glenn, Evelyn, and Roslyn Feldberg. 1989. "Clerical Work: The Female Occupation." In Jo Freeman, ed., *Women: A Feminist Perspective.* Mountain View, CA: Mayfield.

Gunder-Frank, Andre. 1969. *Latin America: Underdevelopment or Revolution.* New York: Monthly Review Press.

Gunder-Frank, Andre. 1972. *Capitalism and Underdevelopment in Latin America.* Harmondsworth: Penguin.

Harewood, Jack. 1975. *The Population of Trinidad and Tobago.* CICRED Series.

Housewives Association of Trinidad and Tobago. 1975. *Report on the Employment Status of Household Workers in Trinidad.*

Inkeles, Alex, and David Smith. 1974. *Becoming Modern: Individual Change in Six Developing Countries.* Cambridge: Harvard University Press.

Iqbal, Janine. 1993. "Adjustment Policies in Practice: Case Study of Jamaica, 1977–91." In Lalta and Freckleton, eds., *Caribbean Economic Development.*

Joeckes, Susan, et al. 1988. *Women and Structural Adjustment: Part II: Technical Document.* Washington, D.C.: International Center for Research on Women.

Larguia, Isabel. and John Dumoulin. 1986. "Women's Equality and the Cuban Revolution." In Nash and Safa, eds., *Women and Change in Latin America.*

LeFranc, Elsie. 1988. "Higglering in Kingston: Entrepreneurs or Traditional Small-Scale Operators." *Caribbean Review,* vol. 16, no. 1.

McClelland, David. 1961. *The Achieving Society.* New York: Van Nostrand

McClelland, David, et al. 1969. *Motivating Economic Achievement.* New York: Free Press.

McKay, Lesley. 1993. "Women's Contributions to Tourism in Negril, Jamaica" In Janet Momsen, ed., *Women and Change in the Caribbean.* Bloomington: Indiana University Press.

McKenzie, Hermione. 1986. "The Educational Experience of Caribbean Women." *Social and Economic Studies,* vol. 35, no. 3.

Massiah, Jocelyn. 1988. "Researching Women's Work: 1985 and Beyond." In Patricia Mohammed and Catherine Shepherd, eds., *Gender in Caribbean Development.* Mona: University of the West Indies Women and Development Studies Project.

Mathurin, Lucille. 1977. "Reluctant Matriarchs." *Savacou,* vol. 13.

Michalopoulus, Constantine. 1987. "World Bank Lending for Structural Adjustment: A

Review of the Bank's Approach and Experience." *Finance and Development*, vol. 24, no. 2.

Mohammed, Patricia. 1987. "Domestic Workers in the Caribbean." In *Women in the Rebel Tradition: The English-Speaking Caribbean*. New York: Women's International Resource Exchange.

Momsen, Janet. 1993. Introduction, in Momsen, ed., *Women and Change in the Caribbean*.

Osirim (Johnson), Mary. 1977. *A Comparative Study of Work and Family Life in the Guyanese Sugar and Bauxite Industries*. Master's thesis, Department of Sociology, London School of Economics and Political Science.

Osirim, Mary J. 1990. *Characteristics of Entrepreneurship in Nigerian Industries That Started Small*. Ph.D. diss., Department of Sociology, Harvard University.

Osirim, Mary J. 1992. "The State of Women in the Third World: The Informal Sector and Development in Africa and the Caribbean." *Social Development Issues*, vol. 12, no. 2/3.

Osirim, Mary J. 1994. "Women, Work and Public Policy: Structural Adjustment and the Informal Sector in Zimbabwe." In Ezekiel Kalipeni, ed., *Population Growth and Environmental Degradation in Southern Africa*. Boulder: Lynne Rienner.

Pantin, Dennis. 1993. "The Role of Export Processing Zones in Caribbean Economic Development." In Lalta and Freckleton, eds., *Caribbean Economic Development*.

Parpart, Jane, and Kathleen Staudt, eds., 1990. *Women and the State in Africa*. Boulder: Lynne Rienner.

Parsons, Talcott. 1966. *Societies: Evolutionary and Comparative Perspectives*. Englewood Cliffs: Prentice-Hall.

Patterson, Orlando. 1969. *The Sociology of Slavery: An Analysis of the Origins, Development and Structure of Negro Slave Society in Jamaica*. Rutherford: Fairleigh Dickinson University Press.

Patterson, Orlando. 1977. *Ethnic Chauvinism: The Reactionary Impulse*. New York: Stein and Day.

Pearson, Ruth. 1993. "Gender and New Technology in the Caribbean: New Work for Women?" in Momsen, ed., *Women and Change in the Caribbean*.

Safa, Helen, and Peggy Antrobus. 1992. "Women and the Economic Crisis in the Caribbean," in Lourdes Beneria and Shelley Feldman, eds., *Unequal Burden: Economic Crises, Persistent Poverty and Women's Work*. Boulder: Westview.

Safa, Helen, and Maria P. Fernandez-Kelly. 1983. *Women, Men and the International Division of Labor*. Albany: State University of New York Press.

Senior, Olive. 1991. *Working Miracles: Women's Lives in the English-Speaking Caribbean*. Bloomington: Indiana University Press.

Sistren Theater Collective. 1987. "Women's Theater in Jamaica." In *Women in the Rebel*

Tradition: The English-Speaking Caribbean. New York: Women's International Resource Exchange.

Walcott, Clotil. 1987. "Domestic Workers Rights." In *Women in the Rebel Tradition.*

Witter, M, and P. Anderson. 1991. "Crisis, Adjustment and Social Change: Case Study of Jamaica." Study prepared for the UNRISD.

World Bank. 1993. "The Caribbean: Exports Preferences and Performance." In Lalta and Freckleton, eds., *Caribbean Economic Development.*

Yelvington, Kevin A. 1993. "Gender and Ethnicity at Work in a Trinidadian Factory." In Momsen, ed., *Women and Change in the Caribbean.*

4

REINVENTING HIGGLERING ACROSS TRANSNATIONAL ZONES

Barbadian Women Juggle the Triple Shift

CARLA FREEMAN

NOT LONG AGO, the classic portrait of the strong Bajan matriarch might have been a buxom woman in colorful prints and gingham, confidently balancing a tray of produce upon her head on her way to market.[1] Today, a slim woman sporting a rayon skirt suit and matching accessories, as she waits for a bus to one of the newly renovated offshore offices, might better exemplify the Caribbean working woman. Contrary to appearances and popular mythologies, the apparent arrival of this professional-looking woman masks those features of her economic life that tie her experience closely to that icon of Caribbean history, the country higgler.[2] This chapter takes as its point of departure the historical continuities marked by women's engagement in formal and informal income-generating activities and explores the ways in which their contemporary forms demonstrate new conditions of an increasingly global arena. It focuses on a group of "pink-collar"[3] workers who dramatically illustrate the Caribbean's particular place within this new transnational era.[4]

As a region populated entirely by "migrants," from European settlers and indentured servants to African slaves and later East Indian indentured laborers, the Caribbean is constituted by complex cultural amalgams. Its economies and social structures have been shaped by international flows of "transmigrants" (Basch et al. 1994), capital, goods, and ideologies for over 300 years. Indeed, the Caribbean has long represented a quintessentially transnational terrain. The fact that virtually nothing about Caribbean culture can be described as pure or indigenous, or without reference to heterogeneous colonial histories (Trouillot 1992), makes this region a particularly fertile crucible for examining what is historically reminiscent and what is decidedly new about today's transnationalism. Several social critics have argued that these cultural flows do not follow a single "core" to "periphery" course but rather reveal twists and turns in which the periphery "talks back" (Hannerz 1992: 265) and punctuates the core itself. The movements are multidirectional and multiformed, and, as such, open up spaces for new local identities and practices across a transnational terrain. For the new informatics workers in Barbados, these identities and practices are formulated through women's simultaneous involvement as transnational producers (processing information as the newest commodity in the foreign-owned offshore sector) and as consumers, blending foreign and local goods, styles, and tastes.[5] The ways in which women combine wage work in new foreign-owned transnational "office-factories" with "informal" craftsmanship and suitcase trade[6] and varying degrees of domestic or reproductive work illustrate complex interconnections between multinational capital and local culture. In practices that blur the boundaries between formal, informal, and domestic economies and between "work" and "leisure," women are fashioning new feminine identities that demonstrate how deeply "local" culture is embedded in the transnational. Their three "shifts" together mark the articulation between transnational processes of production and consumption and the intensification of cultural and economic flows across the Americas. As such, defining "local" culture becomes murky and beckons a return to a concept that has been intimately intertwined with Caribbean studies since the 1950s and 1960s—cultural creolization.[7] Hannerz (1987) has resurrected this concept, derived from linguistics, to describe the intrinsically mixed essence of contemporary cultures and to challenge assumptions of historic purity and homogeneity. Here we will explore new creolized expressions of femininity in the context of cultural flows across the Americas—from kitchens, home sewing rooms, and workplaces in Barbados to corporate headquarters in Dallas, Texas; from discount stores in Miami and shopping malls in San Juan back to the living rooms and fast food restaurants frequented by Bajan informatics operators.

Offshore Informatics and the Transnational Pink-Collar Worker

Following in the path of the global assembly line which has had Caribbean women sewing garments and soldering electronics for multinationally owned industries over the past two decades, the "offshore office" and its new pink-collar service worker represent the latest twist in what many have called the "new international division of labor" (e.g., Frobel et al. 1980, Nash 1983, Fernandez-Kelly 1983, Beneria and Roldan 1987). Offshore informatics makes use of new telecommunications and computer technologies to provide clerical services for head offices in North America in low-wage regions. Data from insurance claims and book manuscripts, consumer warranty cards and credit card applications, are sent by overnight courier or modemed instantaneously from offices in North America to data-processing enclaves in the developing world. Offshore operators, some of whom are located as far away as Ireland and China, receive and manipulate the information within the guidelines established by the client, then send the processed data back to the head office either electronically by modem or by courier on computer disks.

The last five years have witnessed a rapid expansion of the offshore manufacturing sector into the informatics industry, and Barbados has been an international pilot case for governments considering these data enclaves as part of a new development strategy. They mark not only the fragmentation and restructuring of office work and computer-based activity such that white-collar and clerical jobs can now be done in regions far removed from metropolitan head offices, but also the mobilization of new pink-collar work forces. Corporate managers and development officers call these new enterprises "open offices" and hail the plush decor of their futuristically high-tech and air-conditioned working environments. Labor critics, on the other hand, prefer the term "electronic sweatshop" to describe their thinly disguised factory form.

This computer-centered sector signals both an outgrowth of and a departure from the Mexican maquilladora[8] factories and Malaysian electronics plants that dot the global assembly line. Despite many parallels, including incentive packages offered to foreign investors and wage rates that are surprisingly close to those of the neighboring children's wear and cigar factories,[9] the unique management policies and subtle measures of discipline that characterize these data entry operations effectively set them apart from both the local manufacturing sector and the usual offshore assembly plant (Freeman 1993a). Hailed for their innovative use of Total Quality Management and other Japanese-style organizational principles, not to mention their significant potential as job creators and generators of foreign exchange, numerous governments of developing countries see these new industries as the way of the future. For the purposes of this discussion, the informatics sector presents a vivid backdrop for exploring the relationships between formal and informal sectors in the day-to-day lives of its women workers as they come to inhabit a unique transnational ecumene (Hannerz 1992).

Country Higglers and Suitcase Traders: The Informal Sector in the Caribbean Context

Since the 1970s, a growing body of literature addressing women and development has theorized the simultaneous forces and relationships between global movements of international capital and local cultural contexts. Recent theoretical treatments of the global economy have focused increasing attention on the proliferation of the informal sector[10] and its relation to the formal economy.[11] Feminist analyses have best framed our sense of these informal sector activities by relating them both to workers' household compositions and to the formal capitalist economy (Beneria and Roldan 1987, Bolles 1983, Ward 1990). Less well described are the multifaceted relationships between general economic decline, individual/household strategies for saving and getting by, and changing tastes in consumer goods and international fashions—in all of which women play a pivotal role. While workers, and specifically women workers, have long been known to juggle income-earning activities across the boundaries of formal and informal arenas, the case of pink-collar workers in these new informatics industries provides a particularly powerful illustration of the complex connections between economic forces, material realities, and cultural ideologies about women's work as they take shape transnationally.

With economic recession gripping the Caribbean and structural adjustment measures pinching household budgets and testing women's well-known ability to "cut and contrive," regional unemployment figures in the late 1980s and early 1990s ranged between 15 and 25 percent, while the informal sector ballooned dramatically (Harrison 1988, Taylor 1988).[12] Barbados, until as late as 1990, felt itself relatively exempt from the level of economic crisis experienced by Jamaica, Trinidad, Guyana, and much of the developing world. However, severe balance of payments problems and limited foreign exchange reserves have suddenly cast a new light on this regional bedrock of economic and political stability,[13] and new IMF restructuring has brought wage reductions, layoffs, and the possibility of a devaluation of the Barbados dollar.

In the past decade, such downward economic trends have marked an increasingly eroding position for women internationally—rising numbers of female-headed households, greater economic pressures to gain basic provisions for their families, and a swelling of the informal economy as formal employment contracts provide insufficient remuneration (Beneria and Roldan 1987, Ward 1990a). West Indian women have long been known for their creative ingenuity in finding "sources of livelihood" (Massiah 1986). Their involvement in informal economic activities dates back to the days of slavery, when women became "higglers," or informal sellers of agricultural goods. Marketing not only was crucial for the improvement of the nutrition of the slaves and as a mechanism that allowed them to possess property and travel about under otherwise harsh and restrictive conditions but also represented their tenacious independent spirit bound up in everyday expressions of resistance to the degradation of slavery (Beckles 1989: 73, Harrison 1988). A persistent icon of Caribbean culture, the image of the contemporary Bajan higgler is colorfully reproduced on postcards, tourist brochures, and local artists' canvases. She has been the subject of academic theses and political speeches, often embodying a nostalgic and apparently timeless sense of history.[14] Modernization has given new shapes to higglers' goods and methods of trade. Market women now rely on telephone communication, private cars, and minivans for organizing and transporting their produce, though even in new suburban areas the backyard provision garden and the home production of "seasoning," black cake,[15] and other prepared foods remains a strong female tradition.

Along with agricultural and domestic work, needleworking has historically represented another of the primary arenas of income-generating activity for women.[16] Caribbean women's informal economic pursuits continue to include home-based needleworking, assembly work, and food preparation, as both independent and subcontracted labor, in addition to the marketing of imported consumer goods. This last development has undoubtedly taken traditional higglering to new bounds. As in traditional areas of employment contract (e.g., agriculture and manufacturing), changing configurations of the global assembly line have had additionally dramatic effects on vast numbers of women workers who are increasingly juggling triple shifts of formal employment, informal-sector work, and housework. Drawing from Ward (1990), the notion of a triple shift emphasizes the simultaneity of domestic and income-generating responsibilities implied by the now-familiar concept of the "double day" and takes this a step further by acknowledging that a full-time wage-earning job may not preclude additional participation in informal sectors of the economy.[17] In the tradition of the country higgler who has symbolized Caribbean womanhood and the backbone of the informal market (Mintz 1970), many of the fashionably dressed data operators also engage in one or a number of informal economic activities that supplement their formal data entry wage.

Evidence of this burgeoning informal sector is exhibited both within and just outside the mirrored facades of Barbados's newly renovated offshore informatics enclave. As one young data entry operator said about her workplace, "you can just about live inside here—anything you want you can get here." While traveling tradesmen and higglers have long been a part of both rural and town life in Barbados, today a constant stream of minivan traders pull up at lunch time and shift breaks in front of these new offshore enterprises, displaying everything from perfume and fresh produce to shoes, underwear, fashion jewelry, and the latest pirated videos.[18] On the open-office floor itself, perfectly ripe breadfruit and intricate gold jewelry appear from under computer desks and out of fashionable pocketbooks for quick perusal and sale during shift breaks. In addition to marketing consumer goods and produce, women offer each other a wide array of services. Some cut, weave, and braid hair; some promise turkeys in time for Christmas; others can be commissioned to make pudding and souse[19] or a highly decorated cake for special occasions. Given a set of measurements, style preference, and piece of material, others will sew a new skirt suit for work or a ruffled church dress.

Though little substantive research has yet explored these new expansions of traditional marketing practices, a few recent studies in the region make clear the importance of "suitcase traders" as one expression of a changing economic picture, not only within individual women's lives but also of Caribbean national economies more generally (St. Cyr 1990, Taylor 1988, Harrison 1988, Witter 1989). Denoted by her monstrous and heavily packed bags, carried empty and returned ready for the casual market, the suitcase trader generally flies to one of a number of neighboring countries (e.g., Puerto Rico, Venezuela, Panama, Curaçao, and the United States) buying wholesale and later reselling a wide array of consumer items. This growing (and often illegal) practice has been euphemistically named "informal commercial importing" in Jamaica and frequently involves trade in goods that are officially restricted due to nationally limited foreign exchange reserves. Whereas some women may receive startup loans from banks, family members, or informal credit unions, as St. Cyr points out, it is often employment in one of the export processing industries that provides the economic basis or "seed money" for women's entry into this form of informal trade (1990: 8). While the specific ways in which formal and informal sector links establish the basis for this trade vary widely, the predominance of clothing, shoes, and personal and household accessories among female importers is striking, as is the largely female market being catered to.[20] In short, women's participation in informal marketing simultaneously marks innovation (new patterns of material consumption and individual motives and desires) and the endurance of traditional social and economic roles played by Caribbean women.

Of the data entry operators I surveyed, 70 percent are involved in some form of informal economic activity, from trade in clothes and produce to providing services such as babysitting and hairdressing. Internationally, the cash economy has gradually replaced those exchanges and obligations that at one time might have been made in kind (Barrow 1986a: 134). Whether the threat of devaluation and the general belt tightening that now confronts Barbados will create a greater reliance on exchanges and services in kind is yet to be seen,[21] but the expansion of informal services and trade and the predominant role of women in this arena is already apparent. As a response to the recent economic crisis, governments across the region are suddenly hailing the efforts of "entrepreneurs" and "small businessmen"—frequent euphemisms for those who not long ago were considered part of an "underground" economy. In striking acknowledgment of both the proliferation of these practices and their negative implications for local clothing manufacturers and retailers in the formal sector, the minister of trade publicly called for "patriotic Barbadians" to boycott illegal suitcase traders, whose vibrant dealings are contributing to local business woes.[22]

The data workers' informal trade includes selling goods that are both locally produced and grown, selling popular consumer items that have been imported casually, and sewing new fashions and household accessories. A notable dimension of their involvement in the suitcase trade involves the role played by their formal employer in facilitating air travel. Employees of Barbados's largest informatics company may take advantage of travel voucher bonus points (called "thank you cards"), which are earned through high productivity rates or exemplary attendance and team spirit, and fly to Miami, Caracas, San Juan, New York, or any number of other destinations to purchase goods and sewing materials. Travel agents regularly advertise "shopping spree" weekends to these cities, where ground transportation, motel accommodations close to shopping malls, and air travel are included in the package. These shopping tours are popular among Bajans nationwide, particularly over holiday weekends and prior to the Christmas season. Within the informatics zones, these trips are organized as "incentive bonuses" by company managers and independently by groups of women themselves. The excitement of the travel experience—for example, negotiating meals and nightclubs in San Juan with pocket English-Spanish phrase books or trying Cuban restaurants in Miami after an exhausting day at the malls—accounts for much of the pleasure of the higglering trips.[23] Among the informal traders not traveling themselves, many arrange for a relative living abroad to send goods on a regular basis and in small quantities or varied styles so as to avoid suspicions (and duties) of customs officers.

Sewing/fashion design classes and home needlework as well as casual retailing and "suitcase trade" are taking on greater and greater importance, not only for clothing manufacturers, distributors, and the national economy but also in a more cultural sense, in helping to shape popular tastes and styles. Focusing on the experience of women who engage informally in making and selling clothes highlights their participation in this new sort of consumer trade, and their role in shaping and responding to contemporary fashions and styles in an international sphere.

Ward argues that men and women tend to become active in the informal sector with different agendas, women for survival and men for mobility (1990b: 15). By seeing women's activities solely in terms of economic survival, however, we miss other aspects of their experience that are integral to their identities as women and as workers. In the case of these young women whose daily routines often have them running from data factory to sewing machine to housework and childcare or on trips overseas carrying bags heavy with the latest fashions and household goods, I would argue that economic benefit is only one element of their employment in the offshore information industry and of their supplementary needleworking and clothing trade. Just as the adventure of travel is integral to women's energetic income-generating pursuit of transnational trade, they also express other motivating factors behind their commitment to what may seem to be monotonous and dead-end jobs in the data entry industry. While not undermining the central importance of making a living,[24] women's enjoyment of the "cool" high-tech environment, carefully designed ergonomics, and officelike context of work are also integral to their experience. In some cases, those exact characteristics of the job that are resisted and resented by the women (e.g., the strict rules and corporate protocol) are at the same time bound up with aspects of the work experience that give them a sense of identification and even pride (their recognizability as data entry operators whose appearance and connection to computer technology apparently set them apart from other workers in more traditional, less glamorous sectors). Both their formal and their informal economic activities embody a complex of meanings, from meeting the economic "survival" needs of themselves and their households to satisfying their own desires for "professional" status, independence, and personal image making.

Three Women's Stories

In the context of this broad set of economic and ideological relationships, brief portraits of three women who combine work in the data entry industry with the active needleworking trade will illustrate the importance of extra jobs both in expanding their livelihoods and in revealing the contradictions and reinforcing elements of the pervading gender ideologies that underlie them. These women are of interest for the energy and ingenuity displayed in combining varied economic roles, representing varied permutations of the triple shift of formal, informal, and domestic work. They also mark a point of articulation between the international corporate enterprise (their informatics employers) and the local cultural context through their expressions of femininity in the fashions they design, produce, and consume.

Janine

Janine is 26. She and her nine-year-old daughter live at home with her two sisters, three brothers, and parents. Her mother was a home-based seamstress who taught Janine and her sisters to sew when they were young girls. Janine is now taking over her mother's business. Her dream is to become a fashion designer. When she left school, she first got a job in a supermarket, then in a video store. Janine now works at Multitext, a large data entry operation in Barbados, and at her home sewing machine in her "off-time." Janine describes the advantages of combining wage work in data entry with her home-based needlework largely in terms of a guaranteed income. She and every other woman interviewed expressed frustration with the low wages (between U.S.$2.20 and $3.00 per hour, or about $400 per month). But since taking this job, she said,

> I can have a lot of things that I couldn't afford at one time. . . . I can see I can get my bills paid and know I am getting money every month. When I do my own work [sewing] I ain't sure when I gonna get money—cause I ain't sure when people gonna bring the money, when people want something made and what not. So with this job, well I know I will have a certain amount of money every month and I can plan what I gonna do with it when I get it. Since I got this job I've been more aware of how I spend my money. Before I use to just get my money and spend it, but I am more aware now how to budget. Getting paid by the month you have to be able to keep that money to last you for a month and if it run out—you would really be in trouble.

Janine's monthly take-home pay from her data entry job is about $750 (U.S.$375). Her boyfriend gives her $400 (U.S.$200) each month, and she averages an additional $400 (U.S.$200) each month from her sewing (more during heavy months of holidays and weddings, though admittedly this income is insecure and some months bring little income). While she has been combining formal and informal jobs for a number of years, her employment in the data entry operation is significantly more structured and more demanding of her time than her job was in the video store. Janine is a single mother; however, by living "at home," she admits, she has few household or childcare responsibilities. Her mother takes a great deal of the responsibility for her daughter, and Janine said that if she had another child the same would be true. Like her sisters and brothers, she makes a monthly contribution ($100 or more) to the household economy, largely to pay for utility bills and groceries. She is now paying in installments for her bedroom furniture and is saving her money for a trip to Puerto Rico or Venezuela—shopping and eventually selling clothes and accessories when she returns.

Carol Anne

Carol Anne works at Multitext and lives at home with her mother, sister, and two brothers. Her mother works at a garment factory, and her sister works as a keyer at Data Air, the largest data entry operation in Barbados, located next to Multitext. Carol Anne is twenty-seven and is planning to get married next year to her thirty-eight-year-old boyfriend, a primary schoolteacher. They have a piece of land and are having a house built. Carol Anne's father is Vincentian and has lived in St. Vincent since she was very young. The father of her three siblings lived with them while she was growing up, but after years of violence and abuse directed both at Carol Anne and her mother, he was eventually taken to court and moved out of the house. She says they are "living better now." Before getting her current job, Carol Anne worked for another data entry company on the graveyard shift but was eventually laid off. She commutes an hour by bus to work each day, as she lives on the east coast of the island, an area so remote that Bajans are known to refer to it as "behind God's back." She described her days as follows:

When I (am) working nights I find time during the day to wash and cook and clean the house. I am responsible for cleaning the house; we all do our own chores (clothes and cooking) but I clean the house on weekends and during the day when I work nights. On a morning shift, I get up at quarter to five or five o'clock and I have to rush in the bath and rush back out and hurry to get ready because my bus comes at quarter to six and you really have to rush to get ready for that bus. Then I go to work from 7:30 to 3:30 and then now that I'm doing the course (cosmetology) on Mondays, Wednesdays, and Thursdays, sometimes I work overtime till five o'clock and then go up to class. Class finish about eight but sometimes it goes over to about nine or ten. A long day for me. Then I go home at night by bus. Sometimes I get home after ten. Then I have to set my hair in curlers, prepare something to eat—sometimes I make tea and prepare a few sandwiches and go to sleep. . . . when I sit down on that bus and take that long ride home, I just fall asleep—I can't help myself. Saturday I find myself doing a lot of washing; sometimes I wash my hair and then I cook. Every Saturday I do cou cou and something that we call stew food (sweet potatoes and pumpkin and English potatoes . . . stuff like that). My boyfriend comes by me on Saturdays and I cook for him. We might relax and watch television. Sometimes I find myself working and working I don't have time to sleep. I do sewing on weekends—some weekends all I do is sew and some Saturdays and Sundays I have to put time to braid hair. I braid hair on weekends; especially when you're getting to a time when there are bank holidays and stuff, I get a lot of people want their hair braid. I used to do three people in a day, but I find I can't do that now, there's too much to do.

Carol Anne's day dramatically illustrates the triple shift, and adds to it educational pursuits that were part of many other informatics workers' routine as well. While she acknowledged with a long sigh and self-conscious laugh that her life is extraordinarily full, she did not imply that it is particularly remarkable or objectionable. Each set of activities, from her formal job and informal work to her cosmetology course and household and personal chores, was geared toward clear and unwavering ends. In contrast to Janine, her feverish pace both in income generating and domestic duties demonstrates that having other female kin at home may not guarantee a young woman's liberation from household work.

June

June is married and has a six-year-old daughter. Her husband has been a police sergeant for fifteen years and operates a food cart at weekend fetes, cricket matches, and horse races. On a good day he grosses as much as U.S.$1,000 selling hot dogs, cotton candy, popcorn, and drinks. He and June keep chickens and turkeys, selling eggs on a regular basis and turkeys at Christmas time. June has been working at Multitext for three years. Prior to this job, she was an office clerk, then spent a year "at home" making and selling coconut breads on a casual basis to police officers and friends. The combination wood and wall house they live in is owned by her husband's family, and June says that her husband pays for all of the major household expenses. He gives her U.S.$100 a month in addition to her U.S.$425 monthly paycheck. She spends her money on clothes and fabric for herself and her daughter, as well as a number of other household extras such as ceramic ornaments and shelving units for the living room. June began to sew two years ago when a needleworking friend from her village taught her to cut and put together simple patterns. Over the past six months, she has increased her sewing commissions enormously. She made herself four skirt suits for work during her vacation and now sews regularly for a number of her fellow data processors. In time for Christmas, she made new curtains for the living room as well as her black and silver dress for the company party. Weekends and off-time generally find June leaning over her sewing machine, squeezed into a corner of her crowded bedroom. Like other needleworkers, she cuts all her material free-hand and can make a simple suit in a matter of an hour or two. In her four years of marriage, June has experienced several bouts of depression provoked by her husband's "outside" relationships and physically violent episodes. On such occasions she has expressed in sad but resolved terms that as soon as she is able to save enough money and gets a piece of land recently left to her, she hopes to get her own house, leave her husband, and run her own business.

Beyond "Survival": Pleasure and Ingenuity in the Triple Shift

These three cases highlight a number of themes central to women's experience as members of the new high-tech service sector and of families and household groups—saving and budgeting strategies and exercising of personal autonomy and creative ingenuity in income-generating activities. They represent, as well, different stages in their life cycles, a point easily masked by descriptions of offshore workers as generic "pools of young women." Contrary to the pattern within export processing industries in developing countries around the world, the offshore data entry operations in Barbados reveal strikingly low attrition rates (2 percent in the largest foreign-owned operation). This has meant that unlike the profile generally cited of the young, single, childless woman, purported to be the ideal worker, different "generations" co-exist on the data entry floor—the "old guard" who were hired in the first years of the company's existence and the "girls" who are newer recruits, fresh out of secondary school. While the latter group does conform closely to the predictable model, the other represents a group of women who began as young, single, childless women but have stayed in their jobs through the lifetime of the company (eleven years to date) and now occupy different stages in their own life cycles. This is not to say that a major age gap separates these two groups of women or that the "older" women, as they are called within the industry, are in fact very old at all (those who entered their jobs in their late teens would now be in their late twenties and at most in their early thirties). The significance therefore lies in the shift in their life stages—predominantly in their status as mothers and in the composition of their households. Since their initial employment, they may, for example, have gotten married or simply moved into a co-residential arrangement with a partner and children. Of those women surveyed, 53 percent were single and living "at home" with one or both parents or older relatives; 29 percent were either married or in a common-law union; 13 percent described themselves as in visiting unions; and 4 percent were divorced or separated. Regarding their ages, 49 percent were under twenty-five and 51 percent ranged between twenty-five and thirty-five, clustering around age twenty-nine. And, with regard to household headship, of this same group, interestingly, 34 percent cited their fathers or husbands as head of household and the same number, 34 percent, cited themselves or their mother as head (18 percent claiming themselves and 16 percent claiming their mothers as household head).[25]

Female heads of households and poor women generally are more likely than single and married women to work within the informal sector (Ward 1990a). Over 40 percent of Barbadian households are female-headed, and St. Cyr (1990) found that 90 percent of the traders surveyed in the region were supporting dependent children. The three short stories presented here reveal common threads in the lives of Bajan women as well as differences due to their varied household constellations and motivations for engaging in informal work. Ironically, in light of the presumption that motherhood brings with it greater demands and more limited flexibility, of the three accounts, the woman with the greatest economic independence and autonomy is probably Janine. By piecing together sources of livelihood from her formal employment (data entry), informal work (sewing), and contributions from her boyfriend, she is able to save money for the home she and her boyfriend plan to buy and to reinvest in her informal retail enterprise through travel. Because her mother bears the bulk of the responsibility for her child, she has even greater freedom than June, who is married.[26]

All of the women interviewed emphasized the importance of informal fashioning not simply for supplementing their formal wage and increasing their purchasing power, but also in terms of the enjoyment and satisfaction they derive from creating and supplying popular new styles for their friends, family, fellow workers, and themselves. Along with their ready acknowledgment of the necessity and desire they feel to dress well and keep up with the styles was a clear sense that their informal work enhanced their pleasure in fashion consumption both within and outside their formal working lives. Household survival was only one force behind their participation in informal economic activity. While the literature on female operators in traditional multinational factories frequently depicts them as wage-earning delegates working for the maintenance of their families, these women (especially those who were not heads of households) express individual motivations and desires as well. While these desires are seen by parents, religious leaders, and the older managers of the data entry industry as conspicuous consumption endemic within a spoiled "me generation," women themselves express a keen sense of independence derived through fashionable self-expression and entrepreneurship.

"Professionalism" and Feminine Identities

The roles played by the informal needleworker and suitcase trader are significant, therefore, not simply in providing cheaper alternatives to the machine-made clothes in the boutiques mushrooming around the island and clearly enabling fashion to play such a large role in the lives of working-class women; they appear as well to be bound up in a growing globalization of consumption and style. Maria Mies's housewifization theory (Mies 1986), which a decade ago provocatively described women's place within the international division of labor, is now confronted with a radical turn. Mies argued that the international division of labor "worked" only when two conditions were fulfilled: production costs were dramatically lowered by export-oriented enterprises which depended on the cheap labor of docile and malleable Third World women and consumers in the rich industrialized countries were mobilized to purchase these goods produced in the Third World. Both of these strategies, she argued, depended largely on women—Third World women as producers, First World women as consumers. Her analysis of the silent relationship between women on "both sides" of the international division of labor was unusual and important. However, Mies's dualistic model clearly does not characterize the complexities of transnationalism as these young Bajan data processors now experience it. What Mies did not describe was the increasing rate at which Third World women too are consumers, and what makes mass consumption possible among these Barbadian women is their deeply entrenched involvement in informal marketing and trade. Women's formal employment as data processors becomes closely intertwined with informal economic activities and together these place them firmly within an international sphere where they are simultaneously producers and consumers of services, commodities, and styles. Women of developing countries, who just a short while ago provided only the labor behind these consumer goods that Mies claims were meant to tempt and subdue the suburban housewives of the industrialized West and a few elite women in developing countries, now themselves demand these items of adornment and convenience.

In this sense, the fashions designed and produced by women in their homes, as well as those brought in from overseas in the suitcase trade, mark a point of articulation between their formal and informal sector subjectivities. Women's highly styled "professional" wear enhances the corporate image that forms such a potent element of their identity as offshore office workers. The ambiguity expressed by many women as to where the concern for "professional dress" originates (whether integrally part of Barbadian concern for appearances or a foreign corporate prescription) exemplifies the wider complexities surrounding their informal economic activities supplementing an insufficient wage. Two primary explanations were offered to me by managers of foreign-owned companies to rationalize poor rates of pay to women: 1) their wage is supplemental to that of a primary male breadwinner or to a household in which a number of members contribute to the family economy, and 2) Caribbean women are known to be involved in complex exchange and informal economic relations within their communities and therefore can get by on less—an explicit acknowledgment that through these informal activities, women subsidize their formal wage, and thus these industries. In effect, then, the economic strategies exercised by women (e.g., "meeting turns"[27] and trade in goods and services at more reduced rates than in the formal economy) act to remove the responsibility of the state and the employer to bear the expense of both social services (e.g., childcare) and reasonable rates of pay. Further underlying their rationalizations are a number of persistent stereotypes about "traditional femininity" and about the "matriarchal" Barbadian family structure that neatly complement the assumption that women make the best typists (Freeman 1993b). In addition to revealing the continuation of fallacious rationales for "why women make ideal offshore workers," the point here is to emphasize the fact that as women confront greater economic stress and respond with resilience and ingenuity in expanding their sources of livelihood, the state and the corporation are subsequently let off the hook. Workers in the formal sector not only subsidize their formal wage through their informal labor but also absorb greater unpaid reproductive costs and, to top it all off, sustain the mirage of professional prosperity and upward mobility for women that government and the international corporate sector so anxiously assert.

The "pink collar," then, represents a sort of feminine/professional disguise. The data entry operator essentially performs a sort of "blue-collar" work, but in place of the dust and fumes of garment and electronics houses she is situated within a cleaner, cooler "white-collar" setting, and as part of the trade, she is expected to appear distinctly feminine and "professional." As one manager put it, "Women are expected to dress professionally here . . . this is not a production mentality like jeans and tee shirts." Prescriptions for appropriate dress and admonition for "slackness" as cited in an employee produced newsletter include the following:

> Supervisors are concerned about the way you dress; for them it is more than an issue of personal taste. They want you to send the right message, one that projects you as a balanced, responsible person. . . . The dress code relates to all employees. . . . Keep the use of jewelry, ornamental accessories and fancy shoes to a minimum. . . . It was believed that the Company once had no dress code. This was due to the elegant and appropriate dressing of its original staff. The same can no longer be said of today's staff.

The implication of the newsletter's final remarks is that in the early days of the company, women took it upon themselves to maintain an elegantly professional appearance. There had been no formal dress code, but a shared understanding of "appropriateness." The adornment and accessorizing contained in the pink-collar workers' engagement in fashion is very much bound up in a complex of informal economic transactions. The concern about appearance and the desire to look professional, as women uniformly described their dress for work, has as much (or more) to do with demarcating a line which separates them from factory workers as it does with identifying with their foreign employers. It has little or nothing in fact to do with the actual service aspect of their job, as their clients are by definition overseas and invisible. But it has everything to do with the public persona they and their employer wish to cultivate in their own communities. While no one but fellow workers and staff may come in contact with the data entry operator in the course of the working day, many will see her waiting for the bus to get to work, on her lunch break, or on her way home.

The focus on professional dress and appearance by the data entry management also taps into other areas of employee relations. By creating a professional-looking working environment through decor and office ergonomics, managers expect in return not only professional-looking workers but ones who are also willing to put in overtime on demand, as this is what all professionals are expected to do. Corporate imperatives, such as meeting deadlines, accommodating rush orders, or processing inordinately heavy batches of tickets by month's end, demand a great deal of overtime and flexible scheduling on the part of the workforce (e.g., staying late, coming in on a weekends, and working double shifts), and one way of encouraging a willingness to put in "the extra mile" is to make employees feel that it is in their benefit as well (e.g., "as part of the corporate family") to see these goals met. Dress becomes one component of the worker's professional persona. The appearance of the offshore data entry operator therefore is somewhere between the prescribed uniform of the traditional blue-collar worker and the executive woman—like the executive, she has a sense of choosing her style, despite the explicit dress code that is set out and enforced by the company.

Protocol and a pronounced concern about appearances are frequently attributed to Bajans (by themselves and other West Indians), and many attribute this cultural characteristic to the social legacy of English colonialism. Gordon Lewis described the West Indian as a traditionalist who "preserved a Victorian Anglophilism . . . long after those attitudes had waned in Britain itself" (Lewis 1968: 71), and Barbados as the "ultra conservative" and most English of them all (Lewis 1968: 231). While his profile of the "isolated Bajan provincial" hardly characterizes the contemporary context, where travel, tourism, and the electronic media connect all Bajans with the wider transnational scene, the roots of cultural conservatism have held strong.

Bound up in this infamous conservatism are contradicting notions of "ideal" and "real" in the realm of gender identities, where appearances play a central role in defining femininity.[28] In her work about petty traders and higglers in Jamaica, Elsie LeFranc (1989) briefly touches on this relationship between inflated appearances and limited economic wherewithal. She notes the frequent postwar Caribbean literary references to the contrast between the "worthless and/or idle black male and the strong, hard working black woman . . . the economically marginalized and frustrated black male and the coping black female." In a similar vein, she says, has been a black male preponderance for useless "posture on the basis of little substance . . . for example, the ubiquitous but empty briefcase, or the well-dressed young man on his way to nowhere" (LeFranc 1989: 112). Status through appearance becomes a replacement for economic prosperity in a ritualized process whereby structural constraints such as race and class prevent individuals from reaching those goals and values held most highly by the society. She argues that this split between economic appearance (through dress and material display) and real economic means has been supported by the dominant classes as a mechanism for maintaining their own economic control. On the other hand, bound up in their role as primary provider, women are said to be much less vulnerable to this strategy and better equipped to "manipulate the economic system and the split referred to"

(LeFranc 1989: 112). In addition to the hard-to-define pleasures derived from new styles, a new susceptibility among these young fashion-conscious women to this sort of image making relates to both economic and cultural trends. A majority of them are members of households where they contribute to the household economy, but are not sole wage earners, and thus are able to spend a significant portion of their earnings on personal items.[29] Furthermore, they experience increasing exposure to corporate fashion and styles from abroad both from the media and their own overseas travel, and working environments that prescribe feminine "professionalism," even if only as window dressing.[30]

According to a Barbadian fashion designer consultant,[31] the "fashion explosion" began hitting this small island economy in the early 1980s, marking the expansion of mass tourism, Barbadians traveling abroad in greater numbers, the intensification of the Cropover festival, and the influence of American television.[32] This fashion frenzy is represented in a vast continuum encompassing the intensification of informal imports, the growth of small home-based independent needleworkers making everything from school uniforms to corporate-looking suits, extensive production operations for garment subcontractors, and fashion designers who exhibit in local boutiques and international shows. The escalating preoccupation with fashion was even noted in a recent sermon of a Pentecostal preacher, who bemoaned the trend for young people today to come to the house of God merely "to check a style." Needleworkers themselves confirm that they go just about anywhere for new fashion ideas. A great deal of criticism is levied in the press, in popular calypso and dub tunes, and by religious leaders like the one quoted against Barbadian women for their "materialistic" and "obsessive" concern with fashion. However, the two are not necessarily one and the same thing—the desire to "dress hard" and sport the latest styles is not solely an expression of frivolous consumerism. As Elizabeth Wilson notes, "It is quite possible to be critical of the specific form that consumerism takes in capitalist societies and at the same time to defend the practice of bodily adornment. (After all) why should the body not be a bearer of cultural signs?" (1990: 231). Additionally, women's pursuit of or compliance with a particular workplace fashion in the arena of data entry acts both to distinguish the women from one sector of workers (manual, factory workers) and to imitate or integrate themselves symbolically into another group to whom they aspire (office workers and professional women) (Freeman 1995). As McCracken put it, describing women, dress, and work in North America, "Imitation . . . is not the simple pursuit of prestige nor the work of some generalized force; it is a culturally purposeful activity motivated by an appreciation of the symbolic liabilities of one style of dress, and the symbolic advantages implicit in another" (1988: 100).

The contemporary Barbadian needleworker and the suitcase trader who personally selects her styles from overseas straddle local and international aesthetics with great integrity and pizazz. Women workers don their smart "professional" look that bears both an international corporate emblem and a distinctively Caribbean flair, using bright combinations of tropical colors and prints with custom-designed accessories and adaptations of mass-produced patterns.[33] Fashion and dress, defined by both local aesthetics, corporate prescriptions, and transnational imports are symbolic of the more general dialectical relationships that both reinforce and challenge women's subjectivities and gender ideologies in these new high-tech off-shore arenas. In this complex interaction between formal, informal and household realms, the home needlework and suitcase trader mark an historical tradition of female entrepreneurship and creative strategies for making a living. At the same time, the high tech spectacle of the informatics industry, in the midst of what tourist brochures claim to be a timeless tropical paradise, embodies a unique nexus where social and economic practices blend tradition with innovation, self-definition with conformity, and re-fashion "local" into "transnational" cultures. The local becomes transnational and the transnational in turn is "localized" in a frenzied dialectic of new pressures and pleasures across the production/consumption terrain.

NOTES

1. This chapter is based on fieldwork conducted in Barbados between 1989 and 1992. The research was generously supported by grants from Fulbright, the National Science Foundation, the Wenner Gren Foundation for Anthropological Research, and the Organization of American States. I wish to acknowledge the editors of *FOLK: Journal of the Danish Ethnographic Society* for their kind permission to reprint my article "From Higglering to High-Tech and Home Again: Barbadian Women Workers in a Transnational Arena" in this revised form. Thanks to Maria Patricia Fernandez-Kelly, Sherri Grasmuck, Gul Ozyegin, Peter Hervik, Bjarke P. Laursen, Birgitte R. Sorensen, Ninna Nyberg Sorensen, and Alison Greene for their insightful comments and suggestions on various stages of writing and revision.

2. Other names for informal marketeers in the region are "hucksters" and "hawkers." I adopt the term *higgler* following Katzin's usage in her 1959 article "The Jamaican Country Higgler."

3. I use the expression "pink-collar" to denote both the feminine profile of this sector of workers and to distinguish them as a new category that challenges the divide that has long associated blue collar with manual and white collar with mental labor. I return to the point later in the chapter and in more detail in Freeman (1995).

4. A number of recent works have begun to address the question of transnationalism and global culture in terms of migration (Glick Schiller et al. 1992, Basch et al. 1994), cultural flows (Hannerz 1990, Appadurai 1990, Featherstone 1990, Friedman 1990), mass consumption (Friedman 1990a, 1994; Wilk 1990; Miller 1990, 1994; Jackson 1993), national identities (Basch et al. 1994), and gendered divisions of labor (Freeman forthcoming).

5. I argue in more detail elsewhere (Freeman forthcoming) that far from homogenizing and wiping out the distinctiveness of local culture, economic globalization, commodification, and the intensification of cultural flows can also heighten local awareness of (and even invention of) traditional practices, celebrations, foods, etc. See also Miller (1992, 1994) on Trinidad and Wilk (1994) on Belize.

6. A popular euphemism for smuggling goods in suitcases and avoiding import duties.

7. It is impossible to mention creolization in the Caribbean without bringing to mind a long (and recently revived) debate. In essence, the concept gained currency in the 1950s and 1960s surrounding West Indian independence movements in Jamaica, Trinidad, Guyana, and Barbados. Creolization in this context emphasized that Caribbean culture is synthetic, blending cultural elements and practices of European and African origins to create a truly unique cultural tradition. The creolization perspective directly opposed the notion of "cultural pluralism" that portrayed the region as one of fragmented peoples and cultures which could never create nations in a true sense. Creolization therefore became a tool of nation-building and carried with it functionalist elements that emphasized a "melting pot" ideal. More recent uses of the creolization perspective stand in opposition to black nationalist movements that predicate Caribbean/Barbadian authenticity and national identity on race, and equate Barbadianness with blackness, writing out of the national portrait those not of African descent. This recent contest over the utility of the creole concept relates closely to what Hannerz (1991: 5) describes as a process whereby the state may "define away" creolization in its pursuit of a singular "cultural integrity and authenticity."

8. The maquilladora system refers to twin plants established along the U.S. Mexican border where the labor-intensive assembly is performed by low-wage workers on the Mexican side and the white-collar management remains in the United States. This Border Industrialization Program was initiated in 1965 with the hope that new industrialization of this sort would create jobs and bring new skills and technologies to Mexico.

9. According to the Industrial Development Corporation's report in 1989, average wage rates for a sewing machine operator were U.S.$1.60–2.00 per hour and for a data entry operator US$2.00–2.50.

10. First used by British anthropologist Keith Hart to describe the diverse activities of poor city dwellers in Ghana (1973), the notion of the "informal sector" has been debated as a concept and used to encompass a wide variety of income-earning activities outside of but clearly and integrally related to the "formal" economy. I use the term *informal sector* to describe those small-scale production and service activities that generate income outside contractual and legally regulated employment. (See Portes and Walton 1981 for an early explication of the concept, Peattie 1987 for a discussion of its varied uses, and Portes et al. 1989 for an excellent collection of essays discussing the origins, dynamics, and implications of this expanding arena.)

11. See, among others, Ward 1990a, Sen and Grown 1987, Beneria and Roldan 1987, Portes and Walton 1983.

12. From the beginning of this research in 1989 to the latest published reports, the unemployment figures in Barbados jumped from 12 percent to 25 percent. Unofficial estimates place unemployment at closer to 30 percent as of May 1994.

13. In a human development report by the UNDP (1991) Barbados was ranked first for quality of life in the developing world; however, new economic constraints posed by IMF structural adjustment measures are likely to erode this broad category of development.

14. What is sometimes missed in these accounts of strong and resourceful "matriarchs" of West Indian social and economic life is that these women are also represented among the region's very poor. It is important, therefore, not to idealize their "survival strategies" and to contextualize their efforts as part of economic necessity as well as ingenuity and creativity.

15. Seasoning refers to a delicious and highly spiced blend of assorted fresh herbs sold by the jar and generously used in the preparation of traditional fried flying fish (the national dish) and Bajan fried chicken. Black cake is a rum-soaked fruit cake traditionally served at Christmas and on special occasions (e.g., birthdays) decorated with fancy icing designs.

16. Between 1891 and 1921 female labor force participation represented 61 percent, and as Massiah notes, was concentrated in these three areas (1986).

17. Isis Duarte (1989) has argued that the "double day" concept is not always useful for analyzing the conditions of proletarianization of domestic workers or free trade zone workers in the Dominican Republic for two reasons. She says that more important in the study of FTZ workers is the question of factory discipline and the gender-specific strategies enforced in these arenas, and that among the young women incorporated into these industries, their factory jobs actually tend to "liberate" them from their household duties as female kin within the extended family tend to take over their childcare and housework responsibilities. In the Barbadian context, there is evidence for both trends—some women have extended networks of kin and friends who assist them with their household chores and childcare, and some do not. Young women with no children as well as those with children but who are not involved in live-in unions and are living "at home" with other kin, generally have the most flexibility and independence with

regard to both their free time and their earnings. In an effort to represent the widest of women's experiences and to emphasize the links (both economic and ideological) between formal and informal sector work and household membership and responsibility, I employ the notion of "triple shift" here, although with caution in light of the foregoing critique.

18. One advantages for the women workers posed by this informal trade is a customary extension of credit and installment payment.

19. Pudding and souse is a traditional Bajan dish. The pudding is a dark sausage in which pig intestine is stuffed with seasoned sweet potato, and the souse is pig's head, feet, and flesh, cooked and pickled with lime juice and spices.

20. Several women told me that men were more likely to import electronics and tools than housewares and clothing.

21. Bolles (1983) described this expansion of women's informal strategies and exchanges in the face of job losses from export manufacturing industries and general economic decline in Jamaica.

22. *Barbados Advocate*, August 16, 1991, citing Senator Dr. Carl Clarke.

23. Joan French (in Witter 1989: 34–35) describes a similar phenomenon among higglers in Jamaica traveling between Haiti, Curaçao, and Panama who enjoyed not only business expertise across these different cultural locales but also the sense of adventure in their travels.

24. Discussions of the central role played by women in household survival have emphasized their altruism, the fact that they contribute a greater portion of their earnings (smaller though they generally are) than men (Massiah 1986, Grasmuck and Espinal 1993). While this point is important, it sometimes obscures the fact that even among poor women, work and earnings themselves frequently have significance beyond mere survival.

25. There is a substantial literature on female-headed households, which in part addresses the complexities involved in defining these "units" (Massiah 1991). While I have discussed this literature at greater length elsewhere (Freeman forthcoming), I have relied here on women's own bases for defining their households as female-headed (that a female head provides the most significant economic support and represents the "authority" more generally.

26. This corresponds to the pattern noted by Duarte (1989: 198), who argues that export processing industries purposefully employ young women who rely on household support (and childcare if necessary) from other female family members when they take on the burden of factory employment. These young women tend not themselves to be heads of households, and according to Duarte, when they can rely on the help of their extended kin, their exploitation by the formal export processing sector acts to "liberate" them, in turn, from their third (domestic) shift. As the three stories illustrate, this is sometimes the case but is hardly the rule for the Bajan data workers whose participation

in household tasks varies widely and is not entirely predicated on their household constellation.

27. Meetings" or "meeting turns" are widespread in the Caribbean and Africa and refer to informal savings clubs through which women make weekly or biweekly contributions to a common pool, and on a rotating basis each individual claims the total amount. Meeting turns have long been used as an alternative to traditional credit and lending institutions. These women typically contribute $5 or $10 a week for a return of $50 or $100 at the end of the cycle.

28. I allude here to Peter Wilson's much-debated notion of "reputation" and "respectability." See Besson 1993 and Miller 1994 for different interpretations of this gendered dualism.

29. Many of the young women said they gave $100 or more to their mothers (or other older female member of the household), put another portion ($50–100) in a credit union, and had the rest of their pay packet to spend (transportation to work, lunches, and personal expenses such as clothes, toiletries, entertainment, etc.) Obviously, women's expenditures varied according to their position within the household and whether or not they had a child. Those who are without children and live at home with their families or are married to men who absorb responsibility for the household expenses tend to have the most disposable income for personal expense.

30. Miller (1994: 223) also notes that the need for clothes among Trinidadian women was "constantly being linked to the workplace, with individuals going to Caracas to purchase a new wardrobe . . . on hearing they had obtained work."

31. *Weekend Nation*, March 1, 1991.

32. These trends coincided with the emergence of the offshore informatics industry.

33. An expanding new literature on modernity and local and transnational culture has begun to explore ways in which the consumption of imported goods and media enhance and reinvent what is considered to be "local" and traditional culture itself. See Breckenridge (1995) on South Asia and Miller (1990, 1994) on Trinidad.

REFERENCES

Appadurai, Arjun
1990   "Disjuncture and Difference in the Global Cultural Economy." In M. Featherstone (ed.), *Global Culture: Nationalism, Globalization and Modernity*. London: Sage.
1991   "Global Ethnoscapes: Notes and Queries for a Transnational Anthropology." In R. Fox, *Recapturing Anthropology: Working in the Present*. Santa Fe: School of American Research Press.

Barrett, Michele

1980 *Women's Oppression Today.* London: Verso.

Barrow, Christine

1986a "Finding the Support: Strategies for Survival." *Social and Economic Studies,* vol. 35, no. 2: 131–176.

1986b "Male Images of Women in Barbados." *Social and Economic Studies,* vol. 35, no. 3: 51–64.

Basch, Linda, Nina Glick-Schiller, and Cristina Szanton-Blanc

1994 *Nations Unbound: Transnational Projects, Post-Colonial Predicaments, and Deterritorialized Nation-States.* Langhorn: Gordon and Breach.

Beckles, Hilary McD.

1989 *Natural Rebels: A Social History of Enslaved Black Women in Barbados.* London: Zed.

Beneria, Lourdes, and Martha Roldan

1987 *The Crossroads of Gender: Industrial Homework, Subcontracting and Household Dynamics in Mexico City.* Chicago: University of Chicago Press.

Besson, J.

1993 "Reputation and Respectability Reconsidered: A New Perspective on Afro-Caribbean Peasant Women." In J. Momsen (ed.), *Women and Change in the Caribbean.* Bloomington: Indiana University Press.

Bolles, Lynn

1983 "Kitchens Hit by Priorities: Employed Working-Class Jamaican Women Confront the IMF." In June Nash and Maria Patricia Fernandez-Kelly (eds.), *Women, Men and the International Division of Labor.* Albany: State University of New York Press.

Bourdieu, Pierre

1984 *Distinction: A Social Critique of the Judgment of Taste.* Cambridge: Harvard University Press.

Breckenridge, Carol A. (ed.)

1995 *Consuming Modernity: Public Culture in a South Asian World.* Minneapolis: University of Minnesota Press.

Brodber, Erna

1982 *Perceptions of Caribbean Women.* Women in the Caribbean Project, Vol. 4. Institute of Social and Economic Research, University of the West Indies, Barbados.

Duarte, Isis

1989 "Household Workers in the Dominican Republic: A Question for the Feminist Movement." In Elsa Chaney and Mary Garcia Castro (eds.), *Muchachas No*

More: Household Workers in Latin American and the Caribbean. Philadelphia: Temple University Press.

Featherstone, Mike

1990 "Global Culture: An Introduction." In M. Featherstone (ed.), *Global Culture: Nationalism, Globalization and Modernity*. London: Sage.

Fernandez-Kelly, Maria Patricia

1983 *For We Are Sold, I and My People: Women and Industry in Mexico's Frontier*. Albany: State University of New York Press.

Fernandez-Kelly, Maria Patricia, and Anna Maria Garcia

1990 "Power Surrendered, Power Restored: The Politics of Work and Family among Hispanic Garment Workers in Florida and California." In L. A. Tilley and P. Gurin (eds.), *Women, Politics and Change*. New York: Russell Sage.

Freeman, Carla

1993a "Designing Women: Corporate Discipline and Barbados' Off-Shore Pink Collar Sector." *Cultural Anthropology*, vols. 8, no. 2: 169–186.

1993b "Myths of Docile Girls and Matriarchs: Real and Ideal Images of Global Workers." Paper presented at the Ninety-Second Annual Conference of the American Anthropological Association, Washington, D.C., May.

1995 "Traversing the Transnational: Production, Consumption and the Fashioning of Gendered Workers in Barbados." Unpublished paper.

Forthcoming *High Tech and High Heels in the Global Economy: Women, Work and Informatics in Barbados*, Durham: Duke University Press.

Friedman, Jonathan

1990a "Being in the World: Globalization and Localization." In Featherstone (ed.), *Global Culture*.

1990b "The Political Economy of Elegance: An African Cult of Beauty." *Culture and History*, vol. 7: 101–125.

1994. *Consumption and Identity*. New York: Harwood.

Frobel, Folker, Jurgan Heinrichs, and Otto Kreye

1980 *The New International Division of Labour*. Cambridge: Cambridge University Press.

Glick-Schiller, Nina, Linda Basch, and Cristina Blanc-Szanton (eds.)

1992 *Towards a Transnational Perspective on Migration: Race, Class, Ethnicity, and Nationalism Reconsidered*. New York: Annals of the Academy of Sciences, vol. 645.

Grasmuck, Sherri and Rosario Espinal

1993 "Gender, Households and Informal Entrepreneurship in the Dominican Republic." Paper presented at the Eighteenth Annual Convention of the Caribbean Studies Association, Kingston and Ocho Rios, Jamaica, May.

Hannerz, Ulf

1987 "The World in Creolization." *Africa*, vol. 57: 546–559.

1990 "Cosmopolitans and Locals in World Culture." In Featherstone (ed.), *Global Culture*.

1991 "The State in Creolization." Paper delivered at the Annual Meeting of the American Anthropological Association, Chicago.

1992 *Cultural Complexity*. New York: Columbia University Press.

Harrison, Faye V.

1988 "Women in Jamaica's Urban Informal Economy: Insights from a Kingston Slum." *Nieuwe West-Indische Gids*, vol. 62, nos. 3 and 4: 103–128.

Hart, Keith

1973 "Informal Income Opportunities and Urban Government in Ghana." *Journal of Modern African Studies*, vol. 11: 61–89.

Jackson, Peter

1993 "A Cultural Politics of Consumption." In J. Bird et al. (eds.), *Mapping the Futures: Local Cultures, Global Change*. London: Routledge, pp. 207–228.

Katzin, Margaret Fisher

1959 "The Jamaican Country Higgler." *Social and Economic Studies*, vol. 8, no. 4: 421–440.

King, Anthony (ed.)

1991 *Culture, Globalization and the World System: Contemporary Conditions for the Representation of Identity*. New York: Macmillan.

LeFranc, Elsie

1989 "Petty Trading and Labour Mobility: Higglers in the Kingston Metropolitan Area." In K. Hart (ed.), *Women and the Sexual Division of Labour in the Caribbean*. Jamaica: Consortium Graduate School of Social Sciences.

Lewis, Gordon

1968 *The Growth of the Modern West Indies*. New York: Monthly Review Press.

Massiah, Joycelin

1986 "Work in the Lives of Caribbean Women." *Social and Economic Studies*, vol. 35, no. 2: 177–240.

1991 "The Vulnerability of Female Headed Households: Paradoxes and Paradigms—A Caribbean Perspective." Paper prepared for an Institute for Social and Economic Research (ISER) Staff Seminar, University of the West Indies, Cave Hill Campus, Barbados, June.

McCracken, Grant

1988 *Culture and Consumption: New Approaches to the Symbolic Character of Consumer Goods and Activities*. Bloomington: Indiana University Press.

Mies, Maria

1986   *Patriarchy and Accumulation on a World Scale: Women in the International Division of Labor.* London: Zed.

Miller, Daniel

1990   "Fashion and Ontology in Trinidad." *Culture and History,* vol. 7: 49–77.

1992   "Consumption and Culture: The Case of Trinidad." *Caribbean Affairs,* vol. 5, no. 2: 81–95.

1994   *Modernity, an Ethnographic Approach: Dualism and Mass Consumption in Trinidad.* Oxford: Berg.

Mintz, Sidney W.

1970   "Men, Women, and Trade." *Comparative Studies in Society and History,* vol. 13, no. 3: 247–269.

Nash, June

1983   "The Impact of the Changing International Division of Labor on Different Sectors of the Labor Force." In Nash and Fernandez-Kelly (eds.), *Women, Men and the International Division of Labor.*

Peattie, Lisa

1987   "An Idea in Good Currency and How it Grew: The Informal Sector." *World Development,* vol. 15, no. 7: 851–860.

Portes, Alejandro, and Saskia Sassen-Koob

1987   "Making It Underground: Comparative Material on the Informal Sector in Western Market Economies." *American Journal of Sociology,* vol. 93, no. 1: 30–61.

Portes, Alejandro, Manuel Castells, and Lauren A. Benton (eds.)

1989   *The Informal Economy: Studies in Advanced and Less Developed Countries.* Baltimore: Johns Hopkins University Press.

Portes, Alejandro, and John Walton

1981   *Labor, Class, and the International System.* New York: Academic Press.

Safa, Helen I.

1991   "Women and Industrialization in the Caribbean." In Sharon Stichter and Jane Parapet (eds.), *Women, Employment and the Family in the International Division of Labor.* Philadelphia: Temple University Press.

Sen, Gita, and Caren Grown

1987   *Development, Crises, and Alternative Visions: Third World Women's Perspectives.* New York: Monthly Review Press.

St. Cyr, Joaquin

1990   "Participation of Women in Caribbean Development: Inter-Island Trading and Export Processing Zones." Report prepared for the Economic Commission for

Latin America and the Caribbean (ECLAC) Caribbean Development and Co-operation Committee, Kingston.

Taylor, Alicia
1988   "Women Traders in Jamaica: The Informal Commercial Importers." Report prepared for the Economic Commission for Latin America and the Caribbean (ECLAC) Caribbean Development and Cooperation Committee, Kingston.

Trouillot, Michel Rolph
1992   "The Caribbean Region: An Open Frontier in Anthropological Theory." *Annual Review of Anthropology*, vol. 21: 19–42.

Ward, Kathryn (ed.)
1990a   *Women Workers and Global Restructuring*. Ithaca: ILR Press, Cornell University.
1990b   "Reconceptualizing World-System Theory to Include Women." In P. England (ed.), *Theory on Gender/Feminism on Theory*. Chicago: Aldine.
1990c   "Gender, Work and Development." *Annual Review of Sociology*, September.

Wilk, Richard
1990   "Consumer Goods as Dialogue about Development." *Culture and History*, vol. 7: 79–100.
1994   " 'Real Belizean Food': Building Local Identity in the Transnational Caribbean." Manuscript.

Wilson, Elizabeth
1985   *Adorned in Dreams: Fashion and Modernity*. Berkeley: University of California Press.
1990   "The Postmodern Chameleon." *New Left Review*, no. 180: 187–190.

Wilson, Peter J.
1969   "Reputation and Respectability: A Suggestion for Caribbean Ethnology." *Man*, vol. 4, no. 1: 70–84.

Witter, Michael (ed.)
1988   "Higglering/Sidewalk Vending/Informal Commercial Trading in the Jamaican Economy." Department of Economics Occasional Paper Series No. 4, University of the West Indies, Mona, Jamaica.

5

ACROSS THE MONA STRAIT
Dominican Boat Women in Puerto Rico

LUISA HERNÁNDEZ ANGUEIRA

To THINK OF women as multiple subjects marked by internal contradictions opens up the possibility of understanding the differences not only between men and women but also between and among women (Golubov 1994). In Puerto Rico, migrant Dominican women differ from Puerto Rican women (a far more complex opposition than that of women to men) within a society stratified by class, race, ethnicity, and gender. Dominican women represent functions and characteristics that define them as "the other," a condition which benefits the dominant forces of society.

When women belong to marginalized ethnic groups and less privileged social classes, they suffer a "multiple disadvantage" (Rakowski 1987). In such cases, gender prejudice and discrimination aggravate the effects of cultural and economic alienation. Although Dominican immigrant women face many of the same problems that Puerto Rican women do, the lower socioeconomic condition of Dominicans reflects a more acute discrimination to the extent that both racial identity and national origin constitute enormous social barriers between Dominican and Puerto Rican women. This chapter examines the experiences of Dominican women in Puerto Rico in light of gender, ethnic, and class differences. It analyzes the situation of Dominican women by probing their own experiences, specifically, the incorporation of numerous undocumented women into the underground economy, especially those who entered into it through domestic service.

Up to now, studies relative to the informal sector are highly ambiguous. The concept of informality tends to reproduce a dual vision of society. The logic in this binary combination, like formal/informal presupposes that one part of the combination defines the other (Mires 1993). As such, the ideological conception is discriminatory because it determines what is important, what is secondary, what is positive and negative, what has value and what does not. In this sense, the formal defines as negative the informal. Immigrant women are very active in this sector of the economy, especially in domestic service. This chapter will analyze the sexual division of labor and will examine the impact of gender on the informal work of the Dominican woman in Puerto Rico.

Dominican Migrants

The acute economic crisis that the Dominican Republic has faced since the 1980s has forced many Dominican women to risk their lives by journeying across the perilous, shark-infested Mona Channel by boat (*yola*) to establish themselves in Puerto Rico. In doing so, they challenge the dominant discourse regarding women's submission, intuition, and dependence vis-à-vis men.

Our fieldwork in the Barrio Gandul neighborhood of Santurce, located within the capital city of San Juan, Puerto Rico, revealed that close to a third of the Dominican population resides illegally in Puerto Rico. From a sample of ninety-eight Dominicans, thirty-two lacked legal documents to live on the island. Of these, thirty-nine women had papers and fourteen were undocumented (see table 1). More Dominican women than men resided in Santurce, whether legally or not (Duany 1990). Dominican women tended to be young, between twenty and forty years old, with an average eighth-grade education, and of urban origin. Most had not been employed formally in the Dominican Republic; many had left their children behind in the care of their grandmothers or other relatives in their native country. However, most Dominican women supported their children even after they left the country. While Dominican immigration to Puerto Rico tends to increase the proportion of female-headed households (Duany 1990), in New York it seemed to decrease. Women headed close to half (46.7 percent) of the households in 1990 (Necos 1993).

Table 1. Legal Situation by Gender of Dominicans Surveyed in Puerto Rico

	Number of Men (%)		Number of Women (%)		Total Number (%)	
Documented	27	(60.0)	39	(73.6)	66	(67.3)
Undocumented	18	(40.0)	14	(26.4)	32	(32.7)
Total	45	(100.0)	53	(100.0)	98	(100.0)

Source: Duany, Hernández Angueira, and Rey (1995).

Personal narratives of Dominican "boat women" contain keys to understanding the migration of Dominican women to Puerto Rico. On the one hand,
the precarious voyage by boat is the last resort for Dominican women unable
to earn a living at home. Usually the trip is the result of a family decision to
send a young woman abroad to find work and thus contribute to the economic
support of the household. On the other hand, the wages women earn in domestic work barely provide for a woman's economic survival in either Puerto
Rico or the Dominican Republic. Due to legal barriers against obtaining fixed,
well-paid employment covered by Social Security, the undocumented interviewees in Barrio Gandul live in precarious circumstances. For example, Teresa,
who came to Puerto Rico in 1985, explained that after an initial betrayal, she
found household work in an urban center:

> I left on a boat one Tuesday in 1985 with fifteen others. Some were women. We
> reached the coast of Puerto Rico on Friday and landed in Cabo Rojo. My fa-
> ther-in-law brought me, and as soon as we got here he gave me addresses. We
> all scattered, each taking off in a different direction. I walked and walked for
> a long time. Tired and thirsty, I went into a small shop in Cabo Rojo for a
> refreshment. Then I asked for some bread, as we do in the Dominican Repub-
> lic. The woman in charge asked me if I was Dominican. I told her my story,
> that I was alone and had to get to the address I had been given. She offered to
> take me and dropped me off outside of town. I went back later to the cafeteria.
> I was drinking coffee when some policemen came in. I gave myself up. They
> had caught another six people. We went to San Juan. There they told us that
> the government did not have money to pay for our trip back home. They took
> us to the Placita in Barrio Obrero. One of the women went to call a friend to
> come and pick her up. I told her, "Please tell her to let me stay only for tonight."
> I stayed in that house for a whole year. Next day, I found a job as a maid.

After that, Teresa worked in several places. "Now I work in a restaurant in El
Condado together with my son," she explained. "We do all kinds of work."

Gladys, a mother of ten children, also reached Puerto Rico by boat. She related that she "was in very bad shape" in the Dominican Republic. When her
oldest son wanted to take the trip, she told him, "I'm the one who is going first
because if the boat is lost, nothing is lost. You're still very young." Sonia, who
had worked in domestic service in the Dominican Republic, came to Puerto
Rico in 1962, seeking "a better life" for herself and her family. She stayed three
days before setting off for New York. There she worked as a domestic servant,
earning $25 a day. She returned to live in Santurce, attracted by its central lo-

cation and access to jobs. Earlier she was employed as a restaurant worker; at the time of this study, she was working as a domestic servant in a private home for $30 a day. Sonia has three children in New York and a mother in the Dominican Republic. She lives with a Puerto Rican companion and sends remittances regularly to her family. The day before our interview she had sent them $85.

Rosita landed in Puerto Rico by boat in 1980. She came from Santiago Rodríguez, where she was employed both as a factory worker and as a domestic servant. She left her son behind under her mother's care, and she sends them money regularly. She explained that she chose Santurce because her companion had a brother there. She has worked in private homes as a domestic employee but was unemployed at the time of the study owing to the birth, two months previously, of her second child. Rosita desperately needed work but was unable to find anyone to take care of her baby. Her situation was further complicated because her husband deserted her and returned to the Dominican Republic. Although her immediate family also lives there, she decided to remain in Puerto Rico after taking advantage of the amnesty provided to long-term undocumented residents.

In 1973, Luz Divina came to Puerto Rico after her daughter sponsored her legal migration to the island. Before coming to Puerto Rico, she ironed army uniforms. She chose Santurce not only because her two children lived there but also because of its central location. For five days a week, she works in the Miramar section of San Juan as a domestic employee, a job she has held for the past twenty years. Luz Divina claims to be treated and paid well for her work. Her employers pay her Social Security and she pays taxes. From the money she earns, she sends some to a daughter and a sister who live in the Dominican Republic.

The Intersection of Race, Class, Ethnicity, and Gender

Dominican women's migratory experiences entail a continuous struggle to advance and to protect their families. They view Puerto Rico as a place offering job opportunities. After settling in Santurce, all too often they find, as Teresa did, that reality fails to fulfill their expectations. Racial prejudice and stereotypes abound; the women are frequently perceived as strange, untrustworthy, dirty, ignorant, and disorderly. That is to say, their customs and bodies are socially construed as deviant and unmanageable.

Although racism in Puerto Rico is not institutionalized, it is manifested through daily practices (Zenón 1974). Negative attitudes toward migrants can be interpreted as racism, even though a considerable number of the Puerto Rican population is black or mixed. For example, a black Puerto Rican woman of the Barrio Gandul spoke against "those black Dominicans." When a black woman is walking down the street, she may be referred to as a Dominican woman, even though the woman might be Puerto Rican. Racial prejudice means that these migrants are not treated equally. Contrary to Dominican women, many Cuban women migrants do not have problems of cultural assimilation because of their color. Dominicans are also stigmatized for their accent. The Dominican accent is frequently used in slurs and jokes insinuating inferiority.[1] They are also accused of speaking loudly and of listening to loud music, interrupting peace and tranquillity.

Historically, racism and prejudice have denied "different" groups access to jobs. In Puerto Rico, the migrant woman is discriminated against not only because of her ethnicity and race but also because of her class and gender. As a result, domestic labor represents the only job opportunity for the great majority of Dominican women. As a matter of fact, 63 percent of employed Dominicans work in domestic service. Other job sectors available to other immigrants, such as working in stores and at cosmetic counters, are not readily available for black women. Racial prejudice and discrimination against the Dominican women is also manifested in "private areas" such as sexuality, where there is great social repression.

"The majority of us women do not have free control of our bodies," María del Carmen Feijoo has explained. "As with slaves, others make the decisions for us about our needs and our fantasies. These decisions are generally expressed in terms of control of our reproductive potential. This control is apparent in the areas of health, family, medicine, social security. Political decisions focus more on the process of social reproduction or reproduction of the labor force and of increasing or decreasing the demographic potential of countries and the region, than on the people who are the protagonists of these processes and their needs, suffering, happiness, frustrations" (Feijoo 1984).

Prejudice against Dominican women is also manifested in the accusation that they are prostitutes, have too many children, and steal husbands from other women. In this sense, many Puerto Ricans perceive them as undesirable and express hostility toward them. In January 1993, for instance, an anonymous press release circulated in San Juan about "The Dominican Plague":

Now the Dominican population is increasing on the island of Puerto Rico, and no one is talking about Puerto Rico's overpopulation. Dominican women are giving birth like "guimas" in public hospitals. Prostitution is a Dominican bomb. Thousands of Puerto Ricans have already been trampled down by Dominicans. Dominicans insult them, intimidate them, and have forced thousands of Puerto Ricans to move. They are now taking over San Juan, Santurce, and Río Piedras!

As one Puerto Rican informant in Barrio Gandul said, "We used to live better here before." Although both countries share a common history and language, the cultural clash between Dominicans and Puerto Ricans is translated into exclusion and discrimination against the foreigner. Popular reaction to Dominican women is found in such diverse spheres of daily life as jobs, housing, and education. Notwithstanding the precariousness of these women's daily lives, Dominican women struggle to maintain their dignity as human beings.

Gender Differences

For Dominican men, migration tends to be less traumatic. In 1989, El Chino left New York, where he had lived since 1977, for Puerto Rico. In Bonao, his native town, he had worked as a security guard and had supervised three farms. Although most of his immediate family live in Puerto Rico and the mainland, his only son remained in the Dominican Republic because it was too expensive to send for him. In Santurce, he sold aluminum and other metals, a job which his neighbor obtained for him. At the time of this study, he was working as a mason with Dominican contractors who paid social security and provided him with medical coverage. He was happy living in Santurce, sent money regularly to his son, and wanted to move into a more comfortable house.

Josué came to Puerto Rico with a musical group. He decided to stay, finding work as a painter, which he used to do in the Dominican Republic. All of his family live in the Dominican Republic, and he was expected to send home $300 monthly. Although he felt at ease and secure in Barrio Gandul, he expressed a desire to return to live in his country. At the time of this study, he was living with his companion, who worked at a billiard parlor on Ponce de León Avenue, one of the main thoroughfares in Santurce. He found occasional work cleaning ships on the docks of San Juan.

Because of its devastated economy, Apolinar left his country, where he had held two jobs (in a bank and as a newspaper carrier). His journey to Puerto

Rico was arduous. He explained that he waited on a mountain for seven days for a boat to arrive at Higuey, that he drank salt water and went without food. His first job in Puerto Rico was in construction work; later he worked as a security guard and as an independent construction worker. He was earning $5 an hour in construction—equivalent to a month's pay at the same job back home: 500 Dominican pesos. His wife, Altagracia, arrived by boat in 1989. At the time when she decided to leave for Puerto Rico, she was in her second year in college. Because her boat encountered mechanical problems, her trip took longer than her husband's thirteen-hour journey. For $30 a day, Altagracia worked as a domestic servant. The couple rented a small room. Later they moved into a larger apartment, for which they paid $225 a month. Although they had completed some official government documents, the couple had not yet obtained legal residence. They hoped to someday become legal residents and bring their children to live with them. "If I can't solve the problem here," Apolinar said, "I'll leave for New York, where it is easier to obtain legal residency." They sent gifts and money regularly to their children and family, spoke of how expensive it was to live in the Dominican Republic, and held that it was not "worth it" to stay there. Altagracia claimed that she would travel by boat again, if she had to.

In contrast to the Dominican women in Santurce, El Chino, Josué, and Apolinar have had relatively favorable experiences entering the labor market. Like many Dominican males, they found that their occupational skills—they know something about masonry, play a musical instrument, or do occasional construction work (*chivos*)—lead to better-paying, more stable jobs. Nevertheless, many Dominican men must also engage in odd jobs (*chiripear*) and hold two jobs in order to make ends meet. The difference between Dominican men and women in Barrio Gandul is one of degree. The situations of both are precarious.

The interviewees' testimonies suggest that the motivations and migratory experiences of Dominican women differ significantly from those of men. While some came to achieve personal and social aspirations, others "followed their husbands" or their children, as they say. Still others were the first to arrive. They stayed alone temporarily or indefinitely to support their families back home. Once in Puerto Rico, most Dominican women found jobs in domestic service or in small commercial establishments, primarily in bars and cafeterias. Many of the men found better-paying jobs as mechanics, carpenters, and tailors—which offer more social prestige. These notable differences between migrant men and women justify a close examination of the situation of Dominican women in families.

Dominican Families

Dominicans tend to migrate to Puerto Rico as individuals rather than as couples. In most cases, women are the first to migrate (Hernández Angueira 1990). This pattern, where more women than men leave the Dominican Republic for Puerto Rico, contrasts sharply with the migratory patterns one finds in other countries (Grasmuck 1984). Because of Puerto Rico's high demand for domestic servants, Dominican women find jobs more readily than men do. This type of work is not attractive to Puerto Rican women because it has low status and poor prestige, low wages, is temporary, and offers poor working conditions. Thus migration becomes a powerful magnet disengaging conjugal relationships. Women separate from their husbands both prior to and after migrating to Puerto Rico. "The trip cost me a divorce," one woman remarked, "although my marriage was already shaky." The migration process has increased the number of single women, who often speak of themselves as household heads. Under such circumstances, migration is an act of assertion and a positive approach to life.

Some fundamental changes take place in the lives of the migrants at the personal, family, and social levels. Many undocumented women have had to separate from their families, finding it difficult to return to the Dominican Republic. According to some reports, U.S. consuls in the Dominican Republic frequently limit the authorization of visas to only some of one's children and not to others. As a result, many Dominican families in Santurce are incomplete or divided. Women provide an extensive social network of relatives, godparents, friends, and acquaintances stretching from Santo Domingo to San Juan and New York. Eventually, many migrants reconstruct their extended families in Puerto Rico and the United States.

The story of the Alcántaras illustrates several common themes found in the exodus of Dominican families. The Alcántaras came from Moca, in the Cibao, where the husband grew tobacco and yucca on his father's land. With a visa obtained for him by his brother in 1982, the husband arrived first in the United States. In 1985, his wife and five children joined him. Initially they lived in New York, where the husband worked in a factory; but they were not happy there. They moved to Santurce, where they felt closer to relatives living in Puerto Rico

Table 2. Family Structure by Legal Status of Dominicans Surveyed in Puerto Rico

Type of Family	Legal Status of Household Head			
	Documented Number (%)		Undocumented Number (%)	
Single person	7	(24.1)	3	(27.3)
Married couple	13	(44.8)	5	(45.5)
One parent	2	(6.9)	0	(0.0)
Extended family	7	(24.1)	2	(18.2)
Nonrelated persons	0	(0.0)	1	(9.1)
Total	29	(99.9)*	11	(100.1)*

*Totals do not add up to 100 percent owing to the rounding of figures.
Source: Dauny, Hernández Angueira, and Rey (1995).

and in the Dominican Republic. Over the past five years, the husband has worked as a metal classifier (collector). Until the wife became ill with diabetes, she worked consistently as a domestic worker. They regularly sent money home to relatives and have returned several times for visits. They expect to live there someday.

Less than half (44.8 percent) of the Dominican households surveyed in Puerto Rico is a nuclear family (see table 2). A slightly greater percentage (48.2) consists of extend families and single persons. Many extended families consist of a single mother, relatives, and close friends representing several generations. Extended families and single-parent families are generally common among legal and undocumented immigrants in Puerto Rico. As the domestic unit begins to establish itself, its members increase. Work or income is contributed by the children and others close to relatives who arrive and assist with the domestic tasks. In this manner, the extended family begins to act together not only as a consumption unit but also for production purposes.

The Myth of the Male Breadwinner

In Santurce, Dominican women are commonly the main economic contributors to their households, shattering the myth of the passive and dependent woman. The majority of the Dominican women providers in Barrio Gandul were single or separated, although many of them maintained a consensual relationship. Of thirty-five households, twenty-three were headed by women.

This proportion is substantially higher than among Puerto Rican households. Like other migrants, Dominicans internalize the cultural stereotypes of their home society. Dominican culture emphasizes such values as men's honor and women's shame, while segregating male and female public conduct into separate spheres. However, Helen Safa (1995) suggests that Dominican women workers in the Dominican free trade zone have begun to assume more authority in the family. Safa found that 65 percent of the female-headed households in the free trade zone are headed by widowed, divorced, or separated women. She points out that the number of women in consensual unions is twice as high as those legally married, which corresponds to the high level of consensual unions in the Dominican Republic, which reached 33 percent in 1986 (Duarte 1989). We observed that in the Dominican Republic and in Puerto Rico, women in consensual unions often assume greater responsibility for the household and are less economically dependent on men than legally married women.

Authority in the home is derived from women's increased economic contribution to the household, even more significant in the light of declining male wages. This contribution, Safa argues, gives women a basis of resistance to male dominance in the family. My research indicates that in Puerto Rico, as in New York, the migratory process has undermined the Dominican culture's traditional expectations, forcing migrants to maneuver through incompatible and contradictory courses. Thus, many women migrants work outside the home, assert their autonomy, make decisions on their own, have children out of wedlock, and refuse to discuss finances with their husbands. Although it is clear that employment has had an impact on gender roles in the Dominican Republic and in Puerto Rico, this impact is greater at the household level than in the workplace, as Safa suggests. Moreover, Dominican women in Puerto Rico frequently proclaim themselves as heads of household, whether or not there is a man present in the home. Conversely, Puerto Rican heads of households tend to be men even when working women are the main economic providers. Only twenty of seventy-seven Puerto Rican heads of households surveyed were women, and most were single women or divorcees. The census easily conceals their participation in household finances and decisions. It defines "head of household" as the person economically responsible for the domestic unit, that is, "the adult member of the household under whose name the dwelling was bought, or is being bought, or is rented." Dominican women popularly define a household head as one who "defends the house," especially in material terms (Grasmuck and Pessar 1991).

The myth of man as provider and woman as housewife with an insubstan-

tial informal job complementary to her husband's salary is more accepted by
Puerto Rican women than it is by their Dominican counterparts. Many Puerto
Rican women define themselves culturally as housewives when there is a man
in the house, even though they sustain the household economically. Puerto Rican culture has fed this myth more forcefully through its mass media and educational system, both of which reproduce the male-dominant (*machista*) ideology. In the Dominican Republic, one of every three households depends on
the work of a woman (Duany 1990). This percentage is even higher in other
Caribbean countries such as Barbados.

However, in recent decades the percentage of Puerto Rican female-headed
households has increased substantially. In the 1990 census, 23 percent of Puerto
Rican households were headed by women. In Santurce, the percentage increased to 36 (U.S. Department of Commerce 1991). This trend suggests that
many Puerto Rican women perform a variety of nontraditional roles in ways
that are invisible and unrecognized by the society at large. The state tends to
treat female-headed households as deviant in spite of their steady increase in
Puerto Rico as in other Latin American countries. This stereotype furthers the
Puerto Rican society's hostility toward single mothers and their children.

Female-headed households are associated with the feminization of poverty.
In Puerto Rico, nearly 70 percent of female-headed households were below the
poverty line (U.S. Department of Commerce 1991). Among Dominican migrants, the feminization of poverty is even more pronounced. Female poverty
is concentrated among the least-skilled workers, those who receive state welfare
benefits, single mothers, elderly women, and black women; and their poverty
is compounded by a rejection of their ethnic origin and a lack of legal status
in the receiving community. These variables fuse into a process of impoverish-
ment which translates into an inability to find steady employment and income.
Given the low wages of women's formal employment, there is no adequate so-
lution to female poverty. The existing social services are insufficient to raise
women out of poverty. Under these conditions, women usually turn to the informal underground sector as a survival strategy.

Working in the Underground Economy

In previous studies, we have underscored the occupational segregation of male
and female Dominicans in both the informal and the formal economies of
Puerto Rico (Hernández Angueira 1990; Duany 1990). One of every four Dominican male employees in Santurce was a non-domestic worker (see table 3).

Table 3. Main Occupations by Gender of Dominican Immigrants in Santurce,
Puerto Rico (in Percentages)

Occupation	Men	Women	Total
Professionals and technicians	3.3	2.1	2.7
Managers and administrators	3.3	1.1	2.2
Office clerk	1.1	4.3	2.7
Salespersons	16.3	11.7	14.0
Artisans and repair workers	32.6	3.2	17.7
Operators and drivers	15.2	0.0	7.5
Non-domestic workers	27.2	9.5	18.3
Domestic service workers	0.0	68.1	34.4
Farmers	1.1	0.0	0.5
Total	100.1*	100.0	100.0
	(N = 92)	(N = 94)	(N = 186)

*The total of the men column does not add up to 100 percent because figures were rounded.
Source: Dauny, Hernández Angueira, and Rey (1995).

One of every ten Dominican women combined work at home with paid household labor. Like other Latin American women (Rakowski 1987; Berger and Buvinic 1988), Dominican women in Puerto Rico tend to develop informal activities as extensions of their traditional domestic tasks such as housecleaning, childcare, sewing, and cooking. The aging of the Puerto Rican population has been creating a new demand for female immigrants as care providers for the elderly, too. All of these tasks are associated strongly with the underground economy of Puerto Rico and other Latin American countries (Petrovich and Laureano 1987; Cariola et al. 1992).

In Santurce, Dominican men and women are segregated into distinct realms within a traditional division of labor. Men are highly concentrated in retail trade, business services, and repair work. To a lesser degree, they work in construction and transportation. Women by and large work in domestic service and in small businesses, such as cafeterias, restaurants, bars, grocery stores, clothing stores, and beauty parlors. This sexual segregation of labor is typical of a segmented labor market, both in the traditional and informal sectors of many Latin American countries (Duarte 1989; Anderson and Gordon 1989).

In short, women employed in the informal sector tend to concentrate in low-income and unstable economic activities (Rakowski 1987). While the proportion of male-owned businesses is triple that of women-owed businesses, more Dominican men had Puerto Rican and Cuban employers than did Dominican women. The sexual division of labor is clearly expressed in the informal economy, with a predominance of men in the micro-enterprise sector and women in the lower-paying jobs and in poor working conditions.

There are differences not only in the type of workers but also in the way in which men and women incorporate into the labor market. For men it was more important to follow formal mechanisms such as job applications to an unknown employer. Three-quarters of the women obtained their jobs through family contacts and friends as compared to two-thirds of the Dominican men. This variant points to the preponderance of Dominican women in domestic service where informal networks aid in recruiting new employees and contracting new employers.

In sum, the insertion of Dominican migrant women into the Puerto Rican labor market is marked by a multiple disadvantage (Rakowski 1987). Women share with men immense problems in the informal sector as they face insufficient income, lack of labor protection, and few opportunities to advance economically. Moreover, women suffer additional gender-related difficulties, such as scarcity of capital, few opportunities for training, and limited transportation. Like other Caribbean women, they have joined the underground economy as a means to provide for the basic needs of their families (Rivera 1989). In doing so, they have augmented a cheap labor pool willing to occupy the low prestige positions which Puerto Rican women consistently reject for economic and cultural reasons.

The ideological prejudices of patriarchal society uphold images of men as the heads of households even though women are often the principal breadwinners in the home. The concept of household head, however, is perceived quite differently among Puerto Rican and Dominican migrant women. This perceptual difference arises from the effects of social class on the availability of jobs. Most women who reside in Barrio Gandul are limited to jobs in domestic and personal services. This limitation is created by gender, class, race, and ethnic barriers which Dominican women confront daily in Santurce's labor market.

Given the isolation in which domestic service is performed, Dominican migrants become invisible as much to themselves as to those in the receiving society. That is why no Puerto Rican labor union looks out for the rights of domestic workers, as some unions do in Latin America and the Caribbean (Chaney and García Castro 1989). Regardless, the Dominican domestic worker's lack of an organized domestic labor union does not block workers from developing informal networks of solidarity and support. Many interviewees share information about job opportunities, housing, health services, and childcare. These interpersonal networks compensate partly for the lack of access to state benefits available to Puerto Rico's formal workers. Although Dominican women occupy the lower rungs of Puerto Rican society, many reach their aspirations to improve the economic situation of their families through migration.

Dominicans also show less gender inequality than Puerto Ricans in Barrio Gandul. That is because male migrants, just like females, confront intense discrimination based on their scarce economic resources and their national origin. As one can expect, those groups which have greater resources and options have a higher degree of gender inequality. For instance, Dominicans exhibit less economic disparity among men and women than Puerto Rico's more privileged ethnic groups, such as Cubans (Cobas and Duany 1995). Here is clear evidence of the impact of social class on gender relations. As a general rule, the more successful and better educated the man, the less powerful the woman. Although well-educated men may be more aware of inequality than less-educated men, the former can impose their authority even when their companions leave home to work.

Our fieldwork found greater gender inequality among Puerto Ricans than among Dominicans in Santurce. Compared to the Dominican residents of Barrio Gandul, Puerto Ricans occupy a more advantageous socioeconomic position. As a result, Puerto Rican women tend to consider their spouses as household heads, even when they are unemployed or absent from the home. This tendency perpetuates the outworn myth that the "man wears the pants at home."

In Puerto Rico, as well as in other Latin American and Caribbean countries, the female-headed household has increased during the last few decades. Dominican and Puerto Rican female household heads tend to be separated, live in consensual unions, or are single mothers. We have yet to verify the different stages that they go through or their impact on members of the domestic unit. There is, therefore, an urgent need to identify the survival strategies of women throughout their life cycle, considering socioeconomic, cultural, and psychological aspects. For the time being, it is clear that one immediate reason for the increase in female-headed households is the feminization of poverty among both Dominican migrant women and Puerto Ricans.

NOTES

This chapter is a revised version of a chapter of a book written in collaboration with Jorge Duany and César Rey. I would like to thank Elizabeth Hernández and Consuelo

López Springfield for their excellent translation and Jorge Duany, Blanca Villamil, and Lanny Thompson for their editorial comments.

1. This behavior is also evidenced in the Dominican Republic with respect to Haitians and in New York with respect to Puerto Ricans.

WORKS CITED

Anderson, Patricia, and Derek Gordon. 1989. "Labor and Mobility Patterns—the Impact of Crisis." In George Beckford and Norman Girvan, eds., *Development in Suspense: Selected Papers and Proceedings of the First Conference of Caribbean Economists.* Kingston: Friedrich Ebert Stiftung.

Baerga, María del Carmen. 1992. "El sector informal y el trabajo femenino: notas para la reflexión." In Evelyn Otero, ed., *Mujer y estadísticas: Memorias del primer seminario,* pp. 4–14. Cayey: Proyecto de Estudios de la Mujer, Colegio Universitario de Cayey.

Berger, Marguerite, and Mayra Buvinic, eds. 1988. *La mujer en el sector informal: trabajo femenino y microempresa en América Latina.* Caracas: Nueva Sociedad.

Cariola, Cecilia, Luisa Bethencourt, J. Gregorio Darwich, Beatriz Fernández, Ana Teresa Gutiérrez, and Miguel Lacabana. 1992. *Sobrevivir en la pobreza: el fin de una ilusión.* Caracas: Nueva Sociedad.

Chaney, Elsa M., and Mary García Castro, eds. 1989. *Muchachas No More: Household Workers in Latin America and the Caribbean.* Philadelphia: Temple University Press.

Cobas, José A., and Jorge Duany. 1995. *Los cubanos en Puerto Rico: economía étnica e identidad cultural.* Río Piedras: Editorial de la Universidad de Puerto Rico.

Duany, Jorge, ed. 1990. *Los dominicanos en Puerto Rico: migración en la semi-periferia.* Río Piedras: Huracán.

Duany, Jorge, Luisa Hernández Angueira, and César A. Rey. 1995. *El Barrio Gandul: Economia Subterránea y migración indocumentada en Puerto Rico.* Caracas: Nueva Sociedad.

Duarte, Isis. 1989. "Household Workers in the Dominican Republic: A Question for the Feminist Movement." In Elsa M. Chaney and Mary García Castro, eds., *Muchachas No More,* pp. 197–420.

Feijoo, María del Carmen, 1983. "Mujer y política en América Latina: viejos y nuevos estilos". Mimeographed.

Golubov, Nattei. 1994. "La crítica literaria feminista contemporánea entre el esencialismo y la diferencia." *Debate Feminista,* May.

Grasmuck, Sherri. 1984. "Immigration, Ethnic Stratification, and Native Working Class Discipline." *International Migration Review* 18 (3): 692–712.

Grasmuck, Sherri, and Patricia R. Pessar. 1991. *Between Two Islands: Dominican International Migration.* Berkeley: University of California Press.

Hernández Angueira, Luisa. 1990. "La migración de mujeres dominicanas hacia Puerto Rico." In Duany, ed., *Los dominicanos en Puerto Rico*, pp. 73–88.

Mires, Fernando. 1993. *El discurso de la miseria o la crisis de la sociología en América Latina.* Caracas: Nueva Sociedad.

Necos, Belkis. 1993. "Profile of the Dominican Community of Washington Heights." Institute of Dominican Studies, City University of New York.

Petrovich, Janice, and Sandra Laureano. 1987. "Towards an Analysis of Puerto Rican Women and the Informal Economy." *Homines* 10 (2): 70–80.

Rakowski, Cathy. 1987. "Desventaja multiplicada: la mujer del sector informal." *Nueva Sociedad* 90, 134–146.

Rivera, Marcia. 1989. "Women in the Caribbean Underground Economy." In George Beckford and Norman Girvan, eds., *Development in Suspense: Selected Papers and Proceedings of the First Conference of Caribbean Economists*, pp. 161–170. Kingston: Friedrich Ebert Stiftung.

Safa, Helen. 1995. *The Myth of the Male Breadwinner.* Boulder: Westview.

U.S. Department of Commerce, Bureau of the Census. 1991. *1990 Census of Population and Housing: Summary of Characteristics of the Population and Housing, Puerto Rico.* Washington, D.C.: U.S. Government Printing Office.

Zenón Cruz, Isabelo, 1974. *Narciso descubre su trasero: El negro en la cultura puerto riqueña.* Humacao: Editorial Furidi.

6

DAUGHTER OF CARO

RUTH BEHAR

Slowly, inch by inch, the guard in her olive green military uniform inspects my U.S. passport. Like other Cubans living in the United States, I used to have to travel to Cuba with a Cuban passport, a special *gusano* passport for "the worms of the revolution," for which you paid a fee for each year of absence from the mother country. Now the rules have changed, making the *gusano* passport no longer obligatory if you left Cuba before 1970. But the guards sometimes demand to see the Cuban passport anyway. I have it with me, though I finally let it expire, so as not to have to keep paying renewal fees. Just in case, I'm also traveling with a third passport, the passport that offers proof of my innocence, my little-girl passport, the one with which I left Cuba in 1961, just before my fifth birthday.

This is always a tense moment, heavy with inherited paranoia. Will they let me leave the country? Will I be forced to stay against my will? Is that the price I will eventually have to pay for my continued trips back to the island when there's no longer any reason for me to return?

At my feet are various pieces of hand luggage—a suitcase with wheels; a black oversize portfolio case with a snappy red zipper, for the art I've lately taken to buying; a buttery wood sculpture of a male hand and a female hand not quite meeting in space, acquired in a frenzied rainy moment on my last day in Cuba; and my book bag brimming with *Granmas* I never manage to read but keep saving for history. Caro watches me from beyond the yellow line. On my recent return trips, she has accompanied me to the airport. Come to say the last goodbye, the way she did when we left Cuba. My brother was not quite two and he cried and clung to Caro, to Caro who declared when he was born that she wasn't taking care of a second child, no way, she was quitting, but then she'd stayed and, despite herself, come to adore the boy. She cried too. She cried, waiting until our plane took off. Then she took the bus back to El Vedado, to the two-bedroom apartment with its pink bathroom tiles that my parents had left to her. Caro had worked for my parents, newlyweds ten years younger than she, as a *criada*, a live-in maid and nanny, sleeping in the same room with my brother and me. By right of her labor that apartment would now belong to her. But Caro never got to sit in the rocking chair on the balcony, sipping iced pineapple-rind water and letting her pregnancy come to term, as middle-class white women, like my mother, had once been able to do.

Within days the apartment was taken from her. Immediately and violently, they took away that apartment, where she'd scrubbed floors every day with soap, cooked sweet yellow rice, watched over children that were not hers as if they were. Caro fought—she yelled, she screamed, she cried, she cursed. And still she lost the apartment. And lost her firstborn. And lost faith in the revolution, just beginning, which she had expected would speak in her name.

Caro never set foot again in the building in El Vedado.

I glance back at Caro, an uneasy smile on my lips. I don't want to say goodbye to Caro but I also don't want the guard to tell me I can't leave Cuba. Caro's gaze is gentle. She nods her head ever so slightly. She understands my predicament. She's not asking anything of me.

Suddenly I hear the guard calling. You can go, she says. I thank her, a touch too profusely, and leap over my luggage, stretching toward the yellow line, toward Caro. We hug and I notice that in her hand Caro is still clasping the money I gave her in parting. Caro is a black working woman of the Caribbean; this is her inheritance: to come to the airport to wave goodbye to the little white girl inside the well-meaning woman who keeps returning without knowing why.

I keep waving. I cross through the x-ray zone. One last wave. Then another. I look back. Once. Twice. Again. When I am sure Caro is no longer there, I nervously scour the airport stores to see what I might buy during my final hour on Cuban soil—a bottle of rum? a musical tape? a black coral bracelet? a T-shirt of Che Guevara? I am an emigrant white middle-class woman from the Caribbean; that is my inheritance: to keep wanting the things money can buy.

Caro is from the countryside, from the town of Melena del Sur, an hour's drive south of Havana. Now seventy, she grew up, the youngest of nine children, in a wooden house with a yard in back, where the red clay soil gave forth mangoes and bananas, okra and plantains. Like many black women of her generation, she came to Havana to work as a maid in the 1950s. She got her job working for my parents through her older sister, Tere, who was employed by my great-aunt and great-uncle to care for their daughter and son. Tere became deeply attached to the children, and when the son, Henry, became ill with leukemia in 1952 she stayed at his side, refusing marriage offers. Even after our family left Cuba, Tere never stopped visiting Henry's grave in the Jewish cemetery in Guanabacoa, several miles outside of Havana.

Caro came to Havana on various occasions to help Tere. She soon knew the entire extended family on my mother's side. She knew my mother years before she got married. Caro saw my mother first with two long pigtails, then with high heels and fluffed-up skirts. Caro saw my mother marry young, only two weeks after her twentieth birthday. Caro saw how my mother, the daughter of *polacos*, Yiddish-speaking Jews from Eastern Europe, wed the son of *turcos*, Sephardic immigrants from Turkey, and all the problems that caused. How my mother's mother moaned: And how will we speak to them? They don't know Yiddish. Worse yet, my father was of humble origins and went to work as an accountant for my great-aunt and great-uncle, who had a thriving machine shop in Old Havana. I was born later that same year, in 1956. And a year later, when we moved to the apartment in El Vedado, Caro began working for my parents.

During the day Caro and I were alone together. She'd dress me up and we'd go out for lunch, usually to Chinese restaurants. My father worked at the machine shop and my mother would go lend a hand at her parents' foundering lace shop in Old Havana. In the evening, my parents passed the time with friends, dancing at one of the many clubs in the city, or walking along the Malecón. They'd finish off the night with a pounded steak sandwich smothered with translucent slices of onion.

Caro is a witness to my early childhood years, to my first struggles for self-definition. She has told me stories that no one else in the family has told me. She remembers how my father once forced me to sit in my crib against my will and how I let myself out, falling on my head, but free. She remembers how I refused to get into the cab of a taxi driver whom my mother had entrusted to take me, a child of three, from our apartment in El Vedado to the house of my great-aunt and great-uncle in Miramar. My mother couldn't understand why I was being so difficult, but neither she nor anyone else could convince me to get into that cab. The driver, Caro says I later told her, fondled my thighs during the whole trip back and forth from El Vedado to Miramar and I didn't like that. Caro remembers how firmly I knew, even then, to say no.

Caro is a second mother, even from afar. In her neighborhood I am known as *hija de Caro*, daughter of Caro. That I keep returning, with suitcases full of things for her and her family, is a sign of how well she raised me. People say about me, *Mira que bien sabe agradecer la crianza de Caro*—"Look at how well she knows to show her gratitude to Caro for raising her."

One night, when we get to talking about the car accident which happened soon after our arrival in the United States, when I was nine, I told Caro I'd broken my right femur and the family feared I'd never walk normally again. Caro nodded her head. It turned out she knew all about my leg. My cousin had written Tere and told her I was walking with a pathetic limp after being in a body cast for a year. Caro said she made a vow to San Lazaro. She promised to walk to his shrine if he made me well.

Somewhere in the shrine of Lazarus a tin leg hangs; it is my broken leg, left there by Caro.

Growing up in New York in the 1960s and 1970s, I'd accuse my parents, over Sunday brunches, of having been imperialists who colonized a black woman. My mother said I didn't understand. Race relations weren't like that in Cuba, she'd say. And I'd ask: What about all the clubs that blacks couldn't enter? They had their own clubs, my mother would say; blacks didn't want to go to the white clubs. And she'd add: You know there were clubs where they didn't allow us, where they didn't allow Jews. Our arguments would conclude with my mother saying: "Look, Rutie, don't believe me, but Caro wasn't someone you could colonize. Caro made all the household decisions. Caro cooked what she felt like eating. She cleaned when she thought it necessary. She went home to Melena on weekends. Caro was like part of the family . . . " Yet my mother always had to admit that Caro could never be persuaded to sit down at the table and have dinner with us. She ate by herself, when no one was looking.

On my first return trip to Cuba in 1979 I went looking for Caro. I arrived in the afternoon, in a taxi. Caro had been waiting on the corner since morning. I apologized for being late. She said it didn't matter. She knew how to wait.

I found Caro in a small apartment in Miramar. Before the revolution, Miramar was a posh neighborhood of huge mansions and suburban homes with U.S.-style yards in front. It was taken for granted that Miramar was lily white. In a gesture of revolutionary fervor, Fidel Castro ordered that scholarship students from the countryside and black families be sent to live in Miramar. The mansions were turned over to embassies. But soon the students were sent elsewhere, and the black families, with a few exceptions, ended up in the apartment buildings, and garages turned into apartments. Miramar kept its air of exclusiveness and became the neighborhood of choice for those generals and ministers who'd fought with Fidel in the Sierra Maestra.

Caro came to Miramar with her twin sons and daughter to live with Esperanza, a white woman. Caro laughed when I told her I thought she was Esperanza's maid. She and Esperanza were simply friends; they'd started living together after abandoning alcoholic husbands. Esperanza's health was more delicate, so Caro watched over her, but she was not her maid. After Esperanza left Cuba for Miami in 1983, Caro kept the apartment. Esperanza maintains close ties and has been, through the years, the key source for clothes, shoes, and asthma medicine for Caro's children.

In the meantime, Tere had indeed continued to work as a maid, despite the revolution, caring for a young Hungarian girl whose parents were diplomats. When the family returned to Hungary, Tere took another job caring for an older woman who lived in the upstairs apartment from Caro; when that woman emigrated, the apartment was left to Tere. A few years later, Caro's husband died. The two sisters, Caro and Tere, reunited in their old age, now pool all their resources and cook their meals on the same kerosene stove in the kitchen painted a deep sky blue.

Caro's downstairs apartment is the hub, the Times Square, of the neighborhood. Neither Caro nor Tere smokes, so both of them sell the cigarettes they get from their ration books. Someone is always stopping by to buy a pack. Their nephew from Melena brings sacks of okra, plantains, and string beans, which Caro and Tere sell for him. A guy who works at the printing press across the street bought a huge bag of cookies from someone who filched them from a factory and he's also asked Caro and Tere to sell his cookies. Most of the neighbors don't have their own telephones, so they come to Caro's house to make and receive calls. There's a pretty young blond woman, the daughter of an astronaut, who comes twice a week to get her calls from her boyfriend in Spain; one day he'll be her ticket out of Cuba. It is to Caro that the neighbors come to ask if the ration of bread has arrived, if there's fish today at the local *bodega*. Then there are the nighttime regulars like Juana, whose head is always wrapped in a glistening scarf; and there's Anselmo, a black man with a full head of white hair, who guards the building next door and comes in his pajamas to watch the soap operas; and at all times there are friends of Caro's twin sons stopping in to say hello. To the precious Miramar suburban quiet, Caro has brought the open-door neighborliness of the countryside.

Since I have no other family in Cuba except for a distant cousin of my father's, Caro provides my deepest emotional link to Cuba. I have now returned to Cuba nine times, and with every visit I grow closer to Caro and her family. Initially, before I started staying at Caro's house, I booked rooms in hotels and visited Caro and her family in the evenings. Caro insisted I have dinner at her house every night. How are you going to be in Cuba and not come eat at my house, she'd say. I was embarrassed, knowing that with all the hardships and rationing it was easier for me to get food at the hotel. But Caro would prepare such delicious meals it was hard to resist her invitation. Pedrito, the nephew from Melena, always brought fresh plantains, and the rice was always sweet, and there was always a little delicately stewed fish and a salad of cucumber and okra seasoned with lemon. All this food Caro would serve me, alone, on separate dishes, at the dinner table. The rest of the family, and some neighbors, who were regulars at Caro's house, would fan out around the house, eating with plates on their laps. I'd ask Caro why all of us couldn't eat together at the table, but she'd smile and go on serving the way she was used to serving. Sometimes one of her twin sons would sit at the table and eat with me, but no one else would.

Until recently, when only foreigners with foreign passports could enter the dollar stores, I'd accompany Caro to the *diplotienda* down the street from the monstrous Soviet embassy tower and we'd go food shopping. Usually one of her twin sons would come with us and both granddaughters. Those were strange occasions, when I'd become a fairy godmother, buying lollipops and apples for the girls and tomato sauce, meat, cooking oil, and milk for Caro, who was always careful to select the most essential things and those things that cost less. Was this situation, a white woman providing for a black woman, truly any different from the ways things had been before the revolution?

At the same time, life has changed profoundly. As a black woman in Cuba, Caro has gained in strength. There is an old decrepit white woman, Felisa, who comes to Caro's house every night. Caro's daughter-in-law says the woman, who is bone-thin and covered with scabs, looks like a mummy. Felisa was once quite rich and she's well educated, I'm told, but everyone in her family left and she stayed behind alone, taking care of a deaf niece who grew up healthy and strong thanks to her aunt's efforts. The niece married and she and the husband took over the house. Now they confine Felisa to one tiny room and don't let her into the living room or kitchen or bathroom. And they beat her. Felisa smells because she never washes herself. She gathers the almonds from the tree in front of her house and picks leftover food from the garbage. Caro feels pity for Felisa and gives her a plate of food or a *cafesito*, so Felisa comes over night after night. She says nothing; she walks over to the aluminium rocking chair with the armrest that's always falling off, takes her seat, and rocks there, watching television, knowing that Caro won't let her starve.

One night, when there is a full house at Caro's, the conversation turns to the question of immigration. Would you leave Cuba if you had the chance? someone asks. Caro shrugs and says, "I'm not leaving Cuba. Where else would I go? I'll be here with Fidel, until he goes or I go. Let's see who goes first."

During the summer of 1995 I decided to travel to Cuba with my husband and son. I rented an apartment next door to Caro. I wanted to see what it would be like to be neighbors.

A few days before leaving for Cuba I went to a conference in Miami. A friend of my parents, a white man who'd been our neighbor in the Vedado apartment building, drove me. As we approached the hotel where the conference was taking place he said to me, "If you want to take a walk, go that way, where there's a nice mall with good stores. But don't go that way. That's a black neighborhood. It's not safe." And then there I was in Havana next door to Caro. Next door to Caro and her black sons, her black daughter, her black sister, her black neighbors, all of whom watched over us and protected us and gave us their affection.

Caro wasn't feeling her best. Her ulcer was acting up and causing her pain. But she wouldn't let me pamper her in any way. I offered to accompany her to the doctor's and hire a driver to take us to the clinic. She insisted on going to the doctor alone and taking the bus. She worried, instead, about our well-being and sent Guarina, her niece, a sixty-year-old woman who had never married, to cook and clean for us. Guarina came gladly, happily, shooing me out of the kitchen when I'd try to cook or wash the dishes. "Caro says you work very hard with your head all year long and you need to get some rest." There was no way to convince Guarina that we didn't need help. Caro said we needed help and that was that. Did I want to go and argue with Caro?

Caro, indeed, was in charge. When people came selling fish just caught on the Malecón, or eggs, or cheese, or chicken, or a chunk of beef, Caro would send them over to me, so I'd buy these things in dollars. I'd keep a small portion and send over the rest to Caro. In turn, Caro would send over plantains and okra, and before I left she secured three rum-size bottles of the honey I adored from Melena.

Soon I gave up trying to do any household chores. Guarina knew how to wash the floors better than I, with soap and a bucket of water. She understood the drippy ancient refrigerator. When I longed for green vegetables she knew where to go get swiss chard for a few Cuban pesos. Guarina cooked incredible meals, delighted by the electric oven, the rice cooker, and the gas stove that came with the apartment, luxuries that few Cubans could afford. When she learned that my son liked to eat white rice scooped up with fresh plaintain chips, she made sure to prepare this delicacy for him every day. During our month's stay all I managed to cook was a flan, which I prepared early one morning before Guarina arrived.

Each day I asked Guarina to join us at the table for lunch and dinner, but she always refused. She often closed the kitchen door when we were eating, to give us privacy and, I suspect, to give herself privacy too. She said she was used to eating standing up in the kitchen. She ate as she worked. That's how she'd always eaten. She'd worked for a French family and eaten that way. I wondered if Caro had eaten that way when she worked for my parents.

I'd returned to Cuba with the best of intentions, in hopes of undoing racial and class borders, and I'd succeeded in reproducing, in my relationship with Guarina, my mother's relationship with Caro. As for my relationship with Caro, it was clear to me she felt she had to continue to care for me. In Caro's eyes I was still a little girl, a white girl who needed to be served. I was other things, too, of course. I was an anthropologist doing research, a professional woman with an immense network of social ties in Cuba, a poet who'd dedicated a poem to Caro about how she, above anyone else, had made returning to Cuba possible. Caro understood all these roles of mine and expressed her desire to see me succeed in the only way she knew how: by making it possible for me to concentrate solely on my intellectual labors. In that way she was fundamentally no different from my mother, who'd likewise always insisted on doing all the household work so I wouldn't be distracted from reading and writing.

Daughters of Caliban stand tall only when the backs of their mothers stretch wide.

Just before we left Cuba I invited Guarina to go out to a restaurant with us for lunch. She accepted and dressed up in her light yellow culottes and high-heeled sandals. At the restaurant she refused to order the special chicken dinner that my husband and I were ordering because she felt it was too expensive. She ordered an individual pizza for herself, which cost one dollar less. When the bread came, measly rolls that were smaller than the daily ration provided by the state, we each politely ate a piece. There were exactly four miniature rolls.

No one touched the butter. Before the waiter had a chance to take it away, Guarina opened her purse and gently tossed in the yellow wads of fat. "Don't you leave them any soda in your Coke cans," she said. "If you don't want anymore, give it to me." I don't know what possessed us, but we refrained from giving Guarina what was left of our sodas. We gave her the mixer she wanted in order to be able to bake cakes to sell, we gave her lots of used clothing, shampoo, cologne, toothpaste, soap, and money, but something possessed us, and with desperate thirst, as if we'd never have any again, we drank up every last drop of our Cokes.

III

WOMEN AND HEALTH

7

THE POWER TO HEAL

Haitian Women in Vodou

KAREN McCARTHY BROWN

WOMEN'S DIFFICULTIES IN relation to Western medicine, including psycho-analysis, are well documented in feminist literature. The relationships between particular sexist ideologies and medical perceptions, diagnoses, and treatments have been uncovered.[1] Women's difficulties in breaking into the medical profession are equally well known.[2] When women have sought access to the power to heal by becoming doctors, they have met resistance in one form or another in every place and every period of the history of Western scientific medicine.

The root metaphors of Western civilization are more visible in medicine than in many areas of life. On the most basic level, cultures are shaped by their root metaphors. These are the unarticulated yet deeply formative images that direct the flow of thought and action in any given culture. As in any operational thought system, there is a time lag between the root metaphors and current theory of Western medicine. There is a naive empiricism still deep in the medical ethos even though it has been set aside to some extent in medical textbooks. Feminist research, or research in general for that matter, has yet to reveal all the ramifications of Western medicine's intense physicalization of disease or of its view of healing as something done by an heroic actor who "possesses" power to an essentially passive, physical body that has no personal identity, social context, or history.

In Western medicine, healing power, like diseases and patients, is controlled by defining it as a piece of property. The power to heal is understood to reside in things—medical implements, drugs, and machines—whose use is restricted to those who possess other things—diplomas, licenses, and white coats—that indicate their ownership of a particular body of knowledge. It is the view of healing power as material property which can be owned and used by an elite few that I wish to explore in this chapter. Seeing healing power as property, subject to all the dynamics of a capitalist system, is one of the most significant root metaphors of Western medicine and one of the most damaging to women.

It is extremely difficult to become conscious of the root metaphors of one's own people and place. Once grasped, they are even harder to hold on to and pursue through the complex layers of daily life and collective history. It is precisely because they operate below consciousness that these metaphors are so efficient in the processes of culture formation and maintenance. If our root metaphors were available to us easily, if every day we could accept, reject or amend them, there would be no shared culture. Yet to see them as essential to communal life and to see their elusive character as integral to their functioning is not to conclude that they should not be tampered with. Change of the magnitude feminists call for requires that we pursue them. Yet this is not easy. One way to crack open the Western medical system to its root metaphors is to place it in relation to a healing system from another culture which is strikingly different. This is what I propose to do here.

The heart of this chapter is a case study of healing in Haitian Vodou, the African-Catholic religion that grew up on the slave plantations of the eighteenth-century French sugar colony then called Saint Domingue. This case, drawn from a New York–based Haitian healer, will be preceded by a discussion of women healers in Haiti in which I will attempt to uncover the reasons for women's relatively easy access to this power domain and also show something of the women's style, as distinct from the men's, of using power within it. The actual case study will be followed by some analytical comments about healing in the Vodou system which will be used to locate and describe a healing power that cannot be privately owned and tightly controlled. The conclusion will address Western scientific medicine and particularly the feminist critique of it. This section will include suggestions that feminists ought to focus on understanding the oppressive nature of power in Western medicine and on clarifying our own tendency to think of power as property.

Women Healers in Haiti

While in some parts of rural Haiti women can gain recognition and prestige as *manbo* (priestesses) and they can be herbalists and *fèm saj* (midwives) throughout the island, nowhere in the countryside do they effectively challenge the hegemony of the male in the healing sphere. This is not so in the cities, where there are probably as many women as men doing healing work. The urban Vodou context is the heritage of Alourdes, the woman healer who will be described in the case study which is the focus of this chapter. This relatively recent phenomenon of large numbers of women heading Vodou temples is due in part to chance.

Haiti is a poor country with an extremely depressed economy where the agricultural productivity which once made it the "Pearl of the Antilles" is now long gone. The reasons are long-term political corruption, overpopulation, and soil erosion. The large, patriarchal extended family dominated in Haiti's past, and this is still thought of as the ideal family. Even moderately successful men in the countryside can enter into multiple *plasaj* (common-law) unions with women. Each of these women is then set up in a house of her own in which she raises the children born of their union. Having her own household gives the rural woman limited autonomy, and her freedom and responsibility are increased by the fact that it is women who run the markets.[3] In the markets, women sell such things as baskets, candies, and bread along with the family farm produce. A market woman learns selling skills and money management through this work. The small profits she makes from the things she has produced with her own hands are hers to keep as insurance against natural and social catastrophe. These monies are often the only thing that prevents her children from starving.

As more and more young people have been forced off the family land, away from the rural extended families and toward the greater autonomy of city life, women have generally fared better than men. Their adaptable, small-scale market skills are one reason. The preference of piecework factories for women, who are thought to be steadier workers and less likely to cause problems, is another. Women have become breadwinners and their relationships with men, many of whom have significantly less earning power, have become more unstable as a result. Women in the cities have thus found themselves the heads of their own houses, as they were to some extent in the country, but with no supporting (and confining) extended family to back up that household unit.

Urban Vodou is, at its core, an attempt to recreate the security gained from the extended families of the countryside. In the cities, it is the Vodou temple and the fictive kinship network it provides that compensate for the loss of the large rural family. The head of the temple is called "mother" or "father" and the initiates are addressed as "children of the house." The Vodou initiate owes service and loyalty to his or her Vodou parent after the pattern of filial piety owed all parents by their children in Haiti. In turn, Vodou parents, like actual ones, owe their children protection, care, and help in times of trouble. In certain circumstances this help is of a very tangible sort: food, a place to sleep, assistance in finding work.

In rural Haiti the patriarch has unquestioned control, a control that extends to his role as priest when the family serves the Vodou spirits. But in urban Haiti, women's increased autonomy and access to money have made it possible for them to become heads of Vodou "families." Furthermore, I believe that certain aspects of healing and priestcraft have changed as a result of women's greater participation. I do not wish to overstate this conclusion, yet neither do I want to dismiss it simply because it is based on impressions. Starting when I first went to Haiti in 1973 and long before I considered undergoing initiation myself, many male and female friends offered this advice: "If you *kouche* [undergo initiation], do it in a woman's temple. The men will want to use you."

The urban Vodou temples run by men tend to mimic the patriarchal structure of the rural extended families. The authority of the priest is absolute. Also, the urban priest is notorious for fathering many children and recruiting desirable young women to be among his *hunsi* (brides of the gods), the ritual chorus and general workforce of a Vodou temple.[4] He thus creates for himself a highly visible father role which he then extends to all those who serve the spirits under his tutelage. While the priestess who heads a temple is not necessarily more democratic in all of her relationships with those who serve in her house, she does tend to be so in the ways that a mother's role with her children is normally less inflexibly hierarchical than that of a father. For example, some temples headed by women function as day-care centers for the working mothers associated with them. The woman-headed temple tends to reiterate the tone and atmosphere inside the individual home, a place where women have usually been in charge. This is an atmosphere that allows the priestess more flexibility and play in human relationships than the priest who acts out of the more public, and therefore more static and controlled, role of the patriarch.

Thus it has been social change that has created a chink in the patriarchal armor. Women have slipped through and, in urban temples, created "families" of their own modeled partially on the patriarchal family but with important modifications. Women's healing style is subtly but significantly different due to the age-old roles they have played in child rearing and barter marketing. Haitian market women, like many North American black women who support their families, probably have a greater sense of being effective in the world than do the white, middle-class, North American women whose voices dominate in feminist scholarship. This self-assurance is the firm base on which their flexibility operates. Furthermore, the greater flexibility and play of women's roles as compared to those of men have meshed with central attitudes in the larger culture, specifically attitudes toward healing. This meshing has taken place in such a way that key aspects of the character of the people as a whole have been enhanced under the leadership of women. The following study of a woman healer at work will support these observations.

The Soldier Who Was Hungry for Family

Late in March 1984, I went to visit Alourdes[5] at her home in the Fort Greene section of Brooklyn. Alourdes is a Vodou priestess and healer. In this African American spiritual system, the terms *priest* or *priestess* and *healer* are synonymous. Mama Lola, as Alourdes is sometimes called, ministers to the many needs of a substantial immigrant community of taxi drivers, dishwashers, gas station attendants, nurses' aides, telephone operators, and the chronically unemployed. She reads cards, practices herbal medicine, manufactures charms and talismans, and uses her considerable intuitive powers ("the gift of eyes") and the well-honed empathy of a strong woman of fifty who is now a homeowner and head of a sizable household yet spent the first half of her life in Haiti, where at times she was driven to prostitute herself to feed her children. In addition to her personal skills and strengths, Mama Lola also provides her healing clients with access to the wisdom and power of the Vodou spirits, a configuration of African spirit entities loosely identified with Catholic saints, each of whom presides over a particular life domain such as childbearing and child rearing, family roots, anger and assertion, humor and death. (Humor and death necessarily go together in the Haitian view of things.) Alourdes gains access to the spirits through dreams and through possession-trance, which is central in Vodou. In treatment sessions, she will frequently "call" the spirits for diagnosis, insight, or specific instructions as to what is to be done to bring about healing

I have known Alourdes for nearly ten years. She presided over my initiation into Vodou and now calls me her "daughter." We have been working together on a book about her life for the past eight years. I have an easy familiarity in her home. So when we sat at her kitchen table in March 1984, it was not unusual for her to tell me what was currently going on in her healing practice. Alourdes can be discreet if that is what is called for; however, if there is nothing about a client's problem that needs protecting, she sometimes teaches by sharing the details of cases. "I got somebody," she said. "I'm doing some work for him. He

is in the army. Oh boy, Karen! That man so big! When he go downstairs, he got
to go like this." With her usual refusal to reduce a story to words, Alourdes's
stout and squat body sprang up from her chair and hobbled across the kitchen
imitating a tall man in fear of hitting his head on the ceiling. Mama Lola continued:

> He from Virginia, but his mother in New York. She live in Brooklyn. But when
> he come he don't stay with her. He stay in hotel. I say to him, "Why you don't
> stay with your mother? Let her take care of you." He say, "Not me. I not de-
> pendent on nobody. What I need that for? The army is my family. I love the
> army and I going to stay in it until I die . . . er . . . until I retire." That what
> he say. I look at him and I think, "That funny!" because I never meet nobody
> . . . that's the *first* person I meet who say, "I love the army." So you know what
> I think? I think he just hungry for family.

As is the custom, the lieutenant had presented himself to Alourdes with an
introduction from a mutual friend and a nonspecific problem. He had "no
luck." Although she sometimes knows what is wrong with clients as soon as
she meets them, Mama Lola told me she always performs the expected diagnostic card reading so they will not be intimidated by her. She did such a reading for the lieutenant.

As she told me the story I could imagine the two of them in her cramped
altar room tucked away in one corner of the basement, the one tiny window
blocked by a heavy curtain, bunches of odorous herbs and a collection of baskets hanging from the ceiling, smoke-darkened color lithographs of the Catholic saints attached to the walls above altar tables dense with tiny flickering
flames, smooth dark stones sitting in oil baths, bottles of rum, vodka, and perfume, herbal brews and sweet syrups. She would have sat in the big armchair
with the stuffing coming out of one arm, her broad mocha face lighted from
underneath by a candle stub that burned on one corner of the small table in
front of her. I smiled to think of the big army officer hunched on the tiny bench
opposite her where clients always sit.

After a preliminary sign of the cross, Alourdes would have shuffled the cards
and offered them to him to cut. When they were spread in front of her in four
rows of eight, she would already have been in a withdrawn, concentrated state
of mind. After some minutes of silence, Alourdes would have begun to tap the
cards ("heat them up") in an order determined by her inner vision and ask him
questions, such as "You have some trouble in your house? You fight?"

At this stage of the divination process, the healer faces a large number of choices as to the direction of questions. Just as a healer such as Mama Lola is a combination medical doctor, psychotherapist, social worker, and priest, so the "problems" or "bad luck" she is faced with may manifest across a spectrum ranging from the physical to the social to the spiritual. No matter how the bad luck is eventually defined, it will always be diagnosed as ultimately due to a disruption in relationships, whether these are relationships with the living, the dead, or the spirits. The presenting symptom, though carefully articulated and then attended to by the healer, is to some extent arbitrary. In other words, trouble with one's father could equally well result in stomach pains or difficulty on the job. Haitians thus see the person as defined by a relational matrix and disturbance at any point in that matrix can create problems anywhere else.

During diagnostic card readings, the client is free to answer yes or no to the healer's probing questions without prejudice. Thus the client is active in the diagnosis yet does not dictate the description of the problem. When the questions and answers have gone on for some time, a joint definition of the problem will usually emerge. Most clients would acknowledge a significant difference between the problem they thought they came with and the one that was defined through divination. The outsized lieutenant from Virginia was no exception, although it took him awhile to realize this.

After many questions and many negative responses from the lieutenant, it finally came out during his first session with Alourdes that he wanted a promotion to a higher rank in the army and thought one of his superiors was standing in his way. Alourdes was not sure.

> I read card for him, but I don't see nothing. You know some people, they really got bad luck and you just see it. But with him, I don't see nothing like that . . . little thing maybe, but no real big thing in his path . . . nobody at work want to stop him. So I say to him, "How long you feel you got bad luck?" He think . . . he think . . . he think and he say, "Since I was a little boy." I say, "You can't have bad luck since you little boy!" Then I say, "What happened when you was a little boy?" Oh sweetheart, he tell me a story that was so sad . . . so awful.

The lieutenant had grown up in poverty in the Bahamas. A key event happened when he was no more than six or seven. One day his mother had nothing to give her children to eat. Neither did she have money to buy food. "He was so hungry . . . so hungry," Alourdes said. The enterprising and desperate young boy went, without his mother's permission or knowledge, to the factory where his father worked to ask for money for food. The man, shamed in front of his co-workers, turned on the boy with a terrible, hurtful truth that had been hidden until that moment. "Why you calling me Daddy?" he snapped. "I'm not your father." The young boy hid his hurt in anger and retaliated in a way that reveals much about the ideology of male power in Caribbean societies. He yelled at the man he had always thought to be his father: "You going to be sorry. Someday I going to be rich and I going to support you. I not going to be a hungry man like you!" Then, Alourdes said, he went home and cried. But he never said anything to his mother about the incident.

A few years later the boy found out by chance who his real father was. There was a woman who lived not far from his house whom the child had always addressed as Auntie without knowing if she really was an aunt or only a friend given the honorary title as is common in the islands. One day as he walked by her house, a young blonde woman sitting on the porch called him over, took his chin in her hand, lifted his face for careful inspection and said to Auntie: "That brother of yours can't deny this one. Oh no!" Alourdes reported that Auntie then told the boy, "That your daddy's new wife. He marry her in Germany. She come to visit me." That afternoon, for the first time, the boy heard the name of his biological father.

As a young adult already showing signs of promise in an army career, he went to Germany with the intention of looking up his father. But he procrastinated and left the country without making contact. According to Alourdes, her client explained his actions by saying: "What I need to find that man for? He not my father . . . not really."

Alourdes began her treatment, in pace with her client, by addressing the problem the lieutenant had acknowledged: his failure to get promoted. I was temporarily living in Massachusetts, working on Alourdes's biography, so I did not stay in close touch with the details of his case. It is likely that Alourdes gave him a "good luck bath"—herbal infusions and perfume mixed with fresh basil leaves (a general prophylactic) and water—which was spread upward, in small handfuls, over his body. After such a "bath" he would be instructed not to bathe with soap and water for three days.[6] She probably made one or more good luck charms for him as well. Surely she made an herb-doctored cologne that he could wear every day to enhance his luck. If she chose to take his story about the ill will of the senior officer seriously, she may also have manufactured a charm to "tie" or "bind" the supposed enemy. Making these charms is an interesting process, for it requires exhausting amounts of concentration on the part of the client. The lieutenant may well have been given a container of straight pins and told to count out two piles of 101 pins each and then count the piles again, and then again. Once absolutely certain that he had the exact number he would have been instructed to push each one (it takes effort) into a thick wax candle, while repeating aloud his desire that the man get out of his way and doing so in the name of the appropriate saint at each thrust of metal into wax. Among other things, this would have helped the lieutenant get clear as to whether it was his superior officer who was the source of his problems.

Some months after our first conversation about the soldier, Alourdes reported that deeper problems had been uncovered in the course of a subsequent card reading and they were now starting to work on those. It seems the woman known as Auntie had quarreled with the boy's mother not long after the chance meeting in which he learned the name of his father. The now grown man had a dim memory of the boy witnessing an act of magic, the placement of a charm. The boy remembered seeing Auntie write his name several times on a piece of paper and bury it along with a tiny oil lamp beneath one of the trees in her courtyard.[7] Alourdes had to work on a larger canvas now. There were relational problems within the extended family and, since the charm was buried under a tree which everyone knew was the dwelling place of a spirit, the spirits themselves were now involved. This would take time.

Again, I was not in New York and did not observe any of the particulars of the army officer's treatment. But it is unthinkable that it would have gone on without Alourdes calling Papa Gède, Master of the Cemetery, one of the two main Vodou spirits with whom she works. Once this spirit had struggled with and displaced Alourdes's *gro bonanj*, big guardian angel, an aspect of the human soul that is roughly equal to consciousness and/or personality, he would have begun to speak and act through Alourdes's body, slugging down herb- and pepper-laced rum (Alourdes herself drinks little and then only sweet wine or liqueur) and searching about for his bowler hat and his dark glasses with one lens missing.[8] Some say Gède's glasses have only one lens because the penis has only one eye. Others take a metaphysical approach and suggest that Papa Gède sees between the worlds of the living and the dead and that this sense of disjuncture accounts for his randy behavior and merciless joking. Gède delights in going after straight-laced people like the lieutenant who exercise strong control over themselves and their lives. It is likely that Gède teased him relentlessly, though not without point or lesson.

Ezili Dantò, the fearsome dark-skinned spirit associated with the Catholic Madonna known as Mater Salvatoris, may also have made a visit to Alourdes's tiny altar chamber while the lieutenant squatted on the low red wooden stool.

If she did, she did not mince words with a man who neglected his mother and rejected invitations to sleep in her house and eat her food. Ezili Dantò can deliver frightening diatribes.[9]

Whatever its specifics, the treatment went on for some months, with hiatuses when the lieutenant was not able to be away from the base in Virginia. In the course of things, Alourdes got to know her client well and when he came for treatments, she offered him coffee and they sat at the upstairs kitchen table before descending to the basement where the proud soldier had to hunch and squat in order to squeeze himself into the presence of the healing spirits. I asked about him in one of the regular phone calls that went from Cambridge to Brooklyn during the summer of 1984. Alourdes reported a recent conversation she had had with him:

> I talk to him real good. Oh sweetheart, I talk to him. I tell him to forgive his mother. She lie to him and tell him that other man his father. But she say that cause she ashame. So he got to forgive his mother and forgive that man who tell him, "I am not your father." Forgive him, cause he hurt and angry. I tell him, "Even he angry at you and your mother, that not your fault. You was just a child. No child responsible for that. Maybe at first your mother lie to him too. Maybe she say 'I'm pregnant for you,' when it really not his baby. But . . . maybe she hungry. Maybe she got to do that so he could feed her all that time she pregnant. Maybe he not know you was not his baby til after you born and then he hurt and angry. Don't judge her. Women got to do all kind of thing." I know . . . cause when I got Robert [the third of Alourdes's four children and the last one born in Haiti] I tell somebody "I pregnant for you," but it not true. What I going to do? I got to eat or that baby going to die! I tell him, "You got to love your mother . . . do everything to see she happy before she dead . . . she an old lady now . . . send her money . . . go see her." But you know who I hate, Karen? Who the bum? That man who go to England! He the bum! Cause maybe he find out she pregnant and maybe he think that going to be expensive. So he just run away. And you know what? He a racist. He got to go marry a white woman. Black woman not good enough. Ehh!

The course of treatment had been decided on. Healing, forgiveness, and reconnection were the desired ends (as well as disconnection and moral censure for the biological father and his family) and, undoubtedly, Alourdes worked on these goals through her usual combination of prayers and charms and visits from the spirits who would variously tease, empathize, and deliver stern lectures.

To ask whether this clarification of the nature of the problem, when it finally did come, or the cure itself, when that finally was effected, should be credited to Alourdes or to the spirits is to ask a confusing question from the Vodou point of view. Those who serve the spirits do not make such neat distinctions between the person and the *lwa* (spirit) who resides "in" or "around the head" all the time and who "rides" the back of the neck during possession.[10]

Nearly a year later the name of Alourdes's sad and ungainly soldier friend came up in a conversation. "What ever happened to him?" I asked. "Did he get his promotion?" Alourdes responded in a vague and distracted fashion. She thought he did get it. She was not sure. Maybe he did not. "But," and here she brightened up and turned her full attention to me, "when he in New York now, he stay with his mother. His mother the only family he got. That man who raise him dead long time. He don't come to see me no more but he okay now. Don't you worry, sweetheart."

Heating Up: Healing in Haitian Vodou

The word *power* (*pouvwa* in Haitian Creole) is rarely used to refer to the ability to heal. In fact it would hint of associations with malevolent magic if someone were to say of Alourdes, "li genyen pouvwa," she has power. Yet many do say of her, "li genyen konesans," she has knowledge. In Vodou circles *konesans* refers to sacred knowledge, the knowledge of how to heal. It is a word with a wide referential field including complex information about herbs, arcane teachings (including what we might call theology), and, most importantly, open channels of communication with the ancestors and the spirits which provide information as to what is going on at the deepest levels of a person or even what will happen in the future.

"Heating up" is another term used in relation to healing. It is always used in an active mode, as in the following example: "The spirits will not come to help us until the ceremony is *byen echofe*," well heated up. It is only when the singers, dancers, and drummers at a Vodou ceremony have moved beyond the fatigue and preoccupations of their difficult lives and are performing enthusiastically, drawing on a spiritual energy reserve tank, that the spirits will be enticed to "ride" one of the faithful.[11] Yet it is not only large groups that are able to heat things up sufficiently to bring about transformation. Alourdes's own energy can be similarly raised and heated by gazing into a candle flame when she wishes to call one of the spirits for help in performing a treatment. And if charms are expected to work over time, they also must be periodically "heated up" by being focused on and prayed over. Often a candle is lighted by the charm or "point" as part of this process.

With the concepts of "knowledge" and "heating up" we move close to the root metaphors that shape the Haitian understanding of healing power. *Konesans* is a wide-ranging and mostly nonspecific thing. Even those few priests and priestesses who have "the gift of eyes," highly developed intuitive powers, know that this knowledge, like the energy that enables a manual laborer to dance all night, comes from sources beyond themselves and is not something to be counted on in every situation. Thus a Vodou healer can never really be said to "own" such knowledge. Furthermore, heat, even though its presence in the body is a basic life sign and its transformative presence in the hearth makes cooking, eating, and therefore survival possible, is also an evanescent thing. It must be sought again and again, rekindled and recycled. Waxing and waning is part of the nature of heat and so, if healing is accomplished through heating, then it is never appropriate to think of the healer as "having" healing power in the way one can "have" a piece of property. The most that can be said of a Vodou priestess such as Alourdes is that she has mastered some techniques for enticing the heat to rise. In working with the soldier, Alourdes's initial problem was to heat him up enough for the real sources of pain and blockage to rise to the surface.

In Vodou, heat is life energy and it is intimately connected to death, humor, and sexuality. I do not have the leisure here to support these connections by teasing them out of the intricate details of ritual, although this can be done and presents the most convincing case, since there is no scriptural canon or written doctrine in Vodou. I can make a few general comments, however, which will show the connections on a broad scale. The easiest place to begin is with Gède. This spirit is guardian of the cemetery; he is a trickster, and the dance performed for him is a mime of sexual intercourse. During the long and taxing rituals for the Vodou spirits, Gède appears in the interstices, between dramatic and somber possessions that touch deep emotional chords in those gathered to "serve the spirits." His role is not unlike that of a cheerleader who entertains the crowd and gets it revved up for the second half of the game. He also appears at the end of ceremonies, in the early morning hours, when the social and personal wounds cauterized during the long night of spirit contact must be covered with the soothing salve of humor so the participants can return protected to jobs and family. Gède was the humorous but effective medicine most likely applied early in the soldier's cure. Its purpose was to soothe him, but also to energize him, to shake him up.

The word *balanse*, "to balance," has special meanings in Vodou circles. It refers to an active balancing as when something or someone is swung equally far between two poles. When sacred objects are taken off the Vodou altars and introduced into the ritual action, they must first be "heated up." To do this the ritual assistant is directed to *balanse*, dance, with the object in a side to side swinging motion. The word is also used in wider contexts. A Vodou priest once told me about the death of a mutual friend and, in commenting on the grieving family, he said "Gède, Master of the Cemetery, came to the house and balanced it," i.e. sent the household reeling.

Energy is what is sought in Vodou healing ceremonies, but like electricity this energy can be constructive or destructive. It all depends on how it is used.[12] The analogy of electricity is useful and yet, from another perspective, it hides something of the wisdom of the system. Those who serve the spirits do not understand the life energy they work with as morally indifferent so much as they see it as actually created from clash and contradiction. And death is the biggest contradiction of all.

Death and sexuality work together to raise life energy. Without death, there would be no point to sex and birthing. Death and humor go together because humor is the only appropriate and strong response to what is both dreadful and inevitable. Gède's is not an easy dismissive humor based on a false sense of superiority, but one that arises when a person hits rock bottom and rebounds because, put simply, there is nothing else to do. As a result of their cruel history of slavery, oppression, and poverty (Haiti is the poorest country in the Western Hemisphere), Haitians individually and collectively have repeatedly hit rock bottom. The humor and energetic creativity that characterize their culture, and particularly the Vodou dimensions of it, come from acceptance of the conditions of life. "Moun fèt pou mouri," people are born to die, Haitians are fond of saying with a shrug of the shoulders.

Vodou is based on an open-eyed acceptance of the fact of death and, in a related way, all attempts at healing in Vodou begin with the recognition that there are limits to what human knowledge, effort, and will can accomplish. For example, the first determination that a healer makes is whether a problem is "from god" or "from the spirits." God, Bondye, is the distant and omnipotent creator. The spirits are god's "angels" or emissaries in the world. Healers cannot change the mood or will of god. If a problem is discovered to be from god, the healer simply leaves it alone. But healers can feed the spirits, coax and cajole them into being more gentle and forgiving with one of their "children." In the second stage of the soldier's treatment, this is what Alourdes had to do with the spirit whose ill will had been set in motion by the charm "Auntie" buried under the tree in her courtyard.

The Vodou understanding of the multiple dimensions of the human soul parallels the limits the healer faces in problems from god. In addition to several other facets of soul (including the *gro bonanj* that is displaced during possession) there is also *zetwal*, star, a person's fate. At birth, the larger outline of a human life is already determined from beginning to end. All maneuvering, whether it is that of a Vodou healer such as Alourdes or of an ordinary individual, is done within the confines of what is fated to be. Each client is thus a given, someone unique who simply is what he or she is. Clients of Vodou healing do not lose personal history or social identity, and this may partially explain why, at all stages of the cure, the patient is an active participant. The lieutenant from Virginia helped define his problem through his responses to questions during the card reading; he participated in the manufacture of the baths and charms designed to prompt healing; and he engaged in conversation with Alourdes as well as with the Vodou spirits who were called in the course of his healing.

Modern Vodou healers acknowledge other limits to their powers. While most are skilled and effective herbalists, when certain symptoms are present, Alourdes and the hundreds of others like her who serve urban communities where there are scientific medical resources available will recommend that a patient see a medical doctor for x-rays or antibiotics.

Because Mama Lola operates out of a healing system based on an acceptance of limits, she is able to handle the power to heal in a flexible way that is neither grasping nor controlling. In curing the soldier, Alourdes employed a range of powers. She used "the gift of eyes," what I have been calling intuition, for her diagnosis of his problem. She used personal experience and empathy to understand the situation. She drew on community norms for judgment against the irresponsible biological father. She used herbs and charms. She also called on the spirits. Spirit possession when combined with her other skills provided range and flexibility in the postures she could take in relation to her client. At one time she could be a friend whose own experience of having a child in the womb and no man willing to take responsibility for it became the resource for wise counsel and deep compassion for the soldier. At another time she could be an awesome spirit, such as Ezili Dantò, censuring behavior and dictating the terms on which help would be given. This fluidity of roles means that any power a Vodou heater such as Alourdes exercises over a client is applied in a specific place and time, for a specific purpose. Her power as a healer does not adhere to her as a permanent attribute nor does it generalize itself to all her social relations.

Furthermore, because healing power in Vodou cannot be controlled and owned, neither can the object of that power be confined and controlled. Physical problems are taken seriously (and they are treated), but problems are not reduced to their physical manifestations. In Vodou there is a flow between the material and the nonmaterial, the inside and the outside, the intrapsychic and the person, society and history. Charms of the sort described in the story of the soldier's cure are examples of the internal externalized, of the temporary concretizing of a problem in order that it can be addressed directly. The "good luck bath" is an example of the reverse where an olfactory statement about how things *should* be is manufactured, administered, and breathed in by a patient for a period of three days.

In sum, healing power, the process of applying that power, and the problems to which it is applied are all characterized by fluidity and flexibility. And, as I have argued, the power can be held so lightly because those who orchestrate this power are denying neither their own nor another's ultimate vulnerability; nor are they pretending there are no limits to their skills. Facing and accepting (though not surrendering in front of) the givens of the human condition and the limitations on one's own power is the source of the Vodou power to heal, just as death is the source of Gède's humor and drive to propagate life. Acceptance of the rules of the game, the clash of opposites that is life, enhances life energy, heats things up, and heals.

The point of these thoughts is, of course, not to convince anyone to throw over Western scientific medicine and attempt to introduce traditional Vodou healing into the mainstream of North American culture. The purpose of the exercise lies in using the stark contrast with Haitian Vodou to unearth the property metaphor deep in Western medicine (and Western civilization in general) and to examine the tendencies to parcel out, fence in, control, and defend which are fostered in the medical arena by this root metaphor. In Western medicine, unlike Vodou healing, the patient's body is fenced off from his or her identity, history, and social context. We have separate healers to deal with each piece of territory. The physical-psychological-social-historical-spiritual disease cycle is similarly broken apart and parceled out among the experts with few persons paying attention to the interrelations. Within medicine, those specialties which of necessity deal with the interrelations have the least prestige. Think of environmental studies, nutrition, public health, and preventive medicine in general. Furthermore, as a result of being divided, conquered, and colonized, the patient is rendered passive in the curing process.

None of these points is new, nor is it news that women have been especially strongly controlled within such a control-oriented system. If Friedrich Engels was right in connecting the rise of women's oppression with the development of the notion of property,[13] then we can appreciate why women have had so much trouble with Western scientific medicine. This comparative exercise may make a modest addition to the feminist critique of medicine in demonstrating that otherwise diffuse insights into the nature of Western medicine are knit together by the hidden cultural metaphor that defines patients and diseases as pieces of property subject to ownership, use, and alteration.

The more substantial contribution may come in realizing that unlike the fluid and flexible "heat" in Haitian Vodou, the power to heal in Western medicine is also treated like a piece of prime real estate. Doctors own their power as if it were a thing and control access to it through the medical fraternities. One result of this unarticulated assumption about the nature of healing power is that it leaves doctors with a prestigious but rigid and greatly diminished human role. Doctors are required to deny significant portions of their humanity in order to function according to accepted standards. Doctors cannot bring their broader life experiences, their humor, or their own embodiedness into the healing process except as "bedside manner," and that is stage management having nothing directly to do with curing. Furthermore, the role of the Western medical doctor, once defined and controlled, becomes the possession of the person with the diploma, a permanent attribute of that person. This in turn causes the power of the doctor while actually doctoring—a situation in which he or she has awesome power over the vulnerable patient—to generalize itself to other areas of life where it manifests as class status and economic bounty. Along this line, it is interesting that Alourdes strictly follows the unwritten rule of Vodou healing that the healer should never take undue profit from curative work.

Western medical consciousness is carefully controlled like the role of the doctor. Medicine is a science and science enshrines reason, a focused and consistent use of the mind that eschews wider and deeper though less controllable ways of knowing. The supposed universal claim of the well-reasoned argument, its ability to detach itself from the specificity of the person who thought it and function in an equally powerful way no matter where it is applied, is another attempt to reify a power and establish control over it. Western civilization as a whole therefore fears so-called altered states of consciousness (altered from what norm?) of the sort that are central to Vodou possession-trance. For example, while there are substantive reasons for our wariness of "recreational drugs" and alcohol, it is also clear that we fear them because they make people inconsistent and unreasonable. We even apologize when we have a cold for "not being ourselves today." It may well be that one of the reasons Vodou has attracted so many negative stereotypes in this culture is that in heating things up, it brings out the many and not always consistent personae that inhabit each of us. Yet when trance and other altered states of consciousness are discussed in the academic and scientific communities, the question that seems to need answering is why some have chosen to spend time and effort exploring them. Rarely does anyone turn the question around and ask why we, in the Western world, have narrowed our consciousness to such a pure and unflickering beam of light. Erika Bourguignon's work seems to indicate that most groups at most times and in most places have utilized altered states in ways central to their societies.[14] It would seem that our passion for consistent and controlled knowing is more anomalous in the larger human picture than is Alourdes's ability to move in and out of trance states in which spirit entities speak and act through her.

In Vodou healing, the power is not so controlled. Healing power is an evanescent thing raised for the moment through the humor and strength that lie on the other side of an honest facing of death and one's own more short-range limitations. This sense of limits is exactly what we do not have in Western medicine where the doctor is a superhero and every disease is an enemy just about to be conquered, if it has not already submitted to the power of medicine to enforce change. In discussions about abortion and euthanasia as well as in such celebrated cases as that of Baby Jane Doe (an infant born with serious physical deformities), Western culture reveals itself struggling but largely unable to integrate death into life or to acknowledge limits to the power of medicine.

Western civilization has generated a great deal of power and property. This has given us the opportunity to create the illusion that we can avoid the harsh limits that have become the source of strength and healing in places like Haiti. Such a statement is not intended to glorify Haitians, who are as human as any other group, but rather to point to the need for a kind of wisdom in our medical establishments that, among Third World liberation communities, has been called the "epistemological privilege of the oppressed."

One reason it is so difficult for Western medical doctors to face and accept such major limits as death is that we have cut the healing arts off from spirituality, which would provide the only framework large enough and safe enough to make the confrontation possible. When religion and healing are separated, both appear to lose. The humorless, desexed, and death-denying monotheism that we currently pursue in Western culture may well have parallels with the lonely beacon of reason that we follow in scientific thought. But I will leave that connection for others to explore.

Feminists who have found this comparison of healing in Vodou and in Western medicine helpful may wish to ponder the formative powers of the property metaphor at greater length. When we fight the medical establishment for "control of our bodies" or for "control of reproduction," when we identify "our bodies" with "our selves," even when we address a misogynist society by declaring our intention to "take back the night," we sound more as if we are battling over property than changing the terms of the debate. Changing root metaphors is not easy, but we might begin the task by taking a clue from Alourdes and attempting an act of radical empathy with those who wield the power that damages us. It seems to me that it is time for feminists to examine the ways in which we demonize men and male behavior. For a while we have needed to do that to gather strength and reach clarity, but the easy caricaturing of men which passes for humor in some (certainly not all) feminist circles is a thin and brittle humor far removed from the richness of Gède's laugh. If we could look at one male-controlled institution, the medical establishment for example, and see through the heroic antics and controlling ethos to the genuine human hunger for life and life energy from which they spring, then we might be able to do what Alourdes did. She treated the lieutenant from Virginia by exposing his hunger for prestige, power, and independence as what it truly was, a hunger for human connection.

NOTES

1. Among the best examples of this work are G. J. Barker-Benfield, *The Horrors of the Half-Known Life: Male Attitudes toward Women and Sexuality in Nineteenth-Century America* (New York: Harper and Row, 1976), and Barbara Ehrenreich and Deirdre English, *For Her Own Good: 150 Years of the Experts Advice to Women* (New York: Doubleday, 1978).

2. See, for example, Barbara Ehrenreich and Deirdre English, *Witches, Midwives and Nurses: A History of Women Healers* (New York: Feminist Press, 1973).

3. For further insight into market women see Sidney W. Mintz, "The Employment of Capital by Market Women in Haiti," in *Capital, Saving and Credit in Peasant Societies*, edited by Raymond Firth and B. S. Yamey (Chicago: Aldine, 1964).

4. This point needs to be qualified by recognition of the large numbers of homosexual priests who have genuine power and prestige within Vodou. This is somewhat surprising given the homophobia observable in the larger Haitian culture. However, this is only a partial qualification, since many of these same priests would be more precisely called bisexual. They father children and have traditional families over which they exercise more or less traditional forms of power.

5. Alourdes is not yet certain if she wishes her full name to be known. I hope no one will see my use of only her first name in this article as a sign of disrespect.

6. A "bath" is applied in an upward direction, starting at the feet and ending with the head, when it is designed to enhance good luck and in a downward direction when it is supposed to remove bad luck. Leaving the bath on the skin for three days is in my view (I have taken many "baths" myself) a powerful form of aroma therapy. All are pungent. One lives with the smells, waking and sleeping, for a long enough period for them to address the deep self, more technically, the limbic mind where the sense of smell is located.

7. Punitive magic, something not nearly as central to Vodou as its image in North America would lead us to believe, is most often carried out between families or groups. But its target, intentional or de facto, is often the youngest and most vulnerable member of that family. This explains Auntie's charm being directed against the boy even though the quarrel had been between herself and the boy's mother.

8. Possession in Haitian Vodou is not a matter of putting on an act or assuming a ritual posture. It is a deep trance state which most often leaves the one possessed unable to remember anything that happened while being ridden by the spirit. It is a fascinating state from a psychological perspective because the spirit will often contradict and even, at times, severely chastise the very person being ridden.

9. Ezili Dantò is the woman who bears children. Her iconography and possession-performance work through all the permutations of mother-child relations from the most fiercely defensive to the most fiercely rejecting. Dantò is a member of the Petro pantheon of spirits, one of two major groups recognized in urban Vodou. Petro spirits are not evil but they are recognized as having "hot" temperaments and uncompromising standards.

10. The question as to whether persons and spirits are truly separate and distinct is answered in paradoxical ways in Vodou. Beliefs surrounding possession trance and the struggle of the *gro bonanj* with the possessing spirit point to a separation. Yet initiation rituals simultaneously "feed the spirits in the head" of the person and establish a repository for them outside the person. Also, when the ceremony is performed for an ancestor that calls his or her spirit "up from the water" and establishes it on the family altar, that entity is called both by the name of the ancestor and by the name of the chief Vodou spirit with whom he or she worked. Thus reference may be made to "Marie's Dantò" or to "Pierre's Gède."

11. Although the terminology is mine, the notion of a spiritual energy reserve tank is one that is actually quite developed in Vodou. In Vodou belief, one of the dimensions

of the human soul is called the *ti bonanj*, little guardian angel. For a long time I had trouble understanding what this was. Then Alourdes gave me the following example of how it works: "When you walking a long way or you carrying something very heavy . . . and you know you not going to make it . . . then the *ti bonanj* take over so you can do what you got to do."

12. The notion that power has no moral direction of its own and thus can be used either constructively or destructively may account in part for the bad reputation that Vodou has in North America. There are instances of punitive magic being carried out by Vodou priests and priestesses but there is also a strong belief in the overall interconnectedness of things and events which makes them rare. The use of the will to damage another necessarily produces an equally damaging countereffect on the one manufacturing the charm unless that person is either righteous beyond a doubt or very well protected.

13. F. Engels, *The Origin of the Family, Private Property and the State* (New York: Pathfinder Press, 1972).

14. I believe this to be a fair conclusion to draw from Erika Bourguignon's research, even if it must by necessity be an impressionistic one. The reader should know that Bourguignon herself is far too cautious a statistician and researcher to claim to have actually proven anything as sweeping as this statement. See Erika Bourguignon, *Possession* (San Francisco: Chandler and Sharp, 1976), and "World Distribution and Patterns of Possession States," in *Trance and Possession States*, edited by Raymond Prince (Montreal: R. M. Bucke Memorial Society, 1968).

8

MENSTRUAL TABOOS, WITCHCRAFT BABIES, AND SOCIAL RELATIONS

Women's Health Traditions in Rural Jamaica

ELISA J. SOBO

WHEN WE ASK about women's health cross-culturally, we are often answered with lists of statistics.[1] But there is more to women's health than numbers alone can reveal. Health beliefs have profound influences on how we live our lives. They affect the ways in which we treat and evaluate our bodies and the bodies of others. The more we know about the health beliefs of people from different cultures, the more their customs will make sense to us.

Take, for example, a case which occurred while I lived in Jamaica. One evening my neighbor Tasha stepped over a plate of food as she went into her house for a comb with which to fix her aging mother's hair. The plate had been set on a low rock on the ground, for want of a table. The food on the plate was her brother-in-law Joe's dinner. Joe grew angry. He and Tasha exchanged some heated words, and Mother, a nervous woman by nature, pleaded with the two to behave. Tasha went about her business, braiding Mother's hair. Joe sat on the step up to the house, sulking, and he refused to eat.[2]

At the time of the incident, I simply thought that Joe was being difficult and Tasha mean. Now I know better. But in order for others to understand the incident's significance, I would need to tell about the relationship that Tasha had with Joe and with the other women he knows. More important, I would need to tell something about menstrual traditions in rural Jamaica. To understand the short-term and long-term effects that such incidents can have, the reader also needs to know something about intergender relations and sociocultural conditions. I describe these conditions in the next few paragraphs, then outline the general health traditions of Jamaicans. Partly because mothers everywhere are generally the first people sick individuals turn to for help but also because the healing arts were not wrested from women in Jamaica as they were in the

United States, Jamaican health traditions are largely gynocentric, or female-centered; they are based to a large degree on Jamaican knowledge about menstruation and procreation.

The Setting: Jamaica

Like many Caribbean nations, Jamaica was once a colony of Britain. Because of the legacy of slavery, the island is home to people of mainly West African descent, most of whom are poor. People at the top of the class structure generally have light complexions, while people at the bottom are generally dark. This chapter is concerned with members of the latter category, who are a majority in Jamaica.[3]

Unemployment and underemployment run high throughout the island. In 1987, the year just prior to my fieldwork, the per capita income was barely U.S.$1,000.[4] I lived in a village of eight hundred people just east of Port Antonio; one-third of the villagers there could find no work (STATIN 1982). Many engaged in small-scale agricultural pursuits, yet few could manage with this income alone. They also took in wash, hired themselves out for small construction jobs when such work was available, engaged in part-time petty trade (like selling oranges), and relied on relatives for resources.

A typical rural Jamaican village, like the one in which I lived, consists of people brought together by ancestry or because they happen to live near a particular shop or postal agency. In some cases, a village is organized around an estate where villagers sell their labor. Houses generally lack plumbing and electricity and are made of wood planks and zinc sheeting. They are built as far apart as possible but are usually still within yelling distance of a neighbor.

Even though kin solidarity is valued and, ideally, kin (and close friends who are like kin) provide for each other by sharing money and food, the assumption that by nature humans are wicked and covetous leads people to guard their privacy and exert caution in most social dealings.[5] People often secretly resent requests for aid, even when these requests come from kin: in continually draining one's resources, demanding or needy kin impinge on one's liberty and block one's ability to build something for oneself. Nonetheless, giving and sharing are encouraged and kin relations are generally loving and fulfilling.

Ideally, sharing exists not just among kin but between conjugal partners, too.[6] But Jamaican gender relations are typically "consumed by strategies or 'games playing' " (Henry and Wilson 1975, 165). Impoverished men and women often see each other as means to an end. Women are perceived as "smart, clever, and devious" manipulators in "constant search for a male on whom they can rely" (ibid., 193, 172; see also Brody 1981, 187–88; Smith 1988, 142, 192–93).[7] For their part, men are expected to sire many children and to have as much heterosexual genital intercourse as they can.

Ideally, men help provide for their lovers and their children. But boys are brought up to be *irresponsible*[8] by mothers and caretakers who expect such behavior from men (see Clarke 1957, 52). Even for responsible men (and women), jobs are scarce. As a result of these economic and cultural forces, goods that should flow between lovers often do not.

Women resent men for failing to help support their children, and some of this resentment is redirected toward and reflected in a belief in the possibility of being raped and impregnated by the ghosts of dead men. Women's resentment of men's *irresponsibility* and sexual pushiness and men's own resentment of some women's requests for child support (and faithful conjugality) are further reflected in a belief in women's ability to manipulate men through menstrual magic. In both cases (see later discussion), gender-linked role expectations and ideas about the dangers of male-female relationships are expressed and perpetuated in ideas about the body in health and illness.[9]

Health-conscious Jamaicans associate the menses with uncleanness. The association stems partly from the influence of Christianity in the island. But, more important, it has to do with belief in the ability and inclination of women to use their menstrual blood wickedly, to manipulate men. Menstrual symbolism, then, in Jamaica as elsewhere, involves much more than simple physical impurity: the uncleanness associated with menstruants has important moral and social implications. The uncleanness of menstruation and the power of menstrual blood, as well as its physically polluted nature, are linked with Jamaican beliefs about bodies and their bloods.

Traditional Health Beliefs

In Jamaica, the social importance of maintaining the flow of resources between kin and between lovers is related to the physical importance of maintaining the flow of certain substances into, through, and out of the body. Traditionally, Jamaicans see the body as an open system that must stay *equalized*. Ideally, the body maintains itself at a set warm temperature. But because it has pores and is permeable, the body's temperature may be dangerously thrown off by changes in the climate, as when a day turns cold. Still, permeability is necessary for proper heat exchange and for the dispersal of waste matter.

Permeability is also necessary because the body must take in food to build its components and to replenish those lost through work and other aspects of living. Food[10] and drink, or nutriments, go from the mouth through a tube to the *belly*, a large inner cavity that resembles a big bag and holds (among other things) a food grinder. Different nutriments turn into different bodily components as needed, and the purity of these components depends upon the nature of what was ingested.

Blood is the most vital and meaning-invested bodily component of all and it comes in several forms. When unqualified by adjective or context, the word *blood* means the red kind, built from thick, dark liquid items such as read pea soup and from reddish edibles such as tomatoes. *Sinews*, another form of blood, comes from okra, fish eyes, and other light, slimy foods, such as egg whites. Sinews lubricates the joints and facilitates sex and procreation. Our eyes are filled with sinews and they glide in their sockets with its aid. Many call sinews *white blood* in comparison to the red. Both are needed for good health.

Good health is exhibited in plumpness. Because of this, reducing diets seem silly to Jamaicans and in their eyes U.S. fashion models are ridiculously thin (for details, see Sobo 1994). To compliment me (and to compliment the family with which I lived and ate), my friends in Jamaica would tell me that I looked as if I'd gained weight. I had learned early on that this was a good thing. On my first outing to market with Miss Martha, we bumped into her cousin's young wife. To my surprise, Miss Martha smiled and said, "How you grow so fat? You're a big woman!" In the United States this might be hateful, but in impoverished Jamaica it simply means that a person is in good health and is enjoying good living conditions. It also means that they can command respect: mature adults are referred to as big.

Jamaican women, like Jamaican men, generally hold their bodies in ways that maximize their presence, thrusting their hips and bellies forward and standing with legs apart and feet firm on the ground. Still, nobody wants to be too big: as with healthy relationships, a balance between intake and outflow must be maintained. All that gets taken into the body must be used or expelled because unincorporated excess begins to decay. Extra liquids become urine, and solid food turns to *didi*, or feces.

People associate superfluous or unutilized food, fat, sexual energy, and such with filth and the inevitable process of decomposition. People who do not use the toilet often enough literally fill up with waste: Mary asked her five-year-old daughter, Rebecca, why the white missionaries who came through now and then always had such soft and overfat bellies, and the little girl offered that "the tripe [intestines] them fulla didi." Delighted, Mary reiterated: "They fulla shit."

A body that does not efficiently rid itself of excess and waste can turn rotten inside. Many toxins are purged in sweat, which carries waste from the flesh as it makes its way to the skin to exit through the pores. Other toxins are picked up by the blood as it circulates, then are emptied out in bowel movements and urination. Some toxins can get left behind in the blood, and so people take special preventive steps to ensure its cleanliness. *Bush* or herbal teas commonly serve as blood purifiers.[11] The bitterness of a brew indicates how effective it will be. Cerasee (*Mimordica charontia*) tea is an island favorite. Tea of ground bissy (*Cola acuminata*) also removes strong toxins. Most tea brewed for breakfast has preventive, blood-purifying action.

Blood is the primary and most thought-about bodily component, but the most important part of the inner body is the *belly*. This big cavity or bag extends from just below the breast to the pelvic floor. The belly is full of *bags* and *tubes*, such as the *baby bag* and *urine tube*. A main conduit leads from the top of the body through the belly to the bottom (not from bottom to top), with tributary bags and tubes along its length. Sometimes, tube and bag connections are not tightly coupled. A substance improperly propelled can meander off course and slide into an unsuitable tube or bag, then lodge and cause problems.

When Jamaicans think about sickness, they do not think about battles for power and territory being fought between alien enemy forces of germs and armed white blood cells (see Martin 1991). Instead, they think about imbalances and about their bellies. Most sickness starts in the belly because of the central role this space plays in the uptake of substances ingested and in the outflow of foreign matter. Sickness occurs when bodily flow is blocked or otherwise "anomic" (Taylor's term, 1988). Sometimes this is caused when disagreeable foreign substances enter the body; at other times, sickness comes on when something mistakenly slips into the wrong bag or tube and rots there or clogs the system. A lack of attention to proper, timely nutrition and blood that gets unbalanced (too dirty, too full of sugar, too thick, etc.) can also cause problems.

Jamaicans rely on laxative purges, or *washouts*, for maintaining inner cleanliness and for promoting good levels of internal flow and so good health.[12] Taylor (1992) argues that an emphasis on maintaining continuous, unimpeded flow through the body is common among those who obligate people to share

with each other, as Jamaicans do. Individual pathologies, caused by disturbances in the flow of bodily substances, are mirrors of social pathologies,
caused by disturbances in the flow of mutual support and aid.

Washout should be taken about once a month. The model for health, pat-
terned on menstruation, is female-centered, or gynocentric.[13] Periodic cleansing is recommended for all. The purity of the person and of his or her blood
and body as a whole depends on inner cleanliness. Every household medicinal
supply includes a purgative of some sort, such as cathartic herbs or castor oil.

Female Bodies, Sexual Bodies, Bleeding Bodies

The general principles behind reproduction and sex are similar to those just
described. The bodies of men and women differ only in that they have different
sets of tubes and bags (e.g., the female has the *baby bag*) and female bodies are
built to take in semen during sexual intercourse.

Sexual acts that Jamaicans do not condone are referred to as unnatural and
are said to pollute or soil the blood and bring sickness. Such sickness is, in turn,
taken to support the judgment that these acts are morally *unclean*. Anal intercourse is among those acts deemed unnatural and so unhealthy. It contradicts
the social and moral supposition that procreation and kin-group expansion is
the aim of sex. It compromises the body because while the vagina is built to
take in semen the anus is not.

Traditional health beliefs provide ideological or philosophical support for
that culture's recommendations regarding behavior (the same holds true in any
culture). For example, the perceived physical effects of anal sex are seen to indicate the social or moral danger of the act. One Jamaican grandmother, ob-
serving a thin woman with poor posture walking on the road before her house,
declared, "As I look upon the gal's batty [buttocks], I know say the man trouble
the gal's batty. What sin, eh? The lord God did give [her] the batty hole to pass
out the dung—didn't give it for nothing to go into." The "gal's" flat "batty" and
her knock-kneed, pigeon-toed walk indicated her participation, willing or not,
in anal sex.[14]

Semen normally heads to the womb from the vagina. But it can meet a dead
end when ejaculated into the rectum, which does not have an easy opening
(like the vagina) by which unsuccessful semen can drain out. Semen that enters
the rectum almost always ends up rotting there. Ned, my Jamaican "sister's"
boyfriend, claimed that AIDS can result from this.

Ned's inventive use of traditional health beliefs to illuminate what was in

1988 a relatively new health threat is one example of the creative ways that traditional ideas get extended as people attempt to come up with plausible explanations for new problems.[15] Other explanations for AIDS, spun from other cultural notions, also exist. Some Jamaicans suspect AIDS as part of a white plan to exterminate black nations (see Sobo 1995). Some, having internalized the color prejudice engendered by colonialism and slavery, construe the high rate of AIDS among blacks as proof of blacks' inferiority. The idea that AIDS serves as a deserved penalty reflects a common human tendency to cast social and moral lapses as punishable by sickness.

People with AIDS are described as covered with burst sores and pustules full of impurities being worked out of the body through the skin. Twenty-year-old Jean-Bea, who often did laundry for better-off villagers down by the river, told me about a person with AIDS who had to be packaged in plastic wrap before she was transported to a Kingston hospital because her skin sores were so runny. Jean-Bea and others said that AIDS spreads through contact with the decaying matter excreted in such sores as well as through sexual or blood contact.

As with the juice of the sores of persons with AIDS, improperly deposited or disposed-of bodily excretions of any kind are unhealthy. Semen, or *discharge*, is dangerous because, in addition to sperm, semen contains male waste matter. So women *dirtied* by semen that does not go into the formation of a baby must expel at least the portions of it that their bodies cannot absorb.

The waste in discharge notwithstanding, the sperm it contains can fatten women, making them sexually appealing and attractive. To support their claim for the health-enhancing value of sperm, many people say that prostitutes and women who perform oral sex get fat. Persons are often named and reputations can be damaged, as prostitution and oral sex are not condoned.[16]

Sperm cannot always be easily incorporated into a receptor's body to fatten. Blood types differ and those of each lover (or client) that a woman may have cannot always blend. Also, semen can lodge in out-of-the-way spaces, making it inaccessible to the female blood that might otherwise absorb it. And, once cast out, discharge quickly decomposes and, like decaying matter of any sort, can cause sickness if not disposed of. Many say the toxicity or poisonous nature of discharge makes prostitutes and those who perform oral sex lose weight; they refer to specific thin women in making their point.

My friend Altuna's name came up in several conversations about prostitution. At the age of twenty-two she had had three children with three men, which is not uncommon in Jamaica. However, Altuna's aloofness and her tendency to wear trousers made some village women denigrate her. These women supported their prostitution accusations in diverse ways. Some pointed to her (supposed) weight gain, adding that sperm is known to fatten. Others said that she had grown slim since (supposedly) turning to prostitution because sperm sickens and weakens the body. Altuna seemed to me to have neither lost nor gained, but in any case her detractors used health ideas strategically to support their claims that she was acting in what they deemed to be an inappropriate fashion. I did not take note of it and it would be irresponsible of me to suggest it as fact, but I would be willing to bet that the women who said sperm fattens were thin and those that said it sickens were fat. We all use culture to our own advantage when we can.

The sperm debate notwithstanding, the waste that semen or discharge contains is toxic, fouling, and all the more noxious because it was already rejected by another's body. But Jamaicans assume that sex itself necessitates one person's discharging into another. Tradition has it that even women having sex with women couple as "male" and female, the "male" having supposedly stretched her external genitalia into an insertable pseudo-penis with the aid of an oil made for this purpose. This kind of thinking can effectively limit women's sexual repertoires, at least when they have sex with (biological) men. In any case, as long as the person receiving the fouling semen is female all is fine; women can menstruate and so cleanse their inner spaces.

Without intercourse and orgasm, men's discharge can harden in their lower backs, causing pain and sexual problems. Women who stay celibate too long may suffer from nervousness as their sinews balances become undone. Discharging *equalizes* and cleanses the body, promoting as well as signaling good health. People—mostly men—use this knowledge to justify frequent sex and to coerce others into having it with them.

Joe, a twenty-something youth, passes his days playing dominoes in front of the village shop and watching to see who gets on and off the bus from Kingston when it passes by, as it does several times each day. Sarah is twenty-four. She lives with her mother, her sister, and her sister's three children. Sarah, who is ambitious, sent her own child to live with a paternal aunt when she got part-time work as an aide at the health clinic two miles away. Joe wants Sarah to sleep with him, and whenever she leaves her yard to go to the shop for soap or for cooking supplies, he pesters her with stories of the physical dangers of celibacy. Joe also is interested in schoolgirls named Jane, Julie, and Patricia; he plies them with the same information.

Sex is healthy but also dangerous because it *heats* and so *opens* the body, leaving it vulnerable to drafts and the like. *Hot* from *the work* of sex, *blood-strings* or veins and arteries dilate and joints loosen. The opening to the womb—something like the cervix—expands, making pregnancy more likely to happen. The thrusting action of a penis opens women further. This makes the use of condoms risky: they can shoot off of the penis (sometimes called a "gun in a baggie") during sex, move up into the body's inner reaches, lodge somewhere, and rot or lead whatever gets caught behind them to rot. This causes sickness. If a condom happens to get stuck in the vagina itself, infertility and health problems associated with a backlog of blocked, decomposing menses ensue. Understandably, women do not like to use them.

Heterosexually active women cannot avoid discharge, which, from the time it leaves a man until its incorporation into a baby's body, is potentially dangerous and defiling. When male and female bloods or sexual fluids mix and conception occurs, all is well. The kinship bond between a parent and a child is tied with this blood, which, incorporated into the body of the child, physically compels the child to behave in a loving fashion with its parents. People of *one blood* share *one mind* and are of *one accord.*[17]

The creation of kinship is not fixed or finished at conception. The growing fetus eats, with its mouth, its mother's blood and food that she has eaten. If she is having intercourse, the fetus eats the semen that she takes in. Once born, a breastfed baby continues sharing substances with its mother. According to more traditional Jamaicans, breastfeeding can even create a kinship tie between a baby and an otherwise unrelated woman, because breast milk is a bodily substance and kinship ties are based on sharing such substance.

Kinship can be established after birth, experiencing labor pain is key to establishing maternity rights when push comes to shove. A big argument took place when twenty-four-year-old Hennie went into Kingston to claim her nine-year-old son from his father's aunt. The elderly aunt had been caring for the boy because, like many people, she wanted to have a child around the house to help her out as well as "to lively up the place." Hennie had been willing to agree to this, as neither she nor the boy's father had any resources and Hennie already had a two-year-old to feed when the boy was born. But now that the boy was old enough to help in her small garden and with household chores, Hennie needed him back. The aunt tried to keep the boy, noting that she was the one who fed and grew him all those years, but public opinion was on Hennie's side, as she had experienced the *hot* of labor, and she prevailed.

If conception does not occur, no child is born and kinship is not an issue. Gravity *runs* most of the unused semen from the vagina or *tube*. The rest is washed out on a regular basis by the menses. The process of delivering a baby sweeps out impurities that build up within the reproductive bags and tubes even better than the process of menstruation. Because of this, childbearing promotes good health. Mothers can claim "Me clean," insulting childless others by insinuating that they are physically impure, as Glory did to her twenty-year-old daughter, Beverly, when she was angry with her for not cleaning the house one day, and as one very big woman did on the bus to Kingston when a slim young girl stepped on her foot and did not apologize. Postmenopausal women have closed wombs; discharge cannot lodge within to pollute them. It runs out the vagina, unused.

Some believe that intercourse brings on menarche (the onset of cyclic menstruation) as the body tries to protect itself from semen. However, as others observe, menarche can occur before a girl has had sex. In any case, having many lovers is dangerous, as this can cause irregular bleeding. The body, confused by so much diverse semen, purges itself erratically. This, as well as the fact that each partner's penis can force the vagina into a different shape, keeps many women from seeking outside partners, as bodily changes reveal unfaithfulness.

Mister Harvey, who at fifty-five was married to twenty-two-year-old Denise, told me how Jamaican health beliefs support his traditional right to monopolize his wife's sexual services by keeping her fearful of seeking sex from other men. Indeed, as Denise told me later and in private, because her period came early, Mister Harvey almost found out that she had slept with the man hired to paint their house while he was in Panama on business. Luckily she was able to convince him that a month had passed since she had last seen any menstrual blood and that she had not been unfaithful since. She knew that men can justifiably leave mates who keep outside lovers (even if these lovers have been invented to explain what are naturally irregular periods).

Menstrual Taboos

At this point, it may seem that women are the only ones controlled by the strategic use of gender-linked health beliefs. However, men too are subject to the forces of health traditions.

During menstruation, the body heats up slightly and the womb, vagina, and blood vessels open to increase the outflow of cleansing blood. Menstruants should not take washout (laxative purges) because that would increase the flow even more, causing hemorrhaging, and possibly death. Menstruants also must avoid cold baths and drafts: the chances to catch a cold or take in harmful matter increase when the body is hot and open, as it is now. During the rest of the month, wearing panties and keeping one's skirt down and tucked between one's legs when sitting sufficiently shields the vagina's entrance, but now extra precautions must be taken. Menstrual pads, which absorb blood, also offer protection from drafts and other intrusions that might penetrate the vagina and get caught in the womb during this vulnerable period.

While menstrual blood itself is pure and clean, the waste matter and semen carried down by the blood are not.[18] The small dark chunks in menstrual blood contain the actual impurities and waste material being eliminated: toxins picked up by the circulating blood, bunches of semen, and clots of mucus which would otherwise accumulate and block the tubes. Anna, an old and wizened midwife, used an analogy: the river is clean but the mud at the bottom is dirty. The vagina is a riverlike conduit in which water equals clean blood and mud equals semen. The blood of menstruation, like the water of the river, is itself pure and clean; the unclean stuff is what the blood carries.

Cyclic menstruation is desirable (see MacCormack 1985) and menstruating is often called "seeing the health." With the exception of menstrual blood, bodily substances free of toxins and expelled from *clean* people are, in their purity, health-promoting. A clean individual is pure both physically and morally, such as a churchyard healer who practices when just bathed and when spiritually clean from a period of fasting, praying, and celibacy. Clean healers can rub patients' bodies with their own sweat as part of a remedy regime. Churches throughout the island talk of the cleansing, curative action of the blood of Jesus; only the truly pure can, as Jesus supposedly did, share effluvia to cure without endangering those being treated, whose bodies would otherwise reject these fluids as foreign matter.

Healthy bodies are internally clean. If matter that has entered the body is rotten or if it starts to decompose once within, it must be excreted in a timely fashion or the body will have to make extra efforts to regain equilibrium. A body in the process of cleaning itself, as with fever (which, put simply, melts out poisons), is sick. So in addition to claiming to be healthy, menstruants can claim to be sick. Calling menstruation sickness also serves to keep women from pursuing certain activities, and it highlights the pollution they carry. This oppresses women. But there is a flip side to the notion of sickness, which also can be used by women to avoid daily duties. Menstruation's uncleanness is also double-sided, for female power (however limited) flows from it. This power is linked to ideas about unclean or evil deeds and kinship.

Tying

Substances that transport toxins out of the body (e.g., sweat, urine) can cause sickness simply because they are dirty with waste. They can also be used to control the minds of others whose bodies they enter. Women, as a way to tie men to them and thus secure men's love and money, can use their menstrual blood in cooking.[19] Veronica told me that her cousin's friend collected her menstrual blood for this purpose by squatting over a steaming pot (hot steam helps gravity to ease out some of the menses). Sometimes, used menstrual rags or pads are soaked in water to loosen the blood, which is then squeezed or wrung out of them and added to food.

The food most commonly used in tying is *rice-and-peas*, a reddish-brown dish made of rice, coconut milk, and red beans. A woman can steam herself directly over the pot as her rice and peas finish cooking. Red pea soup, stew-peas, and potato pudding are also known as potential menses carriers. All are the correct color and commonly eaten. The mother-child kin-bonding model underlies many of the powerful connotations of blood and amounts for tying's mechanism. As babes are bound to mothers through blood absorbed or eaten in the mothers' womb and at the breast, so too are men who unknowingly eat blood-infused food bound to the women who provide it.

Kinship is material, concrete, and based on shared substances like blood. It can be altered after birth by breastfeeding and other substance-sharing acts. Fed to desired husbands by aspiring or insecure surrogate mothers or wives, menstrual blood works on grown men as blood works on a fetus. The incorporation of a woman's menstrual blood in a man's body ties him to that woman just as shared blood ties an unborn child to its mother-to-be. As shared blood ideally leads children to act lovingly toward their parents, so too should ingested menstrual blood compel men to act altruistically toward the women from whom the blood comes.

Behavioral changes, such as a man's increased generosity toward the woman who cooks for him, can indicate tying. But changes often can be explained situationally, and not everyone becomes aware of them. Whether or not a man has actually been tied, others may draw conclusions based on their ideas about his partner. For instance, the subject of tying came up in a conversation between a group of women during a wake for a man who was known to be quite loyal to his wife—a woman whom very few people liked anyhow. When his tying was implicated, I asked if the man wouldn't know that he was being tied through the taste his food might take on. All the women began to laugh. Fifty-three-year-old Esmerelda explained that it takes only a teaspoon of the fluid to compel, and with a grin she said, "You think that little bit can flavor [the] pot?"

Since a man's behavior is not necessarily a good indicator of tying and menstrual blood diluted in food cannot be tasted, many women might tie their men with nobody the wiser. But if too much of what is essentially decomposing matter and thus noxious poison is eaten by a man, he could become sick enough to notice and even sick enough to die. As with most maladies, this sickness begins in the belly. It is but one form of *bad belly*, a generic gastrointestinal complaint. The bad belly of tying generally looks *funny* (due to its shape, accompanying symptoms, persistence, etc.) and seems to have no cause. Because of its natural quality, ingested blood used for tying cannot be detected even by medical doctors or coroners. This is appreciated by women who would tie men.

Sick bodies signal sick relationships, and a bad belly from tying shows that one's conjugal relations are bad. Take, for example, the relationship between common-law partners May and Uncle. For several months, Uncle sensed a tension in his relationship with May. He then became alarmed by chronic belly pain. One day he stumbled upon a vial of dark, viscous liquid on a little shelf in the shed that served as a kitchen. A visit to a sorcerer confirmed Uncle's suspicion that because she loved him so much and with such jealousy, May had been trying to tie him to her by cooking with her menstrual blood. This explained the belly pain and the ambivalent feelings Uncle had recently had about May's demands and the displays of devotion that she seemed to be coercing from him. Had he not put a stop to things by announcing her sin and leaving her, the buildup of menstrual toxins in his belly would have killed him.

Menstrual rhetoric or talk about menstruation is often used in confirming or legitimizing claims about preexistent, problematic relationships (see Foster 1988). May might have become too demanding or Uncle might have fallen out of love. In any case, Uncle felt that the relationship was no longer a good one. The bad belly physically represented his sense that too many demands were being made of him. Indeed, May's alleged desire to control his decisions regarding what he would do for her brought the sickness on to begin with. Whether or not May had behaved poorly, she was now partnerless and her character had been maligned. Menstrual rhetoric had been used against her by Uncle and by his friends as a way to validate his act of desertion.

Because of their reproductive role, women have access to the most potent means to tie people and so to compel action.[20] Menstrual taboos stem from this "natural" fact. But in May's case, the notion of female might was used to harm a woman rather than to empower her.

Men's quickness to cry "I was tied" stems partly from economic and cultural conditions that make it hard for them to fulfill the expectation that they provide financially for partners and children, leaving men both demoralized and defensive as well as wary of contracting obligations, which any social tie involves.[21] Men's fear of tying also has childhood roots. Children are brought up to be dependent on their mothers. When they start to mature, girls do not grow as ambivalent about this as boys do (Chodorow 1978). They have less fear of the relational bond that tying represents because they lack the male's role expectation of independence (although they can and do attain it). Women also are less wary of tying than men because ascribing more than procreative power to semen is rare.[22] Women can control men with the effluvia of their own bodies but men must work magic with outside power sources.[23]

Men are the strongest supporters of menstrual taboos. These taboos include a ban on sex as well as one on cooking. The ban on sex is used for, among other things, controlling female sexuality. It discourages women from sexual expression, while at the same time and in combination with the idea that menstruants are unclean, it encourages women to feel shame about their genitals. The resultant lack of willingness many women have to even think about their reproductive organs (along with health concerns) leads many women to ignore contraception, which benefits men who want to impregnate them. It also means that many women do not think to ask for sexual gratification, which benefits men unable or unwilling to comply and which helps keep women in relationships from seeking outside lovers.

Fearing women's power to tie, men promote taboos that keep menstruants away from their food and sexually quiescent. But menstrual taboo-keeping is not only of interest to men. It requires the collusion of women, and collude they do—where they see the benefit. A shopkeeper would not close shop, nor would a woman with no one to help cook put away her pot. Taboos can easily be broken because people cannot always know who is menstruating. Women do not advertise their cycles, and dates are easily forgotten.

When women who have helpers (e.g., daughters, sisters, mothers) do see their menses, they can use taboos as a justification for refusing to work. Miss Reeny laughed when asked if menstruating bothered women: "If anything, they glad to see it. Means they can left from fireside [the kitchen]." Besides refusing to cook, women also can refuse men sex. Physically, sex taboos protect women, open from the heat and looseness menstruating entails, from *catching up draft*, or getting colds.[24] But women also may welcome the ban on sex during their periods because of fatigue, its messiness (wash is women's work), or their boredom with a man's technique.

Postmenopausal women stand to benefit in special ways from menstrual taboos. The high status that postmenopausal women enjoy rests, in part, on their cleanliness. They often point out the relative uncleanness of young women who might otherwise usurp their positions. They can exercise power over these young women by demanding they submit to the taboos. By keeping girls ignorant of all but the barest details of menstruation, older women invest the process with the sacredness that accompanies secrecy, making knowledge of it a valuable tool for reinforcing existing patterns of female age stratification.[25]

The food that women are most keen for their men to avoid is the food prepared by their competitors: other women. When I first arrived in the village and was unknowledgeable about many customs, I unintentionally provoked a series of arguments. My neighbor Tess got angry with me and with her boyfriend Franklin when I offered him tea and he accepted. She suspected that because Franklin had a job, making him a good catch, I might try to tie him (coffee is good camouflage for menstrual blood). Further, she believed that he and I had slept together (food sharing between men and women signifies sexual intimacy or such intentions). She gave me the cold shoulder and argued with Franklin daily until he was able to convince her that I was merely ignorant and sociable, not scheming.

By reminding men of the threat inherent in menstrual blood, which they do with direct warnings as by telling little stories about incidents of tying, women try to reduce the chances of their men taking food (and sex) from competitors who might steal the men away by tying them. They encourage men to be sexually and financially faithful.

Women use their knowledge about the menses to control each other and so to maintain their social positions as well as in trying to encourage their men to behave. The threat of tying should work on men like the threat of menstrual irregularity does on women, helping to keep them faithful. But other cultural factors, such as the expectation (upon which male reputations depend) that men have many lovers, undermines the strength of this threat. Further, by supporting menstrual taboos and by perpetuating belief in tying, women unwittingly participate in a patriarchal system of oppression that casts suspicion on their actions, limits their authority, and leads them to consider tying men to begin with.

Spirit Impregnation

Man's most vulnerable bodily opening is the *food mouth*, through which he accepts food that women have prepared. Women's most vulnerable opening is the *buddy mouth*—the vaginal mouth that takes in the *buddy*, or penis, and so takes in semen. Sperm is a kind of food, for it *grows* babies, as does female blood, and it ends up in a woman's belly (where digestion takes place and where babies grow). Foul substances generate sickness and just as they may reach the belly through the *food mouth*, as is the case in menstrual tying, they may reach it through the *buddy mouth*, or vagina, too. Foul substances that can enter the vagina include semen from irresponsible or otherwise contemptible men and bad air or discharge left by spirits.

When men's belly problems seem *funny*, menstrual tying is often suspected. When a pregnancy turns funny—when labor begins very early, when the belly grows too rapidly or in a strange shape, or when a monstrosity emerges in lieu of a humanly shaped baby—people also form suspicions. They might guess that the problem stems from a *witchcraft baby* or *false belly*—from a pregnancy caused or affected by sorcery or supernatural actions.

Women must always beware of male ghosts or *duppies*, for, dead or alive, men are expected to constantly seek sex. Sorcerers can be paid to *set* male duppies to rape women as they sleep, creating unnatural babies; duppies also might rape on their own. Witchcraft baby refers specifically to pregnancies resulting from sorcery-driven rape; false belly is a more generic term that includes pregnancies brought on by duppies of their own accord. The phrases, however, are interchanged regularly.

Some villagers argue that witchcraft babies cannot come from actual duppy ejaculate because, as Jenny explained, "duppy cock it rotten off, don't it!" (the bodies of the dead decompose). But all agree that witchcraft babies can come from the *unclean* or *bad air* that spirits troubling women's bodies leave behind. If the woman attacked is already pregnant, the fetus can be damaged by this air as well as by the trauma of the act.

Sometimes a spirit inserts a miniature creature into a woman's body through her vagina. Placement is usually by hand, but a duppy could place a tadpole, say, on the tip of his penis and, to use a Jamaican term, *shoot* it into the victim.

In such a case, a toad or frog will be "born." One old woman passed a large lizard, which spoke up and told her healer, "I been there since a tot." As the woman's cousin explained, a duppy must have inserted that lizard years ago.

Sometimes a duppy touches or plays with food left unguarded, spontaneously infusing it with his essence.[26] Some of this essence enters the woman's belly as she eats the adulterated food, and it impregnates her or affects a previous conception. A duppy also might punch a pregnant woman in the belly, which can harm the fetus. But women fear vaginal penetration far more than this or troubled food. Sleeping people cannot actively protect themselves from anything. Locked doors do not always deter human rapists; they can never stop duppies.

Duppy leavings enter the vagina and move to the belly, sometimes fertilizing an egg, always making the belly swell (quickly or slowly) as if the woman is pregnant. A spirit pregnancy can mimic a regular one so well that a woman might think it natural until the time of delivery, when only clots of mucus, slimy *sinews*, and bad *gas* or air come out, or when a creature or a monstrosity is "born." Aunt Ginny told Grama Jane and me about froglike creatures, memberless torsos, and children resembling monkeys. She said that Miss Lisa, who lived up the hill, gave birth to a cow head. This kind of statement can have implications for a woman's reputation.

As witchcraft baby is understood to be the unnatural result of sorcery or supernatural actions, spiritual healers are consulted. Healers generally insist on a pregnancy test if a woman seeks healing before labor has begun. Mother Geddes, a churchyard healer, one got ahead of herself in this. During a public service, aflame with excitement, she advised a young pregnant woman in attendance for the first time against buying diapers, as her belly held no baby. An observant church member commented that even though Mother had not *sounded* the woman (felt her body and belly), anyone could tell by looking that the belly held no child: its shape gave that away.

The patient, a mother of three who probably sensed trouble or would not have shown up at the healing yard of the church, agreed. Her common-law husband had run off with her neighbor, and although the patient had had sex with him recently, she believed that she had not conceived. She had no money to feed those children she already had and no man's help to support a new baby. She proposed that the neighbor had set this false belly to make sure that the man, who held a well-paying job, did not return to his rightful wife. This kind of proposition is common in witchcraft baby cases, as competition for "good" men runs so strong in the island. In any case, whether the pregnancy was natural (that is, her husband's progeny) or not, the woman, diagnosed with witch-craft baby, now had a moral right and physical necessity to abort, or *dash away*, the "baby."

False bellies and witchcraft babies do not develop because women wish for children. Most false belly sufferers described to me and those I met were mature adults who already had all the children they desired. The first victim I encountered (we met at a healing) was about forty-five and had long since built her family. Wishes for children are generally answered through the practice of fostering or common-law adoption, as in the case of Hennie and the elderly aunt, mentioned earlier.

The diagnosis of witchcraft baby or false belly can be used to make sense of a miscarriage or of the birth of a monstrously malformed baby. It also can be used to express guilty feelings about adulterous liaisons (and the conceptions they might involve) or about a lust for such partnerings. That is, a lump that comes up in the belly may become the object of a woman's guilty feelings, and it will appear to her (and to those who know about her lapse) as a punishment for having sex out of turn.

The idea of punishment has strong currency with others when a woman with false belly does not have a "good" husband, because in such a case jealousy would not be likely to motivate anyone to set a hex. So her sins are identified, and this often wreaks havoc on her reputation. Unpopular women are generally seen to have committed worse sins. This was the case with Miss Lisa, who gave birth to the cow head. Her condition was seen by others as stemming from her practice of having sex with married men in the village. No doubt, Aunt Ginny said, that one of the wives got vexed and so arranged for the hex.

Sometimes a healthy pregnancy that a women does not want to continue with is called a false belly. Abortion is frowned upon publicly, but with the diagnosis of false belly unwanted babies and babies that cannot be cared for can legitimately be done away with, because now they are seen as unhealthy, unnatural aberrations. Abortion techniques follow from ideas about menstruation and so they mirror the washout: the concoctions traditionally used to induce abortion work by causing the body to break up and purge the blockage that the fetus poses. The blockage is physical, but it also is social: unwanted children undermine family harmony, unbalance already strained budgets, and may be symptoms of failed conjugal relations or of general gender-linked tensions. Although abortions may be seen as antifamily, they often help women maintain the children they already have and so actually support family stability rather than undermining it (Sobo 1992, 1993b, 1996a).

Men "breed and leave" (impregnate and abandon) women so frequently that almost any mysterious swelling of the female belly gets attributed to some man—alive or dead—having left a baby of some kind. In blaming ghosts for pregnancies, men can express resentments about having to support children when jobs are so scarce, and women can express resentments over men's irresponsibility and their often coercive and promiscuous sexuality. For both men and women, casting a baby as a monster can help express inevitable ambivalence or resentments over children's demands. And blaming other women for setting the hexes that lead to witchcraft babies can provide women with a vent for resentments about female competition over husbands and boyfriends, as women are known to set such hexes when they covet other women's men.

The potential danger that sex with men holds for women is expressed in talk about witchcraft babies. Women's fears of being raped by ghosts reflect their fears of living men's potential to force sex and to "breed and leave" them. Methods of healing false bellies or getting rid of witchcraft babies stem from traditional understandings of birth and menstruation, just as understandings about how false bellies happen are linked with understandings of regular conception and gestation. Physical healing is paralleled by social healing as blockages (fetuses, irresponsible and stingy men) are eliminated.

Men's fear of menstrual tying is similarly linked to social and physical fact. The menstruant's power stems from blood's traditional role in reproduction and kinship as well as for internal bodily purification. As I have shown, Jamaican menstrual taboos involve more than simple hygienic fears. Indeed, menstrual blood is welcome in traditional Jamaica and menstruation is considered healthy as it cleanses the reproductive tract. Other cultures have similar beliefs (Browner 1985; Newman, ed., 1985, 15; Skultans 1988). For Jamaicans and possibly for many others, menstrual blood cleanses the body and is itself clean, but the semen it carries is rotten and dirty. Findings in the field of biology may confirm this (Profet 1993).

Despite its good qualities, menstrual blood does have a downside: it can turn a sociable practice—that of sharing food with others—into a manipulative and therefore wicked or unclean deed. Menstrual uncleanness is an idea that points to potential sinfulness in the menstruants themselves, not just to the physical connections between menstrual blood and decay or death. References to such uncleanness may be used to bring down or disempower women. As my friend Sarah said, if a woman gets bright or uppity, one need only "remind her of the last thing she wore": her menstrual cloth or pad. This reminds her, among other things, of her potential for sin. It also reminds her that the power she commands in society is very different from the power that men wield.

Men are careful about what enters their mouths. Likewise, women are as careful as they can be about what they take in through their vaginas. The substances men give women can turn to poison, both figuratively and literally, just as the food women give men can poison them. In both case, nutritive substances are given as gifts through a body opening; but instead of bringing life, as such substances are supposed to do, they cause destruction. The vagina and the mouth, two of the most social openings and the two that are most tightly linked to gender roles, also are the most easily comprised ones. This is no coincidence. The body and the things done to, with, and about it serve as mediums through which Jamaicans, like other people, can express, criticize, and perpetuate their culture.

NOTES

1. F. G. Bailey, William Wedenoja, Mark Nichter, Yossela Moyle, and various anonymous reviewers commented on this chapter; I thank them for their suggestions. The larger study that this chapter is drawn from is described in *One Blood: The Jamaican Body*, published in 1993 by State University of New York Press.

2. The following tale makes clear the dangers associated with things the vagina harbors: A robbery occurred in which several *idlers* stole a large amount of cash from a woman who worked in a foreign country and had returned home to the village for a visit. One of the young thieves gave a big wad of bills to a lover, who decided to take a bus to Kingston. She hid the money inside her vagina, or so the story goes. On a tip, the police stopped the bus, took her in for questioning, and stripped and searched her. They found and confiscated the money. Luckily so, for had they not, each dollar spent would have endangered the life and mind of the one who accepted it because of where it was stashed. For similar reasons, people were aghast at a tabloid account of a corporation whose bosses used the canteen—a place where people must eat—to search women's vaginas for contraband (*Weekend Enquirer* [Jamaica], 1989: 7). They worried over this and not the unfair and exploitative aspects of the practice.

3. The impoverished women whose stories I shall relate live rurally. But many members of the elite class and many urban Jamaicans were raised by women just like them (i.e., nannies) or they come from such ancestry. Accordingly, many elite and urban Jamaicans share, at least minimally, the traditions that I shall describe. Further, although the beliefs and practices that I describe are specifically Jamaican, they also can be found in other African-derived Caribbean or American cultures. They reflect tradi-

tional West African health ways and the legacies of colonialism and slavery. They also bespeak the social tensions engendered by current political and economic conditions in the Caribbean region.

4. Data were collected in 1988 and 1989. Study participants were mainly impoverished rural Jamaicans, most of whom are of West African descent. As is typical in Jamaica, I refer to the villagers with whom I worked simply as Jamaicans because most other islanders also are black, rural (or at least rurally rooted; see Brody 1981; 69, 101), and poor. The data discussed in this chapter were collected as part of a larger study of health, procreation, kinship, and magic (Sobo 1993b). The interviews that the chapter is based on were done with males and females, individually and in both mixed and sex-segregated groups. Some were formally structured, others informal conversations. They took place in community settings and private yards; some were done in clinics. Actions taken in regard to the body and study participants' drawings of its inner workings were also analyzed.

5. Classic works on Jamaica include those by Clarke (1957), Beckwith (1929), Henriques (1958), and Kerr (1963). A collection of life histories is found in Smith, ed. (1986), and health and healing are discussed in Sobo (1993b), Wedenoja (1989), and Laguerre (1987). Other pertinent works include those by Foner (1973), Hudson and Seylor (1989), Seaga (1969), and Wilson (1973).

6. I use the word *conjugal* to denote steady male-female relations, legalized or not. The latter form of marital union (nonlegal) is common among poor Jamaicans, and not all couples live together. Relationships often are unstable and do not last as long as many women might like.

7. In addition to Henry and Wilson (1979), see Justus (1981), Massiah, ed. (1986), Mohammed and Shepherd, eds. (1988), Roberts and Sinclair (1978), and Senior (1991) regarding women's status in the West Indies.

8. With italics, I denote indigenous terms.

9. Notice that while male power is expressed directly (e.g., through rape) women must remain secretive about the control they try to assert over the resources of others (Freilich 1968). Except with children that they have raised, women must resort to manipulations such as menstrual magic-making.

10. Although I use *food* to mean all comestibles, to Jamaicans the word refers only to tubers and belly-filling starches; other edibles have more specific names, such as *meat-kind* and *salting*.

11. Health-related concern over the state of one's blood is also typical among other descendants of the African Diaspora. So is the practice of cleansing it. (See Laguerre 1987; Snow 1974).

12. Such reliance is also found among other African-Caribbean people (Laguerre 1987); it is "legion" among African Americans (Snow 1974, 87).

13. Women take care of primary health needs in many if not most societies (see McClain 1989). The tendency for women's ethnophysiological understandings to be

modeled on their own bodies needs further exploration, as do the effects this has on the household production of health.

14. The woman telling me this had reason to look for negative qualities in the passerby. Some years earlier, the two women had quarreled regarding the ownership of some coconut trees. They had never resolved their differences.

15. In a similar fashion, a group of men attributed a (verified) rise in throat cancer to an increasing slackness with regard to oral sex. The associations seen between insecticide and fertilizer and dirty blood and cancer also demonstrate the creative ways that traditional understandings get used to explain how certain illnesses occur and also to express opinions regarding modernization.

16. Oral sex is overtly nonprocreative and so it is shameful. Sex can be recreational as long as the process of procreation is not hindered. But with oral sex, the white blood lost has almost no chance of finding the right tube and becoming a baby. All who give oral sex are called cannibals; they are antisocial beings who invert the preferred order by eating potential children.

17. Although kin are separate and stand as individuals, their substance remains conjoined conceptually. Rozin and Nemeroff (1990, 221, 219) note that this continuity of substance stems from a history of past contact, through a common ancestor. They argue that kinship loyalty and affection is construable as an instance of contagion—an instantiation of the cognitive style that contagious magic is based on.

18. The belief that semen is polluting exists in other cultural contexts (Eilberg-Schwartz 1990, chap. 7; Gregor 1990; McClain 1989, 75); so does the belief that blood absorbs and carries waste (Farmer 1988; Laguerre 1987).

19. No woman I knew admitted to doing this herself, and all the information I have is hearsay. Whether or not tying occurs often or at all, its islandwide cultural salience and the fear that it inspires make it real enough to warrant discussion.

20. Ingested female discharge can obligate just like menstrual blood. A man performing oral sex (to "eat under the two-legged table") can eat his lover's discharged egg and incorporate it into his own body. Having no womb, he cannot grow it into a baby. He could, however, incorporate it into his body, meshing with what would have been his lover's child, thus becoming like her son (as he would if he ingested her menstrual blood). So cunnilingus can "tie man like donkey" just as menstrual magic can. Men use this knowledge (and also appeal to the danger of ingesting another's waste) to promote genital sex.

21. These conditions include poor job prospects and also the pressures mothers place on grown sons for their loyalty and resources. But, moreover, men are brought up by women who expect them to be—and so treat them as—irresponsible. Social learning leaves men less than fully capable of responsible action.

22. Semen is a relatively weak obligating substance because father-child ties are never as highly charged as mother-child relations. Women can perform fellatio with minimal fear of being tied by semen. Even so, many men say that they do not desire it.

They belittle the women who give oral sex, calling them vampires because they suck blood, and dirty because their bodies are full of unused, rotting semen (taken in vaginally, excess semen runs out). Vampires must take *washout* frequently to avoid sickness.

23. Women do fear being tied through Obeah (sorcery) by men who have nothing to give them but beatings. Many take precautions, such as not drinking from opened bottles that might have had magic powder sprinkled into them and guarding their underclothes, which, if ritually buried in a man's yard, can compel a woman to stay with him. But because women are seen as plentiful and since men tend to overtly express power (while women are often left to manipulate or scheme), the likelihood of this scenario is low and people know it. Men, who must eat from women and whose bodies cannot handle foreign discharge, are not as safe.

24. People abstaining from sex during menstruation avoid subjecting themselves to culturally salient raw odors, associated with decay and death. Sexual sweat and effluvia can be quite redolent—especially in the heat of the day or during or just prior to a woman's menstrual period (female villagers report that their bodily odors become *higher* then). People believe that the pungency of sex lingers to reveal their business. During menstruation, the stench of sweat and sex would be higher, ranker, and even more likely to bring shame. The maintenance of respect necessitates sexual abstinence during this period.

25. Mothers generally tell daughters little or nothing about menstruation before it happens, nor do they inform them about sex. MacCormack and Draper note that a fecund young woman moves into a position to challenge the very status of her mother, who tries to hold onto power by withholding information (1987, 153).

26. Female duppies play with food, too, but I use the pronoun *his* because I am discussing spirit impregnation and not the kinds of interference that female duppies are more often implicated in (see Sobo 1993b, 1996b).

REFERENCES

Beckwith, M.
1929   Black Roadways. Chapel Hill: University of North Carolina Press.

Bock, P. K.
1967   Love Magic, Menstrual Taboos, and the Facts of Geography. American Anthropologist 69(2):213–216.

Brody, E.
1985   Everyday Knowledge of Jamaican Women. *In* Women's Medicine: A Cross-Cultural Study of Indigenous Fertility Regulation. L. F. Newman, ed. Pp. 161–178. New Brunswick: Rutgers University Press.

1981   Sex, Contraception, and Motherhood in Jamaica. Cambridge: Harvard University Press.

Browner, C. H.

1985 Traditional Techniques for Diagnosis, Treatment, and Control of Pregnancy in Cali, Colombia. *In* Women's Medicine: A Cross-Cultural Study of Indigenous Fertility Regulation. L. F. Newman, ed. Pp.99–123. New Brunswick: Rutgers University Press.

Buckley, T., and A. Gottlieb, eds.

1988 Blood Magic: The Anthropology of Menstruation. Berkeley: University of California Press.

Bush, B.

1990 Slave Women in Caribbean Society 1650–1838. Bloomington: Indiana University Press.

Chodorow, N.

1978 The Reproduction of Mothering: Psychoanalysis and the Sociology of Gender. Berkeley: University of California Press.

Clarke, E.

1957 My Mother Who Fathered Me: A Study of the Family in Three Selected Communities in Jamaica. Boston: George Allen and Unwin.

Delaney, J., M. J. Lupton, and E. Toth

1976 The Curse: A Cultural History of Menstruation. New York: Dutton.

Douglas, M.

1975 Couvade and Menstruation. *In* Douglas, Implicit Meanings. Pp. 60–72. Boston: Routledge and Kegan Paul.

Eilberg-Schwartz, H.

1990 The Savage in Judaism: An Anthropology of Israelite Religion and Ancient Judaism. Bloomington: Indiana University Press.

Farmer, P.

1988 Bad Blood, Spoiled Milk: Bodily Fluids as Moral Barometers in Rural Haiti. American Ethnologist 15(1):62–83.

Foner, N.

1973 Status and Power in Rural Jamaica: A Study of Educational and Political Change. New York: Teacher's College Press.

Foster, G.

1976 Disease Etiologies in Non-Western Medical Systems. American Anthropology 78:773–782.

1988 The Validating Role of Humoral Theory in Traditional Spanish-American Therapeutics. American Ethnologist 15(1):120–135.

Freilich, M.

1968   Sex, Secrets, and Systems. *In* The Family in the Caribbean. S. Gerber, ed. Pp.47–62. Puerto Rico: Institute of Caribbean Studies.

Golub, S., ed.

1985   Lifting the Curse of Menstruation: A Feminist Appraisal of the Influence of Menstruation on Women's Lives. New York: Harrington Park Press.

Gregor, T.

1990   Male Dominance and Sexual Coercion. *In* Cultural Psychology: Essays on Comparative Human Development. J. W. Stigler, R. A. Shweder, and G. Herdt, eds. Pp. 477–495. New York: Cambridge University Press.

Henriques, F.

1958   Family and Colour in Jamaica. London: Macgibbon and Kee [1963].

Henry, F., and P. Wilson

1975   The Status of Women in Caribbean Societies: An Overview. Social and Economic Studies 24(2):165–198.

Hudson, R. A., and D. J. Seyler

1989   Jamaica. *In* Islands of the Commonwealth Caribbean: A Regional Study. S. W. Medita, and D. M. Hanratty, eds. Pp. 43–160. Washington, D.C.: Department of the Army.

Justus, J. B.

1981   Women's Role in West Indian Society. *In* The Black Woman Cross-Culturally. F. C. Steady, ed. Pp. 431–450. Cambridge: Schenkman.

Kerr, M.

1963   Personality and Conflict in Jamaica. London: Willmer Brothers & Haram.

Laguerre, M.

1987   Afro-Caribbean Folk Medicine. South Hadley: Bergin and Garvey.

Lawrence, D. L.

1988   Menstrual Politics: Women and Pigs in Rural Portugal. *In* Blood Magic. T. Buckley and A. Gottlieb, eds. Pp. 117–136. Berkeley: University of California Press.

Laws, S., V. Hay, and A. Eagan

1985   Seeing Red: The Politics of Premenstrual Tension. London: Hutchinson.

Lindenbaum, S.

1972   Sorcerers, Ghosts, and Polluting Women. Ethnology 11:241–253.

McClain, C. S., ed.

1989   Women as Healers: Cross-cultural Perspectives. New Brunswick: Rutgers University Press.

MacCormack, C. P.

1985   Lay Concepts Affecting Utilization of Family Planning Services in Jamaica. Journal of Tropical Medicine and Hygiene 88:281–285.

MacCormack, C. P., and A. Draper

1987   Social and Cognitive Aspects of Female Sexuality in Jamaica. *In* The Cultural Construction of Sexuality. P. Caplan, ed. Pp. 143–161. New York: Tavistock.

Martin, E.

1991   Toward an Anthropology of Immunology: The Body as Nation State. Medical Anthropology Quarterly 4(4):410–426.

1987   The Woman in the Body: A Cultural Analysis of Reproduction. Boston: Beacon Press.

Massiah, J., ed.

1986   Special Issues: Women in the Caribbean. Social and Economic Studies 35(2,3).

Meigs, A. S.

1987   Blood Kin and Food Kin. *In* Conformity and Conflict: Readings in Cultural Anthropology. J. P. Spradley, and D. W. McCurdy, eds. Pp. 117–124. Boston: Little, Brown.

Mohammed, P., and C. Shepherd, eds.

1988   Gender in Caribbean Development. Mona: University of the West Indies Women and Development Studies Project.

Montgomery, R. E.

1974   A Cross-Cultural Study of Menstruation, Menstrual Taboos, and Related Social Variables. Ethos 2:137–170.

Newman, L. F., ed.

1985   Women's Medicine: A Cross-Cultural Study of Indigenous Fertility Regulation. New Brunswick: Rutgers University Press.

Olesen, V., and N. Woods, eds.

1986   Culture, Society, and Menstruation. San Francisco: Hemisphere.

Paige, K. E., and J. M. Paige

1981   The Politics of Reproductive Ritual. Berkeley: University of California Press.

Powell, D., and J. Jackson, eds.

1988   Young Adult Reproductive Survey. Kingston: National Family Planning Board.

Profet, M.

1993   Menstruation as a Defense against Pathogens Transported by Sperm. Quarterly Review of Biology 68(3):335–386.

Roberts, G., and S. Sinclair

1978   Women in Jamaica. New York: KTO Press.

Rozin, P., and C. Nemeroff

1990   The Laws of Sympathetic Magic. *In* Cultural Psychology: Essays on Comparative Human Development. J. W. Stigler, et al., eds. Pp. 205–232. New York: Cambridge University Press.

Seaga, E.

1990   Revival Cults in Jamaica. Jamaica Journal 3(2):3–15.

Senior, O.

1991   Working Miracles: Women's Lives in the English-Speaking Caribbean. Cave Hill, Barbados: Institute of Social and Economic Research (published in association with Indiana University Press).

Skultans, V.

1988   Menstrual Symbolism in South Wales. *In* Blood Magic: The Anthropology of Menstruation. T. Buckley and A. Gottlieb, eds. Pp. 137–160. Berkeley: University of California Press.

Smith, H. F., ed.

1986   Lionheart Gal: Life Stories of Jamaican Women. London: Women's Press.

Smith, R. T.

1988   Kinship and Class in the West Indies. Cambridge: Cambridge University Press.

Snow, L. F.

1974   Folk Medical Beliefs and Their Implications for Care of Patients: A Review Based on Studies among Black Americans. Annals of Internal Medicine 81(1):82–96.

Snowden, R., and B. Christian

1983   Patterns and Perceptions of Menstruation. New York: St. Martin's.

Sobo, E. J.

1992   "Unclean Deeds": Menstrual Taboos and Binding "Ties" in Rural Jamaica. In M. Nichter, ed., Anthropological Approaches to the Study of Ethnomedicine. Pp. 101–126. New York: Gordon and Breach.

1993a   Bodies, Kin, and Flow: Family Planning in Rural Jamaica. Medical Anthropology Quarterly 7(1):50–73.

1993b   One Blood: The Jamaican Body. Albany: State University of New York Press.

1994   The Sweetness of Fat: Health, Procreation, and Sociability in Rural Jamaica. *In* Many Mirrors: Body Image and Social Meaning. N. Sault, ed. Pp. 132–154. New Brunswick: Rutgers University Press.

1995   Choosing Unsafe Sex: AIDS-Risk Denial and Disadvantaged Women. Philadelphia: University of Pennsylvania Press.

1996a   Abortion Traditions in Rural Jamaica. Social Science and Medicine 42(4):495–508.

1996b   Pregnancy Loss in Rural Jamaican Tradition. *In* Pregnancy Loss Cross-Culturally. R. Cecil, ed. Berg.

STATIN (Statistical Institute of Jamaica).
1989   Statistical Yearbook of Jamaica 1989. Kingston: Statistical Institute of Jamaica.
1982   Census. Unpublished Portland information.

Stephens, W. N.
[1961] 1967   A Cross-Cultural Study of Menstrual Taboos. *In* Cross-Cultural Approaches. C. S. Ford, ed. New Haven: HRAF Press.

Taylor, C.
1992.   The Harp That Plays by Itself. In M. Nichter, ed. Anthropological Approaches to the Study of Ethnomedicine. Pp. 127–147. New York: Gordon and Breach.
1988   The Concept of Flow in Rwandan Popular Medicine. Social Science and Medicine 27(12):1343–1348.

Wedenoja, W.
1989   Mothering and the Practice of "Balm" in Jamaica. *In* Women as Healers: Cross-Cultural Perspectives. C. S. McClain, ed. Pp. 76–97. New Brunswick: Rutgers University Press.

Weekend Enquirer (Jamaica).
1989   Spread yu legs, mek a si if yu hide anyt'ing up de!! May 5–7, p. 7.

Weigle, M.
1989   Creation and Procreation. Philadelphia: University of Pennsylvania Press.

Wilson, P. J.
1973   Crab Antics. New Haven: Yale University Press.

Wright, A.
1982   Attitudes toward Childbearing and Menstruation among the Navajo. *In* Anthropology of Human Birth. M. S. Kay, ed. Pp. 377–394. Philadelphia: Davis.

Young, F., and A. Bacdayan
1965   Menstrual Taboos and Social Rigidity. Ethnology 4:225–241.

9

WOMEN, HEALTH, AND DEVELOPMENT
The Commonwealth Caribbean

CAROLINE ALLEN

WOMEN'S HEALTH HAS become a major focus of debates on social and economic development in recent years, as policy makers have come to recognize its importance for social and economic development. Women are mainly responsible for the tasks of biological and social reproduction. Biological reproduction "encompasses childbearing and early nurturing of infants," while by social reproduction "is meant the care and maintenance of the household. This involves a wide range of tasks related to housework, food preparation and care for the sick" (Momsen, 1991, 28). In many less industrialized countries, women are directly responsible for the health and education of children; in other countries, they are responsible for ensuring that the child attends school and, whenever necessary, clinic. These tasks are vital to the continuation of economic production and societal value systems, and women are usually expected to provide the services free of charge. Their ability as reproducers is clearly diminished when they are in poor health. Thus women's health underpins the welfare of the entire society. Furthermore, many economies are gradually increasing the employment of women as they increase the production of services (e.g., information processing, tourism, banking) relative to other areas, such as heavy manufacturing (Mitter, 1993). This trend is not restricted to the so-called industrialized countries; indeed, Commonwealth Caribbean economies are increasingly reliant on the production of services. The trend seems likely to continue and gather pace, adding to the functional importance of women's health.

The impetus to promote women's health for practical purposes has been reinforced by women's movements, many arising from the liberation movements of the late sixties and early seventies. These have stressed the rights of women to freedom from pain and disease and to control over their own bodies and reproductive functions. Protection and assertion of these rights is necessary for equitable development (Sen et al., 1994; Germain et al., 1992).

This chapter places data on women's health in the Commonwealth Caribbean within the context of the social and economic forces which affect their lives and their contribution to the development process. A remarkable feature of Caribbean women's lives is that they are largely involved in production as well as in reproduction. Those functions that generate income in cash or in kind are considered productive (Bolles, 1983). As shown in the Women in the Caribbean Project, the work of Commonwealth Caribbean women encompasses the reproductive and the productive, the informal and the formal, and is conducted in both the private and the public domains, while men's work tends to be concentrated in the productive, formal, and public domains, where they occupy the majority of powerful positions (Massiah, 1986a; Gill, 1984; Senior, 1991). Caribbean women might therefore be said to carry the greater burden of tasks related to the development needs of the region, and ill health among women can threaten to jeopardize this development. The weight of the burden itself undermines development when it leads to ill health among women.

My aim is to place the health status of women in the region as a whole in a global context, so I shall concentrate on broad comparisons of health status between the Commonwealth Caribbean and other regions of the world. This is useful for international policy makers within and outside the Caribbean region, especially those concerned with the allocation of funds toward health projects in the Caribbean. Indeed, one of the purposes of this chapter is to show the limitations of health indicators (such as life expectancy) conventionally used to guide the allocation of such funds. Given my interest in the global context and limitations of space, the large differences between countries *within* the Commonwealth Caribbean will be neglected, at least within the prose of this chapter. Those interested in this issue are referred to the tables, which give health indicators for individual Commonwealth Caribbean countries, as well as averages for different regions of the world.

The chapter opens with a brief examination of theories that predict differences in patterns of disease and demographic changes according to the level of economic development, then shows how certain aspects of the Commonwealth Caribbean experience conform to the predictions of these models. I then go on to argue that measures which are conventionally used to measure health in relation to development goals, such as mortality from infectious diseases and life expectancy, do not provide an adequate assessment of women's health in the

Commonwealth Caribbean and can give a misleadingly rosy picture of women's welfare relative to that of their counterparts in other parts of the "developing" world. More detailed analysis of mortality from and prevalence of some specific diseases reveals higher rates among Caribbean women than women in *either* other "Third World" regions or "First World" regions. This has serious effects on development, given the unusually high levels of participation of Caribbean women in the formal and informal labor markets as well as their domestic responsibilities. Hypotheses to explain these patterns of ill health are advanced, based on studies of the roles of women in the region.

Theories of Health and Demographic Change Related to Development

Epidemiologists, who are concerned with patterns of disease in populations, have noted that the transition from an agricultural society to an industrial society is generally accompanied by a change in disease and mortality patterns, in which infectious and parasitic diseases give way to chronic noncommunicable diseases such as heart disease and cancer (Gray, 1993). These chronic diseases are associated with aging and modern lifestyles. Modern life offers opportunities to indulge in various practices which can be bad for health, such as lack of exercise, cigarette smoking, and a high-cholesterol diet. For instance, the dietary risks for both heart disease and cancer are associated with the overconsumption of animal and processed or preserved foods and relative underconsumption of fresh fruits, vegetables, whole grains, and pulses (Hagley, 1987; *Cajanus,* 1994). This is made possible by the development of mass farming of animals and the move away from subsistence agriculture toward large-scale agricultural production for the food industry. The risks of these diseases may be reduced by frequent and regular exercise. Opportunities for this are limited in the modern world as many industrial and service jobs involve limited bodily movement and some involve long hours of work. The process of change from a disease profile dominated by infectious and parasitic diseases to one dominated by chronic, noncommunicable conditions is known as the "health transition" (Frenk et al., 1991).

Demographers have noted that industrialization is also accompanied by a "demographic transition," which proceeds through four stages. The preindustrial first stage is characterized by a high death rate and a high birthrate; the population is concentrated in the younger age groups, and any population growth is slow. In stage 2, the death rate starts to fall but the birthrate remains high, leading to rapid population growth. Stage 3 involves a fall in fertility and a leveling off of the mortality decline. This stage is called the stage of fertility-dominated aging, as it is the decline in fertility which is mainly responsible for the aging of the population. At the final stage the birthrate and the death rate level off at a low level. Any further declines in mortality tend to age the population still further (Gray, 1993; United Nations, 1993a).

There is considerable debate as to how and why industrialization leads to health and demographic transitions. There is debate, for example, on the relative importance of improvements in nutrition and standards of living, the establishment of public health measures such as sanitation and family planning programs, the impact of medical intervention, and progress in medical and contraceptive technology. It is not necessary to enter this debate here (see Gray, 1993, 75–79). The most important point is that the models predict that we can expect the profile of health and fertility in any country to depend on the level of economic development in that country. The Commonwealth Caribbean is generally thought to have achieved a higher level of economic development than most other regions outside Western Europe and North America, though it has not yet reached the levels of development of Western Europe and North America (the so-called "First World"). According to the model, then, the region should stand in an intermediate position between "First" and "Third World" areas, having higher life expectancy, lower rates of mortality from infectious disease, and lower rates of fertility than other "Third World" regions, but lower life expectancy, higher rates of mortality from infectious disease, and higher rates of fertility than "First World" regions.

Examining Evidence for the Commonwealth Caribbean

Limitations of the Data

Before proceeding to examine whether these expectations are borne out in reality, it is important at least briefly to draw attention to major limitations of available data.

Data which can be used for international comparisons give a seriously limited picture of health status, because they are indicators of mortality (death) or population structure and size rather than morbidity (illness) (Gray, 1993). Mortality statistics measure only one extreme of a range of health states (Frenk et al., 1993). This discriminates against a valid assessment of women's health, as death rates among women are generally lower and life expectancy higher than for men, but women suffer the greater burden of illness, much of it associated with their reproductive roles (Althaus, 1991; Germain et al., 1992).

Health data may be incomplete and underreported, particularly as they depend on cases of illness being reported to a medical practitioner, on his/her ability to diagnose, and on his/her efficiency in notifying statisticians (LeFranc, 1990; Beckles, 1992). This applies particularly to morbidity statistics, but mortality statistics also depend on accurate diagnosis of cause of death. Thus health data may be expected to be particularly prone to inaccuracy and underestimation where health services are poor or scanty. This implies that inequalities between rich and poor countries may in fact be even larger than shown in the official statistics. A further tendency for underestimation is introduced in the case of relatively new diseases that require complicated or expensive diagnostic procedures and carry a heavy social stigma; these conditions apply to AIDS.

Nonetheless, it is important and possible to make international comparisons on the basis of the data available. We assume that different regions face roughly similar statistical difficulties, so that it is valid to use the data for broad comparisons.

Conventional Indicators of Health and Development

Table 1 and figs. 1 and 2 present economic and social data which are often used to assess the relative "development" of different countries and regions.

Gross national product per capita differs significantly between regions (see table 1 and fig. 1). On average it is more than four times higher in Europe and North America than in the Commonwealth Caribbean (these differences are statistically significant). On the other hand, the Commonwealth Caribbean is on average richer than other Third World regions such as Africa, South America, and the Spanish Caribbean and Central America, though the differences between the Commonwealth Caribbean and these regions are not significant because of the wide variations in wealth *within* regions. For instance, within the Commonwealth Caribbean the Bahamas has a GNP per capita almost thirty-seven times higher than Guyana's. Such differences within the region should be borne in mind when looking at the health indicators, though it is remarkable that health conditions in the Commonwealth Caribbean do not vary as widely as GNP.

Public expenditure on health as a percentage of GNP (table 1) gives an idea of government commitment of resources to health goals. Note that the rates

Table 1. Basic Economic and Social Indicators

	GNP Per Capita, US$ 1992	Public Expenditure on Health as % of GDP, 1990	Human Development Index, 1992
Caribbean Countries			
Antigua and Barbuda	5,980	M	.796
Bahamas	12,070	3.5	.854
Barbados	6,540	M	.894
Belize	2,220	2.2	.666
Dominica	2,520	M	.749
Grenada	2,310	M	.707
Guyana	330	M	.580
Jamaica	1,340	2.9	.749
St. Kitts and Nevis	3,990	M	.730
St. Lucia	2,920	M	.709
St. Vincent and the Grenadines	1,990	M	.732
Trinidad and Tobago	3,940	2.6	.855
Regional Averages			
Commonwealth Caribbean	3,846	2.8	.752
Spanish Caribbean and Central America[1]	1,661	2.5	.675
South America[2]	2,503	2.3	.776
North America[3]	16,847	M	.929
European Community[4]	17,457	M	.901
Africa[5]	793	2.7	.343
Overall Average	4,649	2.7	.589
Significance Test	***	N.S.	***

Sources: GNP per capita, US$ 1992: World Bank (1994) *World Development Report 1994: Infrastructure for Development;* public expenditure on health as % of GDP, 1990: UNDP (1994) *Human Development Report 1994*; Human Development Index, 1992: UNDP (1994) *Human Development Report 1994.*

Significance test = F-test for significance of differences between means; *** = significant at the 1% level; N.S. = not significant.

M = Missing data

1. Cuba, Dominican Republic, Costa Rica, El Salvador, Guatemala, Honduras, Mexico, Panama.

2. Argentina, Brazil, Chile, Colombia, Ecuador, Paraguay, Peru, Uruguay, Venezuela.

3. USA, Canada, Puerto Rico.

4. Belgium, Denmark, France, Germany, Greece, Ireland, Italy, Luxembourg, Netherlands, Portugal, Spain, UK.

5. Algeria, Angola, Benin, Botswana, Burkina Faso, Burundi, Cameroon, Central African Republic, Chad, Congo, Ivory Coast, Ethiopia, Gabon, Ghana, Guinea, Guinea Bissau, Kenya, Lesotho, Liberia, Madagascar, Malawi, Mali, Mozambique, Namibia, Niger, Nigeria, Rwanda, Senegal, Sierra Leone, South Africa, Togo, Uganda, Tanzania, Zaire, Zambia, Zimbabwe.

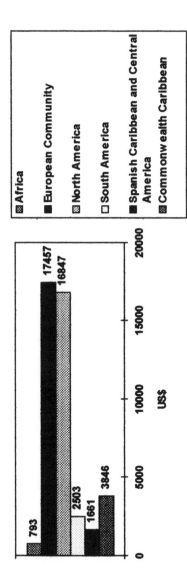

Fig. 1: Average GNP per capita, by region

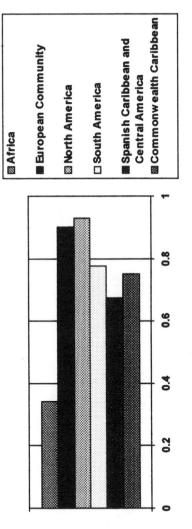

Fig. 2: Average values of the human development index, by region

do not differ significantly between regions. Thus wide disparities in health between regions cannot be said to result simply from lack of "political will" to
commit resources to health (Reich, 1994).

The human development index (HDI) has been devised by the United Nations Development Program in an attempt to find a better, more comprehensive socioeconomic measure than GNP alone. The HDI is a composite of three
basic components of human development: longevity (measured by life expectancy), knowledge (measured by a combination of adult literacy and mean
years of schooling), and standard of living (measured by real gross domestic
product per capita adjusted for the local cost of living, or purchasing power
parity) (UNDP, 1994). Again we see the Commonwealth Caribbean in an intermediate position between the richer and poorer regions (fig. 2). Note also
that South America overtakes the Commonwealth Caribbean despite its lower
income, though the difference between the two regions is not significant.

Table 2 and figs. 3 to 5 present measures commonly used to compare health
and welfare internationally.

Rates of death in the first year of life are much higher in Africa than in other
regions (see table 2 and fig. 3). The Commonwealth Caribbean has lower rates
of infant mortality than other Third World regions, though only the difference
with Africa is significant. As expected, the richer European and North American countries have the lowest rates. As GNP rises, the infant mortality rate
(IMR) falls; this negative relationship is significant. There is also a significant
negative relationship between the IMR and the HDI.

A newborn child could expect to have a significantly shorter life if born in
Africa as opposed to the other regions studied, where on average life expectancy
exceeds 68 years (see table 2 and fig. 4). The average for the Commonwealth
Caribbean is 71 years, ranging from 65 in Guyana to 75 in Barbados. There is a
significant positive relationship between GNP per capita and life expectancy;
higher income tends to bring longer life.

As regards the average number of live births per woman, the Commonwealth Caribbean again stands in an intermediate position, though its rate of
2.3 is significantly different from Africa only (see table 2 and fig. 5). The total
fertility rate (TFR) is negatively related with GNP per capita and the HDI;
higher income levels and "human development" are associated with lower fertility.

The United Nations (1993a) has categorized countries according to the time
period in which stage 3 of the demographic transition model, the period of
significant fertility decline, takes place. "Preinitiation countries" had not
started a decline from a TFR of 5 or more by 1990. "Late initiation countries"

Table 2. Common Measures of Health and Welfare Relating to "Development," by Region

	Infant Mortality Rate, 1985–90[1]	Life Expectancy at Birth, 1992[2]	Total Fertility Rate, 1992[3]
Caribbean Countries			
Anguilla	33.9	M	M
Antigua and Barbuda	24.4	74	M
Bahamas	23.8	72	2.1
Barbados	9.1	75	1.7
Belize	15.1	69	M
Cayman Islands	6.1	M	M
Dominica	18.4	72	M
Grenada	15.4	71	M
Guyana	56.0	65	2.6
Jamaica	13.2	74	2.5
Montserrat	5.0	M	M
St. Kitts and Nevis	22.2	68	M
St. Lucia	18.5	70	M
St. Vincent and the Grenadines	21.7	71	M
Trinidad and Tobago	10.2	71	2.8
Turks and Caicos	24.5	M	M
British Virgin Islands	29.5	M	M
Bermuda	7.8	M	M
Regional Averages			
Commonwealth Caribbean	19.7	71.0	2.3
French- or Dutch- Speaking American Countries[4]	27.9	70.2	M
Spanish Caribbean and Central America[5]	40.8	70.0	3.7
South America[6]	41.7	68.4	3.3
North America[7]	10.5	76.3	1.9
European Community[8]	7.6	76.2	1.6
Africa[9]	104.5	52.1	6.4
Overall Average	55.5	63.3	4.5
Significance Test	***	***	***

Sources: Infant mortality rate: United Nations (1994) *Demographic Yearbook 1992;* Life expectancy at birth: World Bank (1994) *World Development Report 1994: Infrastructure for Development;* Total fertility rate: UNDP (1994) Human Development Report 1994.

Significance test = F-test for significance of differences between means; *** = significant at the 1% level.

M = Missing data

1. Deaths in the first year of life per thousand live births.

2. The number of years a newborn infant would live if prevailing patterns of mortality at the time of its birth were to stay the same thoughout its life.

(*Continued on the next page*)

---

3. Average total number of births per woman.

4. French Guiana, Martinique, Guadeloupe, Haiti, Netherlands Antilles, Suriname.

5. Cuba, Dominican Republic, Costa Rica, El Salvador, Guatemala, Honduras, Mexico, Panama.

6. Argentina, Brazil, Chile, Colombia, Ecuador, Paraguay, Peru, Uruguay, Venezuela.

7. USA, Canada, Puerto Rico, US Virgin Islands.

8. Belgium, Denmark, France, Germany, Greece, Ireland, Italy, Luxembourg, Netherlands, Portugal, Spain, UK.

9. Algeria, Angola, Benin, Botswana, Burkina Faso, Burundi, Cameroon, Central African Republic, Chad, Congo, Ivory Coast, Ethiopia, Gabon, Ghana, Guinea, Guinea Bissau, Kenya, Lesotho, Liberia, Madagascar, Malawi, Mali, Mozambique, Namibia, Niger, Nigeria, Rwanda, Senegal, Sierra Leone, South Africa, Togo, Uganda, Tanzania, Zaire, Zambia, Zimbabwe.

started this decline between 1950 and 1990. "Early initiation countries" began this decline before 1950. According to this classification, less developed countries such as most African countries are "preinitiation countries." Western and Eastern European and North American countries are "early initiation countries." Commonwealth Caribbean countries stand between the two, as "late initiation countries." The average TFR for Commonwealth Caribbean countries was 5.02 in 1950–55 and 2.43 in 1985–90. In Barbados, remarkably, the TFR for 1985–90 was lower than the rate for the USA: 1.62 as against 1.92. Between 1950–55 and 1985–90 there were also improvements in infant health and longevity; in the Commonwealth Caribbean infant mortality rates declined from 99 per thousand live births to 27, and life expectancy at birth rose from 57 to 70 years (United Nations, 1993b).

Thus over time the Commonwealth Caribbean has seen progressive improvements in health, according to these indicators, and seems to be in a privileged position relative to other "Third World" regions. However, note that the indicators tell us little about the welfare of women. GNP is simply divided by population size to give a per capita figure, with few countries attempting to calculate the distribution of GNP between the sexes. UNDP has devised a gender-disparity-adjusted HDI, but so far the absence of collection of some of the component statistics has precluded its calculation for Caribbean countries. Infant mortality and fertility rates undoubtedly affect the welfare of women, but to treat them as the sole indicators would be to treat women solely in terms of their reproductive capacity. Life expectancy is generally higher among men than women, but women suffer the greater burden of illness.

Health programs funded by international agencies have tended to favor the eradication of infectious and parasitic disease via improved immunization and

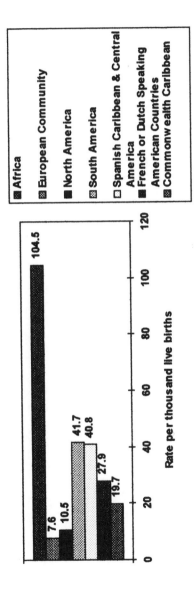

Fig. 3: Infant mortality rate, by region

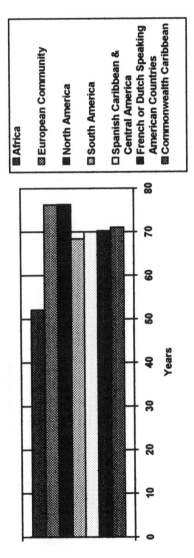

Fig. 4: Average life expectancy at birth, by region

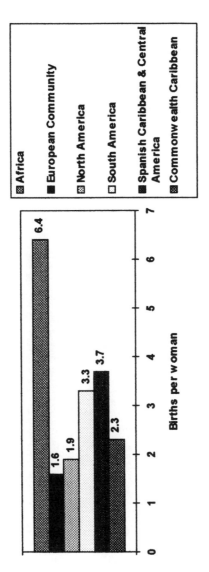

Births per woman

Africa: 6.4
European Community: 1.6
North America: 1.9
South America: 3.3
Spanish Caribbean & Central America: 3.7
Commonwealth Caribbean: 2.3

Fig. 5: Average total fertility rate, by region

sanitation. However, as table 3 and fig. 6 show, women are at less risk of dying from these diseases than men are at any age, in the Caribbean as in other regions of the Americas.

Again, according to this indicator, the Caribbean is in an intermediate position between poorer regions (Spanish Caribbean and Central America, Latin South America) and richer North America. The data are consistent with the epidemiologic transition model, which predicts a negative relationship between income and rates of death from infectious and parasitic diseases.

Chronic Noncommunicable Diseases

The predictions of the epidemiologic transition model have been confirmed thus far. However, when we look at patterns of mortality from chronic non-communicable diseases, the predictions seem to have less validity. The so-called "diseases of affluence," ironically, do not appear to be associated with affluence, and it is the experiences of Commonwealth Caribbean women which particularly challenge the predictions.

At first sight, heart disease appears to conform to predictions (see table 4 and fig. 7). By far the highest crude death rates are in North America, followed by the Commonwealth Caribbean, then Dutch and French speaking territories, Latin South American countries, and lastly Spanish Caribbean and Central American countries. There is a significant positive relationship between crude rates of death from heart disease and GNP per capita, with rates of death from heart disease for both men and women rising as GNP rises. However, the significance of differences between regions disappears when age adjustment is performed, indicating that countries with the highest rates of death from heart disease also have the oldest populations. Women in the Commonwealth Caribbean in fact appear slightly more likely than women in North America to die from heart disease at any age.

Similarly, if we look at overall cancer death rates (table 5 and fig. 8), we see the expected pattern of highest death rates in the richest regions. Again, age adjustment removes the significance of the differences.

However, one particular form of cancer, cervical cancer, gives particular cause for concern, because rates of death from this cancer are higher in the Commonwealth Caribbean than in any other region of the Americas (see table 5 and fig. 9). The pattern of mortality from cervical cancer does not follow that predicted by the health transition model at all; the highest rates are in the Commonwealth Caribbean, followed by French- or Dutch-speaking countries, South

Table 3. Mortality Rates from Infectious and Parasitic Diseases, Caribbean
and American Countries

	Death Rate[1]	Female Death Rate[2]	Age-Adjusted Death Rate	Age-Adjusted Female Death Rate
Caribbean Countries				
Bahamas	16.9	16.7	14.4	13.1
Barbados	19.8	15.5	M	M
Belize	31.1	25.1	28.4	23.1
Dominica	13.2	10.6	14.6	13.5
Guyana	15.6	11.4	15.0	11.7
Jamaica	29.8	28.5	31.1	29.3
St. Kitts/Nevis	47.8	42.4	M	M
St. Lucia	28.6	20.4	M	M
St. Vincent and the Grenadines	18.1	18.5	M	M
Trinidad and Tobago	13.0	11.8	10.9	9.6
Regional Averages				
Commonwealth Caribbean	23.4	20.1	19.1	16.7
French- or Dutch-Speaking[3]	30.6	19.4	17.4	14.9
Spanish Caribbean, Central America[4]	62.9	58.6	63.3	58.8
Latin South America[5]	43.1	39.6	42.8	38.9
North America[6]	9.5	8.7	4.8	4.0
Overall Average	37.5	33.2	36.3	33.1
Significance Test	N.S.	N.S.	*	*

Source: Pan American Health Organization (1990), *Health Conditions in the Americas,*
PAHO/WHO, Washington, D.C. All figures are for the latest year available.
Significance test: F-test for significance of differences between means; * = significant at the
10% level; N.S. = not significant.
M = Missing data

1. Deaths from infections and parasite diseases per 100,000 population.

2. Female deaths from infections and parasite diseases per 100,000 female population.

3. Guadeloupe, Martinique, Curaçao, Suriname.

4. Cuba, Dominican Republic, Costa Rica, El Salvador, Guatemala, Honduras, Mexico, Panama.

5. Argentina, Brazil, Chile, Colombia, Ecuador, Paraguay, Peru, Uruguay, Venezuela.

6. USA, Canada, Puerto Rico, U.S. Virgin Islands.

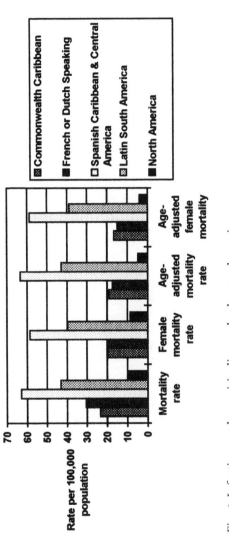

Fig. 6: Infectious and parasitic disease death rates, by region

Table 4.   Mortality Rates from Heart Disease, Caribbean and American Countries

	Death Rate[1]	Female Death Rate[2]	Age-Adjusted Death Rate	Age-Adjusted Female Death Rate
Caribbean Countries				
Bahamas	100.4	96.2	76.4	63.9
Barbados	197.3	198.2	M	M
Belize	58.7	57.5	38.9	36.3
Dominica	140.7	167.1	83.1	81.6
Guyana	93.5	69.5	89.8	69.5
Jamaica	120.0	122.6	78.3	72.3
St. Kitts/Nevis	201.9	177.9	M	M
St. Lucia	159.4	144.3	119.7	94.2
St. Vincent and the Grenadines	158.0	174.0	125.3	124.2
Trinidad and Tobago	165.5	148.3	122.1	99.6
Regional Averages				
Commonwealth Caribbean	139.5	135.6	91.7	80.2
French- or Dutch-Speaking[3]	113.0	112.1	68.7	59.8
Spanish Caribbean, Central America[4]	75.0	69.6	64.9	57.6
Latin South America[5]	115.0	106.9	79.9	67.0
North America[6]	246.7	226.9	93.0	71.1
Overall Average	124.2	117.7	79.0	67.4
Significance Test	***	***	N.S.	N.S.

Source: Pan American Health Organization (1990), *Health Conditions in the Americas*, PAHO/WHO, Washington, D.C. All figures are for the latest year available.

Significance test: F-test for significance of differences between means; *** = significant at the 1% level; N.S. = not significant.

M = Missing data

1. Deaths from heart disease per 100,000 population.

2. Female deaths from heart disease per 100,000 female population.

3. Guadeloupe, Martinique, Curaçao, Suriname.

4. Cuba, Dominican Republic, Costa Rica, El Salvador, Guatemala, Honduras, Mexico, Panama.

5. Argentina, Brazil, Chile, Colombia, Ecuador, Paraguay, Peru, Uruguay, Venezuela.

6. USA, Canada, Puerto Rico, U.S. Virgin Islands.

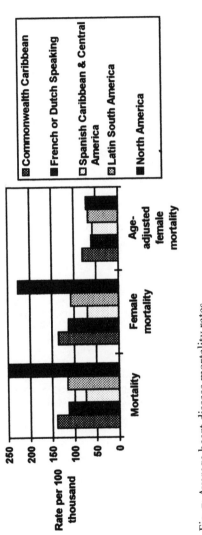

Fig. 7: Average heart disease mortality rates

Table 5. Cancer and Cervical Cancer Mortality Rates, Caribbean and American Countries

	Cancer Death Rate[1]	Female Cancer Death Rate[2]	Age-Adjusted Female Cancer Death Rate	Cervical Cancer Death Rate[3]	Age-Adjusted Cervical Cancer Death Rate
Caribbean Countries					
Bahamas	107.2	81.1	59.8	9.5	6.7
Barbados	160.7	149.4	M	19.2	M
Belize	31.1	28.7	21.6	3.6	2.6
Dominica	72.3	55.7	41.3	15.9	12.8
Guyana	29.9	31.1	29.8	5.4	5.4
Jamaica	90.1	86.4	64.5	12.8	10.9
St. Kitts/Nevis	91.2	84.7	84.7	M	M
St. Lucia	78.2	78.7	57.9	M	M
St. Vincent and the Grenadines	69.5	75.9	63.0	M	M
Trinidad and Tobago	83.3	81.9	60.0	9.3	7.1
Regional Averages					
Commonwealth Caribbean	81.4	75.4	53.6	10.8	7.6
French- or Dutch-Speaking[4]	97.5	89.3	55.6	9.3	6.6
Spanish Caribbean, Central America[5]	50.2	48.5	48.1	5.1	4.9
Latin South America[6]	83.6	78.2	50.0	6.0	5.2
North America[7]	164.8	144.8	59.4	3.0	1.6
Overall Average	83.9	77.6	50.8	7.1	5.4
Significance Test	**	**	N.S.	***	**

Source: Pan American Health Organization (1990), *Health Conditions in the Americas*, PAHO/WHO, Washington, D.C. All figures are for the latest year available.

Significance test: F-test for significance of differences between means; *** = significant at the 1% level; ** = significant at 5% level; N.S. = not significant.

M = Missing data

1. Deaths from malignant neoplasms per 100,000 population.

2. Female deaths from malignant neoplasms per 100,000 women.

3. Female deaths from malignant neoplasms of the cervix uteri per 100,000 women.

4. Guadeloupe, Martinique, Curaçao, Suriname.

5. Cuba, Dominican Republic, Costa Rica, El Salvador, Guatemala, Honduras, Mexico, Panama.

6. Argentina, Brazil, Chile, Colombia, Ecuador, Paraguay, Peru, Uruguay, Venezuela.

7. USA, Canada, Puerto Rico.

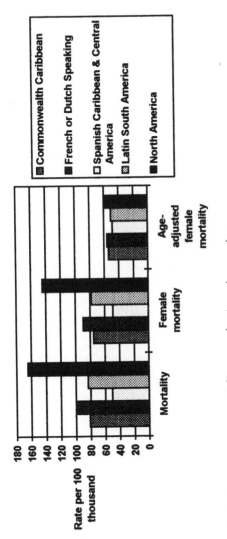

Fig. 8: Average cancer mortality rates, by American region

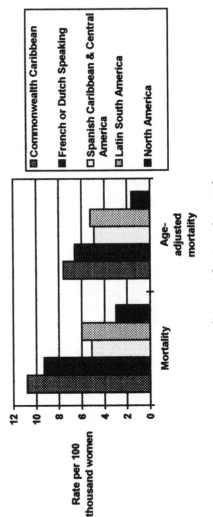

Fig. 9: Average cervical cancer mortality rates, by American region

American countries, Central American and Spanish Caribbean countries, and finally North American countries. The probability of dying from cervical cancer in the Commonwealth Caribbean at any age is 4.75 times higher than in North America. Death from cervical cancer occurs more frequently in the Commonwealth Caribbean than in any other region in every age group from 45–54 upward.

The divergence from predictions is even more striking if we look at rates of death from diabetes (table 6 and fig. 10) and hypertension (table 7 and fig. 11).

Rates of death from these diseases in the Commonwealth Caribbean are significantly higher than in any other region in the Americas, whether measured by crude or age-adjusted rates. Also contrary to expectations, women outnumber men in terms of mortality, and the disparities between the Commonwealth Caribbean and North America are even higher for women; the average female death rate from diabetes is 90 percent higher in the Commonwealth Caribbean than in North America, and the female death rate from hypertension is 203 percent higher. When age adjustments are made, the proportional difference between the Commonwealth Caribbean and North America are even larger. Female death rates from diabetes are significantly higher in the Commonwealth Caribbean than in any other American region in every age group from 45 upward, and the same applies to female death rates from hypertension in every age group from 35 upward. Population studies in Caribbean countries have revealed that of adults over 40 years old, about 30 percent have hypertension and 12 percent are afflicted with diabetes (Hagley, 1987).

Hypertension, diabetes, and cervical cancer death rates, then, do not conform to the expected pattern predicted by the "health transition" model, of highest rates of chronic disease in the wealthiest countries. The data do not fit the predictions. This is important not only because it challenges the health transition theory but also because these diseases have extremely serious implications for women's health and development.

The importance of hypertension and diabetes to women does not lie only in the fact that they are so frequently fatal. They also bring long-term deterioration in quality of life, since they restrict the activities of women and demand rigorous health management routines, such as a special diet. Hypertension and diabetes in pregnancy, though not always associated with preexisting hypertension or diabetes, can have particularly grave effects on a woman's health and that of the fetus. High blood pressure during pregnancy is one of the major causes of maternal mortality in the region (Roopnarinesingh et al., 1991; Matadial, 1988), which official figures show to be ten times higher in the Com-

Table 6.   Mortality Rates from Diabetes Mellitus, Caribbean and American
           Countries

	Death Rate[1]	Female Death Rate[2]	Age-Adjusted Death Rate	Age-Adjusted Female Death Rate
Caribbean Countries				
Bahamas	27.3	35.0	20.4	23.5
Barbados	67.7	85.8	M	M
Belize	18.0	20.3	12.1	14.3
Dominica	18.4	23.9	10.5	11.2
Guyana	17.4	21.0	17.4	20.6
Jamaica	30.8	37.2	21.4	23.3
Trinidad and Tobago	69.0	77.7	52.2	54.2
Regional Averages				
Commonwealth Caribbean	35.5	43.0	22.3	24.5
French- or Dutch-Speaking[3]	16.2	20.2	8.7	10.5
Spanish Caribbean, Central America[4]	10.9	13.0	10.1	11.2
Latin South America[5]	11.3	13.1	8.5	9.0
North America[6]	20.5	22.6	8.8	8.7
Overall Average	18.1	21.6	11.7	12.9
Significance Test	***	***	**	**

Source: Pan American Health Organization (1990), *Health Conditions in the Americas,*
PAHO/WHO, Washington, D.C. All figures are for the latest year available.
Significance test: F-test for significance of difference between means; *** = significant at the
1% level; ** = significant at the 5% level; N.S. = not significant.
M = Missing data

1. Deaths from diabetes mellitus per 100,000 population.

2. Female deaths from diabetes mellitus per 100,000 women.

3. Guadeloupe, Martinique, Curaçao, Suriname.

4. Cuba, Dominican Republic, Costa Rica, El Salvador, Guatemala, Honduras, Mexico, Panama.

5. Argentina, Brazil, Chile, Colombia, Ecuador, Paraguay, Peru, Uruguay, Venezuela.

6. USA, Canada, Puerto Rico, U.S. Virgin Islands.

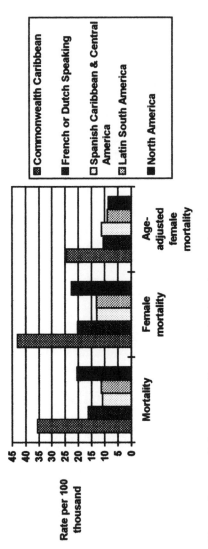

Fig. 10: Average diabetes mortality rates, by American region

Table 7. Mortality Rates from Hypertension, Caribbean and American Countries

	Death Rate[1]	Female Death Rate[2]	Age-Adjusted Death Rate	Age-Adjusted Female Death Rate
Caribbean Countries				
Bahamas	31.7	35.0	23.5	22.7
Barbados	26.8	34.0	M	M
Belize	9.0	13.2	5.6	7.8
Dominica	72.3	87.5	45.2	46.1
Guyana	18.8	19.1	17.5	17.0
Jamaica	32.3	38.0	20.5	21.7
St. Vincent and the Grenadines	87.7	94.4	62.7	63.2
Trinidad and Tobago	28.1	18.8	20.6	18.8
Regional Averages				
Commonwealth Caribbean	38.0	42.5	27.9	28.2
French- or Dutch-Speaking[3]	20.8	25.8	11.3	12.5
Spanish Caribbean, Central America[4]	5.3	5.9	5.0	5.4
Latin South America[5]	9.4	10.1	7.4	7.4
North America[6]	13.9	14.0	6.0	5.3
Overall Average	17.4	19.5	11.8	12.0
Significance Test	***	***	***	***

Source: Pan American Health Organization (1990), *Health Conditions in the Americas*, PAHO/WHO, Washington, D.C. All figures are for the latest year available.
Significance test: F-test for significance of difference between means; *** = significant at the 1% level.
M = Missing data
1. Female deaths from hypertension per 100,000 population.
2. Female deaths from hypertension per 100,000 women.
3. Guadeloupe, Martinique, Curaçao, Suriname.
4. Cuba, Dominican Republic, Costa Rica, El Salvador, Guatemala, Honduras, Mexico.
5. Argentina, Brazil, Chile, Colombia, Ecuador, Paraguay, Peru, Uruguay, Venezuela.
6. USA, Canada, Puerto Rico, U.S. Virgin Islands.

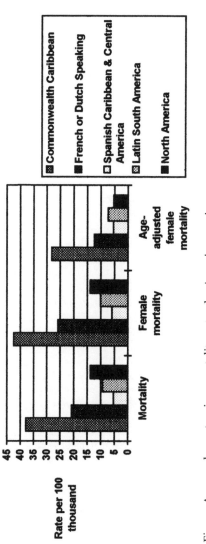

Fig. 11: Average hypertension mortality rates, by American region

monwealth Caribbean than in North America (Allen and Bailey, 1993). It is also associated with low birthweight (Ramsewak et al., 1986) and thus affects infant health. Diabetes is associated with intrauterine growth retardation, recurrent miscarriages, congenital abnormalities, unexplained stillbirths, the birth of oversized ("macrosomic") babies, and poor neonatal survival (Adam, 1988).

Cervical cancer can be cured if women receive treatment at an early stage. However, nearly half the cases in the English-speaking Caribbean present themselves at a stage too advanced for effective treatment. Most of the women eventually die from the disease. Whether or not cervical cancer is fatal, women with cancer suffer enormous amounts of psychological in addition to physical distress, largely because others fear and do not understand the disease. Many Caribbean people still believe cancer to be incurable and treat the woman who reveals she has cancer as if she were dying. Some claim the victim brought it on herself by some unacceptable behavior. There are also people who believe they can "catch" cancer by touching a person who has it (WAND, 1992). As one victim said, "Because of the way other people respond, the first battle you have to win if you have cancer is a battle with yourself not to feel overwhelmed by those responses. It's very hard to feel positive about living when the culture around you says that you are dying" (quoted in WAND, 1992, 37).

These diseases are extremely important to the personal development and self-esteem of women and to the development of society, as they reduce the effectiveness of women in performing reproductive and productive functions. Models of health and development need to take into account the impact of diseases on personal, social, and economic development.

The Challenge of AIDS

The AIDS epidemic has posed grave challenges to conventional wisdom about the links between development and disease. Unlike other infectious diseases, AIDS does not appear to bear any fixed relationship to development. In the Americas, AIDS rates are highest in the richest countries and lowest in the poorest; the positive relationship between AIDS rates and GNP per capita is statistically significant. This contrasts with regions such as Africa, where rates are extremely high in poor countries. Thus it seems we must look beyond crude measures of economic development when seeking to explain differences in prevalence between regions.

Table 8 and fig. 12 show that average regional AIDS rates per million population range from 248 in the Commonwealth Caribbean to 21 in Latin South

Table 8.   AIDS Cases, Caribbean and American Countries

	Total Number to End of 1993	% Perinatal to end of 1993	Cases per Million Population, 1993	Females as % of Total, 1992
Caribbean Countries				
Anguilla	5	M	M	100.0
Antigua and Barbuda	36	16.67	104.5	23.3
Bahamas	1,329	9.71	1,108.2	38.5
Barbados	397	4.28	338.5	25.6
Belize	53	M	143.6	M
Cayman Islands	15	M	0	50.0
Dominica	12	8.33	194.4	M
Grenada	51	3.92	228.3	M
Guyana	359	11.14	122.5	38.5
Jamaica	576	7.47	94.6	32.3
Montserrat	1	M	90.9	M
St. Kitts and Nevis	39	2.56	71.4	25.0
St. Lucia	59	5.08	86.3	50.0
St. Vincent and the Grenadines	54	1.85	72.7	14.3
Trinidad and Tobago	1,404	7.48	190.0	29.4
Turks and Caicos	39	M	1,076.9	M
British Virgin Islands	6	16.67	55.6	50.0
Bermuda	223	M	238.1	29.4
Regional Averages				
Commonwealth Caribbean	259	7.93	248.0	39.0
French- or Dutch-Speaking[1]	817	3.30	104.3	35.0
Spanish Caribbean and Central America[2]	2,935	1.56	50.2	19.5
South America[3]	6,183	1.65	21.1	11.6
North America[4]	173,945	1.00	220.5	9.9
Overall Average	10,375	4.0	141.7	25.4
Significance Test	***	***	N.S.	***

Sources: Total AIDS cases until end of 1993, % perinatal cases until end of 1993, females as % of total AIDS cases, 1992: Pan American Health Organization (1993), *AIDS Surveillance for the Americas Quarterly Report, 10 December 1993*, Regional Prog. on AIDS/STD, PAHO/WHO, Washington, D.C.; 1993 AIDS cases per million population: Pan American Health Organization (1994), *Health Conditions in the Americas, 1994 Edition*, vol. 1, Pan

(*Continued on next page*)

American Health Organization/World Health Organization, Washington, D.C.
Significance test: F-test for significance of difference between means; *** = significant at the
1% level; N.S. = not significant.
M = Missing data

1. French Guiana, Suriname, Netherland Antilles, Martinique, Guadeloupe, Haiti.

2. Cuba, Dominican Republic, Costa Rica, El Salvador, Guatemala, Honduras, Mexico, Panama.

3. Argentina, Brazil, Chile, Colombia, Ecuador, Paraguay, Peru, Uruguay, Venezuela.

4. USA, Canada.

America. However, the differences between the regional averages are not significant, principally because of the very large variations of AIDS rates within
each region. Reported AIDS rates per million population in the Commonwealth Caribbean in 1993 ranged from zero cases in the Cayman Islands to 1,108
cases in the Bahamas.

AIDS is a particular menace to women in the Caribbean, as there are particularly high proportions of women among AIDS victims in the region.
Women in the Commonwealth Caribbean represent higher proportions of total
AIDS cases than in any other region of the Western Hemisphere (see table 8
and fig. 13). In particular, the Commonwealth Caribbean rate is significantly
higher than the South American or Spanish Caribbean and Central American
rates. Perinatal cases, indicating transfer of the virus from mother to fetus, also
represent a significantly higher proportion of cases in the Commonwealth Caribbean than in the latter two regions.

Among heterosexuals with AIDS in the Caribbean, 48 percent of the total
cases recorded since 1985 have been women. Fig. 14 shows that the female proportion of total AIDS cases has tended to rise since 1985 and has hovered between two-fifths and three-fifths of heterosexual cases.

The implications of this pattern for demographic patterns and development
are serious, especially when we consider that it is primarily the most productive
and reproductive age group which is being affected. AIDS cases in the Caribbean are most heavily concentrated in the 25–35 age group. AIDS poses challenges to the demographic transition model as well as the health transition
model; the former predicts that highly developed countries will have low birth
and death rates. By pushing up the death rate in the productive and reproductive age group, AIDS upsets this balance between fertility and mortality, with
unforeseen long-term consequences for population dynamics. The high rates
of prevalence among women and of perinatal transmission pose serious threats
to reproductive health and thus the welfare of generations to come. In small

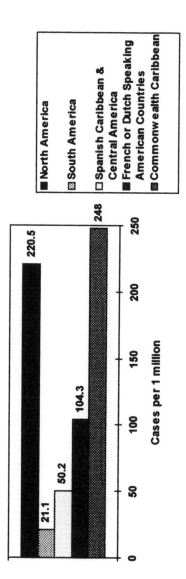

Fig. 12: Average AIDS cases per million, 1993, by American region

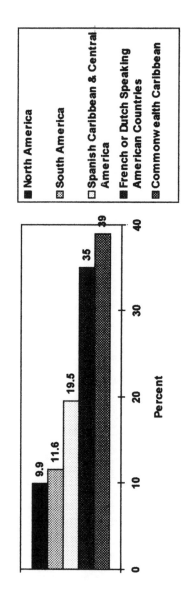

Fig. 13: Females as a percentage of total AIDS cases, by American region

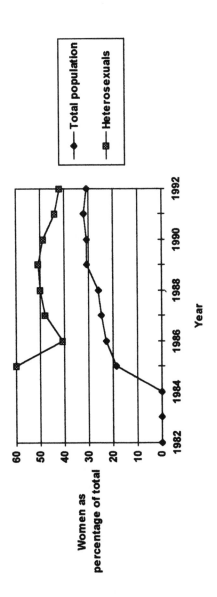

Source: Caribbean Epidemiology Centre, Special Programme on AIDS/STD, CAREC/PAHO, Port of Spain, Trinidad. Our thanks go to CAREC for allowing use of these figures.

Fig. 14: Changes over time in women as a percentage of total adult AIDS cases, for 19 Caribbean countries

developing countries such as those of the Caribbean where demographic structures are already fragile because of migration, AIDS severely upsets the demographic balance, leaving a higher dependent population of children and the elderly to be supported by a shrinking support system.

Diseases of Lifestyle

What prevalent Caribbean diseases such as hypertension, diabetes, heart disease, AIDS, and cervical cancer have in common is a link to the behavior of people who fall victim to the diseases. Models which give a valid picture of epidemiological change need to take account of the rise in so-called diseases of lifestyle rather than just the chronic noncommunicable diseases, since the latter do not include diseases such as AIDS and cervical cancer which are growing in importance, particularly for women in the Commonwealth Caribbean.

Diseases of lifestyle are linked to factors such as sexual and nutritional behavior which cannot be directly controlled by medical or public health intervention. It is clear that to tackle these health problems the health services must be reoriented toward health promotion activities involving programs attempting to modify these factors. However, health education approaches which simply urge individuals to change their behavior are unlikely to meet with much success. Beattie (1991) notes that the word *lifestyle* generally involves the assumption that the individual is primarily responsible for his/her health and does not recognize any collective forces at work. As such the concept has little utility in explaining why one society has a higher prevalence of a certain disease than another society. To understand prevalence, we must understand collective forces such as social norms, the distribution of resources, and macroeconomic policy.

An examination of risk factors related to various diseases which are highly prevalent in the Commonwealth Caribbean shows the importance of collective, societal forces. Hypertension and diabetes are related to dietary factors and lack of exercise. The main dietary factors implicated in hypertension are sodium or salt intake and obesity. Other contributory factors are excessive alcohol consumption, high fat intake, and low fiber intake (Zephirin, 1987). Sodium is widely used in the manufacturing process of many foods which are widely consumed in the Caribbean, being used to preserve fish and meats, in the brine of pickles, and in processed foods such as dried soups, canned soups, vegetables, and fish.

Obesity is a major risk factor in diabetes and hypertension, and at least 60 percent of the diabetic population in the region is overweight. Obesity is more prevalent among women than men and is rising in prevalence. Figures obtained in 1965–71 on prevalence of obesity among women in the Commonwealth Caribbean indicated rates of 39–41 percent; subsequent surveys reveal that these rates are now between 50 and 63 percent (Hagley, 1987). There is some evidence of genetic predisposition to obesity, but overnutrition, including excessive intake of calorific foods such as sugar, is the most important trigger. Sinha (1993a) shows that in 1986–88 calories available per capita were above recommended levels in all Commonwealth Caribbean countries, whereas in 1961–63 seven of the twelve countries had a shortfall in available calories. He also shows (1993b) a significant positive correlation between average per capita total calorie intake by country and mortality rate from diabetes mellitus. A factor which places women at risk is that women who develop "gestational" diabetes during pregnancy are more likely to develop diabetes later in life. Gestational diabetes is also common in the region.

Social Norms and Gender Roles

Social norms governing ideal body types and sexuality need to be given serious consideration if we are to promote optimal health among women. For instance, in a study of Jamaican secondary school students' knowledge, attitudes, and practices regarding obesity, most students correctly identified the causes of obesity. However, many did not think of obesity as a nutritional disease but as a sign of wealth, nobility, or having access to good food. At the same time the study found that lower body (so-called gynoid) obesity was widely thought to be desirable among females, but no sort of obesity was desirable among boys (Bockarie et al., 1994). The pressures on women to conform to these ideals should be considered when designing health promotion packages to prevent diseases such as diabetes, hypertension, heart disease, and cancer.

In contrast with other cancers for which important risk factors are linked to dietary practices, cervical cancer is linked to sexual and reproductive practices. The relative risk of cervical cancer is higher for women who begin sexual activity early and rises with the number of steady sex partners and with the number of live births. Women in the Commonwealth Caribbean tend to begin sexual activity early (Morris, 1988; Remez, 1989; MacCormack and Draper, 1987), have a series of steady sex partners (Safa, 1986) and births per woman are higher on average than in North American and European Community countries (table 1). A history of prenatal care and use of cervical cytology services (pap smears) were shown to be associated with lower risk. Though as yet there is no published research seeking to explain low utilization of pap smear services in the Caribbean, research on utilization of prenatal care shows that less educated women with little social support are more likely to attend late or not at all (McCaw-Binns, 1993a). The sexually transmitted human papilloma virus brings a higher risk of cervical cancer, as does a history of other sexually transmitted diseases (STDs). Because of the links with sexual practices, cervical cancer is now categorized among STDs rather than in the noncommunicable disease category in which other cancers are placed. There is also a significant "male factor" in the development of cervical cancer. Male partners of women with cervical cancer report having significantly more sexual partners and histories of STDs than partners of women without the disease (Herrero et al., 1990; WAND, 1992).

This male factor is also significant in the transmission of AIDS. Women are generally more susceptible than men to STDs for every act of intercourse (Barnes and Holmes, 1984; Padian, 1987), and HIV, the virus which causes AIDS, is "more likely to pass from the male to the female than vice versa because the AIDS virus cannot survive in the normally acidic secretion of the vagina" (Desai, 1989). If we add to this biological disadvantage the tendency of Caribbean men to have more sexual partners than women, we see that women in the Caribbean are more at risk from heterosexual intercourse than their menfolk. As elsewhere, a "double standard of sexual morality" has been found to prevail in Commonwealth Caribbean culture (Barrow, 1982; Massiah, 1986b), indicating that status-seeking behaviors in sexual matters differ between men and women. Norms dictate that men can have multiple sexual partners, whereas women should not (Dann, 1987). The phenomenon of "male-sharing" is common in the Caribbean (Durant-Gonzalez, 1982). Research should now be undertaken specifically focusing on the links between norms governing gender roles and women's health status.

Macroeconomic Forces

Macroeconomic forces also have a vital influence in decisions related to health. The individual, in making decisions about diet and the amount of exercise s/he will take, must be influenced by factors such as the availability and price of certain foods and opportunities for exercise. Trade and macroeconomic forces are largely responsible for the goods available to the consumer and for the division of labor of which the individual is a part. In the Caribbean, where most of the agricultural land is devoted to the production of one or two crops, particularly sugar and bananas, the availability of "healthy" foods such as fruit and vegetables is restricted. A small variety of crops are exported to obtain foreign exchange, while most foodstuffs are imported. In Trinidad and Tobago, one of the larger countries, the contribution of agriculture to the total local food supply is around 30 percent, making the country highly import dependent. The agricultural sector is dominated by the production of sugar and rum for export (McIntosh et al., 1993). Some small territories have very little land to devote to agricultural production and rely heavily on importation of food. In 1991, Monserrat had a total of 2,886 kilocalories of food energy available per person per day, of which 2,698 kilocalories were imported (Food and Agricultural Organization, 1992). This contrasts with a total recommended daily allowance for Commonwealth Caribbean countries of 2,250 kilocalories per day.

Generally it is women who are responsible for obtaining food to keep the family healthy, but they often find that less healthy imported alternatives such as canned and processed foods are cheaper than fresh fruit and vegetables. Women are largely responsible for subsistence agriculture and selling fresh produce on the local market. In Jamaica, women produce 60–75 percent of food for the local market and are responsible for over 80 percent of its distribution (Gomes, 1985). However, the push toward economic development has reduced food production while urbanization has increased. Women provide much of the labor force in urban occupations; they predominate in light manufacturing in Export Processing Zones, data processing, and secretarial work (Antrobus, 1989; Bolles, 1983) and in many of the lower-ranking positions in tourism (Levy and Lerch, 1991). Wages are notoriously low in the Export Processing Zones (Antrobus, 1989; Cowell, 1986; Green, 1990). Others are forced into unemployment, which makes them less able to afford healthy foods. The changing role of women in the international division of labor has implications for food security, the nutritional status of the population, and thus health.

The penetration of Western products and lifestyles is reinforced by various economic mechanisms, such as aid flows to facilitate the establishment of foreign and multinational firms in the Caribbean and "structural adjustment policies" supported by the International Monetary Fund which tend to reduce economic self-sufficiency and increase the proportion of production devoted to exports, sometimes assisted by local governments who may, for example, give "tax holidays" to foreign firms (Antrobus, 1989; Bolles, 1983). Consumption of Western goods and status-seeking behaviors is encouraged by mass media penetration, advertising, and the conspicuous consumption patterns of Western tourists.

McIntosh et al. (1993) argue that the current pattern of agricultural production and food import dependency in Trinidad and Tobago is unsustainable. It has negative impacts on mortality and morbidity from chronic diseases, the prospects for continued livelihood from export of rum and sugar are not good given the imminent dismantling of preferential markets and competition from other sweeteners, and the production of sugar and rum has deleterious effects on the environment and thus health as the annual burning of canefields adds to the emission of carbon dioxide, destroys animal species and organisms on which higher members of the food chain depend and modifies the soil structure adversely.

Thus the individual woman faces multiple external pressures when making decisions about the lifestyle appropriate for herself and her family, even when s/he knows which lifestyle would lead to optimum health. The macroeconomic forces which condition health are largely out of individual control.

We have noted, then, that in order to understand the prevalence of diseases related to lifestyle we need to take account of social and economic factors influencing lifestyle. This suggests that there is a need for more collaboration between social science and medicine in order to identify factors related to lifestyle. Women should play a part in identifying factors which prevent them from achieving optimum health. The implication is that health promotion policies to address the prevalence of these diseases need to move beyond health education to tackle social and economic issues such as trade policies, the sexual division of labour and gender stereotyping.

Economic Crisis and Health

We should also consider the impact of economic policy on health and other services such as education which are necessary to support women's health. As part of the struggle to survive competition from foreign producers, Caribbean governments have tended to channel what resources they have into supporting firms which generate income directly, and away from social services such as health. This has been encouraged by the International Monetary Fund which has pushed governments to emphasize earning foreign exchange in order to repay international debts. In the five-year period between 1981–82 and 1985–86 in Jamaica, real expenditure on health, education, and social security fell by 44 percent (Boyd, 1987). Between 1980 and 1985, all Caribbean countries which had implemented structural adjustment policies under the direction of the IMF experienced a decline in public sector spending on all social services (including education, health, housing, and social security) (Phillips, 1994). They also experienced an aggravation of female poverty (Deere et al., 1990). In Jamaica, the decline in public spending led to deterioration of the sanitation system and less availability of clean water, and there were outbreaks of epidemic proportions of certain infectious diseases—typhoid, gastroenteritis, and measles (Bailey, 1992). In 1989, for the first time in decades, the category "complications of pregnancy" became the leading cause of morbidity requiring hospital admission. In 1979 the rate was 43 per 10,000 discharged. By 1989 the rate had increased to 54 (Allen and Bailey, 1993).

Thus the efforts to adjust Commonwealth Caribbean economies to improve foreign exchange earnings have a number of negative consequences for health. Where they have involved contraction of the economy and particularly cuts in public spending, countries have experienced a resurgence of infectious and parasitic diseases. This conforms to the predictions of the health transition model that poorer countries experience higher prevalence of these diseases. However, the efforts have also had negative consequences for health where they have succeeded in making countries richer. Increased reliance on food imports and declines in subsistence agriculture have gone hand in hand with the export drive, so that the opportunities to adopt healthy nutritional practices are reduced, while the environment can suffer degradation from overreliance on a limited number of crops.

According to certain health and demographic indicators, health status in the Commonwealth Caribbean approaches levels enjoyed in regions with higher average GDP per capita and surpasses that of regions with lower GDP per capita. Infant mortality rates, total fertility rates, and death rates from infectious and parasitic diseases are higher than in richer regions but lower than in poorer regions. People born in the Commonwealth Caribbean are likely to survive to an older age than people in poorer regions but not as long as people in richer regions. Furthermore, health status in the region has, on average, improved over time in line with increases in economic wealth, according to these indicators. These basic findings conform with the health and demographic transition models, which predict that fertility and mortality from infectious and parasitic diseases fall as the economy reaches higher levels of development. Likewise, the finding that rates of death from certain chronic noncommunicable diseases such as heart disease and cancer are relatively high in the Commonwealth Caribbean but not as high as in richer countries conforms to the predictions of the models. These diseases result in part from the aging of the population brought about by the falls in fertility and deaths from infectious and parasitic diseases and in part from lifestyles, particularly nutritional practices, made possible by industrialization and the increased division of labor.

These indicators are often used by international development agencies in deciding on the allocation of funds to health projects around the world. Commonwealth Caribbean countries can expect little sympathy when applying for aid funds to support local health projects because, according to these indicators, poorer countries are more deserving of funds. While not denying the enormous health problems associated with poverty, this chapter argues that concentration on these indicators neglects crucial aspects of women's health status with profound implications for development. The experience of women in the Commonwealth Caribbean in particular is at odds with the health and demographic transition models.

The models may be criticized first of all for paying no attention to the question of distribution. In the Commonwealth Caribbean, women carry out the majority of reproductive tasks underpinning production and are also engaged in productive work to a larger extent than in many other regions. However, they receive lower proportions of the rewards of economic development than men and thus are more likely to be afflicted with physical and mental diseases associated with poverty. The transition to an older population has placed additional burdens on women, as migration of the working-age population is already high and they are expected to provide care for elderly relatives.

The use of mortality statistics to judge the health status of populations discriminates against women, as women tend to die at lower rates than men but suffer the greater burden of morbidity (illness) throughout their lives. Chronic and disabling conditions, often associated with sexual and reproductive functions, are more prevalent among women and tend to last longer. More valid comparisons of the health status of populations would be afforded if morbidity indicators were used in addition to mortality indicators. Unfortunately, in the Commonwealth Caribbean, a picture of morbidity status has to be built up from ad hoc, local reports. Research is urgently needed to establish morbidity surveillance systems throughout the Caribbean and worldwide.

A closer examination of mortality data nevertheless reveals important insights which lead us to question the applicability of the health transition model to the region. The model predicts that the highest rates of mortality from chronic noncommunicable diseases will be in the richest countries. In contrast, rates of death from hypertension and diabetes in the Commonwealth Caribbean are the highest in the Western Hemisphere, surpassing the rates in the richer North American region. They are higher among women than men, and morbidity rates are extremely high. Furthermore, rates of death from cervical cancer are the highest in the Western Hemisphere, with no apparent association with the level of economic development. These diseases, even when not fatal, restrict the activities of women severely and thus hamper their vital contributions to economic and social development. Cervical cancer also exacts large psychological costs.

AIDS poses unanticipated challenges to the model, as it is a fatal infectious disease for which medicine has found no cure or effective vaccine and patterns of prevalence appear to bear no direct relationship with levels of economic wealth. It is an extremely significant issue for women's health in the Commonwealth Caribbean as rates of prevalence among women as compared with men are the highest in the Western Hemisphere and the number of cases is growing faster among the heterosexual population than the population as a whole. AIDS cases in the Caribbean are heavily concentrated in the most productive and reproductive age group 25–35, with serious implications for demographic patterns and thus development.

What prevalent diseases such as hypertension, diabetes, cervical cancer, and AIDS have in common is a link to the behavior of people who fall victim to the diseases. However, in order to understand the prevalence of these diseases we must look at societal factors affecting individual behavior rather than merely targetting individual behavior, as the latter cannot explain why certain diseases are more prevalent in certain societies than others. Their prevalence among women must be seen in the context of the roles and responsibilities of women. Risks of AIDS and cervical cancer are associated with sexual and reproductive practices, both of which are bound by social norms governing the rights and obligations of people according to gender.

The links between the macroeconomic situation and disease need to be explored in their complexity before making pronouncements on the links between economic development and disease. Perhaps the central shortcoming of the health transition model is that it implies that chronic noncommunicable diseases go hand in hand with development, and thus high prevalence of these diseases must be accepted if the society is to develop. Economic development is assumed to bring the expansion of consumer choice, which leads to the adoption of lifestyles conducive to the development of these diseases.

I have argued rather that the high prevalence of these diseases in the Caribbean needs to be examined in terms of the particular model of economic development which has been adopted in the Commonwealth Caribbean rather than explained by economic development per se. This model has involved the prioritization of foreign exchange earnings, which has led to increased reliance on foreign food imports, while increasing urbanization has reduced the opportunities for self-sustaining agricultural production. The availability of fresh fruits and vegetables on the local market has thus become increasingly limited. The status of women and their ability to provide health-sustaining services to their families has been affected; many women have moved out of production and distribution of agricultural products on the local market, for which they were mainly responsible, while facing higher prices for goods which would help sustain health. There is evidence that the majority of the calories available for local consumption in the Caribbean are imported and that they exceed dietary requirements, thus increasing risk of hypertension, diabetes, and other chronic noncommunicable diseases.

Are such lifestyles really an inevitable consequence of development? Little thought has been given in official circles to models of development where alternatives to harmful products and practices are encouraged, for example through the sustained production of healthy food and drink products based on fruits, vegetables, and grains. This would let women in particular draw on their wide experience of food production in order to enhance the development of the country. Sustainable development surely requires that the economy be tailored to the health and subsistence needs of the population, rather than vice versa. Furthermore, attention needs to be paid to the social status of women and thus their capacity to take effective decisions to defend their health; this means emphasizing social rather than just economic development. Health promotion programs should be designed to address gender roles and relationships; they should attempt to raise the self-esteem of women and empower them to defend themselves from sexually transmitted disease and abusive behavior while actively involving males in challenging the norms of masculine behavior which raise the risks of ill health. Since women play major roles in production and reproduction and thus development, their roles and responsibilities must be considered, and they must be involved in tailoring programs of development to meet their needs.

Acknowledgment

Some of the analyses contained in this paper were carried out during my period of employment at the Institute of Social and Economic Research at the

University of the West Indies, Cave Hill Campus, Barbados, from September 1991 to September 1994. My thanks go to the Institute for allowing use of these analyses.

REFERENCES

Adam, M. (1988) "Diabetes in Pregnancy," in S. Roopnarinesingh, ed., *Textbook of Obstetrics*, Paria Publishing, Trinidad and Tobago.

Allen, C., and Bailey, W. (1993) "A Situational Analysis of Reproductive Health in the Caribbean," manuscript, report to the Ford Foundation, Institute of Social and Economic Research, University of the West Indies, Barbados.

Althaus, F. A. (1991) "Reproductive Tract Infections and Women's Health," *International Family Planning Perspectives*, vol. 17, no. 4, 145–150.

Antrobus, P. (1989) "Gender Implications of the Development Crisis," in Beckford, G., and Girvan, N., eds. *Development in Suspense: Selected Papers and Proceedings of the First Conference of Caribbean Economists*, Friedrich Ebert Stiftung/Association of Caribbean Economists, Kingston.

Bailey, W. (1992) "Structural Adjustment and Infectious Diseases in Jamaica, with Special Reference to Typhoid," paper presented to the International Medical Geography Symposium, Charlotte, N.C., Aug. 5–7.

Barnes, R. C., and Holmes, K. K. (1984) "Epidemiology of Gonorrhea: Current Perspectives," *Epidemiologic Reviews*, vol. 6, no. 1.

Barrow, C. (1982) "Male Perceptions of Women in Barbados," paper presented at Women in the Caribbean Project conference, University of the West Indies, Barbados, Sept. 12–16.

Beattie, A. (1991) "Knowledge and Control in Health Promotion: A Test Case for Social Policy and Social Theory," in Gabe, J., Calnan, M., and Bury, M., eds. *The Sociology of the Health Service*, Routledge, London.

Beckles, G. (1992) *The Health of Women in the English-Speaking Caribbean*, Pan-American Health Organization/World Health Organization.

Bockarie, P. M., Taren, D. L., and Patterson, A. W. (1994) "KAP Study of Secondary School Students towards Obesity in Jamaica," *Cajanus*, vol. 27, no. 1.

Bolles, L. (1983) "Kitchens Hit by Priorities: Employed Working Class Women Confront the IMF," in Nash, J., and Fernandez-Kelly, M. P., eds. *Women, Men and the International Division of Labor*, State University of New York Press, Albany.

Boyd, D. (1987) "The Impact of Adjustment Policies on Vulnerable Groups: The Case of Jamaica 1973–85," in Cornia, G., Jolly, R., and Stuart, F., eds. *Adjustment with a Human Face: Country Case Studies*, UNICEF.

Cajanus (1994) "Micronutrients and Cancer: Time for Action," journal of the Caribbean Food and Nutrition Institute, vol. 27, no. 1, University of the West Indies, Mona, Jamaica.

Cowell, N. (1986) "Free Trade Zones: The Garment Sector and Their Impact on Women in Jamaica," report prepared for the Joint Trade Unions Research Development Centre, Kingston, September.

Dann, G. (1987) *The Barbadian Male: Sexual Attitudes and Practice*, Macmillan, London.

Deere, C. D., Antrobus, P., Bolles, L., et al. (1990) *In the Shadows of the Sun: Caribbean Development Alternatives and U.S. Policy*, Westview, Boulder.

Desai, B. T. (1989) "An Ongoing Tragedy: The Acquired Immune Deficiency Syndrome," *Manushi*, nos. 54–55, pp. 44–63 (New Delhi).

Doll, R., and Peto, R. (1981) *The Causes of Cancer*, Oxford University Press, London.

Durant-Gonzalez, V. (1982) "The Realm of Female Familial Responsibility," in Institute of Social and Economic Research, *Women and the Family*, University of the West Indies, Barbados.

Food and Agricultural Organization (1992) *Food Balance Sheets*, United Nations.

Frenk, J., Bobadilla, J. L., and Stern, C. (1991) "Elements for a Theory of the Health transition," *Health Transition Review*, vol. 1, no. 1, 21–38.

Germain, A., Holmes, K. K., Piot, P., and Wasserheit, J. N. (1992) *Reproductive Tract Infections: Global Impact and Priorities for Women's Reproductive Health*, Plenum, New York.

Gill, M. (1984) "Women, Work and Development: Barbados 1946–1970," in Institute of Social and Economic Research, *Women and Work*, University of the West Indies, Barbados.

Gomes, P. I. (1985) *Rural Development in the Caribbean*, Heinemann, Kingston.

Gray, A. (1993) *World Health and Disease*, Open University Press.

Green, C. (1990) *The World Market Factory: A Study of Enclave Industrialisation and Its Impact on Women Workers*, Caribbean People's Development Agency, St. Vincent.

Hagley, K (1987) "Nutrition and Mortality Trends in the Caribbean Region," *Cajanus*, vol. 20, no. 2.

Herrero, R., Brinton, L., Reeves, W. C., et al. (1990) "Risk Factors for Invasive Carcinoma of the Uterine Cervix in Latin America," *Bulletin of the Pan-American Health Organization*, vol. 24, no. 3, 263–283.

Jones, R. (1990) *The Political and Economic Dynamics of Sexual Diseases*, Southern Methodist University Press, Dallas.

LeFranc, E. R.-M. (1990) *Health Status and Health Services Utilization in the English-Speaking Caribbean*, Institute of Social and Economic Research, University of the West Indies, Mona, Jamaica.

Levy, D. E., and Lerch, P. B. (1991) "Tourism as a Factor in Development: Implications for Gender and Work in Barbados," *Gender and Society*, vol. 5, no. 1.

McCaw-Binns, A. (1993a) "Under-Users of Antenatal Care: A Comparison of Non-Attenders and Late Attenders for Antenatal Care, with Early Attenders," Tropical Metabolism Research Unit, University of the West Indies, Jamaica.

McCaw-Binns, A. (1993b) "Women's Health Morbidity Surveillance System," submitted to the Institute of Social and Economic Research, University of the West Indies, Jamaica.

MacCormack, C., and Draper, A. (1987) "Social and Cognitive Aspects of Female Sexuality in Jamaica," in Caplan, P., ed. *The Cultural Construction of Sexuality*, Routledge, London.

McIntosh, C. E., Doni Pierre, G., and Sinha, D. (1993) "Food Consumption Patterns and Their Implications for Sustained Agricultural Development in Trinidad and Tobago," Caribbean Food and Nutrition Institute, University of the West Indies, Mona, Jamaica.

Massiah, J. (1986a) "Work in the Lives of Caribbean Women," *Social and Economic Studies*, vol. 35, no. 2.

Massiah, J. (1986b) "Women in the Caribbean Project: An Overview," *Social and Economic Studies*, vol. 35, no. 2, 1–29.

Matadial, L. (1988) "Pre-eclampsia and Eclampsia," in S. Roopnarinesingh, ed., *Textbook of Obstetrics*, Paria, Trinidad and Tobago.

Miller, E. (1991) *Men at Risk*, Jamaica Publishing House, Kingston.

Mitter, S. (1993) *Common Fate, Common Bond: Women in the Global Economy*, Pluto Press, London.

Momsen, J. H. (1991) *Women and Development in the Third World*, Routledge, London.

Morris, L. (1988) "Young Adults in Latin America and the Caribbean: Their Sexual Experience and Contraceptive Use," *International Family Planning Perspectives*, vol. 14, no. 4, 153–158.

Padian, N. S. (1987) "Heterosexual Transmission of AIDS: International Perspectives and National Projections," *Reviews of Infectious Diseases*, vol. 9, no. 947.

Phillips, D. (1994) "The IMF, Structural Adjustment and Health in the Caribbean: Policy Change in Health Care in Trinidad and Tobago," *21st Century Policy Review*, vol. 2, nos. 1–2.

Ramsewak, S., Roopnarinesingh, S., The, T. (1986) "Obstetric Factors Affecting Outcome in Low Birthweight Infants," *West Indies Medical Journal*, no. 35, 166–169.

Reich, M. R. (1994) "The Political Economy of Health Transitions in the Third World," in Chen, L. C., Kleinman, A., and Ware, N. C., eds. *Health and Social Change in International Perspective*, Harvard University Press, Cambridge.

Remez, L. (1989) "Adolescent Fertility in Latin America and the Caribbean: Examining the Problem and the Solutions," *International Family Planning Perspectives*, vol. 15, no. 4, 144–148.

Roopnarinesingh, S., Ramoutar, P., and Bassaw, B. (1991) "Maternal Mortality at Mount Hope Women's Hospital," *West Indies Medical Journal*, no. 40, 139–141.

Safa, H. (1986) "Economic Autonomy and Sexual Equality in Caribbean Society," *Social and Economic Studies*, vol. 35, no. 3.

Sen, G., Germain, A., and Chen, L. C. (1994) *Population Policies Reconsidered: Health, Empowerment and Rights*, Harvard University Press, Cambridge.

Senior, O. (1992) *Working Miracles: Women's Lives in the English-Speaking Caribbean*, Indiana University Press, Bloomington.

Sinha, D. P. (1991) "Diet and Cancer," *Cajanus*, vol. 24, no. 3.

Sinha, D. P. (1993a) "Food, Nutrition and Health," *Cajanus*, vol. 26, no. 2.

Sinha, D. P. (1993b) Extract from Caribbean Food and Nutrition Institute Annual Report 1993, University of the West Indies, Mona, Jamaica.

United Nations (1993a) *Demographic Yearbook Special Issue: Population Aging and the Situation of Elderly Persons*, Washington, D.C.

United Nations (1993b) *World Population Prospects: The 1992 Revision*, Washington, D.C.

United Nations Development Program (1994) *Human Development Report 1994*, UNDP, New York.

WAND (Women and Development Unit, 1992) "Demystifying and Fighting Cervical Cancer," *Women's Health Journal*, March.

World Health Organization (1993) *World Health Statistics Annual 1992*, Geneva.

Zephirin, M. (1987) "Dietary Considerations in the Management of Hypertension," *Cajanus*, vol. 20, no. 3.

IV

WOMEN, LAW, AND POLITICAL CHANGE

10

THE COLONIAL LEGACY
Gendered Laws in Jamaica

SUZANNE LaFONT AND DEBORAH PRUITT

THIS CHAPTER EXAMINES how culturally inappropriate family laws in Jamaica threaten to disadvantage women. The challenge to women's power through the legal code is the result of laws that do not respond to the lived reality of Jamaican women but rather to the preferred ideal of family life held by the government and the dominant elites. In former colonies such as Jamaica, the imposition of cultural values from the colonial state was partially imparted and enforced through the legal code. Jamaican family law was adopted from British common law with little regard to the dramatic differences between Jamaican society and colonial England. These family laws projected the ethnocentric nineteenth-century model of the patriarchal nuclear family onto the Jamaican family laws, despite its irrelevancy to Jamaican social, family, and gender systems.

This chapter begins with a brief summary of the current state of family relations and the status of women and a historical perspective of social policy and the legal code. It demonstrates that the laws fail to achieve their goal of fostering the nuclear family. In contrast to their intended purpose, inappropriate laws have the potential to exacerbate power struggles between women and men, and in this struggle, it is primarily women and children who are the losers. The chapter concludes with a discussion of the ideological aspect of law in society and its implications for gender relations. It stresses how laws which assume equality and harmony ignore difference and obscure and reproduce inequality.

Characteristic of a plural society with vast economic disparities, Jamaican family patterns vary according to position within the social structure (M. G. Smith 1965). The elite, and to a lesser extent the middle class, approximate the nuclear family held up as the ideal by the colonial elites. Extended kin ties also play an important role. Among the overwhelming majority of Jamaicans, women form the core of the family unit and use generational and lateral kinship ties to assist them with child rearing, housing, and finances.

Despite a preoccupation with the concept of modern, Western romantic love, the conjugal bond is often not the primary alliance (Brody 1981). Legal marriage is the exception rather than the rule, and many Jamaicans who marry do so later in life, often after their childbearing is completed. The 1989 Contraceptive Prevalence Survey found that only 13 percent of women under age thirty were married, despite the fact that almost 40 percent had begun childbearing as teenagers (CPS 1989). Even by the age of forty-five, only around 40 percent of the women in the survey sample were involved in a legal union. Out-of-wedlock birthrates have been rising consistently, from 60 percent in 1886 to 85 percent in 1986 (Hartley 1980, LaFont 1996).

Serial monogamy is the norm, and most women have children with more than one partner. Women age forty and over reported 2.3 child-producing unions (LaFont 1996). Most children are raised in a variety of domestic situations, with LaFont's sample reporting as many as thirty-eight different child-rearing environments (LaFont 1996). Children may live with grandparents, either or both parents, or various relatives at different times during their lives.

R. T. Smith described a cycle of Caribbean familial developmental and identified different patterns of organization at different points in time (1956). This cycle often begins when a woman has her first child while living in the parental home. Eventually she may move into a common-law or legal union, at which time members of her extended family may join her. The woman is most dependent upon her "baby-father" during the period that child rearing limits her economic activity. (*Baby-mother* and *baby-father* are terms unmarried partners use to refer to their child's other parent, i.e., he is my baby('s) father.) When her children mature, leaving her more freedom for economic activity, her dependence on the male decreases. Later, through separation, divorce, desertion, or death, the woman often becomes the head of the household and the center of financial support. As her daughters bear children in her household, the cycle is completed.

Smith (1956) called the Caribbean female-headed domestic domain "matrifocal" and attributed the marginal role of the father to the fact that most low-income men do not have control over economic resources because of racial and class prejudice.[1] They cannot financially provide for a family in the same manner as men of higher social status, who are able to provide full financial support while women stay at home. More commonly, low-income men are important to the functioning of the household only at certain stages of the cycle.

Consequently, many fathers play a marginal role in their children's lives. LaFont found that with the exception of providing financial support (64 percent of the fathers did so), fewer than 50 percent of fathers fit the model of the role of father in the nuclear family in terms of residing with or providing emotional support for their children. Although in her survey she found that both Jamaican women and men stated that fathers were spending less time with their children than in the past, lack of paternal involvement is not a recent phenomenon (LaFont 1996). Forty years earlier, Edith Clarke noted that "the man is satisfied by the proof of his virility [on impregnation] and does not necessarily accept any of the obligations and duties of parenthood. These are generally accepted as the woman's responsibility and there is no public censure if he does not acknowledge or fulfill them" (1957, p. 96).

Given this situation, we have to ask what *father* means in Jamaican society. The concept of father is a cultural construct, embedded in a complex system of meaning and defined by its relation to other concepts, such as mother. Just as gender studies have documented the ways in which the definition of *woman* and *mother* varies between societies and between socioeconomic groups within societies, so it is for *man* and *father* (Leacock 1981). Sex, race, socioeconomics, history, and culture all contribute to constructing identity and status in society.

It is clear that the nuclear family concept of father does not correspond with the behavioral patterns of the majority of Jamaican fathers. Although colonialists sought to promote the nuclear family in Jamaica, it never developed among the majority of the population. African Caribbean women and men have never filled the roles characteristic of British society. Remnants of African cultural traditions, combined with the history of slavery, postcolonial conditions, racism, and economic inequality, mean that the British-style nuclear family is largely irrelevant and inappropriate.

When African women were imported to the Caribbean for slave labor, they were forced to work alongside men in the fields. After the abolition of slavery, widespread poverty necessitated women's involvement in economic activity in the public sphere. Women have had no choice but to seek independent sources of livelihood because dependency on men for economic support has been unrealistic (Massiah 1982). Consequently, women's economic independence translates into considerable power in their relationships with men, and although men are considered to be dominant in Jamaican society, women retain considerable control in the domestic domain (Safa 1986).

The autonomy of Caribbean women has been a subject of discussion among policy makers and social scientists for many years because of women's perceived independence compared to many other areas of the world. The literature is replete with conflicting accounts of female independence and male dominance. Some researchers have said that marriage is the only valued type of union (Blake 1961). Others hold that women do not want to get married because it ties them down to only one man for economic security (Moses 1981). More recently, the theory has been put forth that women may, in fact, acquiesce to male dominance in order to use men to gain financial independence (Barrow 1986). It is difficult to reconcile all these views into one picture of the power women hold vis-à-vis men. Complex relations of production, reproduction, gender, and race combine to shape women's lives. These historical, cultural, and economic features of Jamaican society have led to a tradition of female independence which is in many ways contrary to the ideology of male hegemony held by researchers and Jamaicans themselves.

Indeed, women's power in Jamaica is not uncontested and generates conflict between the sexes as men and women vie for power within their relationships. Sanday (1974) noted that the more freedom women have in a society, the more conflict there is between the sexes. Jamaican gender relations support her theory, and one arena where that conflict is played out is the legal system.

Our description of the Jamaican family structure indicates that it has not been, nor does it appear to be moving toward, a nuclear model, even while the state has enacted laws and policies intended to promote this (postcolonial) ideal. The history of this process warrants a closer look.

In the beginning of the twentieth century, the English government wanted Jamaica (and most of the other British Caribbean colonies) to move toward independence. The colonies had ceased to be economic assets and were draining the ailing coffers of the Crown. Furthermore, Jamaica was torn by social unrest as people repeatedly revolted against an establishment that continued to oppress them economically. With typical colonial bias, the British government sought to construct an independent Jamaican society which mirrored its own structure. Yet the colonial government was confronted with a society which it had stripped of much of its resources and bore little similarity to its own. The Jamaican population was predominantly composed of uneducated and poor former slaves. To aid in devising policy, the post of social welfare advisor to the comptroller of development and welfare in the West Indies was created. T. S. Simey filled that post and produced the document *Welfare and Planning in the West Indies* in 1946. His report informed government social policy for many years, making it an important element in the formation of Jamaican laws and social policy. Indeed, ideas resembling his still permeate current debates.

Simey regarded the nuclear family as essential to the well-being of society and believed that the Caribbean was disorganized and consequently impoverished because of the lack of such a family structure. He stressed the *sine qua non* of the nuclear family and failed to recognize the value of a more fluid family network such as exists in Jamaica. Although he proposed working out the country's problems within a culturally relevant framework, he never relinquished his own cultural assumptions when making policy recommendations. His prejudices are evident in remarks such as his assertion that "looseness of family structure is reflected in a striking weakness in social organization" and constitutes "disorganized human life" (Simey 1946). Many European and North American scholars and public officials shared such views. Their prevalence influenced Caribbean thought to the extent that a decade later a Caribbean-born scholar, Fernando Henriques, referred to Jamaican society as existing in "an acute state of disequilibrium," which he attributed to the "absent or marginal father figure in the home" (Henriques 1953).

Such opinions have informed politicians, teachers, researchers, and generations of Jamaicans as to the nature and value of their family structure. Current debates about the socioeconomic problems in Jamaica often come around to blaming the "lack" of family (read nuclear family). The fact that many low-income Jamaican women and men are unable or unwilling to engage in familial relations as prescribed by the elite continues to fuel arguments about why the Caribbean masses remain what elites call disorganized and impoverished. This scapegoat method of social analysis conveniently masks unequal distribution of wealth, unequal access to opportunity, and sexual and racial discrimination. Yet the belief in the importance of the nuclear family for social well-being is firmly rooted in the ideology of the establishment and continues to predominate.

Gloria Cumper (1972) has discussed the relationship between laws in the Caribbean and the ideology of the dominant class, reporting that "the development of the English Common Law and statutes . . . reflected the conviction that marriage contracted according to the rules of the Church was the only proper basis of family life." The variance in Jamaican mating practices was believed to have "the effect of weakening the monogamous family and thereby threatening the stability of the social organization of the state which is based upon the family unit" (p. 33).

Economically, the classic model of the nineteenth-century British nuclear family was a practical unit of reproduction for industrial society. In the middle-class English family model, husbands worked and supported their wives and children. Wives provided the unpaid domestic labor which allowed men freedom from domestic chores for the reliable production necessary to the growth of the state and economy. Women reproduced the work force by bearing and raising the next generation. It followed that, as the English government sought to ensure the stability of the Jamaican state, it targeted the nuclear family as necessary for social and economic order and enacted laws and policies intended to promote its development.

Yet low-income Jamaicans, who make up approximately 90 percent of the population, did not and do not have the economic and social conditions necessary for the development of this idealized, Western-style nuclear family. Racism and inequality have meant that African-Caribbean men, for the most part, have never earned a family income sufficient to enable women to stay at home and exclusively tend to child care and domestic responsibilities. Even if men were offering to provide such financial support, it is not clear that Jamaican women would relinquish their independence and autonomy for the dependence that characterizes the nuclear family.

Prior to the 1970s Jamaican laws concerning mating unions recognized lawful marriage as the only legally binding union. This meant that, prior to recent amendments, the majority of unions were without benefit of family laws. Even for those who were committed to legal matrimony, the laws were sex-biased. They discriminated against men and women, in different ways, because they were based on the a priori assumption that men were the head of the family and financially dominant. Generally, except for maintenance and inheritance rights, a woman's legal rights, in particular taxation and citizenship rights, were and still are diminished by entering into legal matrimony.[2]

In 1976, Jamaican legislators recognized some of the more obvious discrepancies between the Jamaican social reality and the British-derived legal system and sought legal reforms. The Status of Children Act and amendments to the Guardian and Custody Act, the Maintenance Act, and the Affiliation Act were passed with the intention of reconciling the legal system with the low marriage rates and high out-of-wedlock birthrates in Jamaica.[3] This legislation endorsed three principles: (1) out-of-wedlock children should not be legally discriminated against, (2) men's financial responsibility for their offspring should be based on their income, and (3) unmarried fathers should have equal custody rights. The Family Court was established to handle arbitration of these cases.

Although recent changes in family laws, in particular the amendments to the Affiliation and Maintenance Acts, appear to provide support to women, the amendments to the Guardian and Custody Act, which grants fathers equal custody rights, have the potential to disadvantage women by granting men custody rights without guaranteeing that they fulfill parental responsibilities. This law and accompanying amendments have had conflicting results. The legal stigma of illegitimacy, which represents 85 percent of the population, has been almost eliminated. At the same time, the state has provided women with the ideological and legal justification for the claims they make on their baby-father's income.

While the potential exists for women to be empowered by the family laws, in reality that often does not happen because of the existing power relations between women and men. Being taken to court by his baby-mother is considered shameful to a Jamaican man because it demonstrates that he has lost control over her. Many women report that when their baby-fathers learn of their intention to take them to court, the women are harassed and often beaten, and the father may threaten to steal the child or countersue for custody (LaFont 1996). In many cases, this is sufficient to deter the woman from pursuing her legal rights.

Amendments to the Affiliation, Maintenance, and Custody Acts continue to impose the Western role of father on the Jamaican male population. Yet in a society where power over and control of women brings men prestige, the new legislation has given men a new tool by which to exert that dominance. By legally promoting the role of father as defined by a Western, nuclear family and granting men equal rights to their offspring, the state has eroded the mother's position vis-à-vis her children. Legally requiring fathers to support their children imposes a familial responsibility on men that many fathers have not accepted as anything but, at best, an ideal. It has done so because of the assumption that this is the role men must play if the low-income family structure is to become nuclear and eliminate the cycle of poverty. Unless men accept these responsibilities and, along with them, the rest of the Western concept of fatherhood as social and economic dedication to their children, the legislation is not only culturally inappropriate but potentially harmful.

Although court orders for child support actually assist relatively few women, pursuing legal affiliation and maintenance is perceived by many as an economic strategy of women. Consider the following statement from a local newspaper:

> The Munro College Student Council representative captivated the audience when he noted that the Family Court in Jamaica is now being used as a "business venture" for some young women. He said young women today see it as

"big business" to have five children for five different fathers. These fathers are then taken before the court for maintenance. (*Gleaner*, October 18, 1989)

The fact that Jamaicans believe that women exploit men for child support indicates that financial support of children is a contested issue. Would affiliation cases be seen as a business venture if paternal child support was a norm in Jamaica? If fathers were supporting their children there would be no need to take them to court. Taking five baby-fathers to court for child support is a full-time job, and the amount of money awarded for five children would likely be about the same amount paid to the average helper (maid). Moreover, it is arguably easier to be a helper with defined hours and a guaranteed wage than it is to raise five children and pursue five baby-fathers for support. Nevertheless, the quote indicates that people believe that women use the laws and court system for personal gain.

On the other hand, the amended custody laws have provided men with a weapon of retaliation against women's claims on their income for child support by enabling them to sue for custody of their children. Custody applications are frequently power plays in which children are used as pawns and held in ransom for reconciliations, manipulation, and punishment. Most custody applications involve reasons relating to the relationship between the parents, such as jealousy, rather than accusations of unfit parenting. Children are often transferred back and forth between parents repeatedly in the course of power struggles and are sometimes kidnapped from the other parent.

A case study LaFont collected while working as a counselor at the Kingston Family Court is representative of child custody cases. It involves a twenty-nine-year-old male security guard and his baby-mother.

First session

Mr. Forbes came to court this morning to apply for custody of Theresa, his one-year-old daughter. Although he had custody of the child, Mr. Forbes complained that Miss Evans, his baby-mother, was rude and abusive when she visited the child. During our session Miss Evans arrived. She claimed that when she tried to visit her daughter, she was abused, threatened, and sometimes denied access. Much hostility existed between the couple, and Miss Evans produced a doctor's letter about injuries allegedly inflicted by Mr. Forbes the last time she tried to visit her daughter.

Mr. Forbes reversed his custody request, granted custody of Theresa to Miss Evans, and promised to pay her $200 Ja every fortnight. In return, Mr. Forbes will have the child every third weekend.

Further counseling was requested by both parties.

Second session (ten days later)

Miss Evans kept the appointment, but Mr. Forbes did not. Miss Evans stated that Theresa was in her care, but Mt. Forbes gave her only $100 Ja instead of the $200 Ja he had promised. She claimed that he verbally abused her and refused to pay for Theresa's medication. She believed that he would withhold support in order to get the child back. She stated that she cannot afford to keep the child without his assistance. Hence she planned to return the child to Mr. Forbes until she receives her next paycheck. Miss Evans will then resume custody. She wished further counseling.

Third session (one day later)

Mr. Forbes came in with his adopted sister, who substantiated the claim that Miss Evans exhibits rude behavior when she comes to Mr. Forbes's yard.

Mr. Forbes stated that Miss Evans brought Theresa to his workplace last night. Miss Evans had informed me of this intention yesterday and warned me that Mr. Forbes would be in today saying she dumped the child on him. Mr. Forbes stated that the child was left on the porch like a parcel.

Mr. Forbes admitted that he had not given Miss Evans the promised amount of child support.

Fourth session (twelve days later)

Both Miss Evans and Mr. Forbes kept the scheduled appointment. They appeared quite friendly, sitting together in the waiting room. Mr. Forbes had custody of Theresa and had promised liberal access to Miss Evans. She, in turn, had promised to call Mr. Forbes and inform him beforehand when she wished to visit the child.

Miss Evans appeared to have been sweet-talked into agreeing with all of Mr. Forbes's terms. However, when I spoke with her alone, she stated she was satisfied with the arrangement. Neither partner felt a need for further counseling.

Fifth Session (seven days later)

Miss Evans and Mr. Forbes came in for an unscheduled session. Apparently war had been brewing over the long weekend (three-day holiday). After a long and heated discussion, Mr. Forbes had decided to give Theresa to Miss Evans and deposit $150 Ja fortnightly into Miss Evans's account. He had also agreed to pay half of all medical expenses. He stated that because of Miss Evans's behavior, he wanted nothing more to do with Miss Evans or the child.

Case closed—neither party was seen again during the remainder of my time as a counselor (three more months).

It is easy to see that this case had little to do with the welfare of the child and a lot to do with power, money, and conflicting emotions. Mr. Forbes used securing custody of the child to avoid child-support payments. His concern for his daughter's welfare was questionable. It was his sister, not he, who cared for the child while he had custody and ultimately he decided to discontinue contact with his daughter entirely. It should also be noted that even though he agreed to pay child support, it is extremely rare for the father to continue paying for a child he does not see. The amount and regularity of child-support payments is usually related to the relationship between the baby-mother and baby-father. In fact, 100 percent of LaFont's respondents agreed that once the sexual relationship ends, child support is discontinued. The state has little means to enforce such support payments. When Miss Evans had custody, Mr. Forbes used child-support payments to control her behavior by granting or withholding support payments. On the other hand, Miss Evans was still in love with Mr. Forbes and used the child to gain access to him. The child was transferred back and forth between the couple several times in the course of only one month. It is clear that Theresa and other Jamaican children become the losers and victims in their parents' wars. The Family Court too often has become a mediator of those wars rather than an arbiter of child welfare.

In addition to the price the child pays for parental conflict, the emphasis the state places on the nuclear family may also be detrimental to the self-image of the low-income population. The government's tactics extend beyond legal codes to include media campaigns with posters and television advertisements showing smiling mothers and fathers with their children. If the low-income population internalizes an ideology which advocates marriage and monogamy as a necessity for happy family life, then the majority of Jamaicans will feel short-changed.

The ideology of the elite permeates every aspect of the low-income lifestyle, including the way people view and judge their skin color, their language, and their culture. It assigns a low value to the attributes of low-income Jamaicans, including the family, as inferior to the Eurocentric, upper-class model. Yet poor Jamaicans accept that ideology because it dominates the cultural system that informs them about who they are. Many poor Jamaicans have accepted this evaluation and blame their own family structure for much of their society's problem. The internalization of the ideal of the nuclear family has been nearly complete. Legal marriage, legitimate children, and monogamy are the stated but seldom realized ideals (Barrow 1986, Anderson 1986).

Historical and anthropological research recognizes the importance of the state in reflecting and shaping social ideology (Sewell 1980, Evans et al. 1985). An important mechanism for the state's influence is the legal code. When the laws are based on assumptions and expectations inappropriate to the cultural situation, the results may be unexpected and unintended use of the laws. Legal scholarship has shown that laws help to define what it is to be woman and mother, man and father, and construct notions of appropriate gender behavior (Frug 1992). Laws make assumptions about what kinds of things women and men do, should do, and are capable of doing and may implicitly and explicitly provide incentives geared toward behavior based on those assumptions (Lewis 1993).

Feminist legal scholar Catherine MacKinnon (1989) has described the Western legal code as based on "abstract rights." Equality is linked with rights and pursued by one of two primary tenets. The principle of uniform rights minimizes the differences between women and men and pursues legal equality by distributing rights uniformly. In contrast, the precept of social differences recognizes that sexual and social distinctions exist between people and seeks to achieve social and legal equality in accordance with those differences. Each of these approaches have aspects that encumber the pursuit of equality.

The reality of sexual differences complicates the ideal of uniform equality. The uniform rights approach to law neglects women's special needs as childbearers and mothers, while protection of those needs through special legislation of the social differences tenet may inhibit equality. The challenge lies in how to distribute and protect rights while reconciling sexual and social differences, finding the balance between legal equality, and providing for special needs.

Much of this problem lies in the fact that legal rights are abstracted from social contexts so that the outcome of legal action is not necessarily social equality. MacKinnon notes that "mainstream law of equality assumes that a society is already fundamentally equal" (1989, p. 243). Laws that do not attend to sexual or social differences ignore the socioeconomic and historical conditions creating inequality and work to reproduce that status quo. Laws that reflect existing inequality cannot create social equality. Jamaican family laws provide an interesting case in point.

From the point of view of the uniform rights approach, family laws in Jamaica appear to be moving in the right direction. Each party holds legal rights to custody of the children and each holds a responsibility to care for the children. However, if the social difference perspective is applied, it could be argued that the family laws jeopardize women and children by not protecting women's special needs in the domestic domain.

When the affiliation and maintenance laws were amended in 1976, removing the low maximum payment for child support, it was expected that women would take advantage of the new laws, increasing the number of such cases dramatically. However, contrary to the predictions of social scientists, justice department officials, and popular belief, affiliation and maintenance cases declined yearly. How this legislation is being interpreted, utilized, and reacted to by the populace is not clearly understood. The Eurocentric cultural assumptions that influence laws and policies concerning the obligations of mothers and fathers need to be reappraised.

This is not to suggest that the new laws are without benefit. The Status of Children Act did much to remove legal discrimination against children born out of wedlock.[4] Yet, because they still do not accept the low-income family on its own terms, they have not addressed the needs of children and women in a culturally appropriate and effective manner. By recognizing the rights of unmarried partners yet retaining the nuclear family model, the state has uncovered only one layer of cultural inappropriateness when several are present. Over the last two decades some form of the Status of Children Act and its related amendments has been passed in Jamaica, Barbados, Antigua, Trinidad, Belize, St. Vincent, Cuba, and Guyana and is pending in other Caribbean nations. This makes it imperative that the relevancy of these laws be examined in terms of each cultural context.

NOTES

1. See Gonzalez (1970) and Wilson (1973) for further discussions on this concept.

2. Regarding taxation, husbands may claim their wives as dependents whether they are employed or not. Wives can claim their husbands as dependents only if they are unemployed. In relation to marriage, women have fewer rights than men in matters concerning citizenship and travel under passport. Citizenship for a child born outside of Jamaica is determined by the citizenship of the father. This means that a woman returning to the island with a child born elsewhere, by a foreign father, will have problems with the child's citizenship; not so for men in the same situation. Wives who hold joint passports with their husbands cannot travel alone on that passport, yet the husband is free to do so. The father of a legitimate child must make application for a passport for that child; a mother cannot.

3. The amendments to the Affiliation Act and the Maintenance Act abolished the differences in child-support payments which previously allotted "legitimate" children twice as much support as "illegitimate" children. Prior to its adoption the maximum weekly child support was $4 Ja for "illegitimate" children and $8 Ja a week for "legitimate" children. The amendments also stated that awards would be based on the baby-father's or husband's financial position. Even in 1976, when the Jamaican dollar was worth around U.S. $1.50, $4.00 Ja was a paltry sum.

4. See White and Jackson (1984) and Gibson (1984) for a further discussion on the strengths and weaknesses of the Status of Children Act in Jamaica and similar acts in other Caribbean nations.

REFERENCES

Anderson, Patricia. "Conclusion: Women in the Caribbean." *Social and Economic Studies* 35(1986): 291–325.

Barrow, Christine. "Finding the Support: A Study of Strategies for Survival." *Social and Economic Studies* 35(1986): 131–176.

Blake, Judith. *Family Structure in Jamaica.* New York: Free Press, 1961.

Brody, Eugene. *Sex, Contraception, and Motherhood in Jamaica.* Cambridge: Harvard University Press, 1981.

Clarke, Edith. *My Mother Who Fathered Me.* London: George Allen & Unwin, 1957.

CPS (Contraceptive Prevalence Survey). National Family Planning Board, Kingston, Jamaica, 1989.

Cumper, Gloria. *Survey of Social Legislation in Jamaica.* Kingston, Jamaica: Institute of Social and Economic Research, 1972.

———. "Planning and Implementing the Family Court Project, Jamaica." Mona, Jamaica: Institute of Social and Economic Research, Working Paper No. 27, 1981.

Cumper, Gloria, and Stephanie Daley. *Family Law in the Commonwealth Caribbean.* Mona, Jamaica: University of the West Indies, 1979.

Evans, Peter, Dietrich Rueschemeyer, and Theda Skocpol. *Bringing the State Back In.* New York: Cambridge University Press, 1985.

Frug, Mary Joe. *Postmodern Legal Feminism.* New York: Routledge, 1992.

Gibson, Marston. "Pluralism, Social Engineering and Some Aspects of Law in the Caribbean." *Bulletin of Eastern Caribbean Affairs* 10(1984): 56–87.

Gonzalez, Nancie L. Solien. "Toward a Definition of Matrifocality." In *Afro-American Anthropology,* ed. John F. Szwed and Norman Whitton, 231–243. New York: Free Press, 1970.

Hartley, Shirley Foster. "Illegitimacy in Jamaica." In *Bastardy and Its Comparative History,* ed. P. Laslett et al., 379–396. Cambridge: Harvard University Press, 1980.

Harrison, Faye V. "Women in Jamaica's Urban Informal Economy: Insights from a Kingston Slum." *New West Indian Guide* 62 (1988): 103–128.

Henriques, Fernando. *Family and Colour in Jamaica.* London: Eyre and Spottiswoode, 1953.

LaFont, Suzanne. *The Emergence of an Afro-Caribbean Legal Tradition.* Maryland: Austin & Winfield, 1996.

Leacock, Eleanor Burke. *Myths of Male Dominance.* New York: Monthly Review Press, 1981.

Lewis, Jane. Introduction. *Women and Social Policies in Europe,* Hants, England: Edward Elgar, 1993.

MacKinnon, Catharine A. *Towards a Feminist Theory of State.* Cambridge: Harvard University Press, 1989.

Massiah, Joycelin. *Women and the Family.* Women in the Caribbean Project No. 2. Barbados: University of the West Indies, 1982.

Moses, Yolanda T. "Female Status, the Family and Male Dominance in West Indian Community." In *The Black Woman Cross-Culturally,* ed. Filomina Chioma Steady, Cambridge: Schenkman, 1981.

Powell, Dorian. "Caribbean Women and Their Response to Familial Experiences." *Social and Economic Studies* 35(1986): 83–130.

Safa, Helen I. "Economic Autonomy and Sexual Equality in Caribbean Society." *Social and Economic Studies* 35(1986): 1–22.

Sanday, Peggy R. "Female Status in the Public Domain." In *Woman, Culture and Society,* ed. Michelle Z. Rosaldo et al., Stanford: Stanford University Press, 1974.

Sewell, William. *Work and Revolution in France.* New York: Cambridge University Press, 1980.

Simey, T. S. *Welfare and Planning in the West Indies.* Oxford: Clarendon Press, 1946.

Smith, M. G. *The Plural Society in the British West Indies.* Berkeley: University of California Press, 1965.

Smith, Raymond T. *The Negro Family in British Guiana: Family Structure and Social Status in the Villages.* London: Lowe and Brydon, 1956.

Survey of Living Conditions. Statistical Institute of Jamaica, 1989.

White, Elizabeth, and Leighton M. Jackson. "Status of Children Legislation and the Conflict of Laws." *West Indian Law Journal* 8(1984): 3–25.

Wilson, Peter J. *Crab Antics.* New Haven: Yale University Press, 1973.

❖ 11 ❖

[RE]CONSIDERING CUBAN WOMEN
IN A TIME OF TROUBLES

CAROLLEE BENGELSDORF

SINCE 1989, the island of Cuba has been relentlessly battered by the shocks and aftershocks generated by the collapse of the Soviet bloc.[1] Adrift in a world no longer composed of two separate and powerful economic and political camps and subject to the continuing, undiminished hostility of the United States, Cuba saw its economy decline in size by a drastic 50.2 percent between 1989 and 1993 (Pastor and Zimbalist 1995).[2] The state of extreme crisis which has reigned virtually unabated during these years—designated by the Cuban leadership as the "Special Period in Peacetime"—has redrawn, or at least more starkly outlined, the boundaries of any discussion of women on the island. In conditions of extreme scarcity, characterized by insufficient rations (which often arrive late or not at all),[3] energy shortages and resultant blackouts sometimes scheduled and sometimes unscheduled, transportation cuts which make the simple process of getting to work a daily chore, and the shutdown of whole industries, women's lives have clearly taken on new dimensions. Daily life for everyone on the island is preoccupied with the struggle for survival. Where once an individual looked to the state to ensure such survival, in Cuba today people look to themselves and their families to work out survival strategies. This raises a series of provocative questions about the transitional process in which Cuba has been engaged. These can perhaps best be captured by considering the degree to which the experiences of the Special Period have changed, transformed, or simply revealed or made more visible preexisting patterns and realities. While we are speaking of a period only five-and-one-half years in duration, its ramifications have been traumatic enough to permit us to identify a series of emerging patterns. In what follows, I will attempt to illuminate some of these patterns by taking as my framework the questions of women in the family and women in the public sphere which I used in an earlier article.[4] I will conclude with a discussion of sexuality, which I make no claim of specifically examining in connection with the Special Period. Rather, I try to identify the manner in which specific sexual narratives have been intertwined historically with the narratives of race and nationality which were and remain intensely contested and have already begun to play a central role in the transition in which Cuba in now engaged.

The Family

Since the mid-1970s, as part of its broader emphasis upon molding fixed and permanent institutions with clear purposes, Cuba has stressed the nuclear family as the norm of family organization. This emphasis is clear in laws, in the media, and in the manner in which the state has sought to organize society. The 1975 Cuban Family Code perhaps gives the clearest evidence of this.

The code, which formalized the Cuban Revolution's definition of the family and its role and responsibility in the socialization of children, upholds the nuclear family as the singular "base cell of society" and sets forth the tasks of couples vis-à-vis each other and their offspring.[5] Films such as the wildly popular 1980 *Portrait of Teresa* focus the viewers' attention, as Burton (1981) has pointed out, not on women but upon the *pareja*, the heterosexual couple. Indeed, the pervasive imaging of the nuclear family as the "normal" form of the family is evidenced in the very categories within which Cuban researchers have begun to undertake serious studies of the family. Consider, for instance, recent surveys by the Family Group of the Center of Psychological and Sociological Investigations (CIPS) of the Cuban Adademy of Sciences, which distinguishes "complete" families, defined as those with a mother and father, from "incomplete" families, in which one of the mates is absent (Reca et al. 1990).

This emphasis is particularly curious, given that the nuclear family has not been, either historically or currently, *the* prominent family form in Cuba. Historically and perhaps even more intensely, contemporary families in Cuba tend to function as extended units including kin or fictive kin of more than two generations either living in a single household or in more than one residence. Both single-parent and two-parent households are incorporated into these webs of extended structures.

The very idea of "the family"—that is, that a single family type exists in Cuba—belies what can be observed all across the island. Further, demographic and sociological surveys undertaken since the mid-1980s give some indication of the degree of prevalence of extended families, mainly by surveying the physical presence of different generations in a given household. Reca et al. (1990), using the 1981 census, calculate that nuclear families (both complete and incomplete) living in a single household comprise 53.7 percent of total households and that, interestingly, the percentage is significantly higher in rural than in urban areas.[6] They calculate 56.9 percent of urban households and 66.8 percent of rural households are nuclear. Catasus's earlier survey (1988) of three municipalities—one urban, one suburban, and one rural—echoes the pattern identified by Reca. Reca calculates that 41.9 percent of the total population lives in multigenerational households (i.e., three or more generations). Safa (1995) and the FMC, in their study of women workers in Ariguanabo textile factory in Bauta in the Province of Havana, more or less confirm Reca's and Catasus's findings: 58.9 percent of their sample lives in households of one or two generations; 41.1 percent live in households of three generations.

But these numbers do not reveal the extent to which kinship and fictive kinship, which does not take the form of physical presence in the same household, has functioned in the reproduction of everyday life. What was clear before the Special Period was that, by and large, it was the women within these kin networks who shouldered the tasks. There is some data, for instance, concerning the role that female family members (and, most particularly, grandmothers) have played in childcare. Further, we know from various surveys that while the provisions of the Family Code concerning joint responsibilities of husband and wife for household maintenance and childcare are accepted publicly by the whole population as socially just, they did not in fact produce major changes in who did this work. Indeed, Catasus et al. (1988) calculate from their survey of three municipalities that women continue to do the overwhelming share of household work. In the urban municipality of Plaza de la Revolución in Havana, 81.6 percent of women reported that they did most household tasks; in suburban Buenavista in Cienfuegos, the corresponding figure was 83.8 percent; and in rural Yateras in Guantanamo Province it was 95.8 percent. Reca et al. (1990) provide data concerning leisure time, demonstrating that working women have the least amount of free time, followed by housewives and then by men. But by and large, the actual fieldwork to trace out kinship or fictive kinship networks is just beginning to be done.[7]

If this makes it difficult to grasp, with any precision, how these networks have been affected by the ongoing crisis in Cuba, we can presume that it must underline and intensify the importance of extended families. As the state structures which formerly guaranteed material existence crumble, it is the family unit which has inherited the task of guaranteeing survival. The implications of this are multiple. The time-consuming jobs of standing on lines to get all that is available as it becomes available on rations and of hunting down necessary supplementary food, whether in the newly opened agricultural markets (or agros, as they are called on the street),[8] or on the black market, are better accomplished by families who understand themselves as extended and can divide multiple tasks between themselves. At a time when pesos can add supplemental food at market-determined prices and dollars have become legal tender, extended family structures enable a greater pooling of financial resources to resolve shortages. Further, increasing unemployment resulting from drastic cutbacks and decreasing services means that extended families provide a cushion for those no longer working. In this sense, the Special Period, in making more visible the process of acquiring necessities, has revealed the extent to which it is extended families and friendship and neighborhood networks that accomplish these tasks.

Given all this, why is it that the Cuban Revolution has chosen to enshrine the nuclear family as the norm for the country? There are multiple if incomplete answers to this question.

One answer surely lies in hegemonic ideas concerning what is "modern" throughout the world. The nuclear family appears on the world scene along with capitalism and industrialization. It is capitalism which, for the first time, strips the family of its function in production and creates the dichotomy between what is private and what is public. The Engelsian paradigm, the classical Marxist statement about the family, was shaped in the context of these same nineteenth- and twentieth-century ideas about modernity.[9] Communism, as the Polish sociologist Zygmunt Bauman (1992) has observed, represented nothing if not ultimate adherence to the notions of modernity and progress which have so dominated Western thought since the Enlightenment. The nuclear family is, after all, the "modern" family. Contrary to popularly held views that Marx and Engels advocated free love and the abolition of the family, Engels (1972) gives us, in *The Origins of the Family, Private Property and the State*, a wholly monogamous, heterosexual, and coupled vision of what relationships between men and women will look like once the "world historical defeat of women" which accompanied private property is reversed with its abolition. (See also Sayers et al. 1987.) Cuba's emphasis upon the norm of the nuclear family is, then, perfectly in keeping with Marxist theory and with the practice of socialism in this century.

But the imposition of the nuclear family as the norm in Cuba was, as well, the result of concerns about who in the family would be responsible for the

socialization of children, once the family has been reinserted into the socialization process in the 1970s. Extended families frequently include grandparents,
who are seen as the carriers of traditional values which contradict those of the
revolution regarding everything from work to sexuality. The emphasis on the
norm of the nuclear family underlines the revolution's desire to delegitimize
these traditional values (Lutjens 1994).

Perhaps more critically, the nuclear family can be held up as the norm because it exists in a vacuum: there is virtually no available historical material on
the diverse organization of families in Cuba. While the Caribbean as a whole
became a focus of attention in the late 1950s and 1960s for scholars in the developing field of family studies, the occurrence of the revolution, for a variety
of reasons, effectively removed Cuba from the potential scope of these studies.
Moreover, the literature which emerged in this vein about the Caribbean
tended not to be historical in nature (although surely it contained implications
which could, to some degree, be read or misread historically). And the fact that
the social sciences were literally abolished in Cuban universities from 1970 to
the mid-1980s meant that during that period serious studies touching upon the
family were virtually all demographic in nature.

What we have by way of a social history of families in Cuba underscores yet
another reason why their study might have been ignored by a revolution and a
revolutionary tradition which emphasizes above all, unity and "Cuban-ness."
It becomes clear that one cannot enter into the terrain of family history or related issues in Cuba without discussing the key factor of race.

Cuba was, until the late nineteenth century, a slave society; indeed, the first
half of that century represented perhaps the most intense period of slavery on
the island. Slavery and its effects permeated every aspect of the economic and
social life of the society and certainly had a tremendous impact on family life.
The historical literature that does exist gives us some insight into this and
opens up potentially rich arenas for research and debate. Thus, for instance,
Verena Martinez-Alier's excellent study, *Marriage, Class and Colour in Nineteenth-Century Cuba* (1974), in its examination of the laws governing interracial marriage, gives us a vivid picture of the white family in the nineteenth
century and of the economics of racial "purity," whose object was the preser-
vation of property in the hands of its white owners and whose means to
achieve this was control of women's bodies. The Martinez-Alier study also allows us to glimpse the borders at which racial purity could be "sacrificed" and
the terms of this sacrifice. In so doing, it helps us draw a picture, if impressionistic, of the family and its constitution, particularly for whites and, to some

degree, for wealthy mulattoes, barely a century before the revolution would take power.

It is difficult, however, to arrive at an equivalent picture of life in black families. Here we must rely upon accounts—often excellent—which deal more broadly with black society, both slave and free. Such accounts—Moreno Fraginals's classic study, *The Sugarmill* (1969), or Rebecca Scott's *Slave Emancipation in Cuba* (1985)—begin to define the terms of what remains to be explored. Moreno Fraginals argues, in passing, that given the nature and organization of Cuban slavery—the extreme numerical male-to-female imbalance of slaves on plantations (often two to one, sometimes eight or ten to one) and the housing of slaves in barracoons—"a family unit within the sugar mill was a foreign body, naturally rejected," and plantation slaves "did not know economic, personal or family responsibility because they lacked an economy of their own." Scott questions the terms of Moreno's argument (although it is not her purpose in her book to explore these issues). She points to hospital records, freed slave petitions asking to purchase wives or children, and the limited use of barracoon in Cuba as a basis for questioning Moreno's conclusions. If this begins to sound familiar, it resembles, at least in form, the 1960s controversies concerning the black family in slavery in the United States and suggests that, in a parallel fashion, parish and plantation records may prove a rich and revealing vein for historical research.[10]

Even given its paucity, what we have of historical accounts should be enough to warn us that family norms in Cuba were determined to a great extent by class and racial traditions and that despite the dramatic effects of the revolution from its inception on these traditions, they could not simply have evaporated in one decade or even three. The 1981 census data which divide the population into four racial categories—white, mestizo, Asiatic, and black—seems to indicate that people largely continue to marry into or form consensual unions within their own racial categories. Among whites, 93.1 percent chose whites; among blacks, 90.9 percent chose other blacks or mestizos. Among mestizos and Asiatics, the dividing lines were more blurred: mestizos formed unions mainly with others designated as mestizos (68.7 percent), but a significant percentage (22.5 percent) formed unions with whites. The boundaries between Asiatics and other color groups were even more blurred: while 22.3 percent chose Asiatic mates, 22.5 percent chose mestizos and 50.5 percent chose whites (Reca et al. 1990). These figures would seem to provide tentative support for the hypothesis that historical, traditional patterns of racial separation in marriage have continued into the present and that where mixing has occurred, it has been along the same blurred boundaries between white and mestizo (or Asiatic) to which Martinez-Alier points in her discussion of the nineteenth-century racial mixing in marriage or consensual unions. A current investigation of interracial relationships between young people in an intensely populated and decaying barrio in Central Havana gives some indications that these blurred boundaries are now the product of parental attitudes rather than economic determinations (Fernandez 1994).

Women and the Public Sphere

If the Special Period illuminates patterns within the structure and functioning of Cuban families, in like fashion it provides telling evidence in the debates concerning women's participation in the workforce. The terms of these debates have been fairly straightforward and consistent over the years: all interpretations use the same statistics to draw very different conclusions along three axes.

The first of these axes focuses on the degree to which the Cuban state has been committed to its stated goal (following the orthodox Engelsian paradigm) of getting women out of the house and into the workforce. Here the range of views spans readings which accept the regime's statements about its objectives at face value (see, for example, Randall 1974, 1981) to those who see its efforts to incorporate women as little more than an attempt to generate a reserve labor force and who therefore measure these efforts according to the government's need for labor (see in this regard Bunck 1994, which updates an argument first put forth by Kaufman Purcell in 1973). There is certainly evidence in the statistics to support both arguments. On the one hand, there was, prior to the Special Period, an overall steady growth in the numbers of women employed, which seemed (at least until the late 1980s) to be independent of particular labor needs (see Bengelsdorf 1988). On the other hand, it is true that moments of national mobilization of labor, such as the 1969–1970 sugar harvest, witnessed the most intense efforts to incorporate women into the labor force. This, however, still begs the question of whether such mobilizations were at least in part used as a means to get women into employment outside the house.

The second part of the argument about numbers focuses on the question of whether the revolution has, in the end, actually affected the rate of female employment. Jorge Dominguez (1978) raised this question in the late 1970s, employing as his gauge the percentage of workplace entry of Cuban women in exile in the United States. He uses this to underscore his argument that the process of "modernization" had been well underway in Cuba before the revolution and continued apace among Cuban women on the island and in the diaspora. Casal (1980) directly answered these arguments. Casal effectively pointed to factors Dominguez failed to consider in his decontextualization of the numbers. In particular, she points out that the increases in female employment on the island noted by Dominguez occurred despite the early reeducation programs for domestic servants (who had accounted for 30 percent of female workers before 1959) and prostitutes, despite the enormous expansion of educational opportunities in the 1960s and 1970s, which postponed entry into the workforce for many women, and despite the tremendous disincentive to work, created by the government's guarantee of basic needs and by the dramatic decline in the availability of goods throughout the 1960s (and again, we might add, after 1989).

Dominguez's modernization explanation, set within a different comparative framework, has been reasserted more recently by Bunck (1994). Bunck places the percentage of Cuban women's entry into the workforce against comparable figures for other Latin American countries—in particular, Mexico, Argentina, Venezuela, and Colombia—and concludes that Cuba merely "remained on a par" with other labor forces in the region.

Current economic realities make questions of numbers and genders of workers somewhat moot: a 50 percent decline in an economy cannot, by definition, promote "modernization." Moreover, employment trends in Cuba are virtually impossible to measure with any precision, for several reasons. First, there are no available statistics for overall unemployment: the last unemployment statistics were published in 1989.[11] Second, employment in the Special Period is a constantly shifting scenario, molded and remolded by the fortunes (and misfortunes) of the three targeted sectors of the economy—tourism, sugar, and biotechnology; by Cuba's successes and failures in forming new trading partners; and by the (thus far) piecemeal measures the state has introduced to deal with the economic crisis. But unemployment has grown significantly in response to the downsizing of administrative structures and the closing of workplaces which can no longer be supplied either with raw materials or the energy needed to make them into finished products. The Federation of Cuban Women (FMC) reports (Aguilar and Pereira 1994) that within this painful reality, women have maintained and slightly increased their proportion in the workforce.[12] Even if this is so, further enormous cutbacks in the workforce are inevitable: Cuban officials call this process of cutback a "rationalization" of the economy. Economists on the island estimate that these cutbacks will affect somewhere around 500,000 people, out of a workforce of 4.5 million (Carranza and Monreal 1995). Foreign experts put the figure as high as one third of the total workforce. The criteria for rationalizing will be the number of years on the job and, above all, the efficiency of a given worker. Neither of these categories is gender neutral: given women's household responsibilities and the timing of their entry into the workforce, both will inevitably affect women disproportionately and thereby contribute to an incipient feminization of poverty in Cuba. This is particularly tragic, since one of the most stunning accomplishments of the revolution has been to free women from economic dependence upon men to ensure their survival, by guaranteeing employment for all who wanted jobs, by giving women the opportunity for advanced education and training, and by providing universal free health care and subsidized food. It is bound to be registered most disastrously in households headed by women.[13]

Where will those women who are rationalized out of the labor force go? The idea, in theory, is that they will be absorbed into the growing ranks of those working *por cuenta propria*, the self-employed. The reality is far more clouded and precarious. In fact, *trabajo por cuenta propria* has been, thus far, overwhelmingly male terrain. By March 1994, of the 142,585 officially licensed self-employed workers, some 77 percent were men (*Bohemia*, March 1994).

Moreover, the revolution has been somewhat erratic about what sorts of private occupations will be permitted. For instance, in one area which impacts greatly upon women, in the space of two years, it allowed, banned, and allowed once more the sale and provision of prepared food, particularly in *paladares*, or small-scale, home-based restaurants (but also by street vendors, less visible bakery and sandwich businesses, and even pizza home delivery services).[14]

What becomes clear is that there are tremendous incentives for both men and women to seek work in the amorphous informal or "gray" economy. The state estimates that a number at least equal to those legally licensed for self-employment now moves within the mushrooming, ill-defined territory which makes up this economy. It is surely larger than this. It includes an indeterminate number of people still employed by the state who are moonlighting in second or third jobs, people who have either left or been rationalized out of their state-funded jobs, retirees, and people such as housewives who were never part of the employed labor force. It is their presence in this economy which will, in the end, prove most critical to any measure of the impact of the economic crisis upon women's place in the workforce.

The categories of work *por cuenta propria*, both licensed and unlicensed, begins to engage directly a potentially even more conflicted axis of investigation concerning women and work in Cuba. At its core, again, is the Engelsian paradigm and its assertion that the path to the liberation of women runs through the workplace. In Cuba, as in other countries where the paradigm was adopted as the ideological blueprint for women's self and social realization (see Molyneux 1990), this has, of course, not proven to be true. Its failure can be measured on a number of planes. First, entry into the workforce has has not proven itself to be the route to political equality with men. Overwhelmingly, both before and after the 1986 Third Party Congress (which called, in essence, for an affirmative action campaign for both women and blacks, particularly in relation to political appointments), women were represented politically in proportion neither to their numbers in the population nor to their numbers in the workforce. Practically every article or book chapter dealing with Cuban women makes this clear (see, for example, Perez-Stable 1987, Bengelsdorf 1988, and Bunck 1994). Interestingly, the current crisis has had little effect thus far on women's participation. Despite the political and economic reforms which have marked the Special Period, the patterns in this participation have remained fairly consistent. Even where there appears to be a somewhat significant change in direction, as in the number of women elected as National Assembly deputies (the 1993 elections witnessed a drop in the percentage of women elected from a high of 33.9 in 1986 to 22.8), it is the 1986 figure which seems to be exceptional. The 1986 election followed closely upon the party's conscious articulation of its affirmative action program to increase the number of women in political office. The 1976 and 1981 elections resulted in National Assemblies made up of respectively 21.8 percent and 22.6 percent women (Bengelsdorf 1994).

Most analysts trace this undisputed underrepresentation of women to three sources. The first underlines the continuing "double burden"; that is, despite the Family Code, domestic work and child care remain largely the purview of women. The Communist Party itself gave the first official measure of this in its 1975 Second Party Congress's "Thesis on the Full Equality of Women" (in Stone 1981). In the wake of the 1974 elections in Matanzas Province (which served as a forerunner to the national Popular Power system), in which only 7 percent of those nominated and 3 percent of those elected were women, a party survey revealed that more than half the women questioned would have refused nomination, overwhelmingly because of domestic obligations. Survey after survey in the years following revealed the stark differentials in terms of total working and leisure hours for women, particularly working women as compared to men. The 1980 film *Portrait of Teresa* captured these statistics visually:

the first half of the film is devoted to a grueling portrayal of women's double burden, which is exhausting even to watch (see Burton 1981).

Second, and directly related, the failure of the Engelsian paradigm concerning women and work can be traced to its blindness to the ramifications of a continuing sexual division of labor. Engels and, following him, those countries which called or call themselves socialist never took cognizance of the implications of not challenging a division of labor which assigned women in the public sphere the tasks (or extensions of those tasks) which they had formerly performed in the home. Despite stories about women tractor drivers or cane cutters (Cuban sociologist Marta Nuñez has done the most serious study of women in nontraditional jobs), Cuban women (like their Soviet, Chinese, Vietnamese, and Eastern European counterparts) by and large filtered into employment centering around nurturing and service—concretely, into medicine, teaching, food service, day care—or into those industrial sectors in which they had traditionally worked (textiles and cigar-making in particular). Cuban officials, beginning with Fidel Castro, underscored what was for them the biological bases for such channeling: above all, they continually stressed the primacy of women's role as mothers, or, as Castro phrased it, as "nature's workshops" (*Granma*, December 30, 1973). Such biological determinism and the resultant need to "protect female reproductive organs" found expression in the 1976 Constitution, which asserted that women "should be given jobs in keeping with their physical makeup" (chapter 5, article 43). The ideological premises of the sexual division of labor have provided the soil in which women's double burden has been rooted and have underpinned, in turn, the absence of women in positions of leadership, in both the political and economic structures of the country. For instance, with relation to the party (which has been, since 1975, the single most important political institution), women's access to membership has been structurally inhibited by the fact that party membership is open only to those in the workforce, and then only to those workers who have demonstrated their suitability through exactly the kinds of time-consuming participation in workplace activities that have been and presently are even more intensely difficult for women, given their responsibilities at home.

And since it has effectively operated relatively unchallenged for three decades, the sexual division of labor must inevitably reproduce itself as Cubans move into the legally privatized and the illegal, informal economies. While there are no statistics to confirm it, any observer walking the streets of Havana or provincial cities and towns can note the degree to which women are involved in traditional women's work, centering most particularly on small-scale food

preparation and provision, sewing, beauty care, artisanry, and domestic service. That is, the pattern which seems to be emerging is one in which women
working for themselves or others, whether legally or illegally, are filtering into
exactly the occupations which were theirs before the revolution. And, as in prerevolutionary times, these are generally the least lucrative trades.[15] Without
specific policies which understand the gender implications of licensing different categories of private work—in the form, for instance, of special training
courses for women in plumbing, carpentry, electrical repair, etc.—the shift toward a privatized economy must further encourage and accelerate the feminization of poverty in Cuba.

Sexual servicing is perhaps the most glaring reincarnation of traditional
women's work in the informal economy. The regime's emphasis on tourism as
a major source of foreign currency has seen a dramatic revival of prostitution,
particularly among the young, to service this sector.[16] Despite its early and successful effort to wipe out prostitution, the government has basically ignored its
restitution, treating it as a choice of individual women. Carlos Lage, a Politburo
member and key strategist of the reforms underway on the island, spoke of
prostitution as "the social price we pay for development." To the same end and
at about the same time, Castro asserted that in contrast to prerevolutionary
times, women who prostitute themselves "do it on their own, voluntarily and
without any need for it" (*Washington Post*, January 2, 1993). It was only in
March 1995 that Castro began to acknowledge the economic base of revived
prostitution (*El Habanero*, March 10, 1995).

The final axis of discussion of women's position in the workforce looks to
the nebulous category of inherited male and female prejudices (see Bunck
1994). There is certainly a good deal of material to support interpretations
based on inherited prejudices. For instance, researchers studying Popular Power
at the municipal level in 1989 noted the variation in the percentage of women
elected in different districts and cities across the island. They reported that
in Bayamo, where consistently very few female delegates have been elected,
women themselves "regularly reject their nomination, publicly stating that
their husbands will not allow it" (Dilla and Gonzalez 1991). But the question of
male attitudes, often seen as a reflection of traditional "machismo," leads us
onto a terrain mined with pitfalls. Discussions of male attitudes, or machismo,
are typically decontextualized in the literature and in discussions. This process
of decontextualization enables the portrayal of machismo as a timeless, almost
biological attribute of Latin and, therefore, Cuban men. It can arouse either
fury or laughter, but in the end, exactly because it is timeless and innate, it can

at best be curbed, tamed, or removed from the arena of acceptable conversation. By definition, then, it transcends economic and political crises. Discussions of machismo are rarely situated within the framework of the larger (and necessary) analysis of the manner in which gender and sexuality get constructed in Cuba and the degree to which this process of construction has been changed, or left unaltered, by the experience of the revolution.

Sexuality, Race, and Nation

Discussions of sexuality have, with certain exceptions, always played a subordinate role in the literature about women in Cuba; curiously, this is largely the result of the fact that most of the research on gender in Cuba no matter what its arguments, has adopted the Engelsian paradigm as the framework within which to explore questions of gender. This paradigm, true to the English Victorian setting in which it was formulated, leaves little room for analyses of sexuality.[17] The richest vein of literature concerning sexuality we have is historical in nature, focusing particularly on nineteenth-century Cuba. This literature underscores that the very construction of white or mulatto or black womanhood was embedded in racial narratives. It reveals a rich, conflictive, and contradictory canvas, a heritage against which postrevolutionary realities—for instance, current racial marriage patterns—must be read.

Let us take as the first of these narratives the "traditional" attitudes of "machismo" we spoke of earlier. De la Torre Mulhare's 1969 exploration of white sexual ideology (while problematic, particularly in its assumption of heterosexuality) evokes the traditional stereotypes which paint males as aggressive and sexually active and white females as their opposite: passive and sexually cold. For men, sex was a biological necessity; for women, it was tolerated because of their desire to become mothers. De la Torre Mulhare's Manichean dichotomies, which support a definition of machismo centered on male-female relationships, began to be challenged by Geoffrey Fox in a 1973 article[18] and, even more strikingly, by Verena Martinez-Alier in her 1974 study of the rules which governed marriage in nineteenth-century Cuba and the borderlands where these rules were subverted. Both studies help us to understand that at least in prerevolutionary Cuba and at the moment of the revolution, traditional male "attitudes" were the result not of an immutable male-female face-off, but were the historical means by which men challenged, contested, and bonded with other men, essentially over the bodies of women. That is, women, and most specifically white women, and their "honor" were, in Gayle Rubin's clas-

sical formulation (1976), the objects traded back and forth between men attempting to successfully construct their own manhood and maleness. (Black
women, whether slave or free, virtually by definition had no honor to protect
and were the objects of a different narrative.) Nonetheless, white society defined the hegemonic ideal and set the terms of discourse. Thus the eternal value
of white women's virginity at marriage, faced with the seemingly severely conflicting male sexual imperative, had little to do with men's relationships with
women, but rather was key to their relationships with other men: it was through
the constant contest with other men over the bodies of women that they acquired the status of successful or unsuccessful manhood. If a white man's
honor was invested in the sexual purity of the women in his family—his
mother, wife, sisters, and most particularly his daughters—his social esteem
and position among the male brotherhood was measured by the degree to
which he could undermine another's honor; that is, one's own honor increased
to the degree that the other's diminished. The clearest way, therefore, to deflate
another man's honor was to engage in sexual relations with the women who
fell under that other man's protection, and most particularly with any unmarried woman. The inevitable underbelly of such a system is the assumption of
woman's fundamental weakness: a woman could not on her own be trusted or
expected to shield herself from dishonor; she required the authority of a male
relative to ensure her virtue. Women were thus virtually denied access to or
control of their own sexuality; rather, this sexuality took on meaning only
within the framework of an elaborate game played out by males for whom it
was a pawn in their own quest for increased social status. The prize, as Fox
asserts, "was not the woman, but the esteem of other men." Machismo, then,
must be understood as a discourse of power whose terms were and are set by
men. The frequent assertion, in modern-day Cuba, that machista attitudes are
perpetuated as much by women as they are by men rings particularly false
given this conceptualization.

The frailty of a woman's will to protect her own virtue justified her seclusion within the household (as the saying went, "La mujer honrada, la pierna
quebrada en casa"—the honorable woman: locked in the house with a broken
leg). The custom of female seclusion, as it was practiced in pre-twentieth-cen-
tury Cuba, undoubtedly was indebted to the Moorish institution of the harem
as inherited through a Spanish filter, although it did not take the form of con-
finement to certain areas of the house. Rather, strict social codes determined
when and in what capacity "honorable" women were permitted to be seen on
the streets. The casa/calle (house or home/street) distinction often used to describe the dividing mark between male and female spaces in prerevolutionary

Cuba is much more than a figure of speech; it had a very literal meaning (see Perez 1992 for historical accounts of the social and geographic boundaries of women's lives). The Cuban historian Jose Luciano Franco (whose family was middle class and of racially mixed origin), recalling his childhood in the early years of the twentieth century, asserts that women did not work "in the street." Those employed in tobacco factories worked in their homes and sent the work to the factory. Schoolteachers were accompanied to and from their homes by students or husbands, "because a woman alone on the street was looked upon very badly." Franco remembers a great aunt related to his white father who was considered crazy because she went out alone four times a year (Poumier 1975). This idea that only crazy (white) women roamed the streets is underlined dramatically in the first episode of the 1969 epic film *Lucia*, which deals with women in three eras of Cuban history. In the first vignette, set during the 1895–1898 Cuban War of Independence, a madwoman whom we later learn was a nun (pure) who was raped by Spaniards (the collective degradation of native-born, or *criollo*, males by the colonial regime) and has, as a result, gone insane, wanders the streets of Santiago to the jeers and maltreatment of the population as a whole (which is, of course, male, given that the streets are male space). In the end, she is joined by the first Lucia, who has been driven crazy by the betrayal of her Spanish lover, who uses their relationship to discover the whereabouts of her brother (a *criollo*) and his compatriots, and thus to facilitate their massacre (again the same pattern of male degradation of male, through the violation of female virtue). And in the classical nineteenth-century Cuban novel *Cecilia Valdes*, the only females to roam the streets at will are Cecilia's friend Nemisia, a mulatta, and Maria, a slave who is selling her labor for the financial benefit of her master. When Cecilia herself leaves her house, unaccompanied or with only Nemisia, she is clearly sneaking out, and it is an indication of the "impurity" of her blood.[19] Poumier (1975), in her somewhat fragmentary study of daily life in Cuba in 1898, related that "middle-class" (and therefore mainly white) women never went out on foot or alone; they went in groups and in carriages. If they wanted to buy some novelty from Paris, the storekeeper would bring the article to their carriages: the remainder of the purchases were in the charge of numerous maids. The main outing for women was the "evening promenade," which took place in the late afternoon, to the walks and parks where women of "good society" sunned themselves.

Under these conditions, the possible points of contact of male and female take on particular significance; thus, for instance, the importance of the barred window in *Cecilia Valdes*. The barred window looking out into the street functions as the eyes of females looking out at the world and as a legitimate but at the same time dangerous and restricted frontier. It is through the barred window that Don Leonardo's young daughters first see the child Cecilia, and bring her into their family circle. It is through the barred window that a romance between the eldest of these sisters and a Spanish soldier appears to begin. And it is the barred window which is the scene of most of Cecilia's illicit contact with the young Leonardo (who is not only white but, unknown to either of them, her half-brother). The implication is clear: it is only the barred window which restrains the female from indulging her nature in damaging relationships. (It is interesting to note that the theme of the barred window is taken up in contemporary Cuba in *Portrait of Teresa*. After Teresa, at her husband's insistence, retires from her job as a seamstress and returns to her home as a full-time housewife, we see her once again sewing, this time through the barred windows of her home.)

The concern for a white woman's purity in colonial Cuba had, of course, another dimension in a society which, while already inextricably mixed, sought to retain the myth of racial exclusiveness that provided the basis and the rationale for severe social stratification. Martinez-Alier focuses on exactly this dimension. Control of access to women's sexuality was seen by the white male oligarchy as the key to maintaining the "purity" of the group and protecting it from unwanted outsiders. On this level as well, then, a woman's virginity became a pawn in a sociopolitical and economic game whose rules were determined by men. The upholding of virginity, as Martinez-Alier points out, served to preserve the position of the white oligarchy by precluding the possibility of social equality. This is nowhere clearer than in the laws which came into effect in the 1800s, exactly during the period of the most extensive and intensive slavery in Cuba. With an 1805 royal decree, marriages between "persons of known nobility" and blacks or mulattoes now required both the consent of the father and a license from the civil authorities. The state thus aligned itself directly with the white male oligarchy in its efforts to prevent any dilution of its political and economic monopoly. By the late 1830s, this alignment was complete: any interracial marriage required a dispensation from the state. While the maintenance of *limpieza de sangre*—pureness of blood—was the major official reason raised in opposition to interracial marriages, given the degree of sexual mixing which had already taken place, clearly there were other considerations involved. The dispensations made to the general rule give evidence of exactly what these other considerations were. Generally these exceptions involved white men who were poor and who worked in humble occupations, and "respectable," financially well-off mulattas.

This then brings us face to face with the narrative of black or mulatto women's sexuality. As Jean Stubbs and Pedro Perez Sarduy remark in *AfroCuba* (1993), the literature on race or gender has largely ignored this narrative. While the surveys we have cited, for instance, indicate that marriage continues to be color segregated, the revolution's explanation focuses on the outdated attitudes and values of older generations which will (presumably) die with them. The historical literature, however, gives us some understanding of the centrality of racialized sexuality in Cuba and of its roots in themes which are still very intensely contested. This historical literature—principally the Martinez-Alier book; Reynaldo Gonzalez's *Contradanzas y Latigazos* (1983), a fascinating study of the novel *Cecilia Valdes*; and, most recently, Vera Kutzinski's brilliant *Sugar's Secrets: Race and the Erotics of Cuban Nationalism* (1994)—speaks to the sexual construction of another stereotype: the "Cuban mulatta." The mulatta inhabited and inhabits, at once, the (absent) center and the dangerous borderlands between the races in Cuban sexual ideology.

Gonzalez's point—and it is a powerful one—is that the archetypical mulatta continues to effect and epitomize a dangerous sexuality, which both challenges and sustains the sexual structures of society; that is, the mulatta is (and was) imaged as everything white women were traditionally not: sexually aggressive, immoral, and a threat to the established "rules of the game." Gonzalez and Martinez-Alier both attempt to provide a political economy of race, gender, and class in their discussions of nineteenth-century practices. Kutzinski goes beyond this to spell out a specific construction of mulatta sexuality which lies at the heart of the historical Cuban struggle to imagine itself as a nation.

The question of identity—the very definition of "Cubanness"—was historically, and remains still, bitterly contested terrain. In the nineteenth century, racial realities lay at the heart of heated debates concerning who was and was not Cuban. While the revolution has sought to answer the question geographically (that is, Cubans are those who remain on the island, loyal to it) rather than racially, adopting as its point of departure the assertions of José Martí and Antonio Maceo that to be Cuban is to be "more than white, more than black," there is a narrative of racialized sexuality deeply embedded in this formulation. This "transcendence" of race—actually, the bonding of men across racial lines—which permitted the successful construction of the independence movement and allows revolutionary Cuba to dismiss race as a thing of the past (and consequently blinds it to thinking in terms of racially constructed sexualities) was, literally, written upon the body of the (always absent) mulatta. Kutzinski (1994) points out for instance, that Nicholas Guillen's poem "The Ballad of the Two Grandfathers," one of the "foundational fictions" of the Cuban Revolution, which celebrates the physical bonding of mulatto and white males in the creation of a (racially idealized) Cuban nation, "is predicated upon the erasure—the mis(sing) 'representation'—of a black woman, the one in whose violated body the two races actually met. . . . Once the evidence of messy (that is, sexual) female participation in historical processes of racial mixing is eliminated by being made unrepresentable, mestizaje becomes legitimated as an exclusively male project or the achievement in which interracial, heterosexual rape can be refigured as a fraternal embrace across color (and in this case, class) lines and, significantly across a female body absented by rape." Once more, and in a different sexual narrative, the bonding between men, in Gayle Rubin's terms, takes place through and upon the bodies of women—in this narrative, mulatta women.

If the mulatta provided (and provides) a seductive and dangerous, centrally situated terrain, given the traditions of Cuban sexual codes, the homosexual inhabits a marginal terrain. Homosexuality (which, in Cuba, both historically and at present, refers almost exclusively to males; lesbians are virtually invisible) offers a different basis for male bonding which challenges the "rules of the game." Again, successful manhood, in the dominant paradigm, is written always on the bodies of women. The revolution has had a stormy, revealingly self-conscious set of attitudes toward homosexuals (revealing, perhaps, exactly the degree to which the "rules of the game," in other forms, may still operate). It has moved from understanding homosexuality as criminal and indicative of counterrevolutionary tendencies to considering it a disease or a genetic defect which must be understood and treated as such (see Young 1981 and Arguelles and Rich 1984, 1985].

Curiously, it is only in the context of the current economic crisis (and, perhaps not unrelated, the resurgent tourist industry) that Cuba has begun, as it were, to "come out of the closet." While laws remain on the books which prohibit homosexuals from working in jobs which relate to children, recent short and descriptive articles by North American gays and lesbians document the increasing number of openly gay clubs and cabarets. Perhaps most indicative, a 1993 feature film, *Strawberry and Chocolate*, by the Cuban director Tomas Gutierrez Alea, which is, above all, a statement about intolerance in general but focuses specifically on the issue of homosexuality, has proven to be extraordinarily popular with Cuban audiences and a sign that homosexuality will now be officially tolerated.

As the body of socialism dies elsewhere, Cuba remains virtually alone, its leadership desperately clinging to the skeleton of the past, even as it is forced, for its very survival, to hack away at its own appendages. The most optimistic

Cubans hope that, by the year 2000, Cuba will be functioning (along the lines of the Scandinavian countries) as the first social welfare society in the Third World, having preserved from the fires of capitalist encroachment its tremendous achievements in health and education. The most realistic Cubans know this is unlikely. We have already seen some indications of what all this might mean for Cuban women. We can look at the situation of women elsewhere in the former world of socialism and the price they have paid for freedom from oppressive regimes in terms of basic economic independence and (in Poland and the former East Germany, for instance) fundamental rights such as abortion—that is, control over their own bodies. The degree to which Cuba is able to stop the erosion of its health and education systems will be one key to maintaining Cuban women's capacity to survive with some degree of economic independence. And its ability to slow down or even slightly reverse its economic collapse will, in part, influence its capacity to engage both women and men in the professional employment for which so many have been trained. But given the failure of socialism to challenge, in any fundamental way, the male-gendered nature of the public sphere, it is likely that in the privatized and informal economies, as well as within the state economy and its governmental and administrative structures, traditional patterns of labor and political representation will continue to reassert themselves. And although the revolution dramatically sped up the degree to which women gained rights in their own bodies (in terms of both accepted morality and reproduction), racialized narratives of sexuality, unchallenged or left untouched, are bound inevitably to reassert themselves more openly in some form, as issues of nation and race again become critically contested battlefields in the determination of what a future Cuba will look like.

NOTES

1. Research for this article was done during my participation in the Working Group on Cuban Women, sponsored by the Task Force on Scholarly Relations with Cuba of the Latin American Studies Association and funded by the Ford Foundation.

2. In 1994, this dramatic downward spiral ceased, or at least paused. That year, Cuba recorded a 0.7 percent growth in its gross domestic product. In 1995, this figure rose to 2.5 percent. While the mood in Havana was guardedly less glum in December 1995 and people celebrated the new year for the first time in several years, at least some foreign economic experts argued that the Cuban figures, as a representation of the legal economy, were inflated. The figures are probably more realistic if the informal economy

is taken into account as well. (Information from Andrew Zimbalist at the Conference on the Cuban Economy, Harvard University, December 14, 1995.)

3. The provision of rationed goods worsened as the years of crisis proceeded. In 1994, people received less on their ration cards than in 1993. This meant that virtually the entire population was forced, in order to survive, to seek recourse to the black market—that is, to engage in illegal activities. The October 1994 reopening of agricultural markets across the island alleviated this situation by making a variety of foods available in pesos at prices determined by demand and competition (and therefore not equally accessible). For the most thorough discussions of the rationing system during the Special Period, see Deere 1992 and Mesa-Lago 1993.

4. See Bengelsdorf (1988).

5. The Family Code has been the subject of multiple and not necessarily exclusive interpretations. The first and perhaps most prominent reading of the code celebrates it as a radical statement of women's emancipation. Thus, for instance, Larguia and Dumoulin (1986) see the Family Code as "the center of a direct and massive confrontation with macho patterns and with the foundation of the division of labor between the sexes. Its objective is to free Cuban women's energies for expansion in all areas of social activity so that they can achieve the personal fulfillment which has always been denied them." Croll (1982) and then Deere (1986), Nazzari (1989), and Lutjens (1992) understand it as a product, in part, of conditions of underdevelopment and scarcity; that is, the state found itself without the resources to collectivize in the public sphere household tasks which had traditionally been defined as women's work, through universally available daycare centers, workers' cafeterias, etc. Croll sees the Family Code as an attempt to collectivize these tasks in the private sphere by defining them legally as the responsibility of both husband and wife. For Deere, the code represents the state's recognition that women's emancipation will not result from their inclusion in social production alone but must, as well, involve a transformation of the "traditional reproductive responsibility of women and the burden that it places upon [them]." Nazzari interprets the repercussions of this as support for her argument that the economic changes of the 1970s, by contrast to those of the 1960s, increased women's dependence upon men. She cites here, in particular, the fact that in making parents rather than society responsible for the material support of children, the code "directly contradicted [Fidel] Castro's 1966 statement that a child's subsistence should be determined solely by the 'needs of the child as a human being.' " In this sense, for Nazzari, the Family Code itself was a step away from distribution according to need "toward distribution according to work," and therefore increased the power of men within the family. Withers Osmond (1985) interprets the code as meaning that the code is little more than "an empty beneficent policy," that is, a policy that the state establishes and sanctions without providing any mechanisms for positive implementation (for instance, paternity as well as maternity leave), nor any means of sanction for its violation. Following Nazzari, Withers Osmond concludes that "for Cuban women, intensely involved in the welfare of their children, the Family Code means (a reinforcement of) the traditional preoccupation with family income and maternal responsibility." Gotkowitz and Turits (1988)

provide an even more complex reading of the code, identifying what they understand as its multiple and in some senses conflicting meanings. They note particularly the amount of space devoted in the code to divorce and argue that the document regulates the breakup of the family more than it does its functioning. They further note in it the revolution's consistent tendency to identify women's rights within the context of their role as mothers; in this sense, it is of a piece with labor legislation of the same period which denied women the right to work in range of jobs which might endanger their health as mothers or as future mothers. Finally, they understand the code as the acknowledgment and assertion of the family as a major agency of socialization, most obviously in living arrangements, in household maintenance strategies, and in arrangements concerning the care of children. Bengelsdorf (1988) underscores this last point. She argues that this understanding of the family as the primary agency of socialization was a dramatic reversal of the policies of the 1960s, when the revolution saw itself as the agency of socialization. The family's institutionalization in the Family Code, in this sense, was of a piece with the reversion to a more traditional version of the transition to socialism embodied in the institutionalization process as a whole, a process which dominated the mid-1970s.

All these interpretations, while interesting and suggestive, completely fail to consider its key historical context. The Family Code cannot be understood outside the specific history to which it responds. We mean this not simply in terms of the revolution and its commitment to social and economic egalitarianism. That commitment itself has been molded and shaped by a longer history, as has the Family Code. The code, in this context, climaxes a struggle which has threaded through twentieth-century Cuban history to reform or transform laws governing marriage, divorce, and the rights of women and children. Its path is marked by 1918 legislation which took marriage out of the control of the Church and allowed for what Stoner (1991) labeled "no fault divorce"; by the 1930 termination of the "adultery law," which allowed husbands to kill wives (and their lovers) if they were found in compromising situations and suffer, at most, the penalty of exile; by the 1934 revisions of the divorce law which attempted to strengthen alimony payment procedures; and by the 1940 Cuban constitution which prohibited official classification of children as illegitimate and allowed such children (in cases in which paternity could be proven) to inherit a limited amount of property. In this context, the Family Code marks the realization of efforts of women's groups and radical movements throughout the twentieth century to assure women and their offspring, whether legitimate or illegitimate, equal rights before the law. Its abolition of the category of illegitimacy, its provisions concerning the legal rights and responsibilities of the two contracting partners to each other and their offspring, both within the marriage and in its dissolution, mark the acceptance by the Cuban state and society of the most radical and controversial positions put forth by those women and men who struggled for the better part of a century to overcome women's and children's inequality before the law and to position the state as the guarantor of their rights to support and survival.

6. Also see Ravenet, Perez, and Toledo 1989, and Safa 1995.

7. There is an expectation among Cuban academics who study the family, that (although no data thus far exist) the sheer impossibility of surviving as a single person,

with the multiple tasks such survival now entails, will result in diminished rates of separation and divorce and therefore an increase in two-parent households. This in and of itself will do little to alter the existence and increasing visibility of extended family networks. (Based on discussions at the "Seminar on Families in Cross Cultural Perspective," University of Havana, Faculty of Women's Studies, March-April 1994. See also Sonia Catasus 1994.)

8. The state instituted free farmers' markets for five years, from 1981 to 1986, then abolished them, claiming that they were generating a class of rich middlemen and private farmers. Since shortages became severe and full-scale rationing was reinstituted in 1991, the restitution of these markets has been anxiously awaited by the population as a whole; the resistance to their resurrection is generally thought to come directly from Fidel Castro. On October 1, 1994, farmers' markets, now called *agropecuarios,* were reestablished across the country, stocked by the recently reinvigorated and vastly expanded cooperative farm sector, private farmers, and state farm employees (who were, in 1993, for the first time allotted parcels of land which they could use to grow their own crops). In legalizing the enterprise of food sales, which had been the purview of black marketeers, the state has, to some extent, reinvigorated the peso. With the legalization of the U.S. dollar is July 1993, the black market began to operate only in dollars. By the summer of 1994, the peso was valued at 100 or 120 to the dollar, although the official exchange rate remained 1:1. By November 1994, one month after the opening of the agricultural markets, a dollar was buying only 40 to 60 pesos on the street. By January 1996, the exchange rate on the street and in newly opened state-run exchange agencies was reduced to 25 pesos to the dollar. The state is hoping that the availability of food for purchase in these markets may provide a material incentive for people to work to earn pesos.

9. The Engelsian paradigm, in brief, subordinates women's emancipation to a more generalized emancipation resulting from the overthrow of capitalism, sees women's emancipation as a result of their entry into the productive (that is, waged) workforce (in keeping with the Marxist axiom that human beings realize themselves through work), and postulates that women will be relieved of their work in social reproduction in the household which keeps them subordinated by the socialization of these tasks.

10. This was the kind of research undertaken by Herbert Guttman (1976) in his classic rebuttal of the famous (or infamous) *Moynihan Report.*

11. Statistics on unemployment in 1989 put it at 8 percent (*Anuario Estadistica de Cuba* 1989). Current figures would be significantly higher.

12. The FMC figures are probably misleading. There are, for instance, indications that in the face of the difficulties of daily life, a significant number of women have taken *bajas,* or extended leaves from work (supposedly for medical reasons, often with the cooperation of family doctors who tend to be disproportionately female), to devote themselves full-time to the resolution of domestic problems (reported by Mirta Rodríguez Calderón in the Seminar on the Family in Crosscultural Perspective at the University

of Havana, April 1994). This was certainly true during the tense summer months of 1993 and 1994, which were plagued by scheduled and unscheduled blackouts, shortages in both food and cooking oil, and children on vacation who, with television hours cut back, had little to do to occupy themselves.

13. Percentages for female-headed households vary from 19.7 percent (Reca et al. 1990) to 28. 1 percent (Safa 1995) of the total number of households. Both of these calculations are derived from the 1981 census, and both indicate a substantial increase from the 1953 census. In the Reca study, in 1953, 9.6 percent of households were female-headed. Safa puts the figure at 14 percent. The differences between these two studies may be the result of variations in the definition of who qualifies as a head of household. In her calculations (and in her study of the Aranguanabo textile workers), Safa includes as female heads of households women with their parents and their children under a single roof. Indeed, Safa finds few heads of household who live on their own with their children.

14. When *paladares* were legalized for the second time in June 1995, the state imposed monthly fees for licenses—in effect, taxes—for self-employment. While most can be paid in pesos, *paladares* must pay in dollars—from $100 to $300 each month, depending on the services provided in terms of liquor and food—to be determined by municipal authorities. These fees have now risen and been made more complex and confusing. Given these taxes, it is safe to assume that the legalization of *paladares* will do little to stem the movement of smaller food providers into the unlicensed, illegal informal economy.

15. By February 1994, 135 categories of *por cuenta propria* work had been licensed. The occupations for which licenses were most requested included taxicab drivers, artisanry, carpentry, hairdressers, shoe cleaning, manicurists, and barbers (*Bohemia*, April 1, 1994). Although breakdowns in terms of gender are not available, visual and anecdotal evidence drawn from across the island testifies to the fact that with the exception of food provision and artisanry (which are both male and female terrain), men overwhelmingly dominate those professions—taxicab drivers, carpentry—which are potentially the most profitable.

16. The Federation of Cuban Women estimates that there are some 2,000 prostitutes operating mainly in Havana around the hotel and tourist districts (reported at the Seminar on Women in Cuba, University of Florida, Gainesville, March 1994). Although this figure seems low, the numbers are difficult to calculate, since the line separating young people attracted to the action, the glitz, and the material abundance of the tourist sector and the dollar economy from those actually working that economy as prostitutes is fuzzy.

17. This fact is hardly unique to the Cuban experience; it characterizes, in general, the entire study of women in what were called socialist societies. Maxine Molyneux (1990), one of the few scholars who has attempted cross-cultural analyses of women in former or present socialist societies based in significant part upon her own primary research, has hypothesized that the reason for this has to do with the fact that literature

on women in socialist societies "remained very much outside the mainstream theoretical debates about gender relations and the state as a whole." In Cuba the area of possible exception to this rule has centered on discussions of homosexuality (see in particular, Arguelles and Rich 1984, 1985 Young 1981, and Lumsden 1985).

18. The practice of using fieldwork in communities of exiles which formed in the years immediately following the revolution as a measure of prerevolutionary hegemonic values and attitudes parallels the use made by China scholars of Marjory Wolf's classic *Women and the Family in Rural Taiwan* (1972).

19. In using *Cecilia Valdes* we are keeping in mind Moreno Fraginals's injunction (1983) about treating the novel as historical fact.

REFERENCES

Aguilar, Carolina, and Rita Maria Pereira, 1994. "El Periodo Especial y la Vida Cotidiana: Desaflos de las Cubanas de los 90." Paper presented at the Latin American Studies Association meetings, Atlanta, March.

Arguelles, Lourdes, and B. Ruby Rich, 1984, 1985. "Homosexuality, Homophobia, and Revolution: Notes toward an Understanding of the Cuban Lesbian and Gay Male Experience." Part 1: *Signs* 9:4, pp. 683–699; part 2: *Signs* 11:1, pp. 120–136.

Bauman Zygmunt, 1992. "Living without an Alternative." *Political Quarterly*, January-March.

Bengelsdorf, Carollee, 1988. "On the Problem of Studying Women in Cuba." In Andrew Zimbalist, editor, *Cuban Political Economy* (Boulder: Westview).

———, 1994. *The Problem of Democracy in Cuba: Between Vision and Reality* (New York: Oxford University Press).

Bunck, Julie Marie, 1994. "Castro and the Goal of Sexual Equality." In Bunck, *Fidel Castro and the Quest for a Revolutionary Culture in Cuba* (University Park: Pennsylvania State University Press).

Burton, Julianne, 1981. "Seeing, Being Seen: Portrait of Teresa, or the Contradictions of Sexual Politics in Contemporary Cuba." *Social Text* 4 (Fall 1988), pp. 79–95.

Carranza, Julio, and Pedro Monreal, 1995. *Cuba: La Restructuración de la Economía* (Havana: Ciencias Sociales).

Casal, Lourdes, 1980. "Revolution and Conciencia: Women in Cuba." In Carol Berkin and Clara Lovett, editors, *Women, War and Revolution* (New York: Holmes and Meier).

Catasus, Sonia, 1994. "Características, Sociodemográficas y Reproductivas de la Mujer Cubana." Paper presented at the Latin American Studies Association meetings, Atlanta, March.

————, et al., 1988 *Cuban Women: Changing Roles and Population Trends* (Geneva).

Croll, Elizabeth, 1982. "Women in Rural Production and Reproduction in the Soviet Union, China, Cuba and Tanzania." *Signs* 7:2 (Winter).

Deere, Carmen Diana, 1986. "Rural Women and Agrarian Reform in Peru, Chile and Cuba." In Nash and Safa, editors, *Women and Change in Latin America* (South Hadley: Bergin and Garvey).

————, 1992. "Cuba's Struggle for Self Sufficiency." *Monthly Review*, July–August.

De la Torre Mulhare, Mirta, 1969. "Sexual Ideology in Pre-Castro Cuba: A Cultural Analysis." Ph.D. dissertation, University of Pittsburgh Department of Anthropology.

Diaz, Elena, 1994. "Mujer Cubana: Desarollo Social y Participación." Paper presented at Latin American Studies Association meeting, Atlanta, March.

Dilla, Haroldo, Gerardo Gonzalez, and Ana Vincentelli, 1991. "Participación y Desarrollo en los Municipios Cubanos" (Havana: CEA).

Dominguez, Jorge, 1978. *Cuba: Order and Revolution* (Cambridge: Belknap Press).

Dominguez, Virginia, 1987. "Sex, Gender and Revolution: The Problem of Construction and the Construction of a Problem." *Cuban Studies/Estudios Cubanos* 18.

Engels, Frederick, 1972. *The Origins of the Family, Private Property and the State* (New York: International Publishers).

Fernandez, Nadine, 1994. "Romance in Black and White: Interracial Couples in Cuban Youth." Paper presented at Latin American Studies Association meetings, Atlanta, March.

Fox, Geoffrey, 1973. "Honor, Shame and Women's Liberation in Cuba." In Ann Pescatello, editor, *Male and Female in Latin America* (Pittsburgh: University of Pittsburgh Press).

Funk, Nanette, 1990. "Dossier on Women in Eastern Europe." *Social Text* 9, no.27.

Fuszara, Malgorzata, 1991. "Legal Regulation of Abortion in Poland." *Signs* 17, no.1. (Autumn).

Gonzalez, Reynaldo, 1983. *Contradanzas y Latigazos* (Havana: Editorial Letras Cubanas).

Gotkowitz, Laura, and Richard Turits, 1988. "Socialist Morality: Sexual Preference, Family and State Intervention in Cuba." *Socialism and Democracy* 6 (Spring–Summer).

Guttman, Herbert, 1976. *The Black Family in Slavery and Freedom 1750–1925* (New York: Random House).

Johnson, Kay Ann, 1983. *Women, the Family and Peasant Revolution in China* (Chicago: University of Chicago Press).

Kaufman Purcell, Susan, 1973. "Modernizing Women for a Modern Society: The Cuban Case." In Ann Pescatello, editor, *Female and Male in Latin America* (Pittsburgh: University of Pittsburgh Press).

Kutzinski, Vera, 1994. *Sugar's Secrets: Race and the Erotics of Cuban Nationalism* (Charlottesville: University Press of Virginia).

Larguia, Isabel, and John Dumoulin, 1986. "Women's Equality and the Cuban Revolution." In Nash and Safa, editors, *Women and Change in Latin America* (South Hadley: Bergin and Garvey).

Lutjens, Sheryl, 1995. "Reading between the Lines: Women, the State and Rectification." *Latin American Perspectives.*

———, 1994. "Remaking the Public Sphere: Women and Revolution in Cuba." In Tetrault, editor, *Women and Revolution in Africa, Asia and the New World* (Columbia: University of South Carolina Press).

———, 1992. "Women and the Socialist State: Feminist Questions, Cuban Answers." Manuscript.

Martinez-Alier, Verena [Stolcke], 1974. *Marriage, Class and Colour in Nineteenth-Century Cuba* (London: Cambridge University Press).

Mesa-Lago, Carmelo, 1993. "Cuba's Economic Policies and Strategies for Confronting the Crisis." In Mesa-Lago, editor, *Cuba after the Cold War* (Pittsburgh: University of Pittsburgh Press).

Molyneux, Maxine, 1981. "Socialist Societies Old and New: Progress towards Women's Emancipation." *Feminist Review* 8 (Summer).

———, 1990. "The 'Women Question' in the Age of Perestroika." *New Left Review* 183 (September).

Moreno Fraginals, Mario, 1964. *El Ingenio: El Compleio Economico Social Cubano del Azucar* (Havana: Comision Nacional Cubana de la UNESCO).

———, 1983. "Apendice Valorativo." In Reynaldo Gonzalez, *Contradanzas y Latigazos* (Havana: Editorial Letras Cubanas).

Nazzari, Muriel, 1989. "The 'Women Question' in Cuba: An Analysis of Material Constraints on its Resolution." In Kruks, Rapp, and Young, editors, *Promissory Notes: Women in the Transition to Socialism* (New York: Monthly Review Press).

Pastor, Manuel, and Andrew Zimbalist, 1995. "Waiting for Change: Adjustment and Reform in Cuba." *World Development.*

Pateman, Carole, 1989. "The Fraternal Social Contract." In Pateman, *The Disorder of Women: Democracy, Feminism and Political Theory* (Stanford: Stanford University Press).

Perez, Louis Jr., editor, 1992. *Slaves, Sugar, and Colonial Society: Travel Accounts of Cuba 1801–1899* (Scholarly Resources).

Perez-Stable, Marifeli, 1987. "Cuban Women and the Struggle for 'Conciencia.' " *Cuban Studies/Estudios Cubanos* 17.

Poumier-Taquechel, Maria, 1975. *Apuntes sobre la Vida Cotidiana en Cuba en 1898* (Havana: Editorial de Ciencias Sociales).

Rainwater, Lee, and William Yancey, editors, 1967. *The Moynihan Report and the Politics of Controversy* (Cambridge: MIT Press).

Ravenet Ramirez, Mariana, Niurka Perez Rojas, and Marta Toledo Fraga, 1989. *La Mujer Rural y Urbana: Estudios de Casos* (Havana: Editorial de Ciencias Sociales).

Reca, Ines, 1992. "Social Policy and the Family in Socialist Cuba." In CEA, editors, *The Cuban Revolution in the 1990s* (Boulder: Westview).

———, et al., 1990. *Análisis de las Investigaciones sobre la Familia Cubana 1970–1987* (Havana: Editorial de Ciencias Sociales).

Rosenberg, Dorothy, 1991. "Shock Therapy: GDR Women in Transition from a Socialist Welfare State to a Market Economy." *Signs* 17, no.1.

Rubin, Gayle, 1976. "The Traffic in Women." In Rayna Reiter, editor, *Toward an Anthropology of Women's Liberation* (Stanford: Stanford University Press).

Safa, Helen Icken, 1995. *The Myth of the Male Breadwinner: Women and Industrialization in the Caribbean* (Boulder: Westview).

Sayers, Janet, et al., eds. 1987. *Engels Revisited: New Feminist Essays* (London: Tavistock).

Scott, Rebecca, 1985. *Slave Emancipation in Cuba* (Princeton: Princeton University Press).

Smith, Lois, and Alfred Padula, 1990. "The Cuban Family in the 1980s." In Halebsky and Kirk, editors, *Transformation and Struggle: Cuba Faces the 1990's* (Westport: Praeger).

Stack, Carol, 1974. "Sex Roles and Survival Strategies in an Urban Black Community." In Rosaldo and Lamphere, editors, *Women, Culture and Society* (Stanford: Stanford University Press).

Stone, Elizabeth, editor, 1981. *Women and the Cuban Revolution* (New York: Pathfinder).

Stoner, K. Lynn, 1991. *From the House to the Street: The Cuban Women's Movement for Legal Reform, 1898–1940* (Durham: Duke University Press).

Stubbs, Jean, and Pedro Perez Sarduy, 1993. *AfroCuba* (Australia: Ocean Press).

Tesoro, Susana y Alberto Salazar, 1994. "Harina de Otro Costal," *Bohemia* 1 de Abril.

Withers Osmond, Marie, 1985. "Women, Work and Family in Cuba," Paper presented at the American Sociological Association, Washington.

Wolf, Marjory, 1972. *Women and the Family in Rural Taiwan* (Stanford: Stanford University Press).

Young, Allen, 1981. *Gays under the Cuban Revolution* (San Francisco: Grey Fox Press).

V

WOMEN AND POPULAR CULTURE

"ASÍ SON"

Salsa Music, Female Narratives, and Gender (De)Construction in Puerto Rico

FRANCES APARICIO

Así son, así son las mujeres
Así son, así son cuando se quieren
(Such, such are women
Such are women when you love them)
EL GRAN COMBO DE PUERTO RICO

Quiero que recuerdes para siempre
el momento aquel en que te hice mujer
(I want you to remember always
that moment when I made you woman)
WILLIE COLÓN

FOR ALL OF US in every culture, but particularly in the Caribbean, music has been a strong influence in our formative years, and both song lyrics and the social practice of dancing have had a tremendous impact on the formation of our sexuality. Whispering romantic *boleros* while dancing to their slow melodies, and moving to the fast rhythms of salsa and merengues constitute an important part of my memories of growing up *puertorriqueña*. Indeed, popular music is an important cultural vehicle in defining gender in the Caribbean. Sexual politics also come into play, as popular music reproduces the struggles between men and women in a contemporary urban world where gender identities and sexual roles are being drastically transformed.

This chapter is an exercise in listening woman and listening as a woman. The former posits the task of reading women's representation in Latin popular music, "both the ways in which women are figured . . . and the ways in which such figuring gives representation its force by repressing female desire" (Caughie 1988: 328). The point of listening as a woman is "to challenge masculine appeals to legitimate (textual) meanings and legitimate (sexual) identities." (326) It implies a rereading and a deconstructive stance, "the undoing of ideas about women and meaning elaborated in male discourse" (327; see also Jacobus 1986: 30). While listening woman may suggest a unidirectional mode of categorizing stereotypes and images of women in masculine discourse, my listening as woman, like Showalter's gynocritique, goes beyond an enumerative practice, questioning the very processes of representation and reading.

Listening woman supersedes the "images of women" methodology of the 1970s, which over time has proven static and unidimensional. While twenty years ago this method became the core approach of one of Anglo-American feminism's most urgent imperatives (that of decoding and denouncing literary figurations of women by male authors), in practice many of these analyses were based on the simplistic assumption that texts "reflect" reality, leading to mere psychological or descriptive comments on female characters. In their attempts to uncover women as literary objects, many female critics implicitly reproduced this function. Unfortunately, this flaw was also quite common in the context of Latin American scholarship on women (Jaquette 1973). And it still is. Neyssa Palmer, in her analysis of female characters in the Puerto Rican narrative of the 1940s and 1950s, exemplifies the dangers of this approach:

> Todas estas vidas son trágicas, responden al mundo brutal e injusto que encuentran a su paso, sin otra alternativa que la resignación, pero no hay en ellas degradación moral alguna. Por el contrario, el dolor las enaltece. A través del proceder que develan como personajes, percibimos el profundo conocimiento que posee González de la conducta y reacciones que observa la mujer puertorriqueña frente a la adversidad. (Palmer 1988: 27)
> (All of these [women's] lives are tragic, they respond to the brutal and unjust world around them; they have no other choice but to resign themselves, although there is no moral degradation. On the contrary, *pain exalts them.* Throughout their behavior as characters, we perceive the author's [González] profound knowledge *of the behavior and reactions of Puerto Rican women in the midst of adversity.*) (My own emphasis)

The italicized statement illustrates the ways in which this hermeneutic praxis bypasses the text as a literary construct and insists on a direct correspondence between fiction and reality, what Toril Moi has referred to as "excessive referentialism" (Moi 1985 [1990]: 45). Palmer, indeed, does not take into account that female representation—and by and large any representation—results from the textualization of a constellation of factors such as gender, race, class, and ideology. She does not problematize the process of defining a fixed gender identity for women as well as for men; in fact, she participates in fixing gender identity, in naturalizing women's emotions, even in ascribing patriarchal values to those emotions ("Pain exalts them").

Despite isolated attempts to raise the issue of women's representation in Caribbean popular music and in salsa (Fernández Mirallés 1979; Malavet Vega 1987), salsa lyrics have remained virtually uncontested by women musicians, singers, listeners, and critics. However, two contemporary Puerto Rican women authors, Ana Lydia Vega and Carmen Lugo Filippi, have dismantled constructions of women in salsa in a short story entitled "Cuatro selecciones por una peseta" (Four selections for a quarter) (Vega and Filippi 1983: 127–137). Two women authors, themselves avid readers/listeners of salsa, create four male characters who, while listening to Latin popular music, utter (as authors) their own diatribes against women. The underlying irony in the narrator's voice and the parodic inscription of musical and phallocentric discourses allow this text to participate in the questioning of patriarchal models of being and of social constructs of the feminine. Thus as authors and narrators Vega and Filippi deploy a feminist politics of listening to salsa; they listen woman and they listen as women, undoing and rewriting patriarchal salsa lyrics from a female-centered perspective.

Before analyzing this short story, it is essential to examine salsa music as popular culture and the hermeneutic challenges it proposes for gender studies. Salsa music is a syncretic artistic form born in the Latino barrios of New York City. A conjunction of Afro-Cuban music (el son) and rhythms, of Puerto Rican bombas and plenas, and of African American jazz instrumentation and structures, salsa music has become the quintessential musical marker of *latinidad* in the United States and in Latin America. Not to be conflated with Latin jazz or tropical music—mambo and cha cha chá—salsa is a musical form developed mostly by a Latino proletariat *farándula* (composers, singers, and instrumentalists) (Rondón 1980). As such, it documents and articulates the needs, desires, and perspectives of the Latino working class, of blacks, and of life in the urban barrios of America (from New York to Colombia and Perú). Like other forms of commodified popular culture, salsa music is highly contradictory. While it reaffirms a pan-Latino cultural resistance within the United

States and in that sense can be deemed politically progressive, it simultaneously participates in the patriarchal system of both Latino and North American cultures.

Salsa is produced within a male-dominated music industry. While I agree with Félix Padilla that salsa "results from the interplay between hegemonic determinations on the part of owners of the Latin music recording industry and cultural creative responses by individual musicians" (Padilla 1990: 87), its position as a commercial product under a capitalist superstructure and under a male-dominated industry has excluded women from the areas of production and composition. While some female interpreters have been key figures in the development and popularity of salsa (e.g., Celia Cruz) and recently in the merengue (Sonia López; Milly y los Vecinos; Mayra, Celinés y Flor de Caña; Chantelle; Las Chicas del Can), these women mostly vocalize texts written by men, thus reaffirming the monopoly of patriarchal perspectives and of the male as writing subject.

Nevertheless, the very presence of female interpreters proposes a significantly different listening practice from that of songs uttered by males. When women sing sexist lyrics, the object of the sexism is reversed. It is empowering for many women listeners to see women performers on stage or to listen to female voices on the radio as articulations of a female subjectivity.

Yet why is it that the most recent incorporation of women singers into the music industry has not, as yet, resulted in the dismantling of patriarchal lyrics? While the Cuban singer Celia Cruz has included a number of songs in defense of women—for example, "Las divorciadas" (The divorced women, 1985)—her repertoire in general has not had an impact on Latin women's issues. Indeed, many songs interpreted by women perpetuate fixed gender identities. Milly y los Vecinos in "Ese hombre" (That man, 1990) and Sonia López y su Combo in "Castígalo" (Punish him, not dated) establish gender identities based on dual and oppositional structures—male versus female—that clearly articulate a battle between the sexes. While Anglo feminism may dismiss these songs as examples of gender oppression, in my opinion they must be understood within the cultural, social, and historical contexts of sexual relations in Puerto Rican society. These songs are valuable insofar as they eloquently articulate the struggles of Puerto Rican and Latina women to empower themselves by contesting the dictates of a strong patriarchal system.

The song "Mentira" (Lies) by Mayra and Celinés initially seems to condemn the male subject as liar and traitor, yet its refrain—"estúpida soy" (I am stupid)—reiterates the woman's naiveté for trusting him. Instead of truly inverting the stereotype of the treacherous woman, it reinscribes the construct of woman's lack of knowledge and power, of her supposed "stupidity." That the composer of "Mentira" is Carlo de la Cima partly reveals why these singers are not yet articulating the needs and desires of "real" women.

Another gender-related contradiction in salsa music stands out. Two very progressive salsa composers, Willie Colón and Rubén Blades, who are independent producers, have addressed contemporary issues such as homosexuality and AIDS—(e.g., Willie Colón's recent hit "El gran varón" (The great male, 1989)—yet have not consistently dealt with the situation of women in Latin America. Rubén Blades's "Ligia Elena" (1983), a popular hit in its time, narrates the story of a white, upper-class young woman who elopes with a black trumpet player to the dismay of her family. This song was an initial step in the right direction, yet it still remains an isolated case. Blades's most recent album, *Caminando* (Walking, 1991), suggests that the Panamanian composer's interest in women's issues is on the wane. While most of the songs signal a return to his most politically progressive and denunciatory modes, including a sensitive defense of repressed homosexuality ("El" [He]), the only piece in the album which focuses on women, "Ella se esconde" (She hides), constructs woman as traitor and as *bandolera* (bandit woman), thus uncritically perpetuating the tradition of misogyny in Latin popular music.

The predominance of male composers, singers, and producers is in direct causal relationship to the phallocentric tradition of salsa lyrics, yet it does not constitute an explanation in and of itself. The sociocultural analogy—that machismo is inherent in Latin American culture and therefore popular music reflects machismo values—cannot be held responsible either. The "New Song Movement" is also a cultural product of Latin America, yet its radical ideology, its counterdiscursive stance, and its identification with oppressed groups have allowed for a stronger position on behalf of women's rights, notwithstanding songs that still belittle women in subtle ways. Thus a complex of cultural, economic, and ideological factors come into play when examining the patriarchal positioning of salsa music.

Andreas Huyssen has claimed that the "gendering of mass culture as feminine and inferior," a social, political, and aesthetic project that originated in the late nineteenth century, has become obsolete with the decline of modernism and with the "visible and public presence of women artists in high art, as well as the emergence of new kinds of women performers and producers in mass culture" (1986: 62). This is not the case in salsa and Caribbean popular music. While these musical forms—salsa and merengues—obviously address both male and female audiences as dance music, Puerto Rico's urban musical culture reveals a male-dominated ideal audience. The schism between the *rockeros*, white upper- and middle-class young males who prefer United States and British rock and roll, and the *cocolos*, black and working-class males who listen to salsa, centers on the young male culture. Indeed, the role of entertainment and "escape" ascribed to expressions of popular culture and the ensuing trivialization to which the lyrics and the contents of popular songs are submitted facilitate salsa's patriarchal production and its fast consumption. Owing to this expectation of "escape," men and women listen to Latin popular music "easily" or superficially at dances, as background music, and while driving. We enjoy its rhythms and its interpreters, but many times the lyrics are dispensable to us as receptors, that is, one song could easily replace another. On the other hand, the "disgust for the facile" on the part of scholarship and the educational system directed at popular music is analogous to the social construct of the "easy woman" (Fiske 1989: 121–122; Bourdieu 1984: 486–488). Thus women and lyrics, as signifiers, are trivialized and reduced to univalent objects of consumerism. This prevents salsa songs from assuming a major role as oppositional cultural and social voices. The condescending attitudes toward popular music and the concomitant superficial readings are still signs of the interaction of the modernist "great divide" between high art and mass culture (Huyssen 1986). Moreover, these readings actualize class prejudices. By assuming that all salsa songs are "easy" listening, scholars undervalue the cultural and economic realities of the working class from which they arise.

As to gender-based reception, why have salsa lyrics remained virtually untransformed by feminist social changes? Where are the feminist listeners? Why do women listeners, including feminists such as Vega, Filippi, and myself, enjoy salsa as much as men do despite its patriarchal and misogynist discourse? To answer these questions, it is not enough to examine (and decode) the "ways in which primarily male structures of power are inscribed (or encoded) within our [musical] inheritance," to use Annette Kolodny's words in "Dancing through the Minefield" (1985: 162). In order to really examine the sexual politics of salsa, the ways in which the "discourses which comprise it [reproduce] a struggle equivalent to that experienced socially by its readers" (Fiske 1989: 168), we must consider the dialogic texture of female responses (whether in songs, narratives, or conversations) and the social practice of listening and dancing to salsa, that is, its reception by female and feminist audiences. In other words, a profound gender analysis of salsa must not stop at a denunciation of the absence of the female subject and of the ensuing masculine monologue. As Shelagh Young has posited in her probing analysis of Madonna and feminism:

> we still need to look more closely at the internal contradictions and tensions that affect feminism's relation to popular culture. If feminism is to remain a radical or subversive political force women cannot afford to simply emulate either the old Left's dismissive disdain for mass culture or the new Left's apparently indiscriminate endorsement of anything that appears to be popular. (1989: 177–178)

To this we add the urgency of documenting the voices of working-class Puerto Rican women and their attitudes toward salsa music, a music many of them have listened to growing up in the urban ghettos in San Juan and New York. The views of educated upper- and middle-class *puertorriqueñas* should be considered as well. That these listening practices have not been documented is not a reflection of the assumed passivity with which women listen to patriarchal lyrics but a sign of the elitist disdain toward working-class and female realities. Theoretically, the postmortem approach suggested by Young (1989: 182) would allow for the existence of multiple female subjectivities, thus helping to explain the gaps between feminist listenings of/against salsa (informed by Anglo norms) and the simultaneous acceptance and enjoyment of this music by many Latina women.

A possible venue for the problem of reception is that proposed by John Fiske in *Understanding Popular Culture* (1989). Fiske's thesis is that popular culture "is to be found in its practices, not in its texts or their readers" (45). Contesting the Frankfurt School's vision of mass media as a unilateral vehicle for the ideological forces of domination and of the masses as passive receptors, Fiske approaches popular culture as praxis, as a semiotic exchange between producers and consumers. Indeed, Fiske defines readers/viewers/listeners not as consumers but as "cultural producers" (151) insofar as they activate the "circulation of meanings" in which popular culture consists. His concept of "productive pleasures" is particularly relevant for the problematics of women and Salsa.

For Fiske, productive pleasure is that "pleasure which results from [a] mix of productivity, relevance, and functionality, which is to say that the meanings I make from a text are pleasurable when I feel that they are my meanings and that they relate to my everyday life in a practical, direct way" (57). Thus the receptors of popular culture are empowered by assuming this active role in the process of signification. This also implies that popular texts are polysemic, thus allowing for different and even contradictory meanings to be produced from one text by different readers/listeners.

While Fiske calls attention to the power of the proletariat in creating other meanings from popular texts, his definition of *relevance* proves rather disconcerting when he adds that however we might wish to change the social meanings and textual representations of, say, women or nonwhite races, such changes can only be slow and evolutionary, not radical and revolutionary, if the texts are to remain popular (133). Fiske's interest in explaining the progressive nature of popular culture—its lack of revolutionary potential—leads him to participate in the idea that the proletariat is ultimately patriarchal. This assumption implies, moreover, that the listeners/readers/viewers comprise a monolithic group that identifies with the systems of power. For popular culture to be "popular," it "can never be radically free from the power structure of the society within which it is popular" (134). My contention is that Fiske does not recognize the potential of the media and of music to reach vast audiences and to suggest new modes of consciousness (what the "Nueva Canción," Rubén Blades, Willie Colón, and others have partially achieved).

Despite these reservations, Fiske's concept of productive pleasure helps us approach the question of female reception. As a female reader and listener of salsa, I find many of the lyrics relevant to my own social and personal situation as a Latina. The discursive repertoire, the persuasive strategies, and the rhetorics of love exhibited in salsa songs are, in many cases, analogous to those used by Latino males in personal and romantic relationships. What I am suggesting is that perhaps the "relevance" of salsa music for women resides not in the lyrics themselves but in the ways in which repetitive listening experiences may allow female listeners to reread and reconstruct their own sexual identities and their own relationships to males against the misogynist grain. This liberatory listening, however, may be a function of time, age, and perhaps generation. A woman reflecting on her past may be able to engage in this type of rereading. For a young woman, however, listening to salsa lyrics engages her as a reader of male sexual codes and makes her a participant in a specific musico-cultural "interpretive community" (Radway 1991: 468–470). As such, her capacity to decode male signifiers and sexual puns in the fictive space of music allows her also to decode male language in real life. In this respect, my role as a cultural and feminist critic is to foster a politics of listening to salsa by which women, young and older, acquire an awareness of the ways that the discourse of love, desire, and pleasure are social constructs created by a patriarchal society.

Through this politics of listening and the ensuing critical dialogue established among male composers, feminist critics, and women listeners, a reflexive meta-language flourishes, allowing for the possibility of deconstructing these codes within our own lives.

Let me summarize at this point some of the comments and observations gathered from my interviews of Latina women. I have interviewed twenty women—ten Latina students at the University of Michigan and ten working-class Latinas from Detroit and southeastern Michigan. The interview format consisted of questions about two salsa songs I play for the interviewee: Willie Colón's "Cuando fuiste mujer" (When you became woman) and El Gran Combo's "Así son" (Such are women). It was obvious that young Latina students from upper- and middle-class backgrounds overtly reject salsa on the grounds of its sexism, yet they ascribe these patriarchal values to the "vulgarity," machismo, and lack of education of working-class men (salsa composers and singers). They suggest distinctions between the values of these men and the positions and attitudes of men in their families and within their own educational background. I also observed that for many of these Latinas, salsa—as a marker of national and ethnic identity—ironically has become more culturally significant during their stay in the United States. In other words, they have valued the cultural role of salsa music in their own experiences of displacement and ethnification as recent "migrants." Working-class Latinas systematically accept salsa music as their own and have a knowledge of its history. They overtly state its importance as a cultural marker in their own migration and separation from the island. However, they also exhibit a stronger praxis of "liberatory listening" than do their middle-class counterparts. Most young working-class Latinas reacted in positive ways to these two patriarchal songs because they "selected" those aspects of the love stories that reaffirmed their own sense of independence from men. At the same time, the songs allowed them the space to discuss the negative aspects of male behavior, the double standards, and other issues that they all related to their own personal lives. In other words, they deconstructed sexual roles and masculine constructions of the feminine in texts that articulate just the opposite. This is a clear example of productive pleasure, whereby the woman listener creates her own meanings from a popular text. Even further, she produces a reading that opposes the ideology of the song. This is precisely what Vega and Filippi achieve in the short story "Cuatro selecciones por una peseta." By inserting musical intertexts from salsa into their story, Vega and Filippi position themselves as writing subjects who are simultaneously female listeners/readers of salsa. Through feminist writing strategies of ironic humor and parody, they deconstruct (in the sense of dismantling, undoing) the lyrics that have permeated the lives and loves of their four male characters and of all of us who listen to salsa.

Constructing Gender

Despite the contending ideologemes that salsa contains—patriarchal lyrics, love songs, Christian themes, eroticism, politically progressive texts, nostalgic issues of migration, urban life, reaffirmation of race and ethnicity, AIDS, and so on—this syncretic music has consistently articulated patriarchal and misogynistic attitudes toward women. Many salsa songs express gender-based violence; Héctor Lavoe (1978) sings to a woman in "Bandolera," "te voy a dar una pela / pa' que aprendas a querer / pum pum pum" (I am going to hit you so you may learn to love), and Daniel Santos (1974) sings, "Yo la mato o pide perdón" (Either I kill her or she asks forgiveness). The male desire for violence against women is "naturalized" through utterances such as the following: "mira qué cosas tiene la vida" (that's the way life is, Santos 1974). While "yo la mato" is based on the literalization of a Hispanic colloquialism, the naturalizing effect exonerates the male subject from any responsibility for his expressions of violence. It may be surprising for some readers to note that "Yo la mato" is a *guaracha* written by Don Pedro Flores, the Puerto Rican composer of such Latin American lyrical favorites as "Amor," "Linda," and "Bajo un palmar."

The configurations of feminine identity in salsa are centered on negatively charged images, figures drawn from a topical repertoire rooted in Hispanic and European traditions. The "bandolera" that constantly reappears in salsa songs, for instance, is a figure that can be traced back to European medieval culture. This "bandolera" myth unfolds onto various other textualizations of what could be called the economics of love. (1) The relationship established by the male between love and money, in which the woman is accused of stealing the man's property (Lavoe's "Bandolera," "me buscaste en los bolsillos" [you searched my pockets]), including his heart (Pedro Conga's "Ladrona de amor" [Burglar of Love] (on *No te quites la ropa*, not dated). (2) In Rubén Blades's "Ella se esconde" (She hides, 1991), woman is never to be trusted, for her real self hides behind her smile. This construct of the treacherous woman, an expression of the archetypal association of woman as mystery, ramifies into metaphors of witches and witchcraft (listen to El Gran Combo's "Brujería" [Witchcraft] (1979) and suggests that women cannot be properly read; our bodies and our gestures are signifiers that inexorably lead to misreadings by the male interpreter. (3) In other thematic ramifications of this feminine construct, women appear as merchandise or property to be acquired (through marriage or prostitution).

Other common stereotypes include the dual construct of the promiscuous and sexually superendowed black or mulatta, on one hand, and the adoration of the mother figure and of the virginal female on the other. These figurations are not exclusive to salsa, for they abound in the literature of Hispanic countries as well as in the folklore and literary expressions of other Western countries (Herrera-Sobek, 1990). As Sander Gilman has pointed out, the building of stereotypes "perpetuate[s] a needed sense of difference between the 'Self' and the 'object,' which becomes the 'Other.' Because there is no real line between self and the Other, an imaginary line must be drawn; and so that the illusion of an absolute difference between self and Other is never troubled, this line is as dynamic in its ability to alter itself as is the self" (Gilman 1985: 17–18). This basic need, argues Gilman, leads to the construction of what Stephen Pepper has called "root metaphors," "a set of categories which result from our attempt to understand other areas in terms of one commonsense fact" (22). By establishing analogical values between real-life experiences and the world of myths, stereotypes are associations that may lead to "negative images" or "positive idealizations" (25). At these two poles, indeed, women are positioned and represented within the Hispanic culture.

There is, however, another mode of textualizing women that differs from the above-mentioned stereotypes and figurations. Gender constructions can be found at three levels: first, in the misogynous and violence-laden utterances; second, in stereotypes and images, as we have already summarized; and third, in the power of the male writing subject to concretely articulate the "nature" of womanliness or of the feminine. That is, the power socially and linguistically invested in the male composer/author to create the female. How do men, then, "construct" woman as song (text)?

A discourse analysis of a song by Willie Colón entitled "Cuando fuiste mujer" (Colón 1990) better illustrates this third and most subtle form of gender construction. To listen woman in this song is not enough; it necessitates to be listened as a woman, to be decoded. Its lyrical melody and harmonies informed by the bolero and its "romantic" lyrics establish its condition as "marked writing," what Hélène Cixous has defined as phallologocentrism "hidden or adorned with the mystifying charms of fiction [of lyricism, in this case]" (1980: 249). This is precisely why I have chosen this text as an object of deconstruction. Not only do its lyrics exemplify gender construction at its best, but also its musicality, the slow tempo, and its lyrical tone "plugged" its melody inside my head. I found myself during the summer humming the song over and over again. Its melody is wonderfully and dangerously "seductive."

Cuando fuiste mujer

Conmigo aprendiste a querer y a saber de la vida
Y a fuerzas de tantas caricias tu cuerpo formé.
Tu rostro de pálida seda cambió sus matices
Se tiñó de rubor cuando fuiste mujer, fuiste mujer.
Sentía tu cuerpo temblar sin la noche estar fría
Sentía tu cuerpo vibrar en la noche que ardía.
Sintiendo el gemir de tu amor que me dio su tibieza
Hice mío tu amor cuando fuiste mujer, fuiste mujer.
Quiero que tú sigas siendo niña
aunque en tu alma seas toda mujer
quiero que tu alma y la mía
se unan por amor formando un nuevo ser.

Quiero que tú nunca más te olvides
de tus sentimientos, de tu forma de ser
Quiero que recuerdes para siempre
el momento aquel en que te hice mujer
y fuiste mujer y eres mujer.

CORO: Quiero que tú nunca más te olvides
SOLO: No te olvides del amor que compartimos debajo de la luna cuando dije
        entre mí como esa mami no hay una
CORO: Quiero que tú nunca más te olvides
SOLO: Que comigo aprendiste las cosas de la vida esa noche te juro nunca se
        me olvida
CORO: Quiero que tú nunca más te olvides
SOLO: Quiero que tú sigas siendo niña aunque en tu alma seas toda una mujer
CORO: Quiero . . .
SOLO: que tu alma y la mía se unan por amor formando un solo ser
CORO: Quiero que tú nunca más te olvides
SOLO: Mi recuerdo te desvela, soy el ansia que te llega nunca podrás olvidar lo
        que te enseñé
CORO: Quiero que tú nunca más te olvides
SOLO: Pregunta por ahí quién es el que te ama siempre he sido yo, en la vida
        hay amores que no pueden olvidarse, como nuestro amor
CORO: Quiero que tú nunca más te olvides

SOLO: En una noche encendida tú me entregaste tu cuerpo yo te di todo mi
ser . . .
CORO: Quiero que tú nunca más te olvides
SOLO: Cómo temblamos de alegría, jamás yo me olvidaré

When You Became Woman

With me you learned to love and to know about life
And I molded your body with the power of my caresses
Your pale silk face changed its hues
It blushed when you became a woman, became a woman.

I felt your body trembling when the night was not cold.
I felt your body vibrating in the ardent night.
Feeling your moaning love that offered me warmth
I made your love mine when you became a woman, became a woman.

I want you to remain a little girl
even though in your soul you are all woman
I want your soul and mine
to fuse in love and form a new being.

I don't want you to ever forget
your feelings, your way of being.
I want you to always remember
that moment when I made you into a woman
and you were woman and you are woman.

CHORUS: I don't want you to ever forget . . .
SOLO: Don't forget the love we shared in the moonlight when I told myself
there's no other woman like you
CHORUS: I don't want you to ever forget . . .
SOLO: That I taught you about life that night I swear I'll never forget
CHORUS: I dont want you to ever forget . . .
SOLO: I want you to remain being a girl, even though you are a woman in your
soul
CHORUS: I don't want you to ever forget . . .
SOLO: I want your soul and mine to fuse in love and to form a new being
CHORUS
SOLO: You cannot sleep thinking of me, I am the anxiety that you feel, you
could never forget what I taught you
CHORUS
SOLO: Ask others who could love you, I have always loved you, in life there are
certain unforgettable loves, just like our love

CHORUS
SOLO: In this ardent night you surrendered your body, I gave you my whole
being
CHORUS
SOLO: How we both tremble with joy, I will never forget . . .

The male singing subject addresses a *tú* (you), the implied woman and lover, from the position of master. She acquires her knowledge of love and of life and, indeed, her life itself, only through him. The syntactic location of *conmigo* (with me) as the first word of the song establishes the positionality of the male subject as her initial and primary teacher: "Conmigo aprendiste a querer y a saber de la vida" (With me you learned to love and to learn about life). She is like the blank page upon which the pen(is) utters his desire. She is text, he is author. The reference in the third line to her blushing face full of desire under-lines this interpretation of woman as absence. Her desire is born from a lack of knowledge, from an absence of experience. Sexual intercourse with the master is the bridge between her nothingness and her presence, however imperfect this presence may still be for her (a presence tinged with shame: "rubor"). The male singer further articulates his desire for possession and appropriation when he confesses that: "Hice mío tu amor . . . " (I made your love mine), again rein-forcing the masculine "Yo" as the agent that possesses.

In the recurring theme of remembrance and memory of her first sexual ex-perience, "Quiero que recuerdes para siempre . . . " (I want you to remember always . . .), he ascribes eternity to the transitory nature of the encounter. Through the romantic construction of "no me olvides . . . " (don't forget me), the male subject appropriates for himself not only her love and her feelings, also defined by him ("de tus sentimientos, de tu forma de ser," your feelings, your way of being), but their effects on her, his traces throughout her whole life.

Sexual intercourse and phallic penetration are equated with his making her: both symbolize her initiation into womanhood and being. A causal logic un-derlies the polysyndeton: "el momento en que te hice mujer y fuiste mujer y eres mujer" (that moment when I made you woman and you were woman and you are woman). This gender contouring, reminiscent of the myth of Adam's rib, is earlier revealed in the second line when he suggests giving "shape" to her body through his caresses. Yet the contradictions of his love surface in the opening phrase of that line: "Y a fuerzas de tantas caricias tu cuerpo formé" (And I molded your body by the force of my caresses). Though read as figura-tive language, these "fuerzas" relate to "caricias," so that the *caricias forzadas* (forced caresses) reinscribe the power of the male over the female body, his authority to shape it and to get her "in shape." The power relations suggested in these lines reflect the underlying violence and the suppression of female desire on which the sexual politics of salsa are based.

Woman's desire in this song is far from being hers. It is a sexuality born from the outside, from the man's sense of power over her identity, her body, and her life. While the female desire is once alluded to through the male's voice, it is never defined, marked precisely by the absence of a female utterance. Masculine desire, in contrast, is overdetermined in the anaphoric structure of the verses: the "Quiero" that continuously reiterates itself masked under the pretense of "eternal love": "Quiero que recuerdes para siempre . . . " The dialectics of oblivion and remembrance also allow the male power to be reiterated. The structure of the refrain (*estribillo*) constantly articulates the song itself as a memory of his agency and of his power in the female's own development.

Yet the master's desire confronts a central contradiction. While he expects eternal remembrance as her master and author of her womanhood, he does not truly desire her to be a woman. His position as master will eventually become redundant if and when she grows up and becomes a woman. Thus the male singing subject qualifies female growth: it is only her "soul" that develops into womanhood, not her body. He desires her to remain childlike, though he aspires for a spiritual union between both. The metonymic strategy of body/ child soul/woman is repeated at the end of the song, during the *montuno* section in which the singer improvises upon the previous verses. I argue that because of the improvisatory freedom of this section, the *montuno* may be read metaphorically as the sexual unconscious of the male singing subject. Colón also sings in the *montuno*: "tú me entregaste tu cuerpo/yo te di todo mi ser" (you surrendered your body/I gave you my whole self), illustrating the phallic reduction of woman to object ("tu cuerpo"), a sexual metonymy that objectifies women as woman, and that the male subject counterposes to the construction of his self as totality, as wholesome and whole ("todo mi ser"). The last line of the song, "jamás yo me olvidaré" (I will never forget), introduces the male singing subject as an agent of memory. However, the mutuality suggested between the man and the woman in this last utterance has already been undermined and erased throughout the whole song by the constant reiteration of his will.

"Quince años" (sweet sixteen), a song composed by P. Armas and released by El Gran Combo de Puerto Rico (1991), also exemplifies the construction of woman as sign and object of male patriarchal desires. While the pretext of the song is the laudatory celebration of an older male toward the young girl on her fifteenth birthday, her *quinceañera*, the song is a text which subtly constructs the young girl through the male gaze.

Quince Años

En el campo del amor
cuando nace alguna flor hermosa
siempre hay un ruiseñor
que la mira con pasión deseosa . . . (repite)

La fantasía de tus años comenzó
en una flor hay muchos rasgos inocentes
Dios te bendiga bella hoy, mañana y siempre
que el sol que encuentres
cuide siempre tu esplendor
quince años para contar las estrellas
quince años para empezar a vivir
y habrá muchos caminos esperando
para darte acceso al mundo
que te toca dividir
quince años que se amoldan a tu talle
quince años que cumples para sentirte mujer
Recibe de mi parte quince besos
abrazados al cariño
que hoy en ti deposité
Linda flor, si es que las flores
se merecen siempre flores
de los más bellos colores
para formar su vergel.
CORO: Es una flor en sus quince primaveras
SOLO: apenas sus pétalos comienzan a abrir
            ella significa pureza
CORO: Es una flor . . .
SOLO: Sabe Dios lo que le espera en la vida
            Seguro que cosas malas, cosas buenas
CORO: Es una flor . . .
SOLO: Es una flor que nace sin espina
            que cuando florece se ve muy divina
CORO: Es una flor . . .
SOLO: Que Dios tenga guardadas para ti
            cositas bonitas que te hagan feliz
CORO: Es una flor . . .
SOLO: Y quién diría que aquella niña
            una flor hermosa
            pronto será una mujer

Sweet Sixteen

When a beautiful flower is born
in the fields of love
there is always a nightingale
that gazes at her with desire and passion . . . (repeat)

The fantasy of your age just began
A flower has many innocent traits
May God bless you today, tomorrow, and always
May the sun you encounter
always take care of your splendor
Fifteen years to count the stars
Fifteen years to begin to live
and there will be many paths awaiting
to lead you into the world
that you must divide.
Fifteen years that are fitted to your waist
Fifteen years that make you feel like a woman
Receive from me fifteen kisses
embraced to the affection
that I deposit in you today.
Beautiful flower, if flowers
deserve always flowers
of the most beautiful colors
to complete their garden.
CHORUS: She is a flower in her fifteenth Spring
SOLO: Her petals are barely opening up
        she signifies purity
CHORUS: She is a flower . . .
SOLO: Only God knows what awaits her in life
        Surely good things, bad things
CHORUS
SOLO: She is a flower born without thorns
        and when she blooms she looks divine
CHORUS
SOLO: May God have beautiful things stored for you
        that will bring you joy
CHORUS
SOLO: Who would have thought that this girl,
        a beautiful flower, will soon be a woman . . .

As in Willie Colón's "Cuando fuiste mujer," the male singing subject addresses the topic of the female transition from child to womanhood. "Quince
años," however, employs the rhetoric of religion and the patriarchal imagery

of the "flower," a commonplace signifier in debutante balls and *quinceañera* celebrations throughout Latin America. The phrase "Ella significa pureza" ("She means purity") clearly equates young women with the patriarchal value of virginal sexual "purity" that the young girl is supposed to embody. She is a signifier; purity is the signified. Once again, the male writing subject reads young women as woman, as a univalent text.

Singing simultaneously with this patriarchal, fatherly voice is the voice of male desire. While the former praises her youth and innocence and deems to protect the young woman from unhappiness and suffering, the latter sings the male gaze and articulates his desire. This is achieved by (1) the accumulative effect of references to seeing and to the visual shape of her body: "es una flor que se ve muy divina" (she is a flower that looks divine) according to the male *voyeur*, the "ruiseñor/que la mira con pasión deseosa" (the nightingale who gazes at her with desire and passion); (2) the following detail of the female form: "quince años que se amoldan a tu talle" (fifteen years that are fitted to your waist); and (3) the sexual implications of the flower imagery: "apenas sus pétalos comienzan a abrir" (her petals are barely opening up).

Through the processes of *listening woman* in these two songs and of *listening as a woman*, I have only begun to decode the various ways in which the male singing subject in salsa constructs woman as object and sign. Representations of the feminine in salsa are inscribed not only through topics and stereotypical figures but also through a more subtle discourse of male desire that hides behind lyrics dedicated to womanhood.

As interdisciplinary efforts, my readings of these two salsa songs remain "literary"; they refuse to be complete or comprehensive, for they exclude the musical elements of the song and the heterogeneous reception practices of the texts among their listeners. My readings are informed by my own listening experiences of these particular songs and of salsa in general; you, the reader, have to rely on my verbal translation of that experience. My readings are individual; a more comprehensive study would include a larger number of responses to these musical texts. Despite these material and methodological limitations, I hope this analysis begins to foreground constructions of the feminine in salsa and to contextualize popular music within a system of cultural semiotics and signifying practices that helps to explain its social relevance and popularity among women and men. While salsa songs reinforce the power of males to construct woman according to their gaze and desire, perhaps the same songs also allow female listeners to reread the male language of sexuality and desire, whether present or past, in order to revise their own sexual experiences as social constructs and not as "naturalized" behavior; in other words, to challenge and denaturalize the gender mores of their own generational times. This constitutes a collective sort of "productive pleasure" that could consequently foster a feminist politics of listening to salsa.

Deconstructing

In popular music, meanings are constructed not only through lyrics but also in the conjunction of the lyrics with the music. In some ways, music takes us to the past; it fosters a nostalgia of sorts for our youth or adolescence, in particular for those years when we were, in fact, becoming women and men, when we were both listening and dancing to popular music and associating those lyrics and rhythms with our own lives and with the processes of constructing our own sexuality.

It is not a coincidence that in many Latin American literary texts popular music appears as intertexts that bring forth issues of sexuality and sexual identity alongside cultural and gender politics; examples include Luis Rafael Sánchez's *La guaracha del Macho Camacho* and *La importancia de llamarse Daniel Santos*, Angeles Mastretta's *Arráncame la vida*, Rosario Ferré's "*Cuando las mujeres quieren a los hombres*" and "*Amalia*," Ana Lydia Vega's "*Letra para salsa y tres soneos por encargo*," and Magali García Ramis's *Felices días, tío Sergio* and "*Cuando canten 'Maestra Vida.'*"

Umberto Valverde's *Reina Rumba* (Rhumba Queen, 1981) is an interesting text in this regard. The intertextual presence of the *rumba* and the textual reconstruction of Celia Cruz consistently signal the protagonist's recurring nostalgia or desire for his youth, for the moments when he was becoming a man. Most of the experiences—personal and historical— recounted in the narrative are semantically intertwined with Celia Cruz's figure and presence, and with her songs. Densely phallocentric in its enunciation, *Reina Rumba* articulates the nostalgia for youth while growing old, the need for permanence amid sweeping urbanization in Colombia, and the need for sexual pleasure in loneliness. This is achieved through musical discourse and through the sexual objectification of Celia and her music. Edgardo Rodríguez Julía's *crónica playera* (beach chronicle) "El veranazo en que mangaron a Junior" (1989) is another text that, like El Gran Combo's song and Valverde's novel, textualizes the male gaze and desire within the musical space of a salsa summer beach festival in Punta Salinas, Puerto Rico. This digression regarding musical intertexts in literature illustrates the underlying connections between sexuality and listening to popular music, relations explored by our authors yet still unexamined by literary and cultural critics or musicologists.

In "Cuatro selecciones por una peseta," Vega and Filippi undermine the "productive pleasures" of male listeners of Latin popular music through irony and parody and by subverting their own male codes. The story's epigraph is a well-known refrain of a salsa song by El Gran Combo de Puerto Rico (1979): "Así son, así son las mujeres" (Such, such are women). This refrain anticipates the predominant male perspective that permeates the song and structures the short story.

The male-centered discourse of "Así son" originates from the conjunction of two musical traditions: the bolero and salsa. Boleros—lyrical, sentimental, nostalgic songs—usually express the sufferings of a man due to unrequited love or abandonment. The absence of the loved one causes him pain. In boleros, the male singer assumes the persona of a man who is getting drunk in a bar or club in order to forget his past relationship, "para olvidar" (Malavet Vega 1987: 393–409). Thus the absence of woman is the pretext for many boleros and for salsa songs such as "Así son":

> Tintineo de copas, chocar de besos,
> humo de cigarrillos en el salón,
> El Gran Combo que toca sus melodías
> y gente que se embriaga con whiski o ron.
>
> Yo que me desvelo por tu cariño,
> Tú que me desprecias, ay, sin compasión.
> Andas como una loca por las cantinas
> Brindando a todo el mundo tu corazón.
>
> Clinking cups and the sounds of kisses
> cigarette smoke within the room
> El Gran Combo is playing its songs
> and people are getting drunk on whisky and rum.
>
> I who am sleepless for your love
> You reject me, mercilessly
> You go around the bars like a fool
> Offering your love to all.

The references to drinking, music, and sexuality are established within the male locus of a bar or nightclub, a space in which the male singing subject can enunciate his cathartic accusations against "his" woman, who has now left him and is walking around "loca" (crazy) offering her love to others. Thus the first reference to the woman he loves is a negative one: she is a traitor to his love, while he is her victim.

An analogous space is created in the short story by Vega and Filippi. The ironic subtitle to the text signals the bolero form as one of its subtexts: "Bolero a dos voces para machos en pena, una sentida interpretación del duo Scaldada-Cuervo" (Bolero in two voices for suffering males, a sincere interpretation by the duo Scaldada-Cuervo). While this statement finds its reference in the rhetoric of the bolero tradition, it inverts it. It is, in fact, a contestatory response to this tradition. The "two voices" remit us to the collective authorship of Vega and Filippi, as well as to the implicit male-female opposing voices. There are two female writing subjects who speak, and who speak doubly. While the story is, at first sight, about four males, Eddie, Angelito, Monchín and Puruco, who meet at a bar to express their anger at the women who have either abandoned or betrayed them, the "sentida interpretación" (sincere interpretation) of the subtitle suggests a hidden perspective, a double talk by which the reader is alerted to hidden meanings and subversive strategies of meaning. "Sentida" first translates as "felt" and, derivatively, as sincere, honest, and sentimental. However, it simultaneously echoes "estar sentido," to be hurt or angry, a phrase which, at first glance may remit us precisely to the male protagonists. Yet in the writing of two women subjects this echo reveals the spiteful motivation for the writing itself. We could define it then as a vindictive act toward men, an attempt by women to see and define men from a woman-centered perspective.

The "four selections" remit us to the diatribes uttered by the four protagonists against "their" women, as well as to the musical selections that they choose to listen to on the jukebox. A close analysis of their language reveals, however, that the male utterances and the musical ones constantly contaminate each other. The men's words are not always their own. They use lyrics from songs such as the famous Latin American bolero "Usted" by José Zorrilla and Gabriel Ruiz: "Usted es la culpable de todas mis angustias, de todos mis quebrantos . . . " (You are to blame for all of my suffering, for all my pain . . . , Vega and Filippi 1981: 134), in addition to lyrics from salsa, tangos, and rancheras. All of these musical selections articulate a patriarchal ideology: in them, women acquire value as women only when they love a man or when they allow themselves to be loved. Thus El Gran Combo sings in "Así son": " "Qué buenas son las mujeres, qué buenas son cuando quieren" (Women are so good, so good when they want to) and its variant "Qué buenas son cuando se quieren" (Women are so good when they are loved). The words of men constructing women are the semantic and ideological link between the popular songs in-

scribed in the short story and the *quejas* (complaints) of the four male protagonists. Eddie wanted his wife to be a nurse/slave to take care of his mother; when
she went out of the house for an hour, he beat her up. Because Monchín allowed
his wife to go out to work, he supposedly "lost" her to unions and politics.
Puruco expected his wife to cook him dinner every night and to serve him and
his friends, since he was sensitive enough not to go out to bars, but to have his
friends over. And Angelito, well, he never married.

These four diatribes are textualized forms of "productive pleasures." Their
respective quejas appear interspersed with musical selections from salsa, boleros, tangos, and rancheras: "Qué buenas son las mujeres, qué buena [*sic*] son
cuando quieren (132); "Túuuuuu, sólo túuuuuu . . . " (132); "Usted es la culpable de todas mis angustias . . . " (134). Other indirect references to tangos and
rancheras complete the repertoire of patriarchal lyrics: "No hay como un tango
pa olvidal" (There is nothing like a tango to help me forget, 133) and "Los acor-
des de una ranchera matahembra sobrepoblaron el aire" (The chords of a fe-
male-killer ranchera overpopulated the air, 135). These musical utterances offer
the four working-class Puerto Rican males a mode of catharsis and a patriarchal paradigm for creating and giving meaning to their own experiences. They
actually produce meanings out of the songs, but only out of those lyrics that
are relevant to their position as men abandoned by their wives or lovers. The
four characters represent an interpretive community constituted by working-
class Puerto Rican males who listen to these selected popular songs that re-
affirm and naturalize their socially expected masculine behavior.

In this light, Latin popular music is a code, or a language, for those who lack
one. Eddie, Angelito, Monchín and Puruco constantly depend on the codes of
popular music to define themselves and to define women. As mass media, these
lyrics diffused through the *vellonera* (jukebox) provide the men with a language for catharsis and for expressing their emotions. As what Adorno calls
emotional-type listeners, they react to sentimental music by a "temporary . . .
awareness that [they] have missed fulfillment." This music "permits its listeners the confession of their unhappiness." Yet this catharsis is illusionary. It is
not truly liberating since it actually "reconciles them by means of this release,
to their social dependence" (Adorno 1941: 42). Ironically, the emotional listener
believes he/she is escaping a reality of unhappiness by listening to music. Thus
the ending line of the story: "no hay como un tango pa olvidal" (there is nothing like a tango to help us forget, 137). However, these listeners are participating
in a pattern of social dependence by indiscriminately accepting this musical
discourse as personally theirs. While they may pose as authors of their own

discourse against women, these four men are but the receptors of these messages. This analysis implies a political analogy with the colonial situation of Puerto Rico.

"Cuatro selecciones por una peseta" dismantles the constructions of women in Latin popular music and salsa in particular. The representation of the feminine based on absence, as in Willie Colón's "Cuando fuiste mujer," is now superimposed on the Puerto Rican male, who lacks a language of his own and the necessary cultural and gender codes to deal with his repressed emotions: "Cuando calló Jaramillo el silencio era un bache de lágrimas machamente contenidas" (When Jaramillo stopped talking, silence was a puddle of tears restrained in a macho way, 129). The double discourse of the title, "Cuatro selecciones por una peseta," suggests that the selecciones to be listened to, and to be consumed, are not only the musical ones but also the men's diatribes. The cumulative effect of the ironic, tongue-in-cheek humor of the female narrative voice and the parodic distortions of the male discourse at the level of the signifier propose that this text is a reading not about women but about men. By the end of the story, the reader has gathered that Eddie, Puruco, Monchín, and Angelito either have been unfaithful to their wives (130), are still dependent on their mothers (130), or are politically unsavvy (134) and quite naive about each other as friends (136). "Así son, así son los hombres cuando no los quieren" (Such, such are men when they are not loved) would better summarize what the story is all about: women de(con)structing men.

While much work remains to be done regarding the reception of salsa by both male and female interpretive communities, this interdisciplinary attempt to deconstruct salsa patriarchal lyrics via contemporary female narratives in Puerto Rico is an initial effort in this direction. This chapter, read only as printed matter, as words, excludes the musicality of the songs. The voices of salsa cannot be fully understood or listened to without the music. I urge the reader to become a *cocola/o*, an active listener of salsa and, in the process, to *listen woman* and to *listen as a woman*.

Acknowledgments

I want to acknowledge the support of the National Research Council and the Ford Foundation in the initial stages of this research. I also want to thank Elizabeth Davis, University of Oregon, Eugene, a *cocola* by heart, for the many conversations on Latin popular music and gender issues, and Laura Pérez, University of Michigan, and Suzanne Chávez Silverman, Pomona College, for their helpful suggestions. Sections of the third part of this essay were read as a paper in the 1987 Annual Convention in San Francisco, California.

REFERENCES

Bourdieu, Pierre. *Distinction: A Social Critique of the Judgment of Taste.* Trans. R. Nice (Cambridge: Harvard University Press), 1984.

Caughie, Pamela. "Women Reading/Reading Women: A Review of Some Recent Books on Gender and Reading," *Papers on Language and Literature* 24(3) (1988): 317–335.

Cixous, Hélène. "The Laugh of the Medusa." In *New French Feminisms,* ed. Elaine Marks and Isabel de Courtivron (New York: Schocken Books), 1981, 245–264.

Fernández Mirallés, Elsa. "La salsa, en contra de la mujer?" *El nuevo día, March 7, 1979.*

Ferré, Rosario. *Papeles de Pandora* (Mexico City: Joaquín Mortiz), 1979.

Fiske, John. *Understanding Popular Culture* (Boston: Unwin Hyman), 1989.

García Ramis, Magali. "Cuando canten 'Maestra vida.'" In *Apalabramiento: Cuentos puertorriqueños de hoy,* ed. Efraín Barradas (Hanover: Ediciones del Norte), 1983.

———. *Felices días, tío Sergio* (Río Piedras, Puerto Rico: Editorial Antillana), 1986.

Gilman, Sander. *Difference and Pathology: Stereotypes of Sexuality, Race and Madness* (Ithaca: Cornell University Press), 1985.

Herrera-Sobek, María. *The Mexican Corrido: A Feminist Analysis* (Bloomington: Indiana University Press), 1990.

Huyssen, Andreas. "Mass Culture as Woman: Modernism's Other." In *After the Great Divide: Modernism, Mass Culture, Postmodernism* (Bloomington: Indiana University Press), 1986. Also in *Studies in Entertainment,* ed. Tania Modleski (Bloomington: Indiana University Press), 1986; 188–207.

Jacobus, Mary. *Reading Woman: Essays in Feminist Criticism* (New York: Columbia University Pres), 1986.

Jaquette, Jane S. "Literary Archetypes and Female Role Alternatives: The Woman and the Novel in Latin America." In *Female and Male in Latin America,* ed. Ann Pescattello (Pittsburgh: University of Pittsburgh Press), 1973, 3–27.

Kolodny, Annette. "Dancing through the Minefield: Some Observations on the Theory, Practice, and Politics of a Feminist Literary Criticism." In *The New Feminist Criticism: Essays on Women, Literature and Theory,* ed. Elaine Showalter et al. (New York: Pantheon Books), 1985, 144–167.

Malavet Vega, Pedro. *La vellonera está directa: Felipe Rodríguez (la Voz) y los años 50* (Río Piedras, Puerto Rico: Ediciones Huracán), 1987.

Mastretta, Angeles. *Arráncame la vida* (Mexico City: Océano), 1985.

Moi, Toril. *Sexual/Textual Politics: Feminist Literary Theory* (London: Routledge), 1990 [1985].

Padilla, Félix. "Salsa: Puerto Rican and Latino Music," *Journal of Popular Culture* 24 (1990): 87–104.

Palmer, Neyssa. *Las mujeres en los cuentos de René Marqués* (Río Piedras, Puerto Rico: Editorial de la Universidad de Puerto Rico), 1988.

Radway, Janice. "Interpretive Communities and Variable Literacies." In *Rethinking Popular Culture: Contemporary Perspectives in Cultural Studies*, ed. Chandra Mujerki and Michael Schudson (Berkeley: University of California Press), 1991, 465–486.

Rodríguez Juliá, Edgardo. "El veranazo en que mangaron a Junior." In *El cruce de la Bahía de Guánica* (Río Piedras, Puerto Rico: Editorial Cultural), 1989, 99–130.

Rondón, César Miguel. *El libro de la Salsa: crónica de la música del caribe urbano* (Caracas: Merca Libros), 1980.

Sánchez, Luis Rafael. *La guaracha del Macho Camacho* (Buenos Aires: Ediciones de la Flor), 1976.

———. *La importancia de llamarse Daniel Santos* (Hanover: Ediciones del Norte, 1988).

Valverde, Umberto. *Reina Rumba* (Bogotá: Editorial La Oveja Negra), 1981.

Vega, Ana Lydia, and Carmen Lugo Filippi. *Vírgenes y mártires* (Río Piedras, Puerto Rico: Editorial Antillana), 1983.

Young, Shelagh. "Feminism and the Politics of Power: Whose Gaze is it Anyway?" In *The Female Gaze: Women as Viewers of Popular Culture*, ed. Lorraine Gamman and Margaret Marshment (Seattle: Real Comet Press), 1989, 173–204.

DISCOGRAPHY

Blades, Rubén. "Ligia Elena" in *Rubén Blades' Greatest Hits*, Música Latina Internacional, SP51, 1983.

———. "El" and "Ella se esconde," in *Caminando*, Sony Records International, DCC80593, 1991.

Colón, Willie. "Cuando fuiste mujer" and "El gran varón" in *Legal Alien/Top Secrets*, WAC Productions, JM655, 1989.

Cruz, Celia and Johnny Pacheco. "Las divorciadas" in *De nuevo*, Música Latina Internacional, Vaya Records, 4XT JMVs-106-, 1985.

El Gran Combo de Puerto Rico. "Así son" and "Brujería" in *Aquí no se sienta nadie*, Combo Records, RCSLP 2013, 1979.

———. "Quince años" in *Romántico y sabroso*, Combo Records RSCLP 2054, 1988.

Lavoe, Héctor. "Bandolera," in *Comedia*, Fania Records, JM 00522, 1978.

López, Sonia y su Combo. "Castígalo," in *Sonia López y su combo*, PDC 8701 (not dated).

Mayra y Celinés y su grupo Flor de Caña. "Tanto amor" and "Mentira" in *Mayra y Celinés y su grupo Flor de Caña*, Paradise Records, 3053–4-RL, 1991.

Milly y los vecinos. "Ese hombre" in *14 Grandes Exitos Originales*, Capital Records, H4F 42486, 1991.

Santos, Daniel. "Yo la mato" in *Daniel Santos con la Sonora Matancera*, Panart International.

FACE OF THE NATION

Race, Nationalisms, and Identities in Jamaican Beauty Pageants

NATASHA B. BARNES

IN SEPTEMBER 1986, the Jamaican *Daily Gleaner*, the island's leading newspaper, gave a front-page report of the proceedings of a Miss Jamaica beauty pageant headlined "Missiles Barrage at Beauty Contest."

> Deafening shouts of protest rang through the National Arena. Patrons sprang to their feet screaming and gesticulating their disagreement on Saturday night when twenty-two-year-old Lisa Mahfood . . . was announced winner of Miss Jamaica (World) 1986.
>
> Many in the jampacked arena, estimated to hold about 9,000, booed and shouted, "No . . . no . . . no!" Some banged the metal chairs to the chant "We want Majorie," referring to Majorie Tolloch . . . who placed fourth.
>
> Some patrons in the angry crowd threw crushed paper cups and oranges at the new queen, who was struck in the face with an orange. Others threw bottles, one of which struck a photographer on the side of the head.
>
> Pandemonium reigned. Confusion broke out among those on the platform. The new queen found it impossible to make the usual victory walk. At this stage, the new Miss Jamaica 1986 had to be escorted from the stage by promotor Mickey Haughton-James to prevent further harm to her by flying objects.[1]

How is it that a beauty pageant could arouse such passions? While the Miss Jamaica contest has been both popular and controversial, Jamaican beauty pageants, unlike Reggae Sunsplash concerts and working-class dance halls, are meant to be dignified public affairs; the showcasing of feminine charm and grace is expected to produce an atmosphere of congeniality and good will among contestants and onlookers alike. A fanfare evening patronized by the governor general, choreographed and staged by the prestigious Jamaican Institute of Dance, and featuring a parade of twenty lithe and lovely women in lace bathing suits and lavish evening gowns is hardly the kind of event to conclude with hurled bottles and oranges. A few days later, an interview with Lisa Mahfood clarified the reasons why her unexpected coronation drew such a violent response. Mahfood was white. The daughter of a Lebanese Jamaican entrepreneurial family, she was "European" by the standards of Jamaican racial identity and hence had no business representing what was to many of the Miss Jamaica onlookers a black country. The reporter from the *Gleaner* found her in her family's large suburban home recovering from "shock and surprise" at the outburst of the Jamaican people. "Their behavior . . . ," she stuttered, "and to talk about our [national] motto—Out of many one people . . . and I said to myself how can these people be like this. Jamaica is made up of more than one race. How come they are not living by it?"[2]

Like all good beauty queens, Mahfood wore her crown and represented her country with dignity and grace. Even when she was forced to abandon her coronation walk on the pageant night, she waved and blew kisses at a crowd that was taunting her with racial epithets and assaulting her with oranges. But the fans of the Miss Jamaica pageant felt that they were victims of a larger, more historically rooted insult. A few months earlier, twenty-year-old Lilliana Antonette Cisneros, a woman who declared herself Venezuelan (she was born of a Jamaican father and a Colombian mother), walked away with the Miss Jamaica Universe crown. During the same year, a former contestant, Ruth Cammock, filed a suit in the Supreme Court alleging that as a black woman she was a victim of color discrimination.[3] But the court cases and hurled oranges are only recent manifestations of a crisis brewing within the Miss Jamaica pageant that was hardly new to most Jamaicans. Although images of Rastafarians, reggae music, and tourist brochures have made many of us associate blackness as the very picture of Jamaica, the struggles within the beauty contest reflect the fact that as far as representation on the island goes, Jamaica has yet to assert its identity as a black country. In spite of demographic figures identifying some 90 percent of the inhabitants as black and thirty years of a postcolonial legacy that attempted to shift economic and hegemonic power away from European creole elites to a disenfranchised black mass, many dark-skinned Jamaicans still see their color as a handicap in their efforts to secure good jobs, access to education, decent housing, even polite service from store clerks, bank tellers, etc. For these Jamaicans, the coronation of a white Miss Jamaica is not a trivial matter; nor is it removed from the everyday manifestation of power and privilege on the island. Rather it strikes a violent blow at the very heart of their sense of personhood, viscerally reenacting the failure of the postcolonial promise to give black people their symbolic and material due after centuries of colonial domination. With Jamaica suffering from an unemployment rate at 30 percent, a political party system that has abandoned the social-uplift commitments made during independence, poor inner-city dwellings stunted by neglect and crime, it is the arena of culture—the site of cricket, music, and beauty pageants—that has become the place where black people, resigned to the fact that there will be no piece of the economic pie for them, have come to claim and sometimes violently defend as their own.

To understand how white women and the ideological specter of beauty have come to constitute such a viciously contested terrain of representative power one only needs to look at who beauty queens were in the forties and fifties. In the long and troubled history of beauty pageants throughout the Anglophone Caribbean, it was only the daughters of the white-identified business and plantocratic elite who were encouraged to enter and eventually win the many lavishly financed contests that sprang up. In the colonial Caribbean, where local assemblies hardly provided money for schools let alone cultural events, the extravagant private and governmental sponsorship made affairs like the Miss Jamaica pageant[4] or the "Carnival Queen" contest in Trinidad spectacular public events that dramatized in visceral ways the disenfranchisement of people of color. While the coronation of light-skinned black women today generates the same charges of exclusion and discrimation that surround white winners, in the forties few women whose black or Asian ancestry was obvious, let alone prominent, would have access to these hallowed sororities. When calls for decolonization and black assertiveness became increasingly strident and linked, it became politically expedient to include mulatto, Indian, and Chinese women, but these contestants of color had no illusions about their potential to win. Contemporary commentators rightly argued that the philosophy and practice of such contests made the commodification of beauty a public but decidedly closed affair. Wrapped in a mantle of respectability and civility that was denied to black people in general and black women in particular, beauty contests became the place for the making of feminine subjectivity in a racial landscape where femininity was the jealously guarded domain of white womanhood.

The very infrastructure of the pageants upheld and reflected the fact, often crudely so, that people of color—not just *women* of color—were unfit subjects for national representation, that in spite of their efforts to prove to the contrary, nothing noble and enlightened could be reflected in their image. Beauty contests gave prizes to contestants judged as possessing the "best eyes," prizes that would never be awarded to anyone with brown or black eyes. Prize trips for winning queens habitually included destinations like Miami, Florida, a city that was vehemently Jim Crow at the time. Judges were often members of the island's political and business elites and were closely associated with the sponsors of the competition as well as with the contestants themselves. One reporter for the *Spotlight*, a weekly Jamaican newsmagazine, smitten that the "soft-voiced, olive-colored Peggy Dickard" lost to the white "lux complexioned" winner of the 1948 Buy Jamaican queen contest, noted that although the queen was a "lovely, accomplished and exceptionally pretty miss," she was nonetheless related to one of the "heavily white panel of judges [who] seemed to regard her Nordic beauty as typically Jamaicanesque or West Indian."[5] Likewise Una Marson, one of Jamaica's early twentieth-century black feminists, had ample reason to take the organizers of the pageant to task for their routine choice of blond-haired, blue-eyed women as Miss Jamaicas. As early as 1931 Marson sardonically called attention to the pageant as a segregated arena for the reification of plantocratic dominance and in so doing uncovered the "invisibility" of the its hegemonic work: "[S]ome amount of expense and disappointment could be saved numbers of dusky ladies who year after year enter the beauty competition if the promoters of the contest would announce in the daily press that very dark or black 'beauties' would not be considered."[6]

The tensions expressed here between the contemporary ideals of beauty—which in no way included black women—and the emphasis on the queen as a national representative in a country that was increasingly attempting to identify itself as "black" would reach its crescendo in the Miss Jamaica pageant of the 1950s. It was in this contest that the contrast between a white queen and her public role as a Jamaican representative would become as dramatic as it was fiercely controversial. Unlike previous island beauty pageants where queens would have undefined or limited roles as crowned winners, the Jamaica Tourist Board (with its sponsorship of the Miss Jamaica pageant in 1954) conceived of the queen as a professional of sorts, a cultural broker who would now be charged with a year-long job of "selling" the island to prospective European and white North American tourists. The construction of the queen as a worker, as someone with clearly-defined "professional" and public responsibilities infused the contest with a sense of purpose that changed white women's symbolic function as invisible, leisured wives and daughters whose absence from the rigors of wage-labor work reinscribed the patriarchal privilege of white men. By contrast, the prevailing discourse surrounding black women's public identities as laborers was seen as evidence of black men's inability to assert patriarchal control over the sphere of "home" and "family" and the inevitable consequence of the black family's tendency toward "breakdown" and "pathology." Indeed the concept of the white queen's "work," in its ideological refractions, operated on a number of levels to further antagonize the already hostile relationship between the white owner/managerial caste and an increasingly politicized black labor force—both camps using the rhetoric of masculinity to define and orchestrate their struggle. The white beauty queen's public and well-financed cultural "work" as Jamaica's hostess to the world built and depended upon an eroticized and "exotic" black female presence but outrightly excluded women of color as suitable representatives of this ideal. Miss Jamaica winners not only went on to represent their island at regional and international pageants, but were frequently sent on publicity campaigns to the United States and Canada garbed in the picturesque costume of the creole black women folk—embroidered white blouse, madras plaid head-kerchief and matching skirt, heavy earrings and bead necklaces—to show off the "native" charm of Jamaica's fairer sex. Publicity photographs often showed them superimposed over the map of Jamaica itself inviting their onlookers to read the island as a space of civility and heterosexual pleasure through their white bodies. By the coronation of the second such Miss Jamaica in 1955, the editorial page of the *Daily Gleaner* used the occasion of seventeen-year-old Marlene Fenton's victory to warn the pageant organizers of the growing racial divisiveness that the Miss Jamaica contest was increasingly coming to signify at home through her public image abroad. It rightly identified the Tourist Board's concept of the beauty queen's role as "island ambassadress" as a source of a continuing discrepancy between the insurgent trade union attempts to inscribe Jamaica's postcolonial identity as "proud," "manly," and "black" with the Tourist Board's marking and marketing of the island as "comely," "womanly," and "white." The editorial warned that "constructive care" should be taken "not to let Americans or Canadians or Europeans imagine that this is a Caucasian country. . . . We in countries like Jamaica should not lead the world overseas to think that all the lovely people in the island are of one [racial] sort and the woman on the donkey is of another."[7]

The white beauty queen's high visibility as a symbol of plantocratic hierarchy and racism pitted her against an emergent multifaceted male-identified black labor force that increasingly portrayed her privilege as an insult directed less toward black women, but to black men. Nationalist efforts to regain control over the Carnival festivities in Trinidad in the middle of this century show how the segregated beauty institution formed the axis upon which a competitive struggle between the white colonial managerial elite and an emergent black political force was waged. Between 1946 to 1954, a group of colonial business and political interests organized into the Carnival Improvement Committee attempted to transform the black working class celebrations—celebrations that were remembered as an arena for black women's riotous and disorderly public behavior—into a "decent" and well ordered tourist attraction by initiating the Dimarche Gras Carnival Queen competition, an event which quickly became the most prestigious and well-financed show of the season's festivities. Indeed it is possible to argue that the strategic deployment of white female bodies as Carnival Queens was constitutive of the history of crisis and concession that regulated the evolution of Carnival as an embattled sphere of social culture. If the Canbolay Riots of the late nineteenth century showed that black people would violently resist colonial efforts to ban or threaten the autonomy linked their symbolic "ownership" of Carnival festivities, the colonial elite through a redirected campaign of "refinement" and "Europeanization" successfully, if unevenly, challenged black control of Carnival on precisely this notion of proprietorship. The evolution of the Carnival Queen competition into a beauty pageant (the contest saw its beginnings in the 1920s as a costume competition open to married women and women of color) secured its transformation as a public but "boundaried" social arena, operating within black people's public space but off-limits to them.

By the mid 1950s, the Carnival Queen pageant, like the Miss Jamaica contest, was a lucrative debutante ball for the daughters of Trinidad's white elite, with the winner getting prizes valued at some $7,500—a figure which Gordon Rohlehr estimates was $2,500 more than the prize money given to all the winning masquerade bands put together.[8] In 1957, after unsuccessful attempts to persuade the Carnival Development Committee to substantially raise the value of the Calypso Monarch prizes, the Mighty Sparrow, a young calypsonian enjoying ample career opportunities abroad as a nightclub entertainer in British and American cities, organized a famous boycott of the calypso competition specifically targeting the CDC's unfair privileging of the Carnival Queen show. As his "Carnival Boycott" calypso goes, the promotion of the queen came at the expense of the "real" artistes of the season—steelband players, calypsonians and masqueraders—figures that are identified as black and male. Sparrow's song reflected what a letter writer to the Trinidadian *Guardian* complained of as the unfairness of the " 'Carnival Queen' get[ting] so many prizes [yet] a man who buys a costume for about $200 gets a prize and a silver cup costing perhaps $5. What a reward for showing the skill and art of the natives of our country!"[9]

Perhaps more than any other episode in the history of Trinidadian spectatorial culture are the lines as sharply drawn between the struggle of undeserving white privilege—dramatized here in the body of the debutante queen—and that of an unappreciated and exploited black labor mass—identified in discourse of the controversy as male cultural workers. In spite of the efforts to give the Carnival Queen a public but short-lived "career" as an "ambassadress,"[10] the calypsonian's discourse, using the politicized rhetoric of the emergent labor activism, claims that she is rewarded by the authorities for doing "nothing," while the "real" legitimate cultural workers go unrecognized. As the Mighty Sparrow sang in "Carnival Boycott":

> What really cause the upset
> Is the motor-car the queen does get
> She does nothing for Carnival
> She only pretty and that is all
> But men like me an' you
> Saving money to play "history" and Ju Ju[11]
> All we getting is two case of beer
> And talk up as Band of the Year.

Chorus:
> I intend to keep all my costume on the shelf
> Let them keep the prizes in the Savannah for they own self
> Let the Queen run the show
> Without Steelband and Calypso
> Who want to go can go up dey
> But me ain't going no way

> Calypsonians with the talent
> Hardly getting a cent
> I think its overbearing
> So now give me a hearing;
> Calypso is the root of Carnival
> Steelband is the foot of Carnival
> Without Calypso, no road march could beat
> Without Steelband, I'll bet you don't move your feet.

Sparrow's "Carnival Boycott" identifies the cultural work of the steelbandmen and calypsonians as the motor and machinery that drives Carnival's activity. Indeed Sparrow's eruption into the Trinidad calypso scene in the 1950s and the leadership he brought to the organized boycott inaugurated a period in Trinidadian popular music that was marked by a growing awareness of local music as a source of profit and professionalism. The calypsonians' awareness of themselves as professionals formed a critical dimension of their shifting status in the 1950s and upon which their targeting of the white debutante beauty queen earns its legitimacy. Sparrow's career launched the beginning of the calypsonian's self-definition as professionals, as valued cultural workers whose labor, unlike that of their earlier status as "roving minstrels," could be exchanged and marketed for profit and social veneration. What is established here and in the discourse of Lord Superior's calypso "Brass Crown" is the dangerous symbolic opposition between white female leisure and deserving but unpaid black *male* work. We can see from "Brass Crown" how the dichotomy between the paid Queen who is not, by the calypsonian's estimation, a "real" cultural worker inscribes a dangerous notion of postcolonial culture as being the province of black men—a notion that has serious implications for *all* women's cultural activity:

> They doesn't send the King Calypso
> As far as Tobago
> But the Queen and her family
> Goes to New York city
> When she comes back, before she steps out the plane
> You hear she gone again
> This time, they send she to Stalingrad
> And she can't whistle to represent Trinidad.

From this short history it is not hard to imagine why these beauty contests would become central targets in the efforts of trade unionists, burgeoning anticolonial politicians and black upliftment societies to dismantle the material and psychological effects of colonialism and Eurocentrism. The fact that Jamaica's earliest black feminists rallied against the exclusion of women of color from the contest—rather than the patriarchal structure of the pageant itself—reminds us that the struggle for black women everywhere to be recognized as women, as feminine subjects, is not, as Nancy Caraway puts it, simply "derived from vanity . . . but is a crucial component of a larger collective effort at self definition."[12] The public nature of the Miss Jamaica pageant, the fact that the reigning queen needs validation from the nation's subjects because of her representational status—she goes on to represent Jamaica at an international beauty pageant and hence is to be the embodiment of all that *is* Jamaican—means that a white winner, like the idea of beauty itself, is the site of dangerous contradictions. Like beauty which, as commonly held platitudes on the subject

attest, has no race or class referents—you're either pretty or you're not—the repeated coronation of a white Miss Jamaica lays bare the ugly truth that beauty
is not "natural" but ideological: it has a certain kind of face, certain features,
hair texture, eye color, shape of nose and lips. Indeed, the public scope of the
pageant served to underscore this very fact. Contestants were routinely pa-
raded in Kingston's public places followed by a train of reporters and photographers who eulogized and fetishized the women in newspaper tabloid spreads.
In these flashy pictorials, white women, historically sheltered and made off-
limits to black men and men of color in general, are now flagrantly displayed
and eroticized. Full-page photographs and accompanying copy detail the trap-
pings of power and privilege that they embody: expensively styled "light au-
burn hair," fashionably made-up "grayish-green" and "twinkling sea-blue
eyes"—details that in a highly charged racial atmosphere were read for what
they were: transparent fetishes of the phenotypes associated with whiteness.

Beauty contests in the Caribbean are a continual reminder of both the trans-
parency of race as a historical construction and the concreteness of its social
reality. The first Miss Jamaica, Evelyn Andrade, a woman recognized as white
on the island, was sent as the regional representative to the 1954 Miss Universe
contest held in Long Beach, California. Here Andrade, now Miss West Indies,
was noticed by *Ebony* magazine, which produced a lavish four-page spread of
the photogenic beauty retranslating her as "black": "Jamaican girl is the first
Negro to enter top beauty contest."[13] For *Ebony* blackness becomes identified,
as it usually is the the United States, simply through the presence of a black
progenitor, and hence the proof of Andrade's "Negro" identity is located in
her family: her father, *Ebony* reports, is a "Syrian Jew, well-known in business
circles . . . married to a colored woman in Kingston." But in Jamaica, the
wealth of the Syrian and Lebanese elites had already canceled their prior immigrant and religious identities and the progressive whitening of the island's
elite mulatto castes made individuals of Andrade's background—irrespective
of black ancestry—white to most Jamaicans.

By the late forties the controversies surrounding the Miss Jamaica pageant
and the many other beauty contests organized prior to it led to a well-publi-
cized and spectacular effort to satisfy the public's growing taste for beauty contests while infusing them with a more egalitarian and representative quality. In
1955 the Star, the evening tabloid of the Gleaner, announced its sponsorship of a
"Ten Types, One People" contest organized as part of the island's tercentennial
anniversary of British rule. "Ten Types, One People," echoing what would become Jamaica's national motto—"Out of many one people"—was to celebrate

Jamaican beauty queens stand before a cannon at Fort Charles, Port Royal, Jamaica, in the "Ten Types, One People" beauty pageant, 1955.

Miss Ebony Miss Mahogany Miss Satinwood Miss Allspice Miss Sandalwood Miss Golden Apple Miss Jasmine Miss Pomegranate Miss Lotus Miss Appleblossom the island's racial diversity as well as manage, through the showcasing of race and color "types," concerns about the bias and discrimination that were by now regular complaints about the beauty business. This pageant was in fact made up of a coterie of pageants based on what the *Star* identified as the ten distinct racial types on the island. As the *Gleaner* reported, this was a beauty pageant "break[ing] new ground . . . [by] trying to bring out all the shades and types in one great contest—European, African, Indian, Chinese and those that come from the Near East."[14] Hence there was a Miss Ebony for black-complexioned women, Miss Mahogony for women of "cocoa-brown complexion," Miss Satinwood for "girls of coffee and milk complexion," Miss Golden Apple for "peaches and cream" Jamaican women, Miss Appleblossom for "a Jamaican girl of white European parentage," Miss Pomegranate for "white Mediterranean girls," Miss Sandalwood for women of "pure Indian parentage," Miss Lotus who was to be "pure Chinese," Miss Jasmine for a Jamaican of "part-Chinese parentage," and Miss Allspice for "part-Indian" women.[15] Each winner was to be chosen by a group of twenty judges, ten of whom were to be of the complexion category of the judged—clearly a logistical nightmare for the organizers, who not only had to recruit and categorize the contestants but also match each competition with suitably complexioned judges in an island of only one and a half million people. While the idea of the "Ten Types, One People" contest was as sensational and indeed laughable in 1955 as it sounds to us today, for many of the region's journalists, politicians, and public opinion makers, the fact that this pageant was organized not only to include diverse representation of all Jamaica's ethnicities but also to ensure that a winner would emerge from each group made it a showpiece of racial tolerance to the region and the world. Although the sensationalism of the pageant attracted attention from journalists around the world—both *Life* and *Ebony* magazines sent photographers to cover the event—for Caribbean opinion makers the "Ten Types" contest was a humane and egalitarian way to build racial pride among those communities never represented at beauty pageants. One journalist heralded the pageant for its "revolutionary" potential and declared that it reflected the "culture and civilization" of a peaceful and plural emergent nation. The report in the *Havana Post*, for example, waxed poetic and political:

> I do not know who made up that list of ten names, but it is a masterpiece of poetry, dignity and good taste. The various qualifications are beautifully prepared, and I find myself admiring particularly the little Jamaican girl who does

not protest that it is undemocratic to have a class for "MISS APPLE BLOS-SOM," but who readily admits that she is a "Jamaican girl of black complex-ion" and proudly enters her name in the competition for the title of "MISS EBONY." Such dignity is worthy of the highest praise because it is an accep-tance of reality, of the immutable truth.[16]

The focus on the Miss Ebony contest here is no accidental emphasis. Since Caribbean beauty contests had traditionally denied a place to dark-skinned women, this pageant was envisioned as a social experiment in which black con-testants, and by extension black people in general, would have their dignity and sense of self-worth validated through their access to the institutions that regu-lated cultural norms of physical attractiveness. The very idea that beauty was a quality that could embrace African-descended people and that "black" was a racial description that could be declared proudly and without embarrassment was, in 1955, well before the "black is beautiful" stridency of the 1970s, quite a startling concept. The fourteen finalists for the Miss Ebony title, lithe, well-pro-portioned, and, as a *Spotlight* report remarked, "coal black," drew stares of amazement from white tourist onlookers and smiles of pride and joy from black islanders. Lady Allen, widow of a prominent black Jamaican government minister and member of the Jamaica Federation of Women, brought in to help organize the "Ten Types" contest, told a reporter that the Miss Ebony show was of particular social significance: "[It] brings out some of our really good-look-ing Jamaican girls—if I use the term natives they might not like it, but that is what I mean—it brings out the girls who would otherwise not get a chance."[17] In this spirit contest organizers made a point of recruiting young black women outside of the urban areas to have them photographed for consideration. The *Star* gave its islandwide correspondents hundreds of leaflets advertising both the contest and the date and time that newspaper photographers would be in the area to take pictures. Clifton Neita, a *Gleaner* editorial executive, was ap-pointed to search out such women and even employ some rather unusual tac-tics to coax possible contestants into allowing themselves to be photographed. As he told a *Spotlight* reporter, "Some of the objections those girls made for not coming forward! A favorite was: 'But my hair don't look nice.' I soon learned to squash that by providing comb, brush, mirror, even advice on hair style."[18] The enterprise had its desired effect. Villagers took pride in the fact that the *Star* featured pictures of local women in its pages whether they made it to the finals or not. Young women themselves, emboldened by the fact that their dark skin and "bad" hair did not disqualify them from cultural norms of attractiveness, felt a new sense of confidence and self-worth. As the *Spotlight* editorialized,

"Forever after, the shy servant girls of Little River (St. James) and Bluefields (Westmoreland) could say to their friends: 'I *am* pretty. Didn't you see my picture in the Star?' "[19]

The idea of a racialized beauty contest proudly announcing itself as such took on a decidedly more strident and eventually controversial tone with the introduction of a Miss Chinese Jamaica competition the year after the first Tourist Board–sponsored Miss Jamaica was crowned. Like earlier pageants, the Miss Chinese Jamaica contest had its beginnings as a fund raiser for the Chinese Benevolent Society, the central social welfare institution for people of Chinese descent on the island. Its organizer, Cecil Chuck, then a charismatic member of the younger Chinese Jamaican social set, envisioned the competition as an attraction to the society's already popular annual Garden Party—an outdoor bazaar sponsored by the Chinese Athletic Club and well patronized by a wide cross-section of the Afro-Jamaican public.[20] Like the annual Garden Party, where the Chinese community threw open its doors to the larger public, the Miss Chinese Jamaica pageant soon became a showpiece of ethnic revitalization and pride, a "coming out" of the entire Chinese community enthusiastically received by most Jamaicans. The organizers had no trouble recruiting politicians, ambassadors, and governors' wives as patrons and sponsors, as well as former beauty queens who acted as coaches to the young contestants, instructing them in the finer points of poise, make-up application, and public speaking. Like the "Ten Types" contest, Miss Chinese Jamaica was prominently covered in local and regional magazines and newspapers, a publicity spectacle which proved Cecil Chuck's assertion that "everyone liked Chinese girls."[21]

While Jamaicans may have liked Chinese girls, they may not necessarily have liked the Chinese. Some fifty years earlier the Chinese bore the brunt of the region's most dramatic protest against Asian immigration. During the 1918 Anti-Chinese Riots, a complex social disturbance fueled by a depressed colonial economy that hit working-class black Jamaicans particularly hard, many Chinese shopkeepers were killed or maimed and their properties destroyed by black residents who saw them as unwelcome competitors in strained economic times.[22] While the Chinese have always been seen as a recalcitrant and unassimilated ethnic group, Chinese women entered and were popular contestants throughout the entire troubled history of Caribbean beauty pageants. Dorothy Wong, for example, an entrant in the 1958 Miss Jamaica competition, was the crowd favorite, although she lost to Joan Duperly, a white Jamaican who, a *Gleaner* report enthused, had "the same type of face as Marilyn Monroe."[23] (That same year Wong entered the Miss Chinese Jamaica pageant and won easily.) Indeed, the first time the Miss Jamaica color bar was broken, it was by the Chinese-identified Sheila Chong, whose "Polynesian demeanor" made her the first woman of color to be crowned Miss Jamaica, in 1959. But the presence of Chinese women in these national beauty contests was not without the tensions that have historically surrounded the question of Chinese identity in the Caribbean. In 1958 the Trinidadian representative to the Miss British Caribbean competition, Angela Tong, found herself having to tell reporters that although her father was born in Hong Kong, she spoke no Chinese—a situation that was not repeated for the other regional contestants, who were also members of recently arrived immigrant communities but felt no pressure to explain their legitimacy as Caribbean representatives.[24] Indeed, the crowning of Sheila Chong in 1959 drew a petition signed by several black Jamaican shopkeepers complaining of the fact that since in their knowledge a Jamaican girl was never crowned Miss China, a Chinese woman had no right to be Miss Jamaica.

Clearly it was the color and ethnicity tensions surrounding who was a "typical" Jamaican that led to the inauguration of a Miss Chinese Jamaica pageant in the first place. While such debates about the color and caste identity of the emergent nation were hardly new in the 1950s and certainly not confined to beauty pageants, the spectacle of such competitions had for a long time made such debates ritualized and femininized. Indeed, beauty pageants were precisely the place where public battles over representation and identity would commodity women for a variety of constituent *and* overwhelmingly male interests. By the early sixties the editorials and writers of letters to the editor made the color and caste controversies surrounding the pageants ostensibly about women, but between men. For the island's white elites, caught in a rapidly decolonizing landscape where it was clear that political leadership would soon have a black face, control over the beauty contests was its last effort to preserve Eurocentric social and cultural values. For precisely the same reasons, women of color—black, mulatto, and Chinese—were recruited in these political battles to challenge colonial and European dominance from the podium of the beauty contest.

Something of this effort can be seen in the organization and recruitment practices of the Miss Chinese Jamaica competition. In spite of its popularity among spectators, the organizers of the pageant were quickly faced with the herculean task of finding slim, attractive, and unmarried young women who were willing to enter the contest among a fairly small population grouping.[25] Although many of the older generation were opposed to the idea of parading the community's young women in bathing suits and strapless ball gowns, the

Miss Chinese Jamaica contest was actively supported by the economic and print institutions serving the Chinese community. The *Pagoda*, the fortnightly Chinese Jamaican newsmagazine, soon found itself conducting an active campaign to solicit women to enter the contest—one year the pageant almost had to be canceled because of the lack of entrants—and reward those who did enter with lavish prizes that would normally be awarded only to a crowned winner. In 1955, a particularly sparse year for contestants, a *Pagoda* editorial launched an appeal for entrants that could best be described as desperate, particularly given the fact that in the same year the Star's Miss Ebony contest drew some 1,200 applicants from hopeful dark-skinned women all over the island:

> What have other girls got that the Jamaican-born Chinese girls haven't got? Why do they shy away from beauty contests? These are the questions that must be giving the organizers of the "Miss Chinese Jamaica 1955" contest a big headache. Yet there is no reason why Jamaican-born Chinese girls shouldn't make ideal beauty queens.
>
> I understand this year's winner of the coveted "Miss Chinese Jamaica" title will get a two-week expense-paid trip to Miami. Now every girl dreams of travelling and of being a Beauty Queen, and when the two are offered in one package, there should be a new crop of entrants every year to show up the beauty of Jamaican-born Chinese girls.
>
> And speaking of beauty, the girls have it. I see them every day, in offices, in stores, in their homes, and they have the figure that wins the contests. So girls, why not step out and enter the year's "Miss Chinese Jamaica" contest?[26]

The exhortation drew this letter to the editor from a male reader:

> Although I have never sponsored a beauty contest, I know the difficulties the organizers run into, and I wonder if it's worth all the organizers' time to urge the girls to join in for their own sake. After all, if they are too shy to convince us that there are indeed lovely girls in our community, why should we waste time to get them to do so? We do have lovely girls, yes, but if they want to keep it a secret, let them play hide and seek.[27]

From the rhetoric of this letter the reader mistakenly identifies the pageant as an unmediated parade of beautiful women, separate from the heady political and racial atmosphere which made all such contests on the island embodiments of the decolonization struggle. As this exchange makes clear, the "Miss Chinese Jamaica" competition was not just about the "winning figures" of "our girls," it was about recruiting and investing women with the symbolic worth of the community itself. Soon the pageant became the major public event of

Chinese Jamaica and its popularity drew accolades as well as hostility from some of the island's black cultural nationalists concerned about what the resurgence of Chinese nationalism would mean in a future decolonized landscape. Evon Blake, a popular black journalist and editor of the *Spotlight* newsmagazine, charged the pageant organizers as well as the *Pagoda* itself with making unpatriotic and "un-Jamaican" displays of ethnic pride, even though his magazine featured the Miss Ebony winner on its cover and endorsed her as "our girl," a not-so-veiled reference to the Afro-Jamaican nationalism that he and his magazine promoted. With Jamaican independence on its heels and the ruling party with its strong links to the black trade union movement facing the impossible task of having to fulfill its mandate to a dispossessed black mass while mouthing platitudes about the island's multiracial destiny, Chinese Jamaicans soon realized that the integrity of their cultural institutions would be at risk. To avert charges of divisiveness, not only did the Chinese Benevolent Society and its umbrella institutions—the Sanitorium, the Chinese Public School, and the Athletic Club—have to publicly dismantle themselves, but the Miss Chinese Jamaica pageant had to reinvent itself to survive. But even before independence, the organizers found it expedient to rename the contest from the Miss Chinese Jamaica pageant—a title both calling attention to both the national aspirations of Jamaicans of Chinese descent and signaling their distinct identity—to the less politically charged Miss Chinese Athletic Club. By 1962, the year of independence and the public assertion of Jamaica as a "black" nation, the final Chinese identified beauty pageant was held on the island, an event that marked not just the close of openly racialized beauty contest, but signaled the beginning of the end of ethnically organized cultural activity among the Chinese in Jamaica.[28]

The postindependence period, an era in which black Jamaicans hoped that they could assert economic and cultural dominance, proved to be a difficult and frustrating time in this regard. Colin Palmer, in his essay on black power in independent Jamaica, rightly sees the creation of a distinct racial identity as "one of the most agonizing and protracted struggles" waged by Jamaican people in the last half of this century.[29] Although many racial minorities abandoned their symbolic hold over privilege and power during this period—white-only clubs were desegregated and cultural events like Miss Jamaica were relinquished to government authority—they still maintained a firm, if less visible, hand in the economic affairs of the island. But even as Jamaica was being publicly declared as a "black" or multicultural country, the residual effects of Eurocentric definitions of personhood continued to haunt the nation's psyche well into the present. While such concerns reveal a rather problematic essentialist linkage between race and nation, the vigor in which Afro-Caribbean scholars, artists, novelists, and poets campaigned for the legitimacy and justness of the region's identity as "black" attests to the importance that such racial assertiveness, however one-dimensional, still holds as a political ideal. The real test of the anticolonial struggle was thought to be measured not only in concrete material gains, but in the success that the centuries-old stigma attached to black skin could be eradicated. And it is in this regard that the beauty contest, more so than any other arena of cultural production, was seen as the ideal place where the readiness to accept these values could be tested.

Ideally the postindependence beauty pageant would inscribe Jamaica's new political identity as proud, dignified, and black. In the midsixties sponsorship of the Miss Jamaica pageant was taken over by the government and it was conducted under the umbrella of independence day celebrations. During this period attempts were made to select queens who epitomized the racial ideals of the emergent nation. Jeanette Bartley's study of beauty pageants in this period noted that the preferred contestants were described in newspaper advertisements as "Mahogany Types"—defined as "Jamaican cocoa-brown, neither full black, nor very light-skinned."[30] Although light-skinned and racially mixed women formed the majority of the contestants, virtually no white or Chinese women dared to enter the pageant for fear of the controversy that their presence would inevitably bring. The fact that Chinese and white Jamaicans had to take a back seat in the beauty business—Indian Jamaican women who epitomized the "Mahogany" ideal continued to enter and receive no hostility on account of their race—is indicative of the manner in which these two racial minorites became increasingly linked in the popular Jamaican imagination. The economic success of the Chinese Jamaican community elevated the group into whiteness and in the barter for monetary security the Chinese community had to render itself culturally invisible. Walter Rodney, the most influential Afro-Caribbean intellectual embracing the grassroots politics of Black Power at the time, pointedly excluded the Chinese in his discussions of Afro-Asian regional solidarity. For him, Indian Caribbean people who shared a similar history of oppression had to be embraced within the fold of Black Power; by contrast, the Chinese were an exploiting class who would "have either to relinquish or be deprived of that function before they can be reintegrated into a West Indian society where the black man walks with dignity."[31] Since beauty contests were always a reflection or contestation of prevailing political values, the Miss Jamaica pageants of the late sixties and seventies, although touched by occasional quarrels over class and color, were not events of outright hostility. In this climate the pageants were functioning as they were supposed to: creating consensus about kind of image Jamaica wanted to project of itself.

But the reign of brown-skinned beauty queens of this era was broken in 1973 by a young Chinese Jamaican model, Patsy Yuen. Although reluctant to enter the competition because of her race, Yuen proved to be a successful, if controversial, Caribbean representative because of her willingness to perform Jamaica's ideal of itself. Since her Asian ancestry disrupted the official picture of the country's identity, Yuen's vehement defense of herself as Jamaican gave her an edge in styling herself as a symbol of national pride. But because the nation was already publicly pronounced as "black," Yuen's efforts to prove her Jamaicanness inevitably forced her into a problematic and overzealous denial of her Chinese ancestry. Her efforts in this regard dramatized the fact that the multiraciality of the Caribbean experience was still a problem in the official discourse of national identity. Both at home and abroad Yuen had to remind reporters everywhere that although she may look Chinese, her heart and soul were Jamaican: "I'm Jamaican and I'm proud to be a Jamaican. When I travel and I am asked where I am from, I don't say I'm Chinese. I say I am a Jamaican. Look. I don't even like Chinese food . . . give me my ackee and saltfish any day!"[32] As Jamaica's entry in the Miss World competition in London, Yuen placed third, a feat, in a country intoxicated by the drama of beauty pageants, that elevated her to the status of national hero.

This victory was significant, as it reveals both the paradox of the representation of women within the body politic and the eventual disillusionment with Jamaica's self-styled "black" face. The last time such an event took place was when Carol Crawford, Miss Jamaica 1963, brought home the Miss World crown. Crawford, like all Caribbean women who win international pageants, was given a momentous celebration upon her return to the island, festivities which subdued local arguments about her near-white complexion and her green eyes. In a postindependence climate where women never get representation status as national heroes, the idolatry that surrounds winning Caribbean beauty queens is dramatic and unique: Crawford's image was issued on a series of Jamaican postage stamps and she was given the keys to the city of Kingston, the second woman up to that date—Queen Elizabeth II was the first—who was honored in such a manner. But the troubled political and economic times of the 1980s made the Miss Jamaica enterprise much too expensive for an increasingly impoverished public sector to endure. When the contest was turned over once again to private sponsorship, the focus on choosing queens who were "typically Jamaican" gave way to a new concern over the type of entrant who would have the best chance of winning an international pageant and garnering increased financial rewards for the local sponsors. The fracas over the 1986 coronation of "white" Lisa Mahfood is indicative of the peculiarly post-colonial dilemma facing Third World cultural production in an era of late capitalism. It makes Jamaica's conversation with itself over questions of identity and autonomy as bitter as it is ongoing.

NOTES

1. "Missiles Barrage at Beauty Contest," *Daily Gleaner*, 8 September 1986.

2. Christine King, "Says Lisa Mahfood, Miss Jamaica (World), 'I Did Not Expect to Win' . . . Neither Did the Crowd," *Sunday Gleaner Magazine*, 14 September 1986.

3. "Girl from Venezuela Wins 'Miss Jamaica Universe' amidst Sea of Controversy," *Daily Gleaner*, 12 May 1986.

4. Although there was a series of Miss Jamaicas held before the pageant came under the sponsorship of the Jamaican Tourist Board in 1954, the infusion of cash and sense of purpose that the organization gave to the pageant makes it important to start my discussion from this date. But there were several beauty contests that emerged in the island and ran side-by-side with the Miss Jamaica contest. Many of the earlier events were tied to commercial publicity campaigns with the winner usually sent to regional or international contests, such as the Miss British Caribbean pageant, as a national representative. In 1948, for example, the island witnessed a Buy Jamaican campaign sponsored by the Jamaica Manufacturers Association which featured an island-wide beauty contest and the coronation of a Buy Jamaican campaign queen.

5. "Carload of Queens," *Spotlight* 9, no. 5 (May 1948), pp. 35–36.

6. "Miss Jamaica," editorial, *Daily Gleaner*, 5 December 1955.

7. See Gordon Rohlehr's excellent account of the tensions that surrounded the Carnival Queen competition in the chapter "Calypso: From the Mucurapo Stadium to the Savannah Boycott" in Rohlehr's *Calypso and Society in Pre-Independence Trinidad* (Port of Spain: Gordon Rohlehr, 1990), pp. 401–456.

8. Ibid.

9. Quoted in ibid., pp. 445–446.

10. "Ambassadress" was the title of choice for the organizers and sponsors of Caribbean beauty queens to justify their choice of winning girls and the large sum of money that was spent on the pageants. As the winner of the 1957 Carnival Queen competition, Diana Timps, was described in the *Trinidad Guardian*: "She speaks five languages and will be a perfect Ambassadress for Trinidad overseas." Ibid., p. 447.

11. These are two popular forms of working-class masquerades.

12. Nancy Caraway makes the point that the black female struggle for "cultural acceptance as attractive, 'respectable' beings" has been misinterpreted by white feminists who see this emphasis on "negative imagery" as trivial and politically misguided. Although Caraway's argument is made within the specific contexts of U.S. feminisms, her point here has particular relevance to this discussion. See Caraway's *Segregated Sisterhood: Racism and the Politics of American Feminism* (Knoxville: University of Tennessee Press, 1991), p. 78.

13. "Miss West Indies in Miss Universe," *Ebony*, November 1954, pp. 79–83.

14. Edward Scott, "Beauty Contest of a "Revolutionary Quality," *Daily Gleaner*, 10 August 1955. Although the "Ten Types" pageant was supposed to be held consecutively over a ten-year period, only five of them actually took place: Miss Ebony, 1959, Miss Mahogany, 1960, Miss Satinwood, 1961, Miss Golden Apple, 1962, Miss Appleblossom, 1963.

15. Ibid.

16. Quoted in ibid.

17. Quoted in "Black Beauty," *Spotlight* 20, no. 12 (December 1959), p. 32.

18. Ibid.

19. Ibid.

20. The Miss Chinese Jamaica pageant was only open to members of the Chinese Athletic Club who were members of the Benevolent Society. Although this group comprised both foreign and local-born Chinese people and mixed-race populations of Chinese ancestry, I am not aware of any formal rules concerning the size of the society's mixed-race membership, nor any strict formula about how Chinese ancestry is determined. In a small community like Jamaica's where Chinese-descended people knew each other intimately, Chinese ancestry was frequently determined through kinship lines and it was commonly accepted that an individual needed to be at least one forth Chinese to be considered eligible for membership in Chinese Jamaican social institutions. However, a 1945 article of the memorandum of the Chinese Association of Trinidad stipulated that "at no time must the membership of persons of half or less than Chinese exceed more than 20 percent of total membership." See Trevor M. Millett, *The Chinese in Trinidad* (Port of Spain, Trinidad: Inprint Caribbean Ltd., 1993), p. 78.

21. Cecil Chuck, personal interview, 10 November 1993.

22. The reasons for the 1918 Anti-Chinese Riots are symptomatic of the complex relationship between race, class, and sexuality in colonial Jamaica. According to Howard

Johnson, the disturbances began with a squabble between Fung Sue, an immigrant Chinese shopkeeper, and a black policeman over the attentions of Fung Sue's live-in companion, Caroline Lindo. The feud between the two men quickly led to rumours that the policeman had been murdered by the shopkeeper and some of his Chinese friends. Within a few days the incident drew mobs of local residents who attacked Chinese shopkeeprs throughout the district and looted their stores. See Johnson, "The Anti-Chinese Riots of 1918," paper delivered at the 1979 Postgraduate Seminar, Department of History, University of the West Indies, Mona, Jamaica. Also see Jacqueline Levy, "The Economic Role of the Chinese in Jamaica: The Grocery Retail Trade," paper delivered at the 1967 Postgraduate Seminar, Department of History, University of the West Indies, Mona, Jamaica.

23. "Girl to Stop the Traffic," *Daily Gleaner*, 14 July 1959.

24. "Carib Beauties Reach the U.S.," *Trinidad Guardian*, 17 July 1958.

25. Estimates of the percentages of Chinese-identified Jamaicans at that time range between 6 and 7 percent.

26. "Miss Chinese Jamaica," *Pagoda*, 29 October 1955, p. 3.

27. "Letter to the Editor," *Pagoda*, 6 October 1956, p. 3.

28. The Chinese Benevolent Society still exists, but it has abandoned its social and cultural emphasis and exists mainly as a business organization. However, it is being refurbished and there are plans to revitalize its cultural scope.

29. Colin A. Palmer, "Identity, Race and Black Power in Independent Jamaica," in Franklin W. Knight and Colin A. Palmer, eds., *The Modern Caribbean* (Chapel Hill: University of North Carolina Press, 1989), p. 111.

30. Jeanette M. Bartley, "The Search for a Jamaican Identity," M.A. thesis, University of the West Indies, Mona, Jamaica, 1987, p. 54.

31. The Chinese in the Caribbean were to be distinguished from the Chinese of the People's Republic of China who, for Rodney, a Marxist intellectual, had a long and noble history of antiimperialist and pro-Communist activism. "*Our* Chinese," he writes, "have nothing to do with that movement. They are to be identified with Chiang Kai-shek and not Chairman Mao Tse-tung. They are to be put in the same bracket as the lackeys of capitalism and imperialism who are to be found in Hong Kong and Taiwan." See Walter Rodney, *The Groundings with My Brother* (London and Chicago: Bogle L'Ouverture Publications, Research Associates School Publications, 1990), p. 29.

32. Joan Fairweather, "Patsy Lets It All Hang Out," *Daily News*, 12 August 1973.

WORKS CITED

Caraway, Nancy. *Segregated Sisterhood: Racism and the Politics of American Feminism.* Knoxville: University of Tennessee Press, 1991.

Palmer, Colin. "Identity, Race and Black Power in Independent Jamaica." In Franklin W. Knight and Colin A. Palmer, eds. *The Modern Caribbean*. Chapel Hill: University of North Carolina Press, 1989, p. 111.

Rodney, Walter. *The Groundings with My Brother*. London and Chicago: Bogle L'Ouverture Publications, Research Associates School Publications, 1990.

Rohlehr, Gordon. *Calypso and Society in Pre-Independence Jamaica*. Port of Spain, Trinidad: Gordon Rohlehr, 1990.

❖

CONTRIBUTORS

Caroline Allen is a doctoral student at the University of Warwick, England, carrying out a sociological study of health promotion in the Caribbean. From 1991 to 1994, she worked at the Institute of Social and Economic Research, University of the West Indies, on the Reproductive Health Research Project. She has published papers on health in the Caribbean.

Frances Aparicio is Arthur F. Thurnau Professor and Associate Professor of Romance Languages and American Culture at the University of Michigan, where she also directs the Latina and Latino Studies Program. She is author of *Versiones, Interpretaciones creaciones* (1991) and editor of *Song of Madness* (1985) and *Latino Voices* (1995). She has published articles on U.S. Latino and Latina literatures, Latin American poetry, literature, and music, and teaching Spanish to U.S. Latino/as. Her chapter is part of a forthcoming book on gender, Latino popular music, and Puerto Rican literatures.

Natasha B. Barnes teaches Caribbean literature at Emory University and is completing a monograph on Caribbean cultural nationalism.

Ruth Behar was born in Havana in 1956 and went to live in New York with her family in 1962. She is Professor of Anthropology at the University of Michigan in Ann Arbor. The recipient of many prestigious fellowships, including the MacArthur Fellows Award and a John Simon Guggenheim fellowship, Behar has traveled to Spain, Mexico, and Cuba and written on a range of cultural issues as a poet, essayist, editor, and ethnographer. Her book *Translated Woman: Crossing the Border with Esperanza's Story*, an account of her friendship with a Mexican street peddler, was named a Notable Book of the Year for 1993 by the *New York Times* and was turned into a play by Pregones Theater, a Latino company based in New York. Behar is the editor of *Bridges to Cuba* (1995). She is also co-editor of *Women Writing Culture* (1995). She is writing a memoir about her Jewish Cuban family.

Carollee Bengelsdorf is the author of *The Problem of Democracy in Cuba: Between Vision and Reality* (1994) and co-editor of *Cuban Transition: Crisis and Transformation in the 1990s* (1992). She has written about socialist theoretical traditions, Cuban politics, and women and the Cuban Revolution. She is Professor of Politics at Hampshire College.

Karen McCarthy Brown teaches at the Graduate and Theological Schools of Drew University. She has done continuous field research on Vodou both in Haiti and the Haitian diaspora community in Brooklyn since the early 1970s. She is the author of *Mama Lola: A Vodou Priestess in Brooklyn* (1991) and *Tracing the Spirit: Ethnographic Essays on Haitian Art* (1996), as well as many articles on women, female spirits, and healing practices within Haitian Vodou.

Carla Freeman is an Assistant Professor of Anthropology and Women's Studies at Emory University. Her forthcoming book is entitled *High Tech and High Heels in the Global Economy: Women, Work and Off-shore Informatics in Barbados*. Her research at present addresses modernity, transnational culture, and the changing meanings of consumption in the Caribbean.

Elizabeth Hernández is a Professor of Speech Communication and English at InterAmerican University of Puerto Rico in San Juan, Puerto Rico. Her research focuses on popular music, gender, and communication.

Luisa Hernández Angueira is an Associate Professor of Sociology at the University of Puerto Rico at Río Piedras. Her research focuses on gender, work, and Caribbean migration. She has published in the areas of the needlepoint industry, elderly women in the labor market, gender and the informal economy, and migrant Dominican women in Puerto Rico.

Suzanne LaFont is an anthropologist and Visiting Assistant Professor at Sofia University in Bulgaria under the auspices of the Civic Education Project. She is continuing her research and publishing on women and the state. She is the author of *The Emergence of an Afro-Caribbean Legal Tradition* (1996).

Consuelo López Springfield, a native of Puerto Rico, is an Assistant Dean, College of Letters and Science, at the University of Wisconsin–Madison, where she teaches in Women's Studies. She has published numerous essays on Caribbean literature and political rhetoric and was the guest editor of a special issue of *Callaloo* on Puerto Rican women writers (1994). She is working on a book on Caribbean women's autobiographies.

Cynthia J. Mesh received her Ph.D. in French from Yale University and now works as an independent scholar in San Diego. Her primary interests are Francophone Antillean Literature and Women's Studies. She is working on a translation of Maryse Condé's children's novels.

Mary Johnson Osirim is an Associate Professor of Sociology at Bryn Mawr College. She has served as Coordinator of the Africana Studies Program and Director of the African Studies Consortium at Bryn Mawr College. Her teaching and publications have focused on women and development, gender relations and the family, economic sociology and the role of entrepreneurship in Zimbabwe. She is the recipient of many fellowships and awards, including grants from the National Science Foundation, a Pew Faculty Fellowship in International Affairs, and a Carter G. Woodson Fellowship. She is writing a book on *Women and African Entrepreneurship.*

Lizabeth Paravisini-Gebert is an Associate Professor and Chair, Department of Hispanic Studies, at Vassar College. She is the author of *Phyllis Shand Allfrey: A Caribbean Life* and *Caribbean Women Writers: An Annotated Bibliography.* Her books include *Green Cane and Juicy Flotsam, Pleasure and the Word,* and *Ana Roque's* Luz y Sombra.

Deborah Pruitt works as a consultant developing academic programs for educational institutions and planning for nonprofit community development groups. She specializes in applying anthropological analysis to policy evaluations. With Suzanne LaFont, she has published on "romance tourism" in Jamaica.

Elisa J. Sobo is a Lecturer in the Department of Anthropology at the University of Durham, England. Her book *One Blood: The Jamaican Body* (1993) concerns traditional Jamaican ethnophysiological and ethnomedical beliefs and practices. In addition to Caribbean studies, she is active in the field of HIV/AIDS; her research on condom use and heterosexual relationship ideals is described in *Choosing Unsafe Sex: AIDS-Risk Denial and Disadvantaged Women* (1995).

INDEX

Abortion, 160

Acquired Immune Deficiency Syndrome (AIDS): public health programs, xiv, 14; misconceptions among rural Jamaicans, 148–49; linked to racial prejudice, 149; difficulties in underestimating, 175; proportions in Commonwealth Caribbean, 195–200; in Africa, 195; related to GNP, 195; rates of cases in the Commonwealth Caribbean compared to Latin South America, 195–200; susceptibility among women with STDs, 202; implications for development, 195–207

Affiliation Act (Jamaica), 220–21, 225

Africa: GNP, 176; measures of health and welfare, 177; births, 178; child mortality, 178; AIDS rates, 195

Aging, 174, 205–206

Allfrey, Phyllis Shand, 10–15

Alvarez, Julia, 8

Anal sex, 148–49

Andrade, Evelyn, 293

Anguilla: health and welfare measures, 177; AIDS cases, 196; mentioned, 27

Antigua: health and welfare measures, 177; mentioned, 27, 196

Antrobus, Peggy, 57

Argentina, mentioned, 27, 236

Bahamas: GNP, 175–76; health and welfare measures, 177; mortality rates from infectious and parasitic diseases, 184; mortality rates from heart disease, 186; cancer and cervical cancer mortality rates, 188; mortality rates from diabetes, 191; mortality rates from hypertension, 193; AIDS cases, 197

Barbados: conservative tradition, 84; informatics industry, 68–86; tourism, 84; GNP, 176; health and welfare measures, 177; child mortality, 178–80; mortality rates from infectious and parasitic diseases, 184; mortality rates from heart disease, 186; cancer and cervical cancer mortality rates, 188; mortality rates from diabetes, 191; mortality rates from hypertension, 193; AIDS cases, 196

Barbuda, mentioned, 27, 196

Bartley, Jeanette, 301

Bauman, Zygmunt, 232

Bauxite, 51

Beauty: cultural constructions, xviii; Jamaican beauty pageants, 285–303
—"Carnival Queen," 287–92
—"Miss Jamaica," 292–95, 297, 298, 300, 302–303
—"Miss West Indies," 293
—"Miss Allspice," 295
—"Miss Appleblossom," 295
—"Miss Chinese Jamaica," 297, 298–99, 304n20
—"Miss Ebony," 295–96, 298–99
—"Miss Golden Apple," 295
—"Miss Lotus," 295
—"Miss Mahogony," 295
—"Miss Pomegranate," 295
—"Miss Sandalwood," 295
—"Miss Chinese Athletic Club," 300

Bébel-Gisler, Dany: activism, xv, 8, 16, 18–35; early life, 30; publications, 30, 31, 33–35; school for immigrants, 32–33

Belize: GNP, 176; measures for health and welfare, 177; mortality rates from infectious and parasitic diseases, 184; mortality rates from heart disease, 186; mortality rates from cancer and cervical cancer, 188; mortality rates from diabetes, 191; mortality rates from hypertension, 193; AIDS cases, 196; mentioned, 226

Bennett, Louise, xii

Berleant-Schiller, Riva, xv

Bilingualism, 30–34

Biological determinism, 239

Black Power, 301

Blades, Rubén, 263, 266, 268

Blake, Evon, 300

Boat women, xvi, 97–109

Body: as discourse, 7; violence upon, 16; social constructions of, 99–101, 230, 245–46; identification with property, 140; as a system, 145–62; sexuality and control in Jamaica, 6; in Cuba, 233–47

Bolivia, mentioned, 27

Bolles, Lynn, 172

Bourguignon, Erika, 139

Brazil, mentioned, 27

Breastfeeding, 151, 154

Burgos, Julia, xix

Caliban: literary allusions, xii; related to Caribbean female identity, 119

Calypso: Mighty Sparrow, 290–92; Lord Superior, 292

Cammock, Ruth, 286

Cancer: overall cancer death rates, 183; cervical, 183–95, 200–202, 205, 207

Capetillo, Luisa, 9

Capitalism: global system's effect on Third World's racial, ethnic, and gender relations, 44–45

Caraway, Nancy, 292

Caribbean Basin Initiative (CBI), 41, 52, 60

Caribs: gender roles, 20; battles with French colonizers, 20–21; destroyed in English-speaking Caribbean, 45

CARICOM, 61–63

Carnival Development Committee, 290

Cartagena Portalatín, Aída, 14

Castro, Fidel, 115, 118, 239

Cayman Islands: AIDS cases, 197; mentioned, 27

Cecilia Valdes (novel), 243–44

Celinés, 262–63

Chantelle, 262

Chauvet, Marie, 7, 14, 15

Las Chicas del Can, 262

Childbearing, 152, 171, 226

Chile, mentioned, 27

Chinese: immigrants in Jamaica, 47; violence against, 297

Chinese Athletic Club, 297, 300

Chinese Benevolent Society, 297

Chodorow, Nancy, 156

Chong, Sheila, 298

Chuck, Cecil, 297

Cisneros, Lilliana Antonette, 286

Cixous, Hélène, 269

Clarke, Edith, 217

Cliff, Michelle, 14

Cocolos, 264, 281

Cofer, Judith Ortiz, xiii

Colère (Marie Chauvet), 7

Colombia, mentioned, 27, 236

Colón, Willie, 263, 266, 267, 273, 275, 281

Comte, Auguste, 44

Conference on the Status of Women, 57

Conga, Pedro, 268

Cook, Blanche Wiesen, 11

Cooper, Carolyn, 4, 6, 7

Costa Rica, mentioned, 27

Crawford, Carol, 302

Creole: language as resistance, xii; movement in Guadeloupe, 18–35

Cropover festival, 85

Cruz, Celia, 262, 277

Cuba: informal economy, 116; special period, 229–47; family code, 230–32, 238, 248n5; unemployment, 232; racial categories, 234–35; self-employment, 237–40; women in electoral politics, 238; Popular Power, 240

Cuban Academy of Sciences, 230

Cultural creolization, 69

Cumper, Gloria, 219

Curaçao, 13

Dagenais, Huguette, 28, 33

Danticat, Edwidge, xiii

Data processing: problems with, 53

Davis, Wade, 6

De la Torre Mulhare, Mirta, 241, 246

Development, related to disease, 171–208

Diabetes, 190; risk factors, 200–201; and disease rates, 207

Dickard, Peggy, 288

Diets, 146, 200, 203, 208

Domestic work: in English-speaking Caribbean, 49, 53, 54–55, 62; among Dominicans in Puerto Rico, 97–100, 102, 104, 107–109; in Cuba, 112–20

Dominguez, Jorge, 235–36

Dominica: Women's Guild, 10–12; women's movement, 11–12; GNP, 176; measures of health and welfare, 177; mortality rates from infectious and parasitic diseases, 184; mortality rates from heart disease, 186; mortality rates from cancer and cervical cancer, 188; mortality rates from diabetes, 191; mortality rates from hypertension, 193; AIDS cases, 196

Dominican Republic: military's violence against women, 7; free trade zone, 105; gender roles, 105–109

Dominican women: in Manhattan, 13; resistance to state violence, 7, 10; in Puerto Rico, 97–109; prejudice toward, 99–101; police raids, 98; wages compared to Dominican men in Puerto Rico, 101–102, 107–108
Dress codes, 83–86
Dressmaking: home industries, 48–49
Duchen, Claire, 29
Duperly, Joan, 297
Duppies (male ghosts), 158–60

Earhart, Amelia, mentioned, 11
East Indian labor, 47
Ecuador, mentioned, 27
El Gran Combo, 268, 273, 277–79
Engels, Friedrich, 138
Engelsian paradigm, 232, 235, 238–39, 241, 250n9
English Common Law, 219
Epidemics, 205
Epidemiologic transition model, 183–95
Epidemiologists, 173
Espinet, Ramabai, 16
Ethnocentricity, xviii, 4, 19; in Jamaican family law, 224–26; effects on concepts of beauty, 292, 301
Exercise, means of reducing disease, 173
Export Processing Zones (EPZs), 51–54, 58, 203

Family laws: in Jamaica, xvii, 215–26; in Cuba, 230–32, 238, 248n5
Family networks, xvi, 42, 221
Fashion: concepts of femininity, xvi; traditional Barbadian female clothing, 69; new styles, 80–81; influence of television, 85
Fatherhood: meaning in Jamaican families, 217, 221
Federation of Cuban Women, 236
Feminism: definition, xiv; Caribbean feminism, 3–16; inappropriateness of European models, 5, 19–20; divergence of Caribbean from EuroAmerican, 7–16; in Puerto Rico, 9; rooted to material conditions, 4; French feminist theory, 19, 20, 29
Feminist movements: in Caribbean, 8–9; in Puerto Rico, 9–10; in Dominica, 10–11; in Dominican Republic, 10, 13; among Dominican women in New York City, 13; in Haiti, 14; in Guadeloupe, 18–37
Fenton, Marlene, 289

Ferré, Rosario, 14, 277
Fertility-dominated aging, 174
Fiske, John, 265–66
Flores, Don Pedro, 268
Flores, Juan, xiii
Food production by women, 51, 172, 203
Fox, Geoffrey, 241
Franco, José, 243
French Antilles: research on women, 18–20; independence movement, 23, 25; struggle for women's rights, 18–36
French Ministry of Education, 26
French resistance movement in the Antilles, 21

García Ramis, Magali, 277
Gastroenteritis, 205
Gilman, Sander, 269
González, Reynaldo, 245
Grenada: GNP, 176; health and welfare measures, 177; mortality rates from heart disease, 186; mortality rates from cancer and cervical cancer, 188; mortality rates from diabetes, 191; mortality rates from hypertension, 193; AIDS cases, 196
Guadeloupe: history, 20; inhabitants, 20; imported labor, 21; immigration to France, 22; strikes, 34–35
Guardian and Custody Act (Jamaica), 220–23
Guillen, Nicholas, 245
Gutierrez Alea, Tomas, 246
Guyana: factory work, 48; GNP, 176; health and welfare measures, 177; child mortality, 178; mortality rates from infectious and parasitic diseases, 184; mortality rates from heart disease, 186; mortality rates from cancer and cervical cancer, 188; mortality rates from diabetes, 191; mortality rates from hypertension, 193; AIDS cases, 196; mentioned, 27, 71, 175–77

Hairdressing, 73, 78
Haiti: marriage patterns, 6; voice in the community, 6; cultural ties to Guadeloupe and Martinique, 22–23; practice of healing religion: 123–40
Health: traditions in Jamaica, xvii, 143–62; spiritual healers, xvii; and development programs, xvii, 171–208; traditions in Vodou, 123–40; herbal treatments in Jamaica, 147; health and reproduction, 171–72; difficulties in diagnosing diseases, 175; health risks associated with "male shar-

ing," 202; health problems associated with structural adjustments, 204-205; models in the Caribbean, 205-208

Heart disease, 183

Henriques, Fernando, 219

Herbalists, 124

Heroism, 8, 12, 14-16

Higher education: need for gender equity, 62; universities in Cuba, 233

Higglering, 46, 48, 54, 59; in Barbados, 69-90; among Jamaican villagers, 144

Hodge, Merle, xiii, xiv

Homosexuality: Cuban attitudes toward, 246; addressed in music, 263

Housewifization theory, 81. *See also* Mies, Maria

Housework, 43, 62, 231

Human Development Index (HDI), 178, 180

Huyssen, Andreas, 263

Hypertension, 190, 193

Infant mortality, 178-82

International Monetary Fund (IMF), 58, 203, 205

Ireland, mentioned, 70

Jamaica: village life, 144; unemployment, 144, 287; health traditions, 142-62; GNP, 176; health and welfare measures, 177; mortality rates from infectious and parasitic diseases, 184; mortality rates from heart disease, 186; cancer and cervical cancer rates, 188; mortality rates from diabetes, 191; mortality rates from hypertension, 193; AIDS cases, 196; legal code, 215-26; beauty pageants, 285-305; anti-Chinese riots, 297; Jamaican in "Miss World" beauty pageant, 302; mentioned, 27, 71

Jamaican Federation of Women, 296

Jamaican Tourist Board, 288-89

James, Cyril Lionel R., 9

James, Mabel, 11

Jewish community, in Cuba, 114-15

Kinship relations: assisting and self-esteem, 55; among Haitians, 125-27; in Jamaica, 82, 144-62, 221, 231; bonds formed with blood, 151-52, 154, 161; "fictive kinship" in Cuba, 231-33

Kolodny, Annette, 264

Kutzinski, Vera, 245

Labor movements, in Dominica, 10-13

Lage, Carlos, 240

Lair, Clara, 9

Language: and gender equity, 33

Lavoe, Héctor, 268

Legal codes: in Jamaica, 215-26; Cuban Family Code, 230-32, 238, 248n5

Leiris, Michel, 30

Léonora, l'histoire enfouie de la Guadeloupe (Bébel-Gisler), 8, 33-35

Lesbians, 246

Levins Morales, Aurora, xiii

Lewis, Gordon, 84

Liénart de l'Olive, Guadeloupe, 20

Lifestyle: linked to chronic uncommunicable diseases, 173-95; challenges facing health professionals, 200-201; risk of AIDS, 207

Linguistic discrimination, among Guadeloupean immigrants in France, 31

López, Sonia, 262

Lord Superior, 292

Lucia (film), 243

Lugo Filippi, Carmen, xviii, 261, 264, 267, 268, 278-81

Lydia Vega, Ana, xviii, 261, 264, 267, 268, 277, 278-81

McCracken, Grant, 85

Maceo, Antonio, 245

MacKinnon, Catharine, 225

Mahfood, Lisa, 285-87, 303

Maintenance Act (Jamaica), 220-21

Market women: in Haiti, 6, 125; in Jamaica, 203

Marshall, Paule, 14, 15

Marson, Una, 288

Martí, José, 245

Martinez-Alier, Verena, 233, 235, 241, 244, 245

Martinique, 18-24, 26, 27, 33

Maternal mortality, 190-91

Maurer, William M., xv

Mayra, 262-63

Measles, 205

Medicine: barriers for women, 123; criticism of western medicine, 123-24

Menstrual rhetoric, 155

Menstrual taboos, 152-54, 156

Menstrual "tying," 154-56, 161

Menstruation, 144-62

Mestizaje, xii, 18; in Cuba, 234, 245, 246

Mexico, mentioned, 27, 60, 236

Mies, Maria, xv, 81
Mighty Sparrow, 290–91
Migration: of Dominican women to Puerto
Rico, 96–109; effects of migration on mar-
riage, 103
Milly y los Vecinos, 262
Mitchison, Naomi, 12
Moi, Toril, 260
Momsen, Janet, 28, 171
Monroe, Marilyn, 297
Monserrat, food supply, 203
Morales, Rosario, xiii
Moreno Fraginals, Mario, 234
Motherhood: in Caribbean self-identity, 43;
nannies as "second" mothers, 114

Naipaul, V. S., xiii
Nannies: in Francophone Caribbean, 24; in
Cuba, 113
Needlework, in Barbados, 72–76, 78–81, 85
Neita, Clifton, 296
Newly Industrializing Countries (NICs), 61
Nicaragua, mentioned, 27
Nigeria, mentioned, 46
North American Free Trade Agreement
(NAFTA), 41, 60
Nuñez, Marta, 239
Nuñez-Harrell, Elizabeth, 14, 15
Nursing, 51
Nutritional habits linked to industrialization,
174, 205–206

Obesity, 146, 200–201
Offshore informatics operators, 69–70, 72–86
Oil industry, 51
Overnutrition, 201

Padilla, Félix, 262
Palmer, Colin, 300
Palmer, Nyssa, 260–61
Paraguay, mentioned, 27
Peasant movements: in Dominican Republic,
10–13; in Guadaloupe, 34–35
Pepper, Stephen, 269
Perez Sarduy, Pedro, 245
Peru, mentioned, 27
Pidgin, description, 24
Plaçage, 6
Plantation narratives, 14–15
Polygyny, 6
Portrait of Teresa (film), 230, 244

Poullet, Hector, 26
Priestesses: in Haitian Vodou, 124–40
Prostitutes, 13, 149–50, 240
Prudent, Lambert-Felix, 24
Puerto Rico: Dominican women in, 96–109;
music, 259–81

Quayle, Ada, 14

Racial categories, 234–35
Racial narratives, 241–47
Racism: against Dominican women in Puerto
Rico, 100–101; belief in racist plot to spread
AIDS, 149; in Cuba, 233, 244–46
Reddock, Rhoda, xiv
Reggae, 285–86
Restaurant workers, 99
Reunion Island, 21
Rhys, Jean, 14, 16
Rockeros, 264
Rodney, Walter, 301
Roosevelt, Eleanor, 11
Roqué, Ana, 9
Ruiz, Gabriel, 279
Rum: for export, 203; effects of production
on the environment, 204

Safa, Helen Icken, 105, 231
St. Kitts/Nevis: GNP, 176; measures of health
and welfare, 177; mortality rates from infectious and parasitic diseases, 184; mortality
rates from heart disease, 186; mortality
rates from cancer and cervical cancer, 188;
mortality rates from diabetes, 191; mortality rates from hypertension, 193; AIDS
cases, 196
St. Lucia: GNP, 176; measures of health and
welfare, 177; mortality rates from infectious
and parasitic diseases, 184; mortality rates
from heart disease, 186; mortality rates
from cancer and cervical cancer, 188; mortality rates from diabetes, 191; mortality
rates from hypertension, 193; AIDS cases,
196; mentioned, 27
St. Marteen, mentioned, 13
St. Vincent and the Grenadines: GNP, 176;
measures of health and welfare, 177; mortality rates for infectious and parasitic
diseases, 184; mortality rates from heart
disease, 186; mortality rates from cancer
and cervical cancer, 188; mortality rates

from diabetes, 191; mortality rates from hypertension, 193; AIDS cases, 196
Salsa, 259–81
Sánchez, Luis Rafael, 277
Santos, Daniel, 268
Scott, Rebecca, 234
Sen, Gita, 57
Sewing, 76
Sexually transmitted diseases (STDs), 202
Shakespeare, William: *The Tempest,* xii, xiii
Shopping tours, 74
Simey, T. S., 218–19
Sistren, 56
Slavery: in gender relations, 5; in French Antilles, 21; in English-speaking Caribbean, 41, 45–46; emancipation in English-speaking Caribbean, 47–48; in Jamaica, 217; in Cuba, 233–35; debate over black families, 234
Smith, R. T., 216
Spirit impregnation, 145, 158–62
Stabilization policies, 51
Status of Children Act (Jamaica), 220–21, 226
Stopes, Marie, 12
Strawberry and Chocolate (film), 246
Structural Adjustment Programs (SAPs), 57–61
Stubbs, Jean, 245
Suffrage: in Puerto Rico, 9; in Dominican Republic, 10
"Suitcase traders," 73–75, 77, 82
Summerskill, Edith, 12
Suriname, mentioned, 27

Taboos, concerning menstruation, 152–57
Telchid, Sylviane, 26
Total Quality Management (TQM), 70
Tong, Angela, 298
Tourism: in English-speaking Caribbean, 54–55; in Barbados, 84
Transnational corporations, as forms of imperialism, 51
Transnational identities, 68–69, 73–77, 85–86
Travel agents, 74
Trinidad: dressmaking, 49; import substitution industrialization, 50; domestic workers, 53–54; unions, 55; Women's Bureau, 56; GNP, 176; measures of health and welfare, 177; mortality rates from infectious and parasitic diseases, 184; mortality rates from

heart disease, 186; mortality rates from cancer, 188; mortality rates from diabetes, 191; mortality rates from hypertension, 193; AIDS cases, 196; local food supply, 203–204; carnival, 289; mentioned, 27
Trujillo, Rafael Leonidas, 7, 10
Typhoid, 205

Unions, of domestic workers, 55
United Nations, 26, 178
Uruguay, mentioned, 27

Valverde, Umberto, 277
Venezuela, mentioned, 27, 77, 236
Vicioso, Chiqui, 13
Violence: in songs, 268; against Chinese in Jamaica, 297; against women, 7–8, 34–35; against sugarcane workers in Guadeloupe, 35, 246
Vodou: history of, 124; families, 125–26; temples, 126; in Brooklyn, 127–40; initiation, 127; card readings, 129; charms, 130–31, 137; heat as life energy in healing, 133–35; use of humor, 134–35, 137; belief in fate, 136; use of community norms, 136; negative stereotypes, 139

West Africa, 41, 46
West Indian Federation, 11–12
West Indian women: in the informal economy, 71–73
Wilson, Elizabeth, 85
Witchcraft babies, 158–60
Women in the Caribbean Project (WICP), 42, 172
Women in Development Program (WAND), 56–57, 62
Women's associations: in Dominica, 10–12; in Cuba, 236
Women's movements: in the Caribbean, 3–16; in Guadeloupe, 18–35; impetus to health practices, 171
Wong, Dorothy, 297
World Bank, 58
Wynter, Sylvia, 15

Young, Shelagh, 265
Yuen, Patsy, 302

Zobel, Joseph, 33
Zorrilla, José, 279